Islam and the Everyday World

This pioneering volume goes beyond formalistic analysis of Islamic states and standard discourses of public policy to underscore the actual significance and limitations of the influence of Islamist normative and legalist discourses on key areas of public policy in the Muslim world.

Jomo K. S., Editor of *Islamic Economic Alternatives*

Does Islamic Law affect public policy? The authors methodically uncover the complex interaction between religion and social change in the Muslim world.

Tarik Yousef, Shaykh Al-Sabah Chair in Arab Studies,
Center for Contemporary Arab Studies,
Georgetown University

Public policy determines the scope, limits, and forms of social action. It is the government's means for encouraging, discouraging, or prohibiting certain acts or behaviors. In an Islamic state, the divine law (Shari'a) must be implemented as a means for the realization of the will of God on earth. The Shari'a is, therefore, the code of social conduct and the means of regulating social discourse as well as social change. Since definition of the Shari'a is itself a matter of interpretation, two fundamental issues arise. First, what is the legitimate source and process of interpretation of the precepts of Islamic law, the Shari'a? Second, how are the specific dictums of the Shari'a affected by fundamental changes in the social and technological circumstances of life? This book investigates how Shari'a law affects public policy both theoretically and in practice, across a wide range of public policy areas, including human rights, family law, labor law, commercial law, taxation, and "interest-free" banking. It is an important new resource for anyone seeking to understand Islam and its wider social and political implications.

Sohrab Behdad is Professor and John E. Harris Chair in Economics, Denison University, and also a former member of the faculty of Economics, Tehran University, Iran.

Farhad Nomani is Professor of Economics at the American University of Paris, and is a former member of the Faculty of Economics, Tehran University, Iran.

1. **Trade Policy and Economic Integration in the Middle East and North Africa**
   Economic boundaries in flux
   Edited by Hassan Hakimian and Jeffrey B. Nugent

2. **State Formation in Palestine**
   Viability and governance during a social transformation
   Edited by Mushtaq Husain Khan

3. **Palestinian Labour Migration to Israel**
   Land, labour and migration
   Leila H. Farsakh

4. **Islam and the Everyday World**
   Public policy dilemmas
   Edited by Sohrab Behdad and Farhad Nomani

Islam and the Everyday World

Public policy dilemmas

Edited by Sohrab Behdad and Farhad Nomani

Routledge
Taylor & Francis Group

LONDON AND NEW YORK

First published 2006
by Routledge
2 Park Square, Milton Park, Abingdon, Oxon, OX14 4RN

Simultaneously published in the USA and Canada
by Routledge
270 Madison Ave, New York NY 10016

*Routledge is an imprint of the Taylor & Francis Group,
an informa business*

Transferred to Digital Printing 2010

© 2006 Sohrab Behdad and Farhad Nomani, selection and editorial
matter; the contributors, their own chapters

Typeset in Times New Roman by
Newgen Imaging Systems (P) Ltd, Chennai, India

British Library Cataloguing in Publication Data
A catalogue record for this book is available from the British Library

Library of Congress Cataloging in Publication Data
A catalog record for this book has been requested

ISBN10: 0–415–36823–5 (hbk)
ISBN10: 0–415–45305–4 (pbk)
ISBN10: 0–203–02803–1 (ebk)

ISBN13: 978–0–415–36823–0 (hbk)
ISBN13: 978–0–415–45305–9 (pbk)
ISBN13: 978–0–203–02803–2 (ebk)

Contents

List of contributors   vii
Preface and acknowledgments   ix

1   **Islam, revivalism, and public policy**   1
    SOHRAB BEHDAD

2   **Islamism and economics: policy prescriptions
    for a free society**   38
    TIMUR KURAN

3   **Islam and human rights policy**   66
    ANN ELIZABETH MAYER

4   **Muslim family law: articulating gender, class,
    and the state**   88
    NAHLA ABDO

5   **Islam and labor law: some precepts and examples**   113
    KAREN PFEIFER

6   **Commercial law: the conflict in Shari'a and
    secular law public policy**   141
    WILLIAM BALLANTYNE

7   **Zakat, taxes, and public finance in Islam**   165
    VOLKER NIENHAUS

8   **The dilemma of riba-free banking in Islamic public policy**   193
    FARHAD NOMANI

    Appendix: elements of Islamic law (Shari'a)   224
    SOHRAB BEHDAD

Index   227

Contributors

Nahla Abdo Professor, Department of Sociology and Anthropology Carlton University, Canada.

William Ballantyne Barrister, Visiting Professor, Department of Arab Law, School of Oriental and African Studies, University of London, UK.

Sohrab Behdad Professor and John E. Harris Chair in Economics, Denison University, USA.

Timur Kuran Professor of Economics and Law, King Faisal Professor of Islamic Thought and Culture, and Director of Institute for Economic Research on Civilizations, University of Southern California, USA.

Ann Elizabeth Mayer Associate Professor, Department of Legal Studies, The Wharton School, University of Pennsylvania, USA.

Volker Nienhaus President of Philipps-Universität Marburg and Honorary Professor, Department of Economics, Ruhr-Universität Bochum, Germany.

Farhad Nomani Professor, Department of Economics, The American University of Paris, France.

Karen Pfeifer Professor, Department of Economics, Smith College, USA.

Preface and acknowledgments

Public policy determines the scope, limits, and forms of social action. It is the government's means for encouraging, discouraging, or prohibiting certain acts or behaviors. It is also what governments do or do not do. Laws, decrees, regulations, orders, pronouncements, public persuasion, and propaganda, as well as direct actions of governments, are means of public policy. The socio-political structure determines the process of formulation and implementation, as well as the degree of legitimacy of public policy. In secular democracies, expressions of public consensus, such as elections, polls, and public debates in legislative process and in other forums of political negotiation, lead to the formulation of public policy; and in theory, the majority wins.

In Islamic states, the process of definition and the source of legitimacy of public policy is more complex and potentially more controversial. The complexity arises from applying the interpretations of the divine law, the Shari'a, to contemporary social issues. Islam is concerned not only with the profound theological issues, but just as intensively with the mundane aspects of everyday life. In an Islamic state, the Shari'a must be implemented in its entirety, as a means for the realization of the will of God on earth. The Shari'a is, therefore, the code of social conduct and the means of regulating social discourse as well as social change. Since definition of the Shari'a is itself a matter of interpretation, two fundamental issues arise.

First, what are the legitimate sources and processes of interpretation of the precepts of Islamic law, the Shari'a? In other words, who and in what processes can the "true" precepts of Islam be determined? Second, how are the specific dictums of the Shari'a affected by the fundamental changes in the social and technological circumstances of life? Public consensus and adaptability of the Shari'a to change have been major areas of debate in Islamic public policy. The rise of Islamic revivalism in the past decades has added new dimensions to this politico-theological issue. The problem has evolved into the more fundamental questions of "What is Islam?" and "Whose Islam?" frequently asked by Muslim revivalists groups themselves, who claim that theirs is the "true Islam."

Unavoidably, comparisons are made, approvingly or disapprovingly, by the proponents or opponents of an Islamic state between elements of secular and Islamic systems of public policy. Of course, such comparisons could be made between the ideal, actual, or caricature of each of two forms of state and their system of public policy. Consequently, the number of possibilities that would emerge would be quite large.

The chapters in this collection were commissioned specifically for a volume on Islam and public policy in the *International Journal Review of Comparative Public Policy* (volume 9, 1997). We approached the recognized authorities in each arena of public policy with our proposal. We asked that each article concern itself with the theoretical and practical applications of the issue, and with the controversies that may exist on the interpretation of Islamic precepts on the topic. We have selected a number of the original articles in that volume for this collection. They have been revised and updated to reflect the new developments and account for changes. In this respect, this volume has been planned to be a cohesive and integrated collection.

Obviously, we could have included other topics as well, except for the limitation of space, which has forced us to make some hard choices. Meanwhile, we do not pretend to have a uniformity of methodological approaches and viewpoints in this collection of chapters. We made no attempt in that direction. In fact, we believe that the resulting diversity of approaches and views is a valuable feature of this volume.

Above all, we are grateful to our authors for their contributions and for accommodating our request for revising and updating them for the present volume. We owe our thanks to Professor Nicholas Mercuro, editor of *International Review of Comparative Public Policy* for inviting us to edit the volume on *Islam and Public Policy*, and to Professor Hassan Hakimian, editor of Routledge's *Political Economy of the Middle East and North Africa* series, for encouraging us to bring forth a revised and updated version of the original volume.

Sohrab Behdad wishes to express his thanks to Denison University for facilitating this project, Judy Thompson for secretarial support, and Jasmine Tan for bibliographical assistance.

Sohrab Behdad
Farhad Nomani

1 Islam, revivalism, and public policy

Sohrab Behdad[1]

the detailed structure of social life which ensues from the [Islamic] doctrine is inherently opposed to all others existing in the world. ... [A]ll problems of human life, whether big or small, are viewed and treated by Islam in its own way.

(Sayyid Abul Ala Maududi 1940)[2]

everywhere the best reformers and profound thinkers believe that a glorious renaissance and reconstruction is achievable on the basis of a pure Islamic ideology which planned to organize a society of free men, where exploitation of man by man would not be possible, where monarchies would give place to democratic republics, where feudalism and blood-sucking landlordism would be wiped out, where the State would become a welfare-state and not a police-state and where people would not be tyrannized for thinking freely.

(Khalifa Abdul Hakim 1951)[3]

Islamic revivalism pledges equity, social justice, freedom, and human dignity. It condemns "exploitation of man by man" and attacks not only "blood-sucking landlordism," which has already diminished in most countries, but also "plundering" capitalists and capitalism, imperialists and imperialism, and in recent years "globalism." It demands means of subsistence for all and denounces monopolies and accumulated fortunes. It praises simplicity and discretion in wants and condemns conspicuous consumption. Islamic revivalism, to many, is a march of radicalism, demanding a dramatic change in social structure and the organization of production, often with a heavy handed state in control of the economy. Some revivalists have asked for "Islamic socialism" or a "classless Islamic society."

Yet Islam is also the religion of flourishing bazaars and prosperous merchants. Islam is well-known for promoting trade and entrepreneurship, sanctioning private property rights, accumulation of wealth and profit, and for frowning upon the state's intrusions in the market. It is the voice of the status quo and conservatism in the economic arena. To many, it is laissez-faire capitalism. As Jama'at-i Islami in Pakistan and Taliban in Afghanistan have shown, some Muslim revivalists see Islamization of the economy as promoting free market capitalism.

These extreme representations of Islam closely reflect the universal expression of the range of social contestations in the political arena. It may be argued that Islam, as an encompassing ideology, like other religions, lends itself to a wide range of interpretations (Esposito 2005), reflecting the formation of social forces in the theater of politics in society. There is some truth to this claim since no ideological doctrine can be immune to variations in interpretations arising from differences in social perspectives, or changes in social–historical processes and circumstances. But this assertion, which has gained wide popularity among the post-"Orientalist" Islamicists and Middle Eastern scholars, by way of rejecting the monolithic presentation of Islam put forth by the "Orientalists," reduces any analysis of Islamic ideology to the truism that Islam is what Muslims are. Hence Buddhism is what Buddhists are and socialism is what socialists are, and there have been wide variations among Buddhists and among socialists. Then, one may conclude that "there are as many Islams as there are situations that sustain it" (Al-Azmeh 1993: 1). If so, can one distinguish Islam from Buddhism and capitalism from socialism, as distinct ideological or social systems, in spite of historical and circumstantial variations? Or, to put it differently, is it possible to characterize an ideological system such as Islam in terms of its social ethos and public policy? This is of special interest in an age when Islamic revivalism has become the banner of social change and beacon of a new social order in many Muslim societies.[4]

The contention of this chapter is that the contrasting interpretations of Islam represent two distinct visions of Islamic ideology corresponding to two specific historical circumstances of Islam. The first vision is that of Islam the rebellious, the idol smasher. It is Islam of the *mustaz'afin* (oppressed) and the banner of the mobilized masses. The second is the vision of order in an Islamic state, a class society. It is the Pax Islamicus that lasted for several centuries in a vast empire. While the populism and egalitarianism of Islam of the mustaz'afin generate the revolutionary thunder of Islamic revivalism, Islamic order, reflected in the laws and the historical traditions that ruled over the rigidly stratified Muslim societies of the past, brings together a diversified alliance of the propertied and privileged classes, Islamic or not. In this way, variability and instability of the newly established Islamic states generally reflect the predicaments of transition from Islamic populism to Pax Islamicus (or Islamic order). In this context, formulation of public policy in a newly established Islamic state becomes an arena of confrontation between these two visions of Islam. Whether a newly established state survives, collapses, or degenerates, and how each case may exactly evolve, will obviously depend on the specific of historical circumstances. Yet, the historical legacy of these two visions of Islam defines the terms and format of this social confrontation. The battle is fought in the arena of Islamic jurisprudence.

Let us first consider the two contradictory representations of Islam and their historical contexts.

From Islam the rebellious to Pax Islamicus

Islamic revivalism attempts to establish a social order according to the precepts of Islam, which are stated in the holy book, the Quran, and expressed by the words and actions of the Prophet Muhammad, Tradition (*Sunna*). Moreover, Islam, as a religion, has been a social movement that began when Muhammad preached a new social order while negating the spiritual legitimacy of the idols of the Meccans. In their place, he asked the Meccans to praise no god but Allah. This was a challenge against the dominant clans and families of Mecca and the power and social order that they enjoyed. Mecca was a flourishing commercial center, where merchants were sophisticated financiers and commercial activities were well-developed (Donner 1981: 52). If Muhammad's call to Islam is not to be regarded as merely an expression of a class conflict between the underprivileged and the ruling oligarchy of Mecca, it certainly was true that, as Bernard Lewis suggests, Muhammad drew his support "mainly from the poorer classes" and that his "opposition of the Meccans was largely economic in origin" (Lewis 1960: 39–40). Many chapters (*suras*) of the Quran revealed in Mecca reflect Muhammad's antagonistic confrontation with the wealthy and powerful Meccan clans and families (Rodinson 1971: 69–147). Muhammad brings God's "Woe" for the idolater of Mecca "Who hath gathered wealth" and who "thinketh that his wealth will render him immortal" (Sura CIV: 2–3)[5]. He threatens his own uncle, Abu Lahab, who had joined the opposition boycotting Muhammad's clan, that "He will be plunged in flaming fire," and "His wealth and gains will not exempt him" (CXI: 1–3). And in *Al-Fajr*, a very early Meccan sura, the Meccans are reminded of the fate of Pharaoh and his ilk:

> Dost thou not consider how thy Lord dealt with (the tribe of) A'ad,
> With many-columned Iram, ...
> And with (the tribe of) Thamud, ...
> And with Pharaoh, ...
> Who (all) were rebellious (to Allah) in these lands, ...?
>
> (LXXXIX: 6–11)

They are told that they will receive the "disaster of His punishment," for as the Quran says,

> Nay, but ye ... honour not the orphan, And urge not on the feeding of the poor, And ye devour heritage with devouring greed, And love wealth with abounding love.
>
> (LXXXIX: 17–20)

Muhammad's inability to make progress against the opposition led him to migrate (*hijra*) with his followers to Medina in AD 622. Many citizens of Medina came to the support of Muhammad and his followers, who formed a community of Muslims in that city. Thus Muhammad, an idol smasher, an "anti-establishment" leader of an opposition movement preaching Islam in Mecca, became the chief magistrate of a community, practicing Islam in Medina (Lewis 1960: 41). In fact, it is in Medina that the first Islamic state was formed, and it is the ten years (622–32) of Muhammad's rule over this community that are viewed by Islamic revivalists as the Golden Age of Islam, which they wish either to reconstruct or to view as a model for contemporary social reform.

The revelations of the Quran to Muhammad in this period, too, reflect the change in the position of the Prophet, preaching a new religion, but also the leader of the community, the arbiter among groups and individuals, and the defender of the new community against its enemies. It is in Medina that some very important suras are revealed, such as, *Al-Anfal* (Spoils of War – Sura VIII), dealing with the distribution of the booty of the battle of Badr; *An-Nisa* (Women – Sura IV), dealing mainly with the treatment of women (widows and orphans of the battle of Uhud) and the internal dissidents (*khawarij* – hypocrites); and *Al Ma'ida* (The Table Spread – Sura V), addressing the matter of eating as well as the relations between the Muslims and Christians. The Tradition of Muhammad in this period also reflects the attempt of the Prophet to establish civil order, while trying to maintain social and military preparedness to fend off attacks of the enemy and to score victories against them.

The rule of Muhammad, as well as those of Abu Bakr (632–4) and Umar (634–44), the first two of the Four Rightly Guided Caliphs, was a period of state building and expansion. It was a society in transition and on the make. While the internal order was being established in the face of conflicts and challenges posed against the authority of Muhammad and the caliphs, the realm of Islam was expanding. Two giant imperialist powers, Persia and Byzantium, collapsed under the blow of Islam, which, especially under the rule of Umar, had become a revolutionary thunder (Donner 1981). The booty of the wars certainly helped to empower the Islamic movement and the infant and fragile Islamic state. Soon after his arrival in Medina, Muhammad had begun his predatory raids against the Meccan caravans, both to blockade Mecca and to improve the economic well-being of the community (*umma*) in Medina (Lewis 1960: 44). But taking booty was easily accepted as a custom of the period. What the Quran needed to set straight was that the state receives a share too.

> And know that whatever ye take as spoils of war, lo! a fifth thereof is for Allah, and for the messenger and for the kinsman (who hath need) and orphans and the needy and the wayfarer.
>
> (Sura VIII: 41)

More importantly, as it was the tradition of the Arab tribes, the Quran and Sunna reveal repeatedly that life and property may be taken away in the name of Islam. Many wealthy merchants were killed or taken as prisoners in the raids led by Muhammad. It was made clear that it was legitimate to loot (confiscate) their merchandise (property) and to take them as prisoners and to release them in return for high ransoms (Rodinson 1971: 162–70). The newly instituted state of Islam assumed the right of appropriation of property from whoever threatened the security of the Islamic state.

When caliph Umar was assassinated in 644, Uthman was chosen as the new leader of the Islamic state. The rule of Uthman, the third Rightly Guided Caliph, which lasted until 656, was a period of intense internal conflict in the Islamic state, as the state was transformed from a rebellious Islam to Pax Islamicus of the

Umayyads and Abbasids dynasties. The election of Uthman, a member of the powerful Umayyad family of Mecca, as the caliph, was a victory for the Meccan oligarchy, who benefited from his nepotism in taking many of the high posts of the empire and dominating its commercial relations (Lewis 1960: 59). By the end of Umar's rule, however, the Islamic state was entering a fiscal crisis. The Arab tradition was that the spoils of war would be distributed among the warriors to share with the tribe. This tradition was followed in Muhammad's time and during the rule of Abu Bakr and Umar. In addition to the loot that was carried away from the battlefield, in the Islamic conquests, there were other worthy prizes, namely land, which could be possessed or taxed, and people, who could also be taxed. Until the rule of Umar, the second caliph, these revenues were also distributed equally among the warriors. But by Umar's time it was becoming obvious that the revenue from taxation of the conquered lands was not sufficient to keep the Arab recruits "on the pay roll" (Cameron 1973: 50). Thus, the office of treasurer of the state was established by Umar for regularizing the collection and distribution of the revenues of the state among those who had a right to pension. This imposed the power of the purse on the army, which believed the conquered land, and the tributes from it, belonged to them. Thus, what was viewed by the army as property of the Muslims (*mal al-Muslimin*) became the property of the state (*mal Allah*), or the "public treasury." The large band of warriors of Islam detested this transformation because they now had to depend on the state for their pension (Cameron 1973: 51–2).

Uthman's nepotism and the corruption in the administration of the conquered territory only accentuated the friction that was forming between the state and the opposition groups, particularly those in the army. Uthman put his cousin Marwan in charge of the public treasury and gave him one-fifth of the loot of the North African conquest, offered one brother ("who was proscribed by Muhammad at the capture of Mecca" in 630) the governorship of Egypt, and the other ("who had spat on Muhammad's face") the governorship of Kufa (Cameron 1973: 52). His cousin Mu'awiya, the son of Abu Sufyan and Hind, was already appointed Governor of Syria by Umar.[6] In response to the economic crisis, and unsatisfied with the policies of Uthman, in 656 rebels from Iraq and Egypt moved toward Medina. When the Egyptians arrived, a crowd broke into Uthman's house and the 80-year-old caliph was murdered as he was reading the Quran, one that he had commissioned to be edited and which is considered "the most important and fruitful achievement of [his] reign" (Spuler 1960: 31).

A strong representation of the conflict in the transition of Islam toward Pax Islamicus of the Umayyads (and later that of the Abbasids) is the protests of Abu Dharr and Ali to what they viewed as the betrayal of Muhammad's Islam by Mu'awiya and the house of Umayyads. Abu Dharr was a companion of Muhammad. He objected to the luxurious life of Mu'awiya, and to his misuse of the public treasury. Abu Dharr pointed out to Mu'awiya that the Quran has condemned those who "hoard up gold and silver and spend it not in the way of Allah," and that it warned that "unto them give tiding (O Muhammad) of a painful doom" (IX: 34). Abu Dharr contended that the accumulated wealth at the house of Mu'awiya must be distributed among the poor at once. He claimed that Muhammad told him once that "should this mountain of Uhud be turned into gold for me, I would not wish that the nightfall comes before I have disposed of it all in charity except two carats" (Abdul-Rauf 1979: 14–15). Abu Dharr's troublemaking was unbearable to Mu'awiya, who asked his uncle, Uthman, to recall him to Medina. Thus, Uthman summoned Abu Dharr to Medina and from there sent him to exile to al-Rabadha, where he died in 652 or 653 (Gibb *et al.* 1960: 114–15).

The struggle to establish the pure and unadulterated precepts of the ideology by confronting the "usurpers" and "impostors" who hold political power is not unique to Islam. It is not altogether surprising, therefore, to see that twenty-four years after the death of Muhammad, Uthman, the third Rightly Guided Caliph of the Muslims, is murdered by a group of disenchanted Muslims. The confrontation of Ali, the fourth Rightly Guided Caliph, against Mu'awiya and the house of the Umayyads, and the battle of Husayn (Ali's son) with Yazid (Mu'awiya's son), particularly to the Shi'is, is the continuation of the struggle between Abu Dharr and Uthman, between good and evil, liberation and oppression.

After the assassination of Uthman, Ali became the fourth caliph of the Muslims. Ali was not successful in leading the Islamic state effectively, as Mu'awiya and others, who blamed Ali for Uthman's death, challenged his leadership. In the heat of the tension between Ali and his opponents, Ali was murdered in 661 by one of his former followers. As there was no one to lead Ali's followers, they dispersed. Some historians of Islam suggest that Ali's assassination brought the "eminent danger of a civil war" among Muslims to an end (Spuler 1960: 34). Soon after Ali's death, Hasan (d. 669), Ali's older son, signed a treaty with Mu'awiya abdicating any claim over the caliphate (Momen 1985: 26–8). Thus, Mu'awiya, the son of the most powerful enemy of Muhammad and a member of the Meccan oligarchy, established himself as the caliph of the Muslims and continued to extend the Pax Islamicus, that he had established in Syria, to the rest of the Islamic Empire.

The last effort in reestablishing Muhammad's Islam amongst the populace in these early days of Islamic history was the struggle of Husayn, Ali's second son, and Muhammad's grandson. Mu'awiya, who died in April 680, had arranged for his son Yazid to succeed him. Among the followers of Ali, Yazid was known as a sacrilegious man. Husayn challenged the rule of the Umayyads, regarding both Mu'awiya and Yazid as the impious usurpers of the caliphate. Yazid confronted Husayn in Karbela, where Husayn and seventy-two of his followers were brutally slain by Yazid's forces on October 10, 680 (10 Muharram 61 AH) (Spuler 1960: 39; Momen 1985: 28–33). This proved to be a crucial historical event for the Shi'is, who view Karbela as the theater of confrontation between good and evil and regard Husayn and his followers in that battle among the great martyrs of all ages, symbolizing the selfless, heroic struggle for Islamic justice in a battle with the satanic power of the wealthy, arrogant, and corrupt.

Abu Dharr's confrontations with Mu'awiya and Uthman, followed by Ali's and Husayn's battles against Mu'awiya and Yazid, were the manifestations of the tension in the newly established state of Islam. This tension was between populism, idealism, and egalitarianism that was preached by Muhammad, or at least understood as such by many converts to Islam, and the emerging social order in Medina and in the conquered lands. When the society of Muslims was set up in Medina, and as it expanded into the conquered territories, the imperatives of establishing a viable social order with a legal framework for public policy became clear to the political leaders, the caliphs. The issue became more clearly apparent with the fiscal crisis facing Umar's newly established Islamic empire. The populism and egalitarianism of early Islam, quite compatible with the collectivism of the tribal social order in Arabia, were obviously irreconcilable with the oligarchic order that was being established (or in some cases reestablished) in the new imperial conglomerate of the highly complex agrarian-commercial societies of Mesopotamia, Persia, and Egypt.

The Umayyads succeeded in completing the transformation from Islamic populism to Pax Islamicus, a process which had been begun by Umar and which made Uthman, Abu Dharr, Ali, and Husayn its main casualties. This made the Umayyads seem the principal revisionists and violators of the tenets of Islam to the followers of egalitarian Islamic movements as well as to the orthodox Muslims who believed that the Umayyads (661–750) denigrated the faith while promoting their own power. Obviously the Shi'is, not only from the perspectives mentioned here, but also for their partisan position on the intense and brutal confrontation of Mu'awiya and Yazid with Ali and his son, Husayn, view the Umayyads as the arch enemies of the "true Islam." Even the Abbasids who ruled over the Islamic Empire for more than five centuries (750–1258) in a manner not much different from the Persian kings, and who abandoned enforcing many precepts of Islam, such as the ban against wine drinking (Spuler 1960: 49–52), viewed the Umayyads as adversaries of Islam (Schacht 1982: 23).

But both for the Umayyads and the Abbasids, the main preoccupation of the state was political administration and public policy, and not religious purity. It was in this rather long period, from the seventh to the thirteenth century that Islamic law (*Shari'a*) was fully formulated. The formulation of Islamic law was accompanied with the centralization and rationalization of the system of administration of the state and reforms in public finance, the monetary system, laws of contracts and commercial obligations, inheritance and family laws, and the penal code. Many treatises were written by scholars on these matters, such as that written by Abu Yusuf (1969) at the request of the Abbasid caliph, Harun al-Rashid (786–809).[7] This trend also led to the centralization of the judicial system by the early Abbasid period, when judges (*qadis*) were appointed by the central government, and the position of the Chief Justice (*qadi al-qudat*) was created. The caliph, who ruled over the state as the sovereign, was expected to possess the same attributes as those of the qadis and to be constrained in the same way by the Shari'a. But the caliph also had the power to legislate in matters of public policy to promote the welfare of the state. By the early Abbasid period this came to be known as *siyasa* (Schacht 1982: 50–4).

Siyasa: public policy

Development of the concept of siyasa was the manifestation of a fundamental transformation in the institution of societal leadership, from prophethood to kingship. Caliphs were gradually evolving into kings or sultans, if not in name at first, at least in practice. Dynasties were established. First the Umayyads and Abbasids, and then Fatemids and Ayyubids, before the Seljuks and the sons of Changiz took over the caliphate. One may regard this transformation as "monarchization of the caliphdom." This transformation was accelerated especially by the influence of the theories of administration espoused by Iranians, who reflected upon the administrative practices of the courts of the Persian kings. Yassin Essid (1995) examines the significance of the administrative literature, known as "the Mirror for Princes" written by scholars, wazirs, or kings in the first centuries of Islamic rule. Among these are *Adab al-Kabir* (circa 750)[8] of Roozbeh (Abd Allah) Ibn al-Muqaffa', *Kitab al-Sultan* (889) of Ibn Qutayba, *Siyasat Nama* (1091) of Nizam al-Mulk, and *Nasihat al-Muluk* (1105) of Imam Muhammad Ghazali. In about 1121, al-Turtushi (also known as Ibn Randaqa) wrote *Siraj al-Muluk* in an attempt to present an Arabized mirror (Essid 1995). These treatises are discourses on a wide array of subjects dealing with the conduct of the affairs of the state. Their range is from the protocol of the court of the king, the manners of conducting the administrative duties of the sovereign, and the intricacies of power plays in the court, to justification for the power of the sovereign, discussion of the social stratification and occupational composition of society, and means of achieving prosperity and social tranquility.

If these treatises reflect the discourse on the principles and wisdom of governance of the sovereign, the institution of *hisba* and the position of the *muhtasib* provide the means for implementation of public policy in the public space, namely the market (*suq*). The institution of hisba was to maintain law and order, to ensure collective welfare of the community (umma). It was responsible for regulating market activities by guarding against fraud, dishonesty, and extortion. It was to guard the orderly flow of commerce and maintenance of market stability and, most importantly, the availability of food staples and stability of their prices. In addition to commercial activities, the office of hisba was the guardian of public morality.[9] In other words, the office of hisba was to promote good – *ma'ruf* – and to suppress evil – *munker* (Khan 1982: 135). Thus, the office of hisba was to provide both temporal tranquility and spiritual purity in the Muslim city, as a corollary of the unitary conception of Islam (Essid 1995: 138).

The rules of conduct of the market were presented as the "laws of the market" (*ahkam al-suq*). The first known treatise of this kind was written by Ibn Umar (1975) in the third century of Islam (Essid 1995: 123). The responsibilities of the office of hisba were carried out by the muhtasib. He was expected to be a man "with a high degree of integrity, insight, reverence and social status," to oversee the organization of religious rituals, market activities, and the administration of affairs of the municipality (Khan 1982: 137). Thus, the muhtasib was to see that commerce was flowing smoothly, without any dishonesty, that no immoral acts or other disruptive behaviors were being demonstrated, that building codes and zoning restrictions were observed, that public passages were not obstructed, and that roads were clear and streets were safe.

These duties of the muhtasib reflected the high degree of sensitivity of government to urban tranquility and its fear of "enemies of the interior," and acts of protest and violence that the population of the suq had a tendency to exhibit, especially in response to acute shortage of provisions and the sharp increase of their prices (Essid 1995: 129–30). The muhtasib was also responsible to see that riba was not practiced, weights were not short and scales were accurate, no transaction was carried out with children and mental incompetents, and hoarding was not exercised. One of the most significant aspects of the duties of the muhtasib was maintaining price stability. This was done although price regulation is a highly controversial issue in Islam.

Market and prices

In spite of much controversy about price regulations, it is accurate to say that Islamic jurisprudence and scholarly discourse express a clear preference for a smoothly functioning and stable free market, where the main provisions of life are provided at a "reasonable price," and where profitability for the merchant and adequate livelihood for the populace are guaranteed. All of this is expected to be the general norm of a free market with no intervention by the government. The cornerstone of the opposition to price regulation in Islam is a hadith (statement) by Muhammad. It is reported that on the occasion of rising prices some asked him to fix prices. He replied,

> God is the Taker, the Disposer, the Succourer and the Controller of prices. I very much hope that when I meet God no-one will claim against me for an injury I have caused in blood and property.
>
> (Ibn Taymiya 1982: 35)

There is some doubt about the validity of this hadith which is not reported in *Muwatta'* of Imam Malik or *Sahih* of al-Bukhari (Essid 1995: 153). Bernard Lewis asserts that "it is obvious that the Prophet said no such thing, for such a question could hardly have arisen in western Arabia during his lifetime" (Lewis 1974: xxi). Lewis adds that this "theological statement of laissez-faire economics... has been the predominant view among the professional men of religion, since virtually all the traditions dealing with prices take this line" (Lewis 1974: xxii). It could very well be that this is a fabricated hadith, but the reliability of its source and the chain of transmitters aside, one cannot reject it for its historical context and meaning.[10] Medina was a city much dependent on imports of goods, and it is well-known that any economy reliant on imports is susceptible to exogenously induced price fluctuations. This could be the statement of a ruler of a city relying heavily on imported provisions. (With a high dependence on agricultural output, the statement could also be true in reference to unpredictability of the climate.) If this is in fact Muhammad's statement, it cannot be construed simply as fatalistic submission to God's will. For a man who spent much of his life in the world of commerce, he was well aware of the workings of the market. Thus, this statement may mean that under normal circumstances the market price is "fair" and "just" (Essid 1995: 153). It may be also viewed as a way of discouraging the public from expecting the government to fix prices any time they rise because there are many cases in the market when price control is ineffective and even possibly counterproductive.

Al-Maqrizi (d. 1442) points out that price fixing would be counterproductive because the merchants would view it as arbitrary and abusive, and will tend to react by overstocking their merchandise (Essid 1995: 153). It is on this basis that the Hanbali and Shafi'i schools of Islamic jurisprudence reject price fixing. Ibn Qudamah al-Maqdisi, a Hanbali scholar, states that government has no business fixing prices because it is an injustice inflicted upon the owners of the merchandise who have the right to sell their property at any price that they agree upon with the buyer. Furthermore, he argues that price fixing will in itself cause prices to increase. That is so, he states, because when government fixes prices in a market, merchants will not bring their goods into that market and those who have goods in that market will keep them in stock. But as the buyers cannot satisfy their demand, they bid up the price. Therefore, price increases and the buyers and sellers will both suffer. For this reason Ibn Qudamah maintains that price fixing is prohibited in Islam (Islahi 1988: 95).

Taqi al-Din Ahmad Ibn Taymiya (d. 1328), a prominent Hanbali theologian and jurist, however, underscores the views of some scholars who approve some price regulations.[11] He maintains that "if people refuse to sell what they are under obligation to sell," or if they refuse to sell at a "fair price," they may be ordered to do so and be punished for noncompliance (Ibn Taymiya 1982: 50). In this way, Ibn Taymiya maintains that rejecting price regulation by relying on Muhammad's statement above is a mistaken interpretation. He does not refute the authenticity of the statement attributed to Muhammad, but argues that it is a "particular judgment, not a general pronouncement," and is mainly related to the situation of Medina where there was little that the Prophet could do about the effects of fluctuations in import prices (Ibn Taymiya 1982: 51). Ibn Taymiya seems well aware of the price mechanism and is not disposed to price regulation when a price increase is the "natural" outcome of the dynamics of the market. He states that

> Rise and fall in prices is not always due to an injustice (*zulm*) by certain individuals. Sometimes the reason for it is deficiency in production or decline in import of the good in demand. Thus if desire for the good increases while its availability decreases, its price rises. On the other hand, if availability of the good increases and the desire for it decreases, the price comes down. This scarcity or abundance may not be caused by the action of any individuals; it may be due to a cause not involving any injustice, or sometimes, it may have a cause that does involve injustice. It is the Almighty God who creates desires in the hearts of the people.
>
> (Islahi 1988: 88–9)[12]

This and other similar passages indicate that Ibn Taymiya understood the dynamics of price determination and appreciated that prices may go up and down, depending on availability (supply) and desire (demand). He, too, attributed this to Almighty God who creates desires in our hearts. Thus, even the restrictive interpretation of Ibn Taymiya calls for the market to work freely.

Whether or not one accepts the validity of the hadith by Muhammad on free fluctuation of prices, Muslim scholars are generally proponents of a free market. Ibn Taymiya and all the other proponents of price regulation call for the intervention of the government only to rectify the effects of market irregularities (imperfections), such as monopoly and hoarding, on the price of the main provisions demanded by the public. Thus, the muhtasib is entitled, as Ibn Taymiya sees it, to compel the hoarders or the monopolists to sell their merchandise at their "fair value" (Ibn Taymiya 1982: 31–3). When price stability is disturbed for any exogenous reasons, such as bad harvest or high price of imports, Ibn Habib suggests that the ruler should bring together all the merchants of the market and ask them how they buy and sell. Then the ruler may bring their price down to where it is acceptable to the merchants and the public (Ibn Taymiya 1982: 50). This is a form of mediation between the conflicting interests of the merchants and the public in order to evade a crisis. This voluntary price fixing among the merchants, under the sanction and control of the ruler, brings into focus the reconciliation of individual freedom of enterprise and the collective well-being of the society.

The proposed conditions for government's control over prices are the most intrusive aspects of an Islamic ruler's market intervention in Ibn Taymiya's controversial views, which have gained him recognition as a maverick reformer in the long succession of great Muslim scholars (K. Ahmad 1982; Islahi 1988). The proposed criteria of Ibn Taymiya for market intervention are, however, not only insignificant in comparison to the "just price" doctrine of Medieval Christianity and the pre-Industrial Revolution mercantilist policies in Europe, but they are quite mild even in contrast to the restraints imposed on enterprises in their pricing and other business practices in the market economies of the post-Industrial Revolution, and especially in modern capitalism. Predatory pricing, cornering the market, fraud, and extortion are business practices that hamper the efficiency of the market and, more importantly, subvert its legitimacy. These practices are unequivocally condemned in Islam as they are viewed illegitimate in modern capitalism.

On the determination of wages and the rights of workers, Islam sanctions the dynamics of the labor market as defined in classical capitalism. As long as the laborers are paid the wages that they agreed upon with their employer and are aware of the going wage rate in the market in reaching their agreement, there is little reason for the government to intervene. Therefore, an Islamic state may not be expected, according to the Shari'a, to intervene in setting wages or determining the conditions of employment in any ways such as determining the hours of work and minimum wage rate, or restricting child labor. Nor is the Islamic state expected to create any of the restrictions that the states of many modern capitalist economies (developed or otherwise) impose (Behdad 1989, 1992). The mechanism of the market is expected to maintain the wellbeing of the Muslim state except when special circumstances arise, for which special policies may be enacted. (For elaboration of labor law, see Pfeifer, Chapter 5, in this volume.)

Public interest, urgency, and public policy

When the society is functioning within its "normal" course and individuals live as devout Muslims, with honesty, decency, benevolence, and in accordance with the rules of the Shari'a, minimal intervention of the state in the market will be necessary. The state will collect taxes for making public expenditures and will supplement the charity and alms giving of the individuals to help the poor and destitute. But should the need arise, an Islamic state may implement new or exceptional policies in order to deal with new or extraordinary circumstances. Theoretically, *ijtihad* (the process of deducing new laws from the basic sources by a qualified Muslim scholar, *mujtahid*) should be relied upon to deal with new circumstances. However, in the opinion of the major schools of Sunni jurisprudence, the "gates of ijtihad" have been closed since the fourth century of Islam (Schacht 1982: 69). That is, by the time this view gained dominance, all essential questions dealing with the Shari'a had been dealt with by the great mujtahids of the past.

Therefore, according to this view, there is no need for independent reasoning in the Shari'a and the jurists are limited to the interpretation of "the doctrine as it had been laid down once and for all" (Schacht 1982: 71).[13] But since societies would confront new and extraordinary circumstances, the provisions of *istihsan* (juristic preference), *maslaha mursala* (unrestricted public interest), and *istislah* (consideration of public interest) have been devised by the major Sunni schools of jurisprudence (Paret 1978: 255–9; Khadduri 1989: 738–40).[14] These juristic practices involve setting aside an existing law, when its enforcement may harm the society of Muslims, in favor of an alternative ruling which would serve public interest better (Kamali 1991: 247). Imam Muhammad Ghazali (d. 1111) articulated the juristic concept of maslaha by suggesting that the "ultimate purpose of the Shri'a ... [is] the maintenance of religion, life, offspring, reason and property. 'Anything which furthers these aims' ... is maslaha" (Khadduri 1989: 739). Thus, in extraordinary circumstances, most importantly in the conditions of "urgency" (*daruriyyat*),[15] the objectives of the Shari'a may be relied upon in order to pursue public interest. Public interest here means safeguarding religion, life, future of the society, sanity, or property against an imminent danger in any of these regards for society. Ghazali points out that anything which furthers these aims is maslaha and anything which runs contrary to them is "mafsada" and cites the example of unbelievers shielding themselves among Muslims. He notes that the killing of innocent Muslims in this case is permissible in order to preserve Islam (Khadduri 1989: 739). Kamali, however, emphasizes that maslaha is invalid if it has been "nullified either explicitly or by an indication that could be found" in the Shari'a (Kamali 1991: 273). Therefore, for example, the argument that in modern times usury (riba) could be justified based on maslaha, because it is necessary for Muslims to engage in usury to participate in the world market, would not be acceptable because usury is explicitly prohibited in the text (*nass*) of the Quran (Kamali 1991: 274–5).

Thus, as long as a ruling is not contrary to the text of the Quran and the objectives of the Shari'a, it could be upheld for the reason of expediency if it is viewed by Islamic jurists, or the Islamic state, that it is to the public interest (Kamali 1991: 280). With the wider scope of ijtihad in Shi'ism, a Shi'i state would have less need to rely on istihan, maslaha, or istislah, which Shi'i scholars have rejected altogether (Kamali 1991: 246). But even a Shi'i state, when it needs to violate a primary rule of the Shari'a finds a way of legitimizing its action in the name of public interest and preservation of the Islamic state. In a context similar to that expressed in Imam Ghazali's example, Ayatollah Khomeini in 1981 let the Consultative Assembly (Majlis) of the Islamic Republic of Iran invoke "secondary rules" (*ahkam thanaviyya*) in a condition that was declared "urgent," to redistribute land and take other actions, in violation of "primary ruling" (*ahkam avvaliyya*) which guarantees property rights (Behdad 1995a). This is similar to the example of Imam Ghazali, which is viewed as a troublesome case of maslaha by some Muslim scholars (Kamali 1991: 275). In each case, a specific injunction of the Shari'a is violated: in Ghazali's case the sanctity of life of innocent Muslims, and in Khomeini's case the sanctity of property. When Khomeini encountered the opposition of the jurists in the Guardian Council to the passage of laws by the Majlis, even on grounds of urgency, and only for the temporary duration of the urgency, he constituted in 1988 the Expediency Council (*Majma'-e Tashkhis-e Maslahat*) for reconsideration of the rulings of the Guardian Council.

The issue points to the conclusion that in urgent circumstances an Islamic state can implement any policy measures to preserve itself, because the state views itself as the guardian of religion, life, and even sanity and property, and any state claims that its collapse will bring chaos and destruction. This divinely sanctioned means of political expediency is especially convenient for the states defining themselves as Islamic.

Reformism and revivalism

From the tenth century (fourth century AH) to the fall of the Ottoman Empire after the First World War, Islamic public policy was practiced within various local or national state entities based on what may be called traditional jurisprudence. This is viewed by many as the period of imitation (*taqlid*) and decline in Islamic jurisprudence, when original ijtihad was discouraged and scholars were preoccupied with writing commentaries on the works of the great theologians of the past (Kamali 1996: 67). From the late nineteenth century, a movement began to reform and rejuvenate (*islah*) Islam. This movement was mainly in response to the colonial domination of Europe over the Muslim societies of the Middle East, and a reaction to the advances of Europe in science, technology, and, most importantly, in acquiring an enviable economic affluence, in contrast to the poverty and stagnation of the Middle Eastern economies. Sayyid Jamal al-Din Afghani (d. 1897) is the pioneer in the path of Islamic reformism and anticolonialism. As a political activist he traveled throughout the Middle East, and to India and England as well. He struggled to take away the control of the traditional ulama over the faith and to make Islam a means of political mobilization and a "source of solidarity" against Western imperialism (Keddie 1994: 23). The reformist trend, especially in promoting rationalism and a scientific outlook, was pursued by such influential thinkers as Muhammad Abduh (d. 1905) in Egypt (Kerr 1966), and Shariat-Sangalaji (d. 1944) and Ahmad Kasravi (d. 1946) in Iran (Richard 1988).[16]

In the early decades of the twentieth century, a strong current in Islamic reformism evolved into a movement for the revival or renewal (*tajdid*) of Islamic social order.[17] That is, the Islamic movement, instead of attempting to "rationalize" Islam, so that it would become compatible with the modernity and industrialism of the West, came to rely on the precepts of Islam to invigorate the umma toward construction of an ideal society, in accordance with the blueprints drawn from the Golden Age of Islam. As John Voll (1986: 168) observes, "revivalism is inherent in the logic and experience of Muslims in history," for Muhammad's Tradition (Sunna) is a pillar of the Shari'a and Islamic belief. The society that Muhammad organized in Medina, and the rule that he and the Rightly Guided Caliphs extended to the new territories of Islam, have been viewed by Muslims as examples of equitable and just societies to be followed. Moreover, the prosperous and powerful Islamic state of the Umayyads, the Abbasids, and other Islamic dynasties that followed them on the vast territories spreading from India to Spain, and the great scientific contributions of Muslim scholars in medieval ages, when Europeans were struggling with the fanatical rigidities of the Christian church, have given many Muslims a sense of chauvinistic religious pride. This is in the face of the indignities imposed upon them by colonialism, foreign domination, and, not the least, by their own poverty and technological underdevelopment.

Thus, an utopianism, a wish, and even a struggle to return to the morally upright, politically successful, and economically prosperous golden ages of Islamic rule seems only a "natural" response to these circumstances. The reaction to the top-down, and at times coercive, secularization policies of the state in Turkey, Iran, and Egypt, pursued particularly from the late 1920s, and the economic and social dislocations resulting from the industrialization and the subsequent urbanization of these and many other Middle Eastern societies, gave the urban and rural underclass and the traditional petty producers and merchants ample reason to congregate under the unifying green flag of Islam. This congregation longed for two principal objectives. Foremost, it expressed a strong yearning for the values and morality of the "old-time religion." It opposed the "immorality and social decadence" that had been brought about by the secularization policies of the state and the encroachment of Western culture upon the Muslim society. Bureaucratic corruption, use of intoxicants, and sexual immorality were the main areas of concern, for all of which the state was held responsible. None of these maladies was new, except possibly the last. The objection was raised to the assertive and even coercive effort of the state, particularly in Turkey and Iran, in "bringing" women into the public space by de-veiling them and making available to them some educational and occupational opportunities.

No less significant, particularly to the urban and rural underclass, was the Islamic pledge to social fairness and economic justice. The peasants yearning for access to land, generally held by large landlords, the discontent of the recently urbanized laborers, working for meager wages with the constant fear, and often the reality, of chronic unemployment, and the struggle of the artisans and shop-keepers to survive the destructive waves of domestic or foreign competition and market instabilities, made any promise of social justice attractive.

Islamic revivalism and socialism

The Islamic revivalist movement was deeply influenced by the spread of socialism as an ideological and a revolutionary movement, and by the Cold War between the capitalist and socialist camps in the post-Second World War decades. This influence was particularly accentuated by the anticolonialist and anti-imperialist movements that many Muslim societies were engaged in for much of the twentieth century. As early as 1912, Mushir Hosain Kidwai, an Indian Muslim, an opponent of British rule over India, and the Honorary Secretary of the Pan-Islamic Society of London, wrote *Islam & Socialism*.[18] This may be the first pamphlet published on Islam and socialism. Kidwai advanced a thesis that later became a prevalent position among many radical Islamic revivalists. He claims that the "idea of Socialism in Islam is not less than thirteen centuries old and cannot be attributed to European influence" (Kidwai 1912: ii). He states on the cover of his pamphlet that "[t]o us (Musalmans) Socialism means an organized, continuous and harmonious co-operation of individuals in all the affairs of life." He refers to the many verses of the Quran, Tradition of Muhammad, and the examples of the Rightly Guided Caliphs to demonstrate what he views as the many socialistic aspects of Islam. In Kidwai's view (1912: 33), Islam would have had a brilliant history if Ali had not been assassinated, for he would have ruled "on truly Socialistic lines." But he adds that "Muhammad had so profusely imbued Musalmans with Socialism that its spirit lingered tenaciously," even after the "destruction of democratic Muslim Socialism" by "the despotism of [Mu'awiya], the first Muslim 'king'" (Kidwai 1912: 33, 66).

Ansari (1986) has studied the impact of socialism on Indian Muslims engaged in the struggle against the British rule in India in the early decades of the twentieth century. In the years following the end of the First World War, anti-British, pan-Islamist Muslims who left India to organize opposition to the British rule in India became aware of the October 1917 Revolution in Russia and the communist ideology. Many of these *Muhajirin* (expatriates) became converts to socialism. Some became the founders of the Communist Party of India. Many of these Muhajirin, communist or still remaining Muslim, believed that there was much in common between Islam and communism. An important example is Maulana Barkat-Allah. He was a pan-Islamist Muslim, with tendencies very similar to

Jamal al-Din Afghani (with whom he had met), and with a belief, as early as 1905, that the British rule over India was the cause of poverty of the Indian people (Ansari 1986: 515, 519). Maulana Barkat-Allah, who remained a believer in Islam all his life, wrote strong words in support of communism in his *Bolshevism and the Islamic Body Politick* (Ansari 1986: 519). For example, "Oh, Muhammedans listen to this divine cry. Respond to this call of liberty, equality and brotherhood which Comrade Lenin and the Soviet Government of Russia are offering you" (Ansari 1986: 519). Shaukat Usmani, one of the founders of the Communist Party of India, stated that "Islam preaches equality, so does Communism. That is why I am a Communist" (Ansari 1986: 530).

Muhammad Iqbal (d. 1938), the great poet and the Pan-Islamic intellectual leader of Pakistan/India's independence movement, wrote in admiration of Karl Marx, Lenin, and the Russian Revolution (M. Iqbal 1955). He wrote in the *Song of the Worker*, "Let us overturn the foundation stones of old taverns" (Gordon-Polonskaya, 1971: 119) and *To the Panjab Peasant*

> Break all the idols of tribe and caste,
> Break the old customs that fetter men fast!
> Here is true victory, here is faith's crown –
> One creed and one world, division thrown down!
> (M. Iqbal 1955: 56)

He calls for a social revolution and summons the dispossessed to

> Rise and arouse the poverty-stricken,
> And shake the foundations of the palaces of the rich.
> Warm up the blood of the slaves with the fire of faith
> And make the sparrow dare to fight the eagle.
> The time of sovereignty of the masses has arrived;
> Wipes away all traces of ancient law and customs.
> (Malik 1971a: 138)

One wonders if Iqbal wanted to echo the International: "Arise ye prisoners of starvation/Arise ye wretched of the earth/For justice thunders condemnation/A better world's in birth" (IWW 1976). It is well-known, however, that to him, socialism was quite compatible with Islam. He wrote to Muhammad Ali Jinnah, the political leader of Pakistan's independence, "[f]or Islam the acceptance of social democracy in some suitable form is not a revolution but a return to the original purity of Islam" (Hassan 1971: 154).

The enthusiastic celebration of socialism by Indian Muslims soon evolved into a general negation of communism and skepticism toward socialist ideals. This was an understandable evolution in the face of the declared atheism of the communist parties, the spreading of the news of the brutality of Stalinism in the Soviet Union, and the Cold War that was waged in the post-Second World War decades. Thus, Islamic revivalist movements, in India, Pakistan, and elsewhere, evolved toward a third worldist, "Neither East, Nor West" ideology, with a clear attempt to draw the lines of demarcation of the Islamic movement with capitalism, on the one side, and with socialism, on the other. On the "left," Islamic reformists such as Khalifa Abdul Hakim (1953), Ghulam Ahmed Parwez (1968), and Nasir Ahmad Sheikh (1961) have taken a position similar to Kidwai that socialism, in its best form, is the innovation of Islam. They all, however, concentrate on the issue of land ownership and the conditions of peasants and pay little attention to industrial production and wage workers (Malik 1971b: 70–4).

On the "right," however, some important conservative Islamic revivalist organizations emerged as anticommunist forces confronting the spread of socialist ideology in the Muslim world. Notable among these were Ikhwan al-Muslimin (Islamic Brotherhood) of Hasan al-Banna (d. 1949) in Egypt (Ramadan 1993), Fada'ian-e Islam (Warriors of Islam) of Mojtaba Navvab-Safavi (d. 1956) in Iran (Behdad 1997), and Jama'at-i Islami of Abul Ala Maududi (d. 1979) in Pakistan (Nasr 1994). To these revivalists, communism and its negation of God, religion, and private property rights are manifestations of the decadence of the West.

Ali Shariati in Iran and Abul Ala Maududi in Pakistan have been the most eloquent proponents of these two tendencies in Islamic revivalism. The clear line of distinction between these two visions of an ideal Islamic society is the provision of social justice and the organization of the relations of production. Shariati recognizes Islam as the religion of liberation, and Islamic revivalism as a move toward formation of a classless society. On the other hand, to Maududi the foundations of an Islamic society are the principles of capitalism, where people's behavior has been modified by the Islamic rules of conduct. Here I will examine these two visions of Islam.

Vision I: monotheistic classless society

Ali Shariati began his political activism in the late 1960s by giving a series of lectures at Mashhad University and the Hoseiniyeh Ershard (Tehran). He died in June 1977 in London, as the early signs of the revolutionary movement in Iran were becoming apparent. Shariati, who had received a doctorate in sociology from the University of Paris like his precursors in Iran, Kasravi and Shariati-Sangalaji, rejected religious fanaticism and condemned political conservatism of the clergy (Behdad 1994). To Shariati, Islam is a rational and progressive worldview, and a "a philosophy of liberation" (Shariati 1978a, 1980a: 73).

The most fundamental and controversial aspect of Shariati's thought is his conception of history, which may be regarded as a Quranic expression of Marx's historical materialism. Shariati (1979: 98) sees the war between Cain and Abel as "the war between two opposing fronts that have existed throughout the history, in the form of a historical dialectic." To him, the killing of Abel by Cain represents the end of the stage of communal ownership of a pastoral society (primitive communism) and the advent of private ownership of an agrarian society (a class society). He adds that this was the beginning of a permanent war between the owners and the dispossessed, the oppressors and the oppressed, the party of Cain and that of Abel. Then, he carries on a distinctly Marxian analysis of class formation and accepts Marx's formulation of the successive stages in the development of social formations, from primitive communes to advanced capitalism, and finally to "the triumph of the proletariat" (Shariati 1979: 98–114). However, he contends that Marx is "confused" in his formulation of these stages since, according to Shariati, societies can have only one of two possible social structures. They can be a classless society, as in primitive and advanced communism. That would be "the structure of Abel." Or they can be a class society, as in slavery, feudalism, and capitalism. This is "the structure of Cain" (Shariati 1979: 112, 1980b: 37).

Shariati, then, concludes that the weapon of both Cain and Abel has been religion. Polytheism (*shirk*), the religion of a class society, is the religion of Cain. Monotheism (divine unity, *towhid*), the religion of a classless society, is the religion of Abel (Shariati 1979: 106–9). In Shi'ism this opposition, according to Shariati, is manifested in the struggle between Alavi Shi'ism (attributed to Imam Ali), the religion of struggle and liberation, and Safavi Shi'ism (attributed to the Safavid kings[19]), the religion of alienation and oppression. Shariati maintains that the existing (prerevolutionary) Shi'i clergy represents Safavi Shi'ism, and expounds a conservative interpretation of Islam. It promotes religious fanaticism and trivializes the teaching of the Quran and Muhammad. This, he claims, is done to preserve the existing structure of social oppression. Shariati, thus, calls upon the Iranian intellectuals to understand Shi'ism as a religion of liberation and not as a stale and degenerated dogma (Shariati 1981a). He calls for an Islamic Protestantism, an Islamic reformation, toward the revival of Alavi Shi'ism with its revolutionary ideals and rejection of the establishment of the clergy (Shariati 1981b: 56).

Shariati is an Abu Dharrian revivalist. He praises Abu Dharr for "fighting exploitation and capitalism" (Shariati 1980b: 29), and in a voice not unlike William Godwin or Pierre Joseph Proudhon, negates private property rights as the basis and the manifestation of polytheism. He contends that Islam is in opposition to "capitalism, private ownership and class exploitation" (Shariati 1978b: 147). Thus according to Shariati (1981c: 296), Islamic liberation is accompanied with rejection of private property and the struggle toward establishing a monotheistic classless society.

Many young followers of Shariati found themselves ideological and political sympathizers of the Organization of Mojahedin Khalq Iran (hereafter, the Mojahedin, a plural noun). A small number of these young activists joined this underground, Islamic revivalist, guerrilla organization, many of whose members were either killed in armed confrontations or spent long times in the Shah's prisons, if they were not summarily executed (Abrahamian 1989). The Mojahedin were remarkably blunt in their regard for Marxist epistemology and methodology (Mojahedin 1972, 1980a). They accepted Marxist social thought but rejected atheism and emphatically objected to the charge by their Muslim opponents of being eclectic Islamic-Marxists (Mojahedin 1980b). In any case, the Mojahedin believed that in a monotheistic society "class contradictions" would have been resolved, "commodity relations" eradicated, the economy demonetized, and a "classless society" established (Mojahedin 1980a: 14, 22–3).

Shariati called for a "genuine socialist" society, which unlike the dictatorial-bureaucratic socialism, was not to be unidimensional in its materialism. Instead, it was to be a society for human liberation, where the essentiality of humanism is recognized (Shariati 1978a: 83–5, 1982: 222). Does Shariati see a contradiction between his Islam, and socialism, and Marxism? He clearly does not. The resolution of the contradiction between the historical materialism of Marxism and the metaphysics of Islam is more essential. Riffat Hassan, in an effort to explain the same issue about Muhammad Iqbal, points out that in the contrapositioning of Marxist materialism and Hegelian idealism we are led to the dichotomy of matter and spirit. However, Hassan points out, in materialism "the reality of thought and other mental phenomena is not denied, only their primacy" (1971: 154). Thus, to Shariati historical materialism and Islam are not necessarily contradictory. The resolution of socialism and Islam is much simpler for him. The life and statements of Muhammad, Ali, and Husayn, to him are all clear proofs that collectivism and egalitarianism are integral parts of Islam. To Shariati, Abu Dharr, Muhammad's Companion, who dared to say in condemnation of private property what even Proudhon did not (Shariati 1980b: 29), was simply following Muhammad's teaching and Tradition. Mojahedin brought Shariati's thought into the Iranian revolution.

Vision II: Islamic capitalism

Seyyed Abul Ala Maududi (also transliterated as Mawdudi or Maudoodi), the Pakistani Muslim revivalist, has been regarded by some as a "Muslim Adam Smith" and a champion of "laissez faire economy" (Malik 1971b: 75). Maududi (1903–79) founded the Jama'at-i Islami in 1941, and following the independence of Pakistan as an Islamic state, carried on a campaign for the formulation of an Islamic constitution based on the Shari'a (Maududi 1969; Nasr 1994). Maududi believed that the "Islamic Movement . . . has to change the whole pattern of living: it has to change the politics, ethics, economics, and the civilization of the world" (S. R. Ahmad 1976: 26–7).

Maududi elaborates on his political theory in a speech delivered at a meeting of the Inter-Collegiate Muslim Brotherhood in Lahore in 1939. He states that sovereignty in the state belongs to God, and no "person, class or group, not even the entire population of the state as a whole, can lay claim to sovereignty." Furthermore, the real lawgiver is God and "the authority of absolute legislation vests in him." From this it follows that the state must "in all respects, be founded upon the laws laid down by God through his Prophet," and no independent legislation can be made, nor can God's laws be modified, "even if the desire to effect such legislation or change in Divine laws is unanimous" (Maududi 1969: 132).

Maududi, however, suggests a redefinition of the Shari'a. In a speech delivered at the Law College in Lahore in 1948 he points out that one is not compelled to "accept any and every saying or expression of opinion by an authority on fiqh, or anything and every thing written in a book of fiqh" (Maududi 1969: 104). This is an obvious fact to any student of Islamic jurisprudence (*fiqh*) because of the existence of many contradictory positions that have been taken by various jurists (*fuqaha*) on many minor and some major issues over the centuries of Islamic rule in various historical, social, and geographical circumstances. According to Maududi, only the following can constitute elements of Islamic law: (i) "an explicit commandment of God" in the Quran; (ii) Muhammad's Tradition (explanations of Quranic verses or his explicit order or prohibition); (iii) juristic interpretations of the Shari'a "on which there has been a consensus (*ijma'*)" of the umma, or "the majority decision of the ulama which has been accepted by an overwhelming majority of our own people"; and (iv) a consensus reached by "our own men of learning and authority" (Maududi 1969: 104–5). Here Maududi reaffirms the tenets of Islamic law accepted by the majority of jurists in various schools of jurisprudence, except placing "our own men of learning and authority" at par with the ulama. This implies that jurisprudential determinations are not in the monopoly of the ulama. The category ulama (or ulema) is, however, a vague concept. It is a plural noun meaning "the learned," as a distinction from lay persons. But it also means the clerics and it is in this context that the word is generally used. However, a cleric may be the lowly mullah of the village officiating at weddings and burials, or a grand mufti or ayatollah with the authority to make jurisprudential judgments and with millions of followers. On the other hand, anyone who goes through the training of Islamic jurisprudence (*fiqh*) can attain the authority of a jurist, whether he (only men qualify to be jurists) is a member of the clergy or not. However, generally, only the clergy go through the training necessary for becoming a jurist, and they generally reject those outside of their rank attempting to break into the circle. Maududi himself is an example, which may explain some of the antagonisms between Maududi and the Muslim clergy in India and Pakistan. But aside from this issue, there is little difference between Maududi and the Islamic orthodoxy on any matter of jurisprudential significance.

According to Maududi (1969: 48), the Shari'a is "a complete scheme of life and an all-embracing social order where nothing is superfluous, and nothing is lacking." This follows the presumption that it is an eternal and universal system of law, which may be applied with some minor variations in different circumstances, but can never be modified in terms of its principle, "even if the desire to effect such legislation or change in Divine laws is unanimous." Moreover, as Maududi asserts (1969: 48–9), "the scheme of life envisaged by the [Shari'a]" constitutes "an organic whole." Thus, no judgment can be passed on any parts of this system before the entire scheme of Islamic life has been established. He attributes many of the "misunderstandings" about the Shari'a to the "faulty attitude" of judging its parts separately (Maududi 1969: 49). As an example, he cites the Islamic penalty of amputating the hand of a thief. He argues that "this injunction is meant to be promulgated in a full-fledged Islamic society," where the Islamic tax of zakat is paid, everyone is provided with "equal privileges and opportunities," and people are "God fearing," love their neighbors and provide for the needy, and so on. This injunction is not for the present society where,

Maududi says, "the economic system only leads to enrichment of the few at the cost of crushing poverty and intolerable misery of the many," and where the government promotes "injustice, class-privileges and distressing economic disparities." He then goes even so far as to say that in these circumstances "it is doubtful if theft should be penalized at all, not to speak of cutting of the thief's hand" (Maududi 1969: 50).

This is the patented response in the revivalists' debate with their secular opposition. A similar point is generally made about stoning to death for adultery, and Maududi finds himself compelled to address that issue, too, on the same pages. On these issues, and also on the issue of women's rights, Muslim reformers like Shariati find themselves in serious difficulty. They do not believe that such injunctions are viable in the modern circumstances; however, many of these injunctions are either explicitly stated in the Quran or are established as Muhammad's Tradition, and therefore, their negation (*naskh*) is not permissible. In this situation, Muslim reformists attempt to present a positive interpretation of these injunctions and to view them as similar to Islam's injunction about trade in, and treatment of, slaves, an issue no longer relevant. But Maududi, true to his revivalist position, does not question the viability of these injunctions. Instead, he suggests that such injunctions may not be carried out before the complete Islamization of society. This position, however, raises a theoretically relevant, and a politically crucial issue in the newly established Islamic states. That is, at what point may the society be regarded Islamic, when the various injunctions of Islam can be carried out? Or rather, at what pace and order should the Islamization of society take place? Clearly, Islamization would be a process, and society may approach its utopian ideal only, and at best, asymptotically. Maududi, too, believes that Islamic law may be introduced gradually, as Muhammad himself did not implement it all at once (S. R. Ahmad 1976: 110). It is, however, a curious fact that the implementation of the penal code of Islam, with flogging, amputation, and stoning to death, and coercive imposition of veil on women has been among the first acts of Islamization in the newly formed revivalist states. Sudan, Pakistan, Iran, and Taliban's Afghanistan are the most vivid examples.

Maududi has been quite explicit on the economic features of an Islamic society. In an address delivered in 1941 at the Muslim University in Aligarh, he states that the economic problems of human society begin when "natural selfishness of man exceeds the limits of moderation,... with the aid of certain other immoral habits and... further support from an inherently defective political system" (Maududi 1978: 13). Then, Maududi proposes his Islamic solution by delineating the line of demarcation of the Islamic economic system with those of capitalism and socialism. To him, the "uncontrolled economy of capitalism" which allows individuals to pursue their gains in any ways that they wish, gives rise to evils of capitalism, such as the unemployment of "hundreds of thousands of workers" and in the continuation of "the curse of artificial soaring prices, and regularly planned scarcities of commodities," or in short, in the persistence of the "disease of Trade Cycle" (Maududi 1977: 49–50, 55). The excessive accumulation of wealth by the rich "would injure" society, as they neglect the deprived individuals and engage in "artificial and self-created requirements of their self-indulgence" and as they get engaged in adultery, which necessitates "an army of prostitutes" and "another army of... musicians, dancing girls, drum beaters," and many other wasteful uses of society's resources by the "pleasure-loving" wealthy people (Maududi 1978: 15–16). Maududi asserts that it is true that socialism may eliminate some of the evils of capitalism "but at the cost of huge losses of life and property and open rebellion against morals and religion," and will also "suppress individual freedom totally" (Maududi 1977: 55).

While Maududi distinguishes Islamic order from capitalism and socialism by criticizing both, his opposition to socialism and his affinity with capitalism are fundamental. In a treatise on *Interest* written in the 1950s, Maududi articulates his epistemological and ideological commitment to individualism. He states as one of the fundamentals of the "Islamic Solution,"

> Islamic point of view attaches real importance to the individual and not to any party, nation or society... No party, nation or society in its entirety is accountable before God, rather every individual singly and in his personal capacity is answerable to Him for his deeds. ... Collective life here does not necessarily mean the collective prosperity but individual welfare. ... [T]he criterion of goodness... of a social order is the degree to which it can help individuals prosper and develop their potentialities.... Islam does not approve of any form of social organization or any measures aimed at Collective welfare.
>
> (Maududi 1977: 55)

Maududi is explicit that economic freedom is the central tenet of the Islamic order, which converts the "oppressive" and "uncontrolled economy" of capitalism into a "free economy" in accordance to the limits Islam defines for such freedom. The most controversial issue in the arena of economics is the limits on property rights. He states that

> Islam recognizes, like other proprietary rights, the right of individual owner-ship of land. ... And there is no limit placed on such ownership; it may be thousands of acres. If it has come in his possession legally, it is his lawful property.
>
> (Maududi 1977: 61)

Maududi's acceptance of unlimited private property rights is in striking con-trast to the view expressed by Shariati and the Mojahedin in Iran some years later. But more significant is Maududi's acceptance of unlimited land ownership in the Zamindari system (landlordism) of Pakistan in the 1950s, when many Muslim reformers were promoting a land reform (Hakim 1953; Sheikh 1961; Parwez 1968). But Maududi adds that the problems of "the feudal system" in Pakistan "are neither purely the outcome of the Zamindari system nor call for the drastic measures of abolition of the individual ownership of land, or need such limitations as are being advocated by 'lay -practitioners' of the day." In his view, application of the Islamic law of inheritance and restriction on land allowed to remain fallow would be sufficient to take care of the land problem in Pakistan (Maududi 1977: 61, 1994).

Thus, to Maududi ownership of private property is certainly legitimate as long as the subject of ownership has been acquired legitimately. Moreover, by rejecting revolutionary acts he suggests that once an Islamic state is established, all the wealth that had been previously acquired would be safe from confiscation, even if the wealth had been acquired "unlawfully." This, Maududi claims to have been the policy of the Prophet and the victorious Muslims who took "no cognizance... of the past deeds of once usurers, brothel-keepers and highway robbers" and raised no question about "previous hoardings or that all the unlawfully earned wealth ought to be confiscated" (Maududi 1977: 59–60). Great Islamic jurists, Abu Yusuf in *Kitab al-Kharaj*, Abu Ubaid al-Qasim in *Kitab al-Amwal*, and Ibn al-Qayyim in *Zad al-Muad*, provide proof for the above assertion (Maududi 1994: 135–6). Maududi, however, points out the restrictions that Islam imposes on ownership, even on lawfully earned property. One may not "spend his wealth on illicit and dissolute pastimes." Drinking of alcoholic beverages, gambling, adultery, making free persons slaves and selling them to the wealthy to "fill their harems with female slaves," are all prohibited. But "if a man desires to utilise his surplus wealth to earn more wealth, he can do so only by practicing a lawful business" (Maududi 1994: 112).

Maududi spells out the general organizational principles of an Islamic economy, where interest on loans, hoarding, speculation, and fraud are prohibited, and "as far as possible" industry and commerce "should be open to free competition." Maududi believes that the application of the law of inheritance of Islam (dividing the assets of the deceased among the heirs in specific proportions), imposition of 2.5 percent tax on "annual assets" of "industrialists and businessmen" (zakat), 5–10 percent tax on agricultural products (*kharaj*), 20 percent tax on "the wealth obtained from mines and buried treasures" and "of the war spoils," and the charity of "the businessmen, industrial magnates and other traders," and "landlords and cultivators" would take care of extreme inequalities in society (Maududi 1977: 59–60).

The role of the state in society is the guardianship of the Shari'a, to ensure compliance of the members of the community with its restrictions and to facilitate the virtuous activity of the pious. In the economic domain the state would safeguard freedom of economic activities and would guarantee that the principles enumerated earlier, and those necessary for the Islamic conduct of affairs in any specific circumstances, prevail. Here, Maududi expresses certain suspicions about the activity of the industrial sector. While he condemns government's control over the economy in the "Nazi fashion," he gives the state the role of "guidance and co-ordination, so that the industries and commerce may not enter wrong channels and there may be complete harmony among various phases of economic life." Even more specifically, he states that no application of labor-replacing technological changes by "industries and other businesses" should be allowed before "thorough stock has been taken as to how many hands it is going to render idle and that ample provisions has been made for them" (Maududi 1977: 62–3). While the state has no responsibility to provide employment for "each and every one of its citizens," the state "has to provide dole" to those who are out of work or are disabled, and to children with no guardians (Maududi 1977: 64–5).

On July 5, 1977 General Zia-ul Haq staged a coup d'etat against Prime Minister Zulfiqar Ali Bhutto and his People's Party of Pakistan. In a program for "Islamic justice" Bhutto's government had nationalized some large enterprises, carried out a land reform, and promoted unionization of workers (Nomani and Rahnema 1994: 121–6). Bhutto's government had come under criticism for trying to impose socialism on Pakistan. Immediately following the coup d'etat, Zia imposed martial law. Worker's strikes were broken, some of the striking workers were shot dead, and "thousands of tenants were forcibly evicted" from the land that Bhutto had distributed (A. Iqbal 1984: 107). Jama'at-i Islami applauded the coup and joined Zia's government which committed itself to set up the Islamic system (*Nizam-i Mustafa*). Zia's Islamization entailed imposition of zakat and *ushr* (tax on trade), elimination of interest and enforcement of the Islamic penal code (*hudud*). The imposition of zakat and ushr confronted many practical difficulties (Clark 1986; Mayer 1986; Nienhaus, Chapter 7 in this volume), and the elimination of interest was no more than cosmetic changes, renaming of banking practices, and application of "legal tricks" (Nomani and Rahnema 1994: 126–9, Nomani, Chapter 8 in this volume).

The enforcement of the Islamic penal code was, however, swift. In 1979 the laws dealing with Offenses Against Property, Offenses of Zina, Offenses of Qazf, and Prohibition were put into effect (A. Iqbal 1984: 113). The law on offenses against property provides for amputation of the right hand of the offender for the first offense, the left foot for the second offense, and life imprisonment for the third offense. The offense of *zina* (extramarital sex) can result in stoning to death or one hundred stripes, and *qazf* is the penalty for false accusation of zina, in cases of charges of adultery and rape, punishable by eighty stripes. Ironically, women victims of rape can become charged under the qazf provision for not being able to convince the court of their claim of rape, and then becoming themselves charged and punished for zina. Finally, the Prohibition Ordinance makes drinking intoxicants punishable by thirty stripes and three years in prison (A. Iqbal 1984: 113).

All these penalties were enforced in spite of Maududi's earlier statement that the penal codes would not be enforced until the Islamization of society is completed and "injustice, class-privileges and distressing economic disparities" have been rectified. Perhaps the impositions of penal codes for zina and the consumption of intoxicants and promotion of Islamic religious practices are themselves indications of Islamization of society and elimination of injustice, class privileges, and economic disparities. After all, that is how for centuries caliphs, kings, and governors and their qadis and muhtasibs proceeded to rule what everyone viewed as an Islamic society, except occasional voices of reformist dissidents who, following Abu Dharr and Husayn, asked for returning to the "true Islam" of Muhammad. The stories of Abu Dharr and Husayn have become legends in the liberation movement of the oppressed Muslims, and those who dared following their examples met the fate of their heroes. The Iranian revolution of 1979 appeared to be the first victory of an Abu Dharrian Islam over the Mu'awiyas and Yazids of the time. Alas, it too proved to be a failed utopia.

The revolutionary Islam (the rule of the oppressed)

The 1979 Iranian revolution claimed to establish the rule of the oppressed. The slogans, songs, posters, and the resolutions of the revolution, Islamic or not, were all on the high tempo of social justice and liberation of masses. The revolution demanded "the guarantee of the rights of workers and peasants to the full benefit from the product of their labor," an end to "the exploitation of man by man," and elimination of "exploitive profiteering and economic domination which will result in accumulation of great wealth, on the one hand and depravation and poverty, on the other" (Khalili 1981).

The revolutionary movement enjoyed powerful popular support and was deeply influenced by the radical agenda of the left, both secular and Islamic (Behdad 1995a, 2000). The views of Shariati and the Mojahedin overshadowed those of the conservative clergy. The revolutionary movement soon accepted the slogans demanding elimination of the "system of dependent capitalism." Fighting "dependency," "dependent capitalism," and "dependent capitalists" soon became a part of the revolutionary agenda of nearly all Islamic and non-Islamic groups. Khomeini, who opposed the materialist interpretation and the classless society of Shariati and the Mojahedin, nevertheless asked the seminary students, prior to the revolution, not to denounce those who have such beliefs, because "Islam is for justice" and "for class balance" (Khomeini n.d.: III, 222). It was after the revolution that the Mojahedin were banished as hypocrites (*monafeqin*)[20] and Shariati received severe condemnations.[21]

An Islamic Republic was established in the insurrection of February 1979. The various "revolutionary organizations" of the Islamic Republic championed the expropriation movement that accompanied the revolution. Within a few months, most of the large manufacturing establishments and all the banks and insurance companies were declared nationalized by the Revolutionary Council. The Revolutionary Islamic Courts also condemned "lackeys of imperialism and of the Pahlavi regime" and those who had "embezzled public funds" as "Corrupt on Earth" and confiscated their properties. The Revolutionary Islamic Courts acted swiftly in the Muhammadan spirit in confronting the enemies of Islam and collected a grand treasure of war booty, possibly unparalleled in the history of Islam. It constituted a significant part of the national wealth, including the entire assets of the Pahlavi Foundation (the largest conglomerate in Iran), many factories, farms, and a huge collection of highly valuable real estate properties belonging to the prerevolutionary Iranian oligarchy at the national and local levels. This large booty of the war of Islam against its "enemies" was placed, with the order of Ayatollah Khomeini, at the custody of the Bonyad-e Mustaz'afan (the Foundation for the Oppressed), which was formed for this purpose, independent from the structure of the Islamic state. Khomeini, in a posture not unlike that of Muhammad in Medina, proclaimed in the early months of the Revolution that "We will deal with those capitalists, whose capital and wealth could not have become so large from legitimate sources" (Khomeini n.d.: VIII, 470). And "even if we assume that someone has legitimate properties but the Islamic judge or *vali-ye faqih* realizes that an individual having so much will adversely affect the welfare of Muslims, he can expropriate those properties" (Khomeini n.d.: X, 481). Khomeini had stated in his treatise on *Islamic Government* (1971) that Islam does not allow masses to remain hungry and deprived while plundering oppressors live in opulence (Khomeini 1971). The Abu Dharrian followers of Khomeini, many of whom were the young students of the Shariati and the Mojahedin school of Islam, proceeded to "conquer," with a revolutionary fervor, every fort and fortress of the arrogant (*taghoti*) enemy.

The Constitution of the Islamic Republic reflects this ebullient spirit. It asserts that "the Iranian Revolution...has been a movement aimed at the triumph of all oppressed and deprived persons over the oppressors," and condemns "concentration and accumulation of wealth and maximization of profit" (*Constitution* 1980: 19, 21). The Constitution diminishes the place of private sector in the economy as the residual that will supplement the state and cooperative sectors (Article 44), and puts the private sector completely out of certain economic activities, most importantly, foreign trade. Although the Constitution recognizes "legitimately acquired" property (Article 47), it sets such a vague set of criteria (Article 49) that any properties, especially those acquired prior to the revolution, may be declared illegitimate.

A clear conflict surfaced when in 1981 the newly established Islamic Consultative Assembly (Majlis) attempted to establish the legal structure of the Islamic Republic. The confrontation was between the populist forces gathered around an Abu Dharrian interpretation of Islam, promoting an interventionist state and a widespread social welfare policy, and a conservative alliance of privileged classes, particularly the bazaar merchants, upholding Islam's recognition of the sanctity of private property. The latter alliance had the strong support of a large segment of the high ranking clergy, including all Sources of Imitation (*Maraje' Taqlid*), except Khomeini, who tried to balance the two factions.

With the Mojahedin banished as hypocrites, the radicalized young activists of the Islamic movement adhered to some variations of the Mojahedin's view. Habibollah Peyman's radical interpretation of Islam on property ownership was the most attractive alternative for these Islamic activists.[22] Peyman, in a scholastic interpretation of the Islamic notion of God's ultimate ownership argues that since all natural resources belong to God, everyone has the right to take advantage of them, and, therefore, individuals may not be allowed to possess any more of the fruits of nature than they need (Peyman 1979: 32). Furthermore he argues that since tools are products of advances in human civilization and are an inseparable part of the labor process and since everyone has the natural and social right to engage in productive work, everyone has the right to own tools of production (Peyman 1979: 66).

On this basis, Peyman sees capital accumulation as the means for exploitation of workers, which is only possible when many workers do not own their tools of production or do not have access to the natural resources (Peyman 1979: 71) Therefore, he argues that only what is received as the result of one's direct labor is legitimate. This leads Peyman to a Sismondian utopia of small family firms, supplemented by the state or cooperative ownership of those industries that have to be large because of the technological necessities of the modern age (Peyman 1979: 137–8, 273).

Many populist leaders of the Islamic Republic adhered to a less radical interpretation of the Islamic social order by Ayatullah Muhammad Baqir Sadr, an Iraqi Shi'i mujtahid who was executed by the Iraqi government for supporting the Iranian revolution. To Sadr, the contemporary Islamic economic system would be a market economy with mixed ownership, where an interventionist state imposes some limits on economic activities and maintains the Islamic "social balance" (Sadr 1971: vol. I, 354). The interventionist activity of the state is legitimized by Sadr on the basis of God's ultimate ownership. That implies that private property rights are subject to fiduciary principles, and individuals can exercise "their" property right as long as they look after society's welfare, as determined by the Shari'a. Since the Islamic state is the guardian of the divine law, it can limit the exercise of private property rights to maintain the social balance required by Islam (Sadr 1978: vol. II, 32–3). Sadr, then, argues that technological changes now necessitate existence of an interventionist state to maintain the social balance mandated by Islam. This is necessary because, in Sadr's opinion, with the modern technology there are no limits on the amount of resources that individuals can bring under their control. Thus, the Islamic social balance may be easily disturbed, and, therefore, the state may have to limit the scale of certain activities which were not limited by Muhammad (Sadr 1978: vol. II, 34–44, 57–8, 209–10).[23]

It is important to note that Murtaza Mutahhari (d. 1979) had apparently reached a similar conclusion toward the end of his life.[24] Mutahhari, a student and disciple of Khomeini, and one of the principal theoreticians and ideologues of the Islamic Republic, was the major defender of Islamic orthodoxy in opposition to Shariati.[25] Mutahhari relied on the conservative Islamic tradition to refute Shariati's radical interpretation as a dangerous ploy that threatens Islam (Mutahhari 1978: 34). In the early 1980s, some manuscripts of Mutahhari were published posthumously. In these manuscripts Mutahhari states that "new capitalism is a separate, independent and unprecedented phenomenon and requires separate and independent jurisprudential considerations" (Mutahhari 1983: 57). Here, Mutahhari, similar to Sadr, argues that advanced machinery has changed the character of relations of production, and since, as Peyman points out, technology is the product of human civilization, no individual can claim the "surplus" that it creates. Hence, Mutahhari suggests that with modern technology production is not the outcome of individual's actions and its output must be owned collectively (Mutahhari 1983: 191–2).[26] This was strong support from a reputable source for the proponents of an interventionist state, an issue of intense debate in the Islamic Republic. The publication of Mutahhari caused an uproar in the Seminaries and the bazaar. Since his critics could not challenge the authority of Mutahhari, they questioned the authenticity of the manuscripts. Some claimed they are counterfeits, others, when Mutahhari's handwriting was published, regarded them as Mutahhari's notes to himself and therefore inconsequential. The book was soon banned and taken out of the market.[27]

The orthodoxy on the Islamic social order was presented by a group of seminary teachers (*modarresin*) who were officially charged, as a part of the Cultural Revolution, with the responsibility for Islamization of various academic disciplines (Behdad 1995b). They constituted the Center for Cooperation of Seminaries and Universities (Daftar-e Hamkari-ye Hozeh va Daneshgah) and published their principal views on the economic system of Islam in a volume in 1984. The Modarresin reject, unequivocally, the radical views of Shariati and the Mojahedin, the populist-statist interpretations of Peyman and Sadr, and the newly revealed ideas of Mutahhari about private property rights and market activities. The Modarresin, relying on the traditional jurisprudential scholarship and juristic practices, argued that there is no limitation on accumulation of capital and wealth acquired from legitimate economic enterprises (Daftar 1984: 186–7). The domain of legitimacy is limited only by prohibition of riba, production of goods that are forbidden in Islam (mainly intoxicants and pork), speculation, monopoly, fraud, deception, and similar practices that are banned by Islam. In this way, the Modarresin's vision of an Islamic economy is similar to Maududi's outline presented some forty years earlier. The Modarresin, however, find the discourse of modern mainstream economics quite useful for justification of private property rights and for promoting limited government intervention in the economy (Behdad 1995b).

The scholarly and intellectual debate on the Islamic economic order was only an extension of the political disputes in the Islamic Republic and the actual skirmishes on the frontiers of property rights in the society. Khomeini's attempt to play a balancing act, by calling for the unity of the whole (*vahdat-e kalameh*) did not resolve the problem; it simply postponed its resolution. To avoid a jurisprudential confrontation between himself and the other Grand Ayatollahs, who opposed the nationalization policies, Khomeini packed the Guardian Council with proponents of Islamic orthodoxy and let them fight a populist-statist Majlis. But the Guardian Council kept rejecting the laws passed by the Majlis.

Even Khomeini's delegation of the power of the *vali-ye faqih* (the juriscounsult) for recognition of urgency (*darura, zarorat* in Persian) to the Majlis in October 1981 (which enabled this body to pass laws that may be in opposition to the Primary Rules of Islam) did not settle the issue. Finally, in December 1988 Khomeini established the Expediency Council to intervene in the conflict between the Majlis and the Council of Guardians. Khomeini died in June 1989 without resolving the conflict between the populist-statist proponents of an Islamic social order and the uncompromising front of the Islamic orthodoxy. This conservative front was firmly constituted by the alliance of the Grand Ayatollahs, their religious seminaries, and the propertied class, especially the bazaar merchants, who have had traditional ties with the religious establishment and have served as its concentrated source of financial contributions.

With the death of Khomeini, the Islamic Republic began a process of transformation. Frustrated from the destructive impacts of a prolonged war with Iraq, a sharp glut in the oil market between 1985 and 1989, which wiped out much of the Iranian source of livelihood, and an unyielding orthodox opposition, and faced with an intense economic crisis, the populist-statist faction began abandoning its revolutionary slogans. The search for an ideal Islamic society, the struggle for establishing the rule of the mustaz'afin (oppressed) had come to its dead end. Instead, a pragmatic coalition of conservatives and reformed populists was formed. The experts of the World Bank and the International Monetary Fund were invited to serve as the source of guidance, and they were happy to oblige. They offered to the Islamic Republic their usual remedy, a strong dose of an economic liberalization, which entails denationalization and privatization of state enterprises, elimination of many social programs and subsidies, and "rationalization" of the markets, including decontrolling prices and a free floating foreign exchange rate. This policy is a clear repudiation of all the revolutionary claims of the Islamic Republic (Behdad 2000). That is an issue that has not been easily accepted by those who had formed the popular base of the regime, and as the warriors of Islam, very much in the tradition of Muhammad, had received an enticing share of the booty. They find it hard to see that the sons of Abu Sufyan and Hind are placed in positions of consultation and power. The major proponent of the liberalization policy, Ali Akbar Hashemi-Rafsanjani, found himself, similar to Uthman, in a precarious situation and tried to reach the end of his two-term presidency in 1997 without confronting Uthman's fate. Muhammad Khatami, elected on a platform of cultural liberalization, pursued practically no economic agenda (Behdad 2001). More than twenty-five years after being established, the Islamic Republic has not been able define its public policy framework. In 2005, Mahmoud Ahmadinejad, elected president on a populist platform, promised to fight corruption and nepotism in the Islamic Republic and to bring the oil revenues of Iran to the Iranian tables. It is clear, however, that the heyday of the revolutionary Islam of Abu Dharr and the mustaz'afin is over in Iran. Pax Islamicus, Islamic orthodoxy, is being established within a social order that exhibits little difference with what existed prior to the revolution, except the coercive imposition of certain Islamic cultural norms and rules of social conduct.

Conclusions

Islamic revivalism is a movement for renewal of Islamic social order. It is an utopian struggle to return to what it perceives as the morally upright, politically successful, and economically prosperous golden ages of Islam. The experience of Islamic revivalism in the twentieth century reveals two clearly distinct and completely opposite presentations of Islam. One is the popular image of an Abu Dharrian social order, in which an egalitarian system of social justice would prevail, where there would be neither any "excessive" accumulation of wealth nor any suffering from deprivation. This utopia, this social order of Ali and Husayn, is the heaven on earth for the mass of urban and rural populations of Muslim societies. These are the people who in the past century have suffered social and economic dislocation in the face of acute social inequalities.

The story of Abu Dharr's opposition to the luxurious life of Mu'awiya, and Husayn's martyrdom at the hands of Mu'awiya's impious and arrogant son, Yazid, are vivid representations of the contradiction between justice and oppression, "social balance" and disparity. This is the vision of Islam, the rebellious, the idol smasher, the hope of the mustaz'afin (oppressed), the banner of the mobilized masses. This is the Islamic populism that conquered the temples of the wealthy, arrogant, and corrupt, and the shrines of polytheism (shirk) in Mecca and later in the empire that Muhammad and his disciples constructed. This is the Islam that its towhid (monotheism) means not only the oneness of God, but also oneness of the umma. It was the collectivism of the band of warriors of Islam, who distributed the booty of the war among their ranks and left some for the newly formed state of Islam only when the Prophet presented them with God's words (Sura Al-Anfal). This is the Islamic populism that has the power of mobilizing the poor and destitute, the unemployed and the low wage urban workers. These followers of Islam are also delighted to see a return to Islamic morality and rules of social conduct, so that corruption, fraud, addiction, and prostitution would disappear, so that their sons and daughters could live a decent and moral life, so that they would have a job, a house, a family, and social respect. This is the vision that populist theorists of Islamic revivalism present, from Parwez, Hakim, and Sheikh in Pakistan to Shariati, Mojahedin, and Peyman in Iran. The case of Islamization of Iran is of special interest to us because it presents the most radical and the most articulate expression of the Abu Dharrian Islam. Moreover, the Iranian Islamic movement grew out of the 1979 popular revolution, which provided it with a forceful momentum for establishing a new social order.

The experience of Islamization in Iran shows that the Abu Dharrian vision of Islam soon confronts another interpretation of Islam, one that is a vision of order in an Islamic state, a class society, Pax Islamicus. This is the Islam that protects property rights and its muhtasib maintain order in the suq, where a brisk market would offer merchandise of competing entrepreneurs to desirous buyers. The presence of the muhtasib guarantees that contracts are honored, transactions are honest, and weights and measures are accurate. Fourteen centuries of Islamic jurisprudence is the legal means for the conduct of affairs in the class societies of the Islamic world in a long historical span that began during the rule of the Umayyads and extended to those of the Ottoman Empire and the Saudi Kingdom. In this vision, too, adherence to the moral values of Islam, chastity and thriftiness, modesty and veracity are valued. They are valued for the hard-working, well-disciplined, and productive members of a society who do not expect, nor demand, any more than what they work for and the sustenance that God has set aside for them. This vision, whether presented by Maududi or the Modarresin, is a call for returning to the moral values and norms of conduct of the Islamic societies of the past, while supporting the status quo in the social relations of production. This is the Islamic order of the Saudi Kingdom and the Emirates of the Persian Gulf.

The power of Islamic revivalism is in its populism, in mobilizing masses under the green flag of Islam raised to fight injustice, oppression, and exploitation. As vague as these terms are, they are even appealing to Maududi and the Modarresin who subscribe to them to attract the poor and destitute. The conservative vision of Islam that Maududi and the Modarresin propagate corresponds closely to the traditional jurisprudence of Islam. This is the vision of Islam that receives the seal of approval from the mujtahids or muftis who are the guardians of the legal structure developed by generations of great theorists such as Abu Yusuf and Imam Ghazali. This vision is also supported by an alliance of propertied class, particularly its traditional segments, the bazaaris, who find the vision of suq and muhtasib especially appealing since it tends to limit, at least temporarily, the freedom of action of the large modern oligopolies, who have enjoyed, for decades in some Muslim countries, the support of the secular state.

Any attempt toward Islamization of society, whether by a newly established Islamic state, as in Iran, or by a secular state attempting to accommodate some of the demands of a revivalist movement, as in Egypt or Algeria, would provide an arena of contestation between the two visions of Islam. Clearly, there are sufficient ambiguities in the Quran and Muhammad's Tradition to inspire the believers to design a wide range of models for the social order. It is also understood that the "true Islam" that would be established in any Muslim society would be most fundamentally a reflection of the social balance existing in that society. It must be recognized, however, that the ulama, the guardians of the jurisprudential tradition (*fiqh*), in their alliance with the privileged classes, form an incredibly strong force in the determination of the outcome of the struggle within the revivalist movement. In the absence of a thundering opposition to the Islamic hierarchy and the traditional jurisprudence, there is little to expect from the Islamization efforts in terms of changes in the social order, except those that have to do with appearance. Even Ayatollah Khomeini, riding strong on the waves of a popular revolutionary movement, did not manage to win over this fourteen-century-old fortress. The failure of the Islamic revolutionary movement in Iran, undoubtedly, has weakened the populist dimension of the revivalist movement. This would imply weakening of the social welfare orientation of the revivalist movement and its proposed public policy agenda. In the recent decade, the shift in the Islamic movement has been toward cultural and symbolic dimensions of Islamization, and incorporation of modern concepts and categories into the system of Islamic jurisprudence. The problem would be more in dealing with issues such as segregation of the work and educational space of men and women, organization of an interest-free banking system, and a speculative-free stock market, control of foreign satellite transmission of un-Islamic television programs in the national space, and redefining the categories and forms of Islamic taxation. In this change of emphasis, there is little promise for improvement of the lot of the Muslim masses, while limitation of human rights, particularly for women, religious minorities, and secularists appears to be the main outcome.

The internationalization of the revivalist movement by Osama Bin Laden and his ilk, in declaring war against global decadence, immorality, and modernity manifested in the cultural values of the West, has fortified the bastion of a conservative vision of Islam. This movement seeks to replace the discourse of social welfare and economic justice with one having to do with chastity and sexual fidelity, and the debate on human and democratic rights within the Muslim societies with one on promoting female domesticity and traditional "family values" as means of mass mobilization. This strategy seemed to have been working, at least for a time, in attracting and engaging the urban and rural poor, without posing a danger to the domestic social hierarchy of the Muslim societies. It is no wonder that the Islamic fundamentalism of the likes of Bin Laden was not only tolerated, but was also nurtured and supported, by the Saudi, Pakistani, and other reactionary political establishments. But now that this fundamentalist movement for establishing a traditionalist utopia has gone dangerously off the expected track, in the international political arena of the post-9/11 period the "war on terrorism" has become the dominant discourse on Islam, Islamism, and Islamic revivalism. While this has fed the fire of the Islamophobes and political opportunists in promoting "a clash of civilizations," it has also brought in the recognition of the need to understand the general characteristics of Islam as a system of ideology. Hence we now hear of "Good Muslim Bad Muslim" (Mamdani 2004), and "moderate Muslims" who are "wrestling Islam from the extremists" (Abou El Fadl 2005), and the recognition that Islam has an identifiable theological and ideological "corpus" that is shared "absolutely consistent[ly]" even by "Globalized Islam" (Roy 2004: ix).

Be it as it may in the international arena, in the domestic political theater of predominantly Muslim societies public policy debates continue to revolve around the mundane matters of human existence, such as internal and international migration, urban and rural poverty, employment and unemployment, human rights, rights of women and religious minorities, family laws, and labor laws. Those who contend that Islam is the answer are obligated to find their solutions.

Notes

1 This study was supported by a Faculty Development Grant from Denison University. I would like to express my appreciation for this financial support. I would also like to thank Bahram Tavakolian and Farhad Nomani for their comments and corrections. I am responsible for the opinions expressed and errors remaining.

2 From the English translation of *Tajdid-o-Ihya-i-Din* published in Urdu. See Maududi (1972: 17–18).

3 See Hakim (1953: x–xi).

4 See also Rahnema and Behdad (1995: 1–18).

5 The Quran is quoted from Pikthall (N.D.).

6 Abu Sufyan was a leader of Meccan opposition to Muhammad. He was murdered by Abdallah ibn Unays, who received a prize when he threw Abu Sufyan's head at Muhammad's feet. Hind is known for expressing her hatred for Islam by tearing out and eating the liver of Hamza, Muhammad's uncle, in the battle of Uhud (Rodinson 1971: 189, 295). Umar appointed Mu'awiya to the governorship of Syria in an effort to "associate the Meccans with the cause" (Lewis 1960: 59).

7 Aharon Ben Shemesh in his translation of Yahya Ben Adam's *Kitab al-Khraj* (1967: 4–6) notes that there are references to twenty-one treatises titled *Kitab al-Kharaj* or *Kitab Risala fi al-Kharaj*.

8 He had a number of other books that did not survive: *Kitab Siyar Muluk al-Ajam* (Chronicle of Kings of Persia), *Kitab al-A'in* (on customs of the court), and *Kitab al-Taj* (on the life of Anoshirawan Sassanid). Only the last of these titles survived. Others are quoted in segments in the works of others.
9 Yassine Essid (1995: Part II). This is an excellent source on the study of hisba. It also provides references to the original Arabic treatises. See also Khan (1982).
10 On fabrication of hadith see Kamali (1991: 65–8) and on the sources of hadith in general see Siddiqi (1993).
11 On Ibn Taymia see Islahi (1988), Lewis *et al.* (1971: 951–5), and Maududi (1972: 63–9).
12 The original source for this statement is Ibn Taymia (1963: vol. 8, 583).
13 Some scholars of Islamic jurisprudence view the closing of the gate of ijtihad as fiction. See for example Aghnides (1969: 124) and Hallaq (1984).
14 Among the four major schools, Hanafis, Malikis, and Hanbalis have validated and practiced one or more of these methods, but the Shafi'is have refused to accept such juristic practices. (Kamali 1991: 245–82).
15 The other possibilities are "need" (*hajiyyat*) and "improvement" (*tahsiniyyat*). Since there is less "urgency" in these cases, it is more difficult to invoke maslaha in dealing with them (Khadduri 1989: 739).
16 For example, Abduh suggested including modern sciences in the curriculum of al-Azhar (the center of religious learning in Egypt) (Ramadan 1993: 153) and Kasravi (1990) condemned most religious ceremonies.
17 For a discussion of the necessity of tajdid by a leading revivalist see Maududi (1972) and for an analysis and review of literature in the Arab world about this topic see Haddad (1986).
18 The pamphlet does not have a date of publication. The "Explanatory and Discursive" introduction of the author is dated 1912. I learned about the existence of this pamphlet from Ansari (1986).
19 They ruled from 1502 to 1736, and made Shi'ism the official religion of the court.
20 Starting summer of 1981, many were killed in armed confrontations or were executed in prison. Many others fled to exile.
21 Although the extreme popularity of Shariati prevented the Islamic Republic from criticizing him sharply in the mass media, some strong condemnations were issued by the clergy. See, for example, Abolhasani (1983).
22 On property ownership in Islam see Behdad (1989).
23 Sadr's main point is about *taqrir* in Tradition, meaning Muhammad's silence about actions taking place around him with his knowledge. For a discussion of the issue see Sadr (1978: vol. II, 44–9) and Behdad (1994).
24 Mutahhari was assassinated in May 1979 by members of Forqan, a group which claimed to be followers of Ali Shariati.
25 On the debate between Mutahhari and Shariati see Behdad (1994), Nomani and Rahnema (1994), Dabashi (1993), and Abolhasani (1983).
26 For a more detailed discussion of the issue see Behdad (1994).
27 Occasionally parts of the manuscripts have been published in the newspapers or magazines (e.g. *Kayhan Hava'i* in December 1986) supporting the populist faction of the Islamic Republic.

Bibliography

Abdul-Rauf, M. (1979) *The Islamic Doctrine of Economics and Contemporary Economic Thought; Highlight of a Conference on Theological Inquiry into Capitalism and Socialism*, Washington, DC: American Enterprise Institute for Public Policy.
Abolhasani (Monzer), A. (1983) *Shahid Mutahhari*, Qum: Entesharat-e Eslami.

Abou El Fadl, K. (2005) *The Great Theft: Wrestling Islam From the Extremists*, New York: Harper San Francisco.

Abrahamian, E. (1989) *Radical Islam: The Iranian Mojahedin*, London: I.B. Tauris.

Abu Yusuf, Y. (1969) *Kitab al-Kharaj*, translated, with an introduction and notes by A. Ben Shemesh, published as *Taxation in Islam,* vol. III, Leiden: E.J. Brill.

Aghnides, N. P. (1969) *Mohammedan Theories of Finance with an Introduction to Mohammedan Law and a Bibliography*, New York: AMS Press.

Ahmad, K. (1982) "Preface," in Ibn Taymiya (ed.) *Public Duties in Islam: The Institution of the Hisba*, Leicester: Islamic Foundation, 5–11.

Ahmad, S. R. (1976) *Maulana Maududi and the Islamic State*, Lahore: People's Publishing House.

Ahmed, I. (1987) *The Concept of an Islamic State: An Analysis of the Ideological Controversy in Pakistan*, New York: St. Martin's Press.

Ansari, K. H. (1986) "Pan-Islam and the Making of the Early Indian Muslim Socialists," *Modern Asian Studies*, 20 (July): 509–37.

Arjomand, S. A. (ed.) (1988) *Authority and Political Culture in Shi'ism*, Albany, NY: State University of New York.

Al-Azmeh, A. (1993) *Islam and Modernities*, London: Verso.

Behdad, S. (1989) "Property Rights in Contemporary Islamic Economic Thought: A Critical Perspective," *Review of Social Economy*, XLVII (2): 185–211.

Behdad, S. (1992) "Islamic Economics: A Utopian-Scholastic-Neoclassical-Keynesian Synthesis!" In *Research in the History of Economic Thought and Methodology*, 9: 221–32.

Behdad, S. (1994) "A Disputed Utopia: Islamic Economics in Revolutionary Iran," *Comparative Studies in Society and History* 36 (4): 775–813.

Behdad, S. (1995a) "The Post Revolutionary Economic Crisis," in S. Rahnema and S. Behdad (eds) *Iran After the Revolution: Crisis of an Islamic State*, London: I.B. Tauris.

Behdad, S. (1995b) "Islamization of Economics in Iranian Universities," *International Journal of Middle East Studies* 27 (2): 193–217.

Behdad, S. (1997) "Islamic Utopia in Pre-Revolutionary Iran: Navvab Safavi and the Fada'ian-e Eslam," *Middle Eastern Studies* 33 (1): 40–65.

Behdad, S. (2000) "From Populism to Economic Liberalism: The Iranian Predicament," in P. Alizadeh (ed.) *The Economy of Iran: The Dilemmas of an Islamic State*, London: I.B. Tauris.

Behdad, S. (2001) "Khatami and His 'Reformist' Economic (Non-)Agenda," *MERIP Press Information Notes*, no. 57, May 21 (www.merip.org/pins/pin57.html).

Cameron, A. (1973) *Abu Dharr al-Ghifari: An Examination of His Image in the Hagiography of Islam*, London: Royal Asiatic Society/Liuzac.

Clark, G. (1986) "Pakistan's Zakat and Ushr as a Welfare System," in A. M. Weiss (ed.) *Islamic Reassertion in Pakistan: The Application of Islamic Laws in a Modern State*, Syracuse, NY: Syracuse University Press.

Constitution of the Islamic Republic of Iran (1980) translated from Persian by H. Algar, Berkeley, CA: Mizan Press.

Dabashi, H. (1993) *The Theology of Discontent; The Ideological Foundation of the Islamic Revolution in Iran*, New York: New York University Press.

Daftar-e Hamkari-ye Hoze va Daneshgah (1984) *Daramadi bar Eqtesad-e Eslami*, n.p.: Salman-e Farsi.

Donner, F. M. (1981) *The Early Islamic Conquests*, Princeton, NJ: Princeton University Press.

Esposito, J. L. (2005) *Islam: The Straight Path*, New York: Oxford University Press.

Essid, Y. (1995) *A Critique of the Origin of Islamic Economic Thought*, Leiden: E.J. Brill.

Gibb, H. A. R., Kramers, J. H., Lévi-Provençal, E., Schacht, J., Lewis, B., and Pellat, C. (1960) *The Encyclopedia of Islam*, new edition, vol. I, Leiden: E.J. Brill.

Gordon-Polonskaya, L. R. (1971) "Ideology of Muslim Nationalism," in H. Malik (ed.) *Iqbal: Poet-Philosopher of Pakistan*, New York: Columbia University Press.

Haddad, Y. (1986) "Muslim Revivalist Thought in the Arab World: An Overview," *The Muslim World*, LXXVI (1): 143–67.

Hakim, K. A. (1953) *Islam and Communism*, Lahore: Institute of Islamic Culture.

Hallaq, W. B. (1984) "Was the Gate of Ijtihad Closed?" *International Journal of Middle East Studies* 16 (1): 3–41.

Hassan, R. (1971) "The Development of Political Philosophy," in H. Malik (ed.) *Iqbal: Poet-Philosopher of Pakistan*, New York: Columbia University Press.

Ibn al Muqaffa', R. (1964) *Al-Adab al-Saghir wa l-Adab al-Kabir*, Beirut: Dar Sadi.

Ibn Taymiya, A. (1963) *Majmu' Fatwa Shaik al-Islam*, Riyad: Matabi' al-Riad.

Ibn Taymiya, A. (1982) *Public Duties in Islam: The Institution of the Hisba*, translated by Muhtar Holland. Leicester: Islamic Foundation.

Ibn Umar, Abu Z. (1975) *Ahkam al-Suq*, Edited by Abdelwahab. Tunis: STD.

Iqbal, A. (1984) *Islamisation of Pakistan*, Delhi: Idarah-i Adabiyat-i Delli.

Iqbal, M. (1955) *Poems from Iqbal*, translated by V. G. Kiernan, London: John Murray.

Islahi, A. A. (1988) *Economic Concepts of Ibn Taimiyah*, Leicester: Islamic Foundation.

IWW (Industrial Workers of the World) (1976) *Songs of the Workers*, Chicago, IL: IWW.

Kamali, M. H. (1991) *Principles of Islamic Jurisprudence*, Cambridge, UK: The Islamic Text Society.

Kamali, M. H. (1996) "Fiqh and Adaptation to Social Reality," *The Muslim World*, LXXXVI (1): 62–84.

Kasravi, A. (1990) *On Islam and Shi'ism*, translated from Persian by M. R. Ghanoonparvar, Costa Mesa, CA: Mazda.

Keddie, N. R. (1994) Sayyid Jamal al-Din "al-Afghani," in A. Rahnema (ed.) *Pioneers of Islamic Revival*, London: Zed Books.

Kerr, M. H. (1966) *Islamic Reform: The Political and Legal Theories of Muhammad Abduh and Rashid Riza*, Berkeley, CA: University of California Press.

Khadduri, M. (1989) "Maslaha," in C. E. Bosworth, E. van Donzel, B. Lewis, C. Pellat, and W. P. Heinrichs (eds) *The Encyclopedia of Islam*, new edition, vol. VI, Leiden: E.J. Brill.

Khalili, A. (1981) *Gam be Gam ba Enqelab*, Tehran: Soroush.

Khan, M. A. (1982) "Appendix: Al-Hisba and the Islamic Economy," in A. Ibn Taymiya (ed.) *Public Duties in Islam: The Institution of the Hisba*, translated by Muhtar Holland, Leicester: Islamic Foundation.

Khomeini, R. (1971) *Hokomat-e Eslami*, n.p.: An English translation of this treatise appears as Islamic Government in [Khomeini] (1981).

Khomeini, R. (1981) *Islam and Revolution; Writings and Declarations of Imam Khomeini*, Translated and annotated by Hamid Algar, Berkeley, CA: Mizan Press.

Khomeini, R. (n.d.) *Sahifeh-ye Noor*, CD-ROM, second edition, Tehran: Zafar Rayaneh.

Kidwai, S. M. H. (1912) *Islam & Socialism*, London: Luzac & Co.

Lewis, B. (1960) *The Arabs in History*, New York: Harper and Row.

Lewis, B. (ed.) (1974) *Islam from the Prophet Muhammad to the Capture of Constantinople. Volume II: Religion and Society*, New York: Harper & Row.

Lewis, B., Ménage, V. L., Pellat, C., and Schacht, J. (eds) (1971) *The Encyclopedia of Islam*, new edition, vol. III, Leiden: E.J. Brill.

Malik, H. (ed.) (1971a) *Iqbal: Poet-Philosopher of Pakistan*, New York: Columbia University Press.

Malik, H. (1971b) "The Spirit of Capitalism and Pakistani Islam," in The Canadian Association for South Asian Studies (ed.) *Contributions to Asian Studies*, Leiden: E.J. Brill.

Mamdani, M. (2004) *Good Muslim, Bad Muslim: America, the Cold War, and the Roots of Terror*, New York: Three Leaves Press.

Marty, M. E. and Appleby, R. S. (eds) (1993) *Fundamentalism and the State, The Fundamentalism Project,* vol. 3, Chicago, IL: The University of Chicago Press.

Maududi, A. A. (1969) *The Islamic Law and Constitution*, translated and edited by K. Ahmad, Lahore: Islamic Publications Ltd.

Maududi, A. A. (1972) *A Short History of the Revivalist Movement in Islam*, translated by al-Ashari, Lahore: Islamic Publications.

Maududi, A. A. (1977) *Capitalism, Socialism and Islam*, translated by S. A. Khan, Kuwait: Islamic Book Publishers.

Maududi, A. A. (1978) *The Economic Problem of Man and its Islamic Solution*, Lahore: Islamic Publications.

Maududi, A. A. (1994) *Economic System of Islam*, edited by K. Ahmad and translated by R. Husain, Lahore: Islamic Publication.

Mayer, A. E. (1986) "Islamization of Taxation in Pakistan," in A. M. Weiss (ed.) *Islamic Reassertion in Pakistan: The Application of Islamic Laws in a Modern State*, Syracuse, NY: Syracuse University Press.

Mojahedin-e Kalq-e Iran (1972) *Shenakht (Metodolozhi), Ideolozhi, Part 1*, n.p.: Mojahedin-e Kalq-e Iran, September/October.

Mojahedin-e Kalq-e Iran (1980a) *Tabyin-e Jahan (Qava'ed-e va Mafhoom-e Takamol); Amoozesha-ye Ideolozhik*, n.p.: Entesharat-e Sazman-e Mojahedin-e Khalq-e Iran.

Mojahedin-e Khalq-e Iran (1980b) *Elteqat va Ideolozhiha-ye Elteqati; Majmo'eh-ye Seh Sokhanrani*, n.p.: Anjoman-e Daneshjoyan-e Mosalman-e Kompiyoter.

Momen, M. (1985*) An Introduction to Shi'i Islam*, New Haven, CT: Yale University Press.

Mutahhari, M. (1978) *Elal-e Gerayesh be Maddigari*, Qum: Entesharat-e Sadra.

Mutahhari, M. (1983) *Barresi-ye Ejmali-ye Mabani-ye Eqtesad-e Eslami*. n.p.: Entesharat-e Hekmat.

Mutahhari, M. (1985) *Fundamentals of Islamic Thought: God, Man and the Universe*, translated from Persian by R. Campbell, Berkeley, CA: Mizan Press.

Mutahhari, M. (1986) *Social and Historical Change: An Islamic Perspective*, translated from Persian by R. Campbell, Berkeley, CA: Mizan Press.

Nasr, S. V. R. (1994) *The Vanguard of the Islamic Revolution; The Jama'at-i Islami of Pakistan*, Berkeley, CA: University of California Press.

Nizam-al Mulk (1960) *The Book of Government or, Rules for Kings: The Siyasat-Nama or Siyar al-Muluk*, translated from the Persian by Hubert Darke, New Haven, CT: Yale University Press.

Nomani, F. and Rahnema, A. (1994) *Islamic Economic Systems*, London: Zed Books.

Paret, R. (1978) "Istihsan and Istislah," in E. van Donzel, B. Lewis, C. Pellat, and C. E. Bosworth, (eds) *The Encyclopedia of Islam,* new edition, vol. IV, Leiden: E.J. Brill.

Parwez, G. A. (1968) *Islam: A Challenge to Religion*, Lahore: Idara-e-Tulu-e-Islam.

Peyman Paydar, H. (Circa 1979) *Bardashtha'i dar Bareh-ye Malekiyyat, Sarmayeh va Kar az Didgah-e Eslam*. n.p.: Daftar-e Nashr-e Eslami.

Pikthall, M. M. (n.d.) *The Meaning of the Glorious Koran; An Explanatory Translation*, New York: New American Library.

Rahnema, A. (1998) *An Islamic Utopia: A Biography of Ali Sahriati*, London: II.B. Tauris.

Rahnema, S. and Behdad, S. (eds) (1995) *Iran After the Revolution: Crisis of an Islamic State*, London: I.B. Tauris.

Ramadan, A. A. (1993) "Fundamentalist Influence in Egypt: The Strategy of the Muslim Brotherhood and the Takfir Group," in M. E. Marty and R. S. Appleby (eds) *Fundamentalism and the State, The Fundamentalism Project,* vol. 3, Chicago, IL: The University of Chicago Press.

Richard, Y. (1988) "Shari'at Sangalaji: A Reformist Theologian of the Rida Shah Period," in S. A. Arjomand (ed.) *Authority and Political Culture in Shi'ism,* Albany, NY: State University of New York.

Rodinson, M. (1971) *Mohammed,* Harmondsworth, UK: Penguin.

Rodinson, M. (1981) *Marxism and the Muslim World,* New York: Monthly Review.

Roy, O. (2004) *Globalized Islam: The Search for a New Ummah,* New York: Columbia University Press.

Sadr, M. B. (1968) *Iqtisaduna,* Beirut: Dar al-Fikr. The references in the text are from the Persian translation: *Eqtesad-e Ma,* vol. I, translated by M. K. Mosavi-Bojnordi (1971), vol. II, translated by A. Espahbodi (1978), Tehran: Entesharat-e Eslami.

Schacht, J. (1982) *An Introduction to Islamic Law,* Oxford: Clarendon Press.

Shariati, A. (n.d. Circa 1978a) "Chegooneh Mandan," in *Majmo'eh-ye Asar,* vol. 2, Daftar-e Tadvin va Enteshar-e Asar-e Bradar-e Shahid Doktor Ali Shariati dar Oropa.

Shariati, A. (n.d. Circa 1978b) "Khodsazi-ye Enqelabi," in Shariati *Majmo'eh-ye Asar,* vol. 2, above.

Shariati, A. (1979) *On the Sociology of Islam,* translated from Persian (excerpts from *Eslamshenasi,* Shariati, 1981b, 1981c) by H. Algar, Berkeley, CA: Mizan Press.

Shariati, A. (1980a) *Marxism and Other Western Fallacies: An Islamic Critique,* translated from Persian (*Ensan, Marksism va Eslam.* Qum: n.p., 1976) by R. Campbell, Berkeley, CA: Mizan Press.

Shariati, A. (1980b) *From Where Shall We Begin? and The Machine in Captivity of Machinis,* translated from Persian by F. Marjani, Houston, TX: Free Islamic Literature.

Shariati, A. (1981a) *Tarikh va Shenakht-e Adyan, (1) Majmo'eh-ye Asar,* vol. 14. Tehran: Sherkat-e Sehami-ye Enteshar.

Shariati, A. (1981b) *Eslamshenasi (1) Majmo'eh-ye Asar,* vol. 16, Tehran: Entesharat-e Qalam.

Shariati, A. (1981c) *Eslamshenasi, (2) Majmo'eh-ye Asar,* vol. 17, Tehran: Entesharat-e Qalam.

Shariati, A. (1982) "Mazhab Aleyh-e Mazhab," in *Mazhab Aleyh-e Mazhab, Majmo'eh-ye Asar,* vol. 22, Tehran: Enesharat-e Sabz.

Sheikh, N. A. (1961) *Some Aspects of the Constitution and the Economics of Islam.* Surrey, UK: Working Muslim Mission and Literary Trust.

Siddiqi, M. Z. (1993) *Hadith Literature; Its Origin, Development & Special Features,* Cambridge, UK: The Islamic Text Society.

Spuler, B. (1960) *The Muslim World: A Historical Survey; Part I: The Age of the Caliphs,* Leaden: Braille.

van Donzel, E., Lewis, B., Pellat, C., and Bosworth, C. E. (eds) (1978) *The Encyclopedia of Islam,* new edition, vol. IV, Leiden: E.J. Brill.

Voll, J. O. (1986) "Rivivalism and Social Transformation in Islamic History," *The Muslim World,* LXXVI (3–4): 168–80.

Yahya B. A. (1967) *Kitab al-Kharaj,* translated and edited by A. Ben Shemesh, published as *Taxation in Islam Volume I,* Leiden: E.J. Brill.

2 Islamism and economics

Policy prescriptions for a free society

Timur Kuran

A visible triumph of the ongoing global movement known as Islamic fundamentalism, Islamic revivalism, or Islamism[1] has been the spread of Islamic banks. Throughout the Islamic world, the successes of Islamic banking have alarmed many supporters of secularization, modernization, and economic development. One worrier was Uğur Mumcu, a widely read Turkish columnist who was assassinated in January 1993 for his outspokenness.[2] Mumcu saw the advent of Islamic banking as part of a sinister ploy to advance Islamism, isolate Muslims from global civilization, and force Muslim nations into a despotic political union established on Medieval principles.

To readers familiar with the actual practices of Islamic banks, Mumcu's fears may seem hysterical. The typical Islamic bank is a commercial enterprise whose choices are sensitive to market pressures. Notwithstanding the utopian claims of Islamist ideologists, its practices differ only cosmetically from those of conventional banks. Where an ordinary bank charges interest openly and unabashedly, the Islamic bank charges a commensurate "commission." A Malaysian observer of Islamic banking puts it more bluntly: "The only difference is whether the man behind the counter is wearing a religious hat or a bow tie" (*Economist* August 7, 1993: 57).

The notion that Islamic banking differs minimally from its conventional counterpart is not inconsistent, however, with the assertion that the spread of Islamic banking is socially disruptive. Even if inherently beneficial to commerce and investment, it may serve a potentially harmful political and cultural mission. Going beyond Islamic banking, this essay offers reasons for concern about the spread of Islamist economic teachings and practices. It also proposes responses to the challenge of Islamism. The first policy prescription is to disseminate information about flaws of the Islamist economic agenda. The second is to show that Islamist leaders tend to overstate their popular support. The final prescription, to which secularists of Mumcu's persuasion might object, is that close attention should be paid to Islamist concerns. Many Islamist misgivings about modernity, including various socioeconomic grievances, stem from genuine policy failures.

The social significance of Islamic banking

In and of themselves, Islamic banks pose no challenge to a free economic order. As long as they are sustained by private capital, governments give them no special privileges, their clients are free to use conventional banks, and their operations will not violate economic freedoms. Moreover, at least where these conditions are met, the very success of Islamic banking implies that it meets an apparent social need; so it should be tolerated, given full protection of the law, even welcomed.

It has been argued that in its ideal form, Islamic banking encourages certain classes of depositors, such as the retired, to carry risks better borne by others. It has also been argued that Islamic banking necessitates excessive monitoring of commercial and industrial borrowers.[3] Though justified, such criticisms are besides the point. If a septuagenarian chooses to risk her savings by placing them in a variable-return account, third parties have no reason to object – provided they will not be forced to support her in the event her investment turns sour. Likewise, if a private bank chooses to tie the returns on its industrial loans to the profits from the financed projects, third parties need not be concerned – provided, again, they are not obligated to keep the bank solvent.

Every society gives its members wide latitude to make decisions that observers might characterize as wasteful or silly. Americans are free to purchase nutritionally worthless, even harmful, food. Granting Muslims the liberty to "misspend" resources in running their finances according to an alleged Islamic tenet is no different, in principle, from allowing Americans to "misspend" resources on unhealthy food. Even if Islamic banks are inefficient, in itself that is no reason to oppose their existence.

The alarmists would agree that the practice of Islamic banking presents no reason for concern;[4] many recognize that a religious hat is no more threatening than a bow tie. They would hasten to add, however, that Islamic banking is motivated by more than the provision of a neglected financial service. A common alarmist theme is that Islamic banking represents not simply a new financial instrument but also a conspicuous, lucrative, and symbolically potent instrument of Islamism. Mumcu considered Islamic banking an affront to Atatürk's vision of a secular and Westernized Turkish Republic. In the same vein, Islamist Egyptian writers view it as both a source of financial support for Islamist activities and a vehicle for creating financial ties among Islamist activists (Ayubi 1991: chap. 8, esp. p. 192).

The link between Islamic banking and Islamism is anything but imaginary. The founders and executives of Islamic banks see themselves as contributing to the reestablishment of the primacy of Islam in the lives of Muslims. Some want the entire social order restructured according to Islamic criteria, not only economic relations but also gender roles, education, the mass media, government, and much else. An appliance manufacturer might launch a new line of refrigerators or enlarge his workforce without intending to change the basic framework of the economy, to say nothing of revising the high school curriculum or reordering male-female relations. By contrast, Islamic bankers commonly view themselves as both profit seekers and agents of social renewal. They do not ask merely to be left alone, to be permitted to withdraw from the economic mainstream. They want to be noticed and to inspire. They wish to make their preferred financial practices the norm. They consider themselves in the vanguard of a struggle to cleanse the economy, indeed the whole social system, of harmful secular influences.

The vast literature that falls under the rubric of "Islamic economics"[5] confirms that Islamic banks are meant to serve a broad social mission. The literature holds that the prevailing capitalist and socialist economies generate injustice, corruption, inequality, poverty, and discontent. A major source of all these problems is interest, which pushes distressed borrowers into poverty, allows lenders to make risk-free gains without exerting any effort, and weakens social ties. By offering an alternative to interest, Islamic banking will contribute, so claims Islamic economics, to making the economy fairer, more egalitarian, and less harmful to the social fabric. But the objective is not simply to make Islamic banking more accessible. It is to make all banking Islamic. Certain campaigns against conventional banking have been successful, at least in the sense of making "interest-laden" banking illegal. In Pakistan all banks were ordered in 1979 to purge interest from their operations within five years, and in 1992 the Shari'a court removed various critical exemptions.[6]

The religious justification for prohibiting interest has been that the Quran bans all its forms, irrespective of the prevailing institutional framework and the nature of the involved loan. Actually, what the Quran bans is riba, an ancient Arabian lending practice whereby defaulters saw their debts grow exponentially. Although the notion that all interest amounts to riba has never enjoyed unanimous acceptance among Islamic authorities, to say nothing of skepticism on the part of laypeople (Rodinson 1973), Islamic economists[7] treat the issue as settled, and they consider anyone who questions the wisdom or feasibility of prohibiting interest as misguided, corrupt, or ignorant. They feel justified, moreover, in compelling everyone, including Muslim skeptics and even non-Muslims, to abide by a ban.

For many proponents of Islamic banking, its religious rationale is far more important than its economic justification. Indeed, some respond to criticisms of the methods of Islamic banking by saying that its economic merits are secondary to its contribution to the revival of Islam. For them, the overriding objectives are the reassertion of Muslim identity, the reaffirmation of Islam's relevance to the modern world, and the restoration of Islamic authority. Islamic banking defies the separation between economics and religion. It invokes religious authority in a domain that modern civilization has secularized. Moreover, by promoting the distinctness of Islamic economic behavior, it counters the absorption of Islamic civilization into Western civilization. Many leaders of Pakistan's Jama'at-i-Islami support Islamic banking as a vehicle for replacing the cautious and limited Islam of Iqbal and Jinnah with one that is relatively assertive and intrusive (Ahmed 1994: 688–9).

The broader Islamic subeconomy

"True Muslims," wrote Sayyid Mawdudi, the Pakistani thinker who founded Islamic economics in the 1940s, "merge their personalities and existences into Islam. They subordinate all their roles to the one role of being Muslims. As fathers, sons, husbands or wives, businessmen, landlords, labourers, employers, they live as Muslims" (Mawdudi 1985: 115, translation edited). Following in Mawdudi's footsteps, contemporary Islamists consider Islam a "complete way of life," a source of guidance and inspiration in every personal and social domain. This position obviously clashes with the secularist goal of keeping religion out of public realms such as science, law, politics, and economics.

To discredit the notion that Islam's relevance is limited to matters of personal faith, Islamists have needed to demonstrate its comprehensiveness as a way of life. Islamic economics emerged, through the writings of Mawdudi and others, as one component of a broad philosophical attempt to meet this challenge.[8] With the literature growing rapidly, concrete applications were quick to follow. Sustained efforts to exhibit the practicality, distinctness, and wisdom of Islamic economics got underway in the 1960s, and the world's first Islamic bank went into operation in 1975.[9] Subsequently, Islamic banking spread to more than sixty countries, putting it at the center of the campaign to prove the superiority of Islamic economics over secular economic traditions. The practical demonstrations of Islamic economics, which go much beyond banking, may be grouped in four categories.

The first consists of efforts to give an Islamic identity to existing economic activities, mainly through symbolism. Islamic banking falls into this category. From a substantive standpoint, Islamic banks do not operate very differently from their conventional counterparts. In making loans, they adhere mainly to financial criteria. Contrary to the stipulations of Islamic economics, they tend not to give priority to long-term development projects over projects aimed at quick profits. They do not limit their business to pious Muslims, or even to Muslims. And they show no appreciable bias against projects with heavy social costs, such as high-polluting factories. They differ from conventional banks primarily in appearance. Their operations are formally under the control of a religious council. Their quarters often feature signs of Islamic piety: verses from the Quran on the walls, veiled female and bearded male tellers, prayer rooms, and breaks during times of prayer. Finally, and as already noted, they give and take interest under various religious disguises.

Cosmetically, Islamic variants have emerged for other types of businesses too. There are now Islamic retail outlets, Islamic investment companies, and even Islamic conglomerates (Göle 1999; Özcan and Çokgezen 2003). What makes all such enterprises Islamic, observes Nazih Ayubi, is essentially that their owners have taken to "wearing white gowns, growing thick beards, and holding long rosaries" (1991: 188–9). Indeed, the substantive differences between Islamic and ordinary firms are minor. Self-consciously Islamic firms tend not to deal in commodities considered un-Islamic. Thus, an Islamic grocery store does not sell pork or liquor, and an Islamic boutique does not cater to the needs of discotheque patrons. Another difference involves beneficiaries of the firm's charitable contributions. Where an ordinary firm donates to secular causes – an art show, a scholarship program, a sports team – the Islamic firm tends to favor explicitly Islamic causes.

If employees of Islamic firms were asked what makes their operations Islamic, a common response would be that they avoid interest. In fact, most Islamic enterprises deal in interest as a matter of course, though usually under Islamic garb. In no essential respect do their business practices differ systematically from the norm. Though serious research on Islamic enterprises is in its infancy,[10] work to date suggests that they are not exceptionally honest in their dealings with clients unlikely to be repeat buyers. Some are known to have overstated their assets to incumbent and potential shareholders. Nor do they appear any less prone than ordinary firms to tax evasion, or to be especially generous toward their employees. Though Islamic economics is highly critical of the prevailing standards of honesty, trustworthiness, and fairness in contemporary economies (Siddiqi 1972; Naqvi 1981), nothing suggests that established Islamic enterprises behave substantially differently from ordinary enterprises.

Efforts that form this first category of Islamic economic activity do no great harm. In refusing to stock dancing outfits, an Islamic boutique does not keep dancers from taking their business elsewhere. Islamists also try, however, to prevent economic choices they find objectionable, sometimes by force. Such efforts form a second category. They include attacks on establishments deemed to foster moral laxity: video stores, theaters, bookstores, dance clubs, bars, hotels that cater to "naked" tourists, and restaurants that serve food during fasting times (Rashwan and Gad 1993). The attacks are aimed at destroying certain economic sectors, and the consequences have hardly been insignificant. In Egypt and Indonesia, attacks against tourists and tourism establishments have lowered foreign exchange earnings, harming investment and growth (Murphy 1992; Al-Hamarneh and Steiner 2004). Such attacks serve to differentiate Islamic economic values from non-Islamic ones. They also signal that the goals of preserving and advancing Islam take precedence over such objectives as individual liberty, financial opportunity, hospitality toward visitors, and economic development.[11]

Economically harmful attempts to establish the primacy of Islam have not been limited to violent attacks against morally controversial sectors. In various countries it is now common for employees to be pressured to attend communal prayers several times a day. During Ramadan, employees have been forced to fast, often with adverse effects on productivity. Communities have been discouraged from spending resources on nonreligious social services, lest these reduce the amount available for the construction of mosques and Quran schools (Gürsoy-Tezcan 1991).

The third category of economic instruments for advancing Islamism consists of nongovernmental Islamic social services. Such services include hospitals, clinics, legal-aid societies, schools, dormitories for college students, youth centers, summer camps, and sports facilities. Benefiting primarily the poor, they demonstrate that organizations infused with an Islamic spirit can tackle various social problems more adequately than the government. Also, by giving a religious dimension to traditionally secular services they lend credibility to the claim that Islam is a complete way of life. In Egypt, mosque-affiliated clinics are delivering health services at rock-bottom prices, generally more efficiently than overburdened health facilities run by the government. Where a poor Egyptian might wait three months for an X-Ray at a government facility, at an Islamic clinic access to the procedure typically takes much less time.[12] For another example, thousands of underprivileged Turkish teenagers have attended Islamic summer camps, their expenses paid by Islamist organizations (*Cumhuriyet* July 10, 1993: 1, 15; August 7, 1993: 1, 17).

It is costly to run services like camps and hospitals. By contrast, the final category of economic instruments consists of services that bring Islamists net financial gains. The most important instrument is zakat, a religious tax on wealth and income. By tradition, zakat proceeds serve partly to deliver poor relief and partly to finance "praiseworthy activities," defined to include religious education and pilgrimage. In several countries, including Pakistan, zakat has become a legal obligation, and the government now organizes both its collection and its disbursement. In most parts of the Islamic world, however, zakat is collected and disbursed in a decentralized manner by local religious organizations (Kuran 2003, 2004: 19–29). Whatever the pattern, substantial shares of zakat revenue are used to finance Islamist activities. Another source of income for Islamist causes is the hides of sacrificial animals. In Turkey, such hides traditionally went to the Turkish Aviation Society. Since the early 1990s a large share, in some localities the lion's share, goes to Islamist collection agencies, which have taken to spreading the word that it is sinful to make donations to a secular authority (*Cumhuriyet* July 19, 1993: 1, 15).

No one knows the total income of Islamist organizations. What is known is that Islamists derive revenue from many channels, including not only zakat and hides but also donations from Islamic businesses, individuals sympathetic to Islamic causes, and unsympathetic individuals hedging their bets. There is also reason to believe that many Islamist organizations receive funds from foreign governments. The governments of Saudi Arabia, Libya, and Iran, among other countries, deliver much help to Islamist organizations throughout the world.[13] Some of the diffuse income supports Islamic services, but part of it supports an array of political activities. In predominantly Muslim countries that have meaningful elections, the candidates of Islamist parties regularly receive financial support from Islamist organizations whose primary purposes are nonpolitical.

All told, the economic activities of the Islamists hardly amount to a radical reordering of economic relations. They serve either to raise resources for Islamist advancement or to demonstrate that Islamists are capable of solving entrenched social problems. True, Islamists talk of radical change. Yet, the ongoing economic activities associated with Islamism generally do not represent major departures from the economic status quo.

It is essential here to remember that Islamic economics did not originate from a need to reorder economic relations. Rather, it arose out of an impulse to demonstrate the distinctness, continuing social relevance, and priority of Islam. From this perspective, Islamists have been remarkably successful in pursuing their economic objectives. They would have been less successful, perhaps, had they advanced a detailed, coherent, and comprehensive plan for truly revolutionary economic restructuring, because that would have identified many potential losers. As matters stand, the vagueness of Islamic economics allows Islamists to appeal to diverse constituencies without triggering widespread anxieties about the economic consequences of an Islamist takeover. It also gives Islamists the flexibility to adjust the content of Islamic economics to changing needs and opportunities.

The domino effect

Successful Islamization in one domain lends credibility to Islamization attempts in other domains. So a significant consequence of the economic activities undertaken in the name of Islam is the support they give to the broader Islamist agenda. The economic accomplishments of Islamism encourage activists to press new demands. They also discourage resistance from opponents and embolden Islamist movements elsewhere. Hence, the economic advances of Islamism may lead, through a domino effect, to further victories in both economic and noneconomic domains.

When Islamists insist, then, on the inseparability of economics, family structure, dress, and education, they do not mean only that in the minds of believers these domains are interlinked. They mean also that every move toward Islamization facilitates further moves. The spread of Islamic commerce discourages women from dressing immodestly in public settings. Conversely, as veiling becomes more common, Islamic economics is taken more seriously, and its opponents become less vocal.

In pursuing power, any political movement will rely on two complementary strategies. The first is to promote understanding and acceptance of its objectives, the second to pressure individuals of all persuasions, including skeptics and potential opponents, into supporting the objectives. Each of these strategies is apparent in the economic activities of Islamists. A philosophical contribution to Islamic economics serves primarily to persuade. By contrast, a profitable Islamic bank and an efficient clinic serve both to persuade and to build political pressure. On the one hand, they show that Islam can make valuable economic contributions. On the other, they boost the perceived power of Islamism, thus compounding pressures to support Islamist positions.

Bolstering a movement's perceived strength is not riskless: it can induce a major reaction. The military response to the imminent victory of the Islamic Salvation Front in Algeria's legislative election of 1991–2 illustrates the point (Roberts 1994). Yet, under the right set of contingencies a pro-Islamist turn in public opinion will make fear change sides: people who were reluctant to appear sympathetic to Islamism will become reluctant to appear unsympathetic. This scenario is being played out in Iraq, where politicians who endorsed Saddam's anti-Islamist policies have endorsed various Islamist objectives (Nasr 2004). Thus, a shift in public opinion may weaken the anti-Islamist resistance, make it equivocate, and eventually crush it. Islamist leaders can never be certain about their hidden support or about their opponents' susceptibility to social pressure. Like all political players, they face uncertainty regarding the appropriate timing for action. Nevertheless, they all recognize that the likelihood of overcoming resistance is likely to grow with increases in Islamism's perceived strength (Kuran 1995: chaps 15–18).

In some places, Islamism in general and Islamic economics in particular already derive critical support arising from fears of being stigmatized as un- or anti-Islamic. Though many Pakistani leaders have serious misgivings about Islamic economics, few have gone on record with their reservations. In fact, they generally make a point of claiming that their own economic programs are consistent with, if not derived from, the economic teachings of Islam. Zulfiqar Ali Bhutto, who once questioned the feasibility of organizing a modern society according to Islamic principles, began asserting in the mid-1970s that the inspiration for his socialist ideas had come from Islam (Ahmad 1991: 474–9). A decade later, his daughter Benazir Bhutto refrained from denouncing the ban on interest, even as the Jama'at-i Islami was conspiring to topple her government. Such episodes are at once a manifestation of, and a contributor to, social pressures to appear supportive of Islamism.

All fundamentalist objectives, not simply those associated with attire, gain legitimacy and immunity to criticism when a political leader appears in an election poster with her head fully covered and reading the Quran (Ahmed 1994: 687). So, too, they all benefit when Pakistani statesmen, bureaucrats, intellectuals, and professionals exhibit reticence to take issue with the claims and practices of Islamic economics.

To sum up thus far, Mumcu's point that Islamic economics is part of a broad mission is unassailable. Islamic economics serves to differentiate the Islamic social order from prevailing social orders, to signal the strength of Islamism, and to make potential opponents practice self-censorship. As such, schemes such as zakat and Islamic banking are both objectives in their own right and instruments of the wider Islamist cause. Opponents of the Islamist agenda are justified, then, in treating Islamic economics as more than a quaint doctrine.

If this point is granted, the obvious next question is, "How should non-Islamist policy makers respond to the economic activities undertaken in the name of Islam?" I will offer three suggestions after making two additional points. I will note that Islamism has been grappling, not always unsuccessfully, with some deep social problems. And I will then suggest that Islamism – like other fundamentalisms – carries the potential of harming the global economy.

Islamism as economic instrument

Given that the rise of Islamic economics was driven largely by noneconomic factors, it is unsurprising that it has solved no major economic problem. A half-century after the publication of Mawdudi's seminal writings, Islamic economics has not made Muslim economies more equal, more productive, or more innovative. Nevertheless, for reasons essentially unrelated to the principles of Islamic economics, Islamism has helped alleviate certain discontents of rapid urbanization. In particular, it has enabled metropolises like Cairo, Istanbul, and Karachi to cope with historically unprecedented demographic changes.

Because of rampant government corruption and widespread dishonesty in business relations, many businessmen of the Islamic world find it difficult to succeed without bribing government officials or deceiving their suppliers and clients.

Their inevitable moral compromises give rise to guilt, a condition for which Islamism offers an array of cures. By holding savings in an Islamic account and making a point of shopping at Islamic stores, a businessman can achieve the feeling that he is doing his best to live as a good Muslim. Likewise, by donating money to a mosque and time to a Quran school, he can satisfy himself that, despite the adverse conditions, he is doing his share to improve the moral climate. He can alleviate his guilt also by assuming an Islamic identity for *his own* business.

It would be simplistic, then, to portray the businessmen who contribute to Islamic causes and participate in the Islamic subeconomy as mere tools of Islamist leaders, although there are those who take such actions under real or imagined social pressures. Many of the businessmen who have fueled the growth of the Islamic subeconomy derive important personal benefits from their activities. To them, Islamism is not just a social force to be accommodated. It serves also as a vehicle for fitting into a hostile economic culture (Özcan and Çokgezen 2003).

A related consequence of rampant dishonesty is that it makes it advantageous to join a subeconomy that fosters trustworthiness. Relative to businessmen who must constantly guard against being cheated, those who can count on timely deliveries and payments incur lower costs of operation. In particular, they spend less time, energy, and money on negotiating, drafting, monitoring, and enforcing agreements (Williamson 1985; Rauch and Casella 2001). New urbanites have immediate access to networks built on ties of kinship and regional origin. As a rule, however, these networks provide fewer benefits than those comprised of longtime residents, because members of the former tend to be poorer, less experienced, and politically powerless. The newcomers would like to break into the most lucrative networks. They seldom can, however, if only because they lack the proper education and the requisite social etiquette. The Islamic subeconomy offers a second-best alternative. Within it, they are able to establish business ties with ambitious but culturally handicapped people who, like themselves, are excluded from the economic mainstream. Their shared commitment to Islam provides a basis for mutual trust. Their costs of doing business are thus lower than those of the typical newcomer operating outside the Islamic subeconomy.

The networks of the Islamic subeconomy are not limited to the private sector. Throughout the Islamic world they extend into various levels of government. Islamists elected or appointed to positions of government authority are known to grant financially valuable political favors to those outside government. They make it cheaper for Islamist businessmen to learn about regulations, obtain licenses, avoid tax audits, and pass inspections.

Hence, low standards of honesty fuel Islamism through two channels: by creating a need for guilt relief and by making the economically insecure seek a vehicle for forming networks based on trust. The Islamic world displays low standards of honesty partly because overregulation and mis-regulation provide officials, high and low, with vast opportunities for earning bribes (Rowley *et al.* 1988). Also, governments have been ineffective at their most essential task, namely, providing the legal foundations of a complex, dynamic, and increasingly impersonal economy. In most parts of the Islamic world, the legal system fails to furnish low-cost instruments for collecting overdue debt. Traders thus have strong incentives to join private networks for protection against being cheated.[14] Explosive urbanization has compounded the incentives by stretching government services, including legal services, to the breaking point.

In populous countries like Egypt and Turkey, there was a time when the government could employ every high school graduate in need of a job. Now it cannot even hire every applicant with a university degree. In Cairo, a university graduate may wait a decade for a low-paying, entry-level position. At the same time, today's young job seekers have much higher aspirations than those of earlier generations. Populist ideologies, schooling, and mass communications have all raised their expected living standards way above what is feasible. Yet many must wait until they are around thirty to get a stable job, rent a place, and get married. In the meantime they remain sexually and emotionally frustrated, and they feel robbed of honor and dignity.

This brings us to still another way in which contemporary Islamism helps marginalized urbanites cope with frustrations. In promoting a puritanical lifestyle, it gives the deprived a justification for accepting a bad situation they are powerless to change. In effect, it offers both sexes the means for adjusting their aspirations to their possibilities – much like the fox who decided the grapes he could not reach had to be sour.[15] Islamists communicate to their adherents that to get married and have children, one need not wait for financial security. One can live as a "good Muslim," they say, even without fancy clothes, a private home, and modern amenities. They add that today's popular lifestyles are in any case immoral and un-Islamic. In some Egyptian Islamist circles, a prospective bride demands nothing from her future husband but a deep commitment to Islam. Moreover, before she accepts and her family agrees to the marriage, the groom must prove, usually through an oral quiz, that he has sufficient religious knowledge.[16]

Against this background, the Islamist obsession with veiling may be seen as another effort to alleviate the frustrations of marginalized urban youths. The veil reduces women's need to compete socially by keeping up with changing fashions. It also makes a statement against the materialism of modern civilization. Yet another of its functions is to protect the dignity of men socialized into measuring their manhood by how well they protect their women. City life offers great opportunities for the mixing of the sexes, and overcrowding in poor urban communities drastically limits family privacy. Under the circumstances, the veil attenuates the vulnerability of culturally conservative men, young and old (Ayubi 1991: chap. 2).

By no means do all veiled women belong to economically deprived segments of the urban population. Some come from upwardly mobile families that live in posh neighborhoods and have the financial means to keep up with fashions. For such women, the motivation for veiling lies primarily in its political and religious symbolism. This observation is supported by the emergence of an Islamic fashion industry which even stages fashion shows that display the latest styles in Islamic dress (Saraçgil 1993; Sullivan 1994: 58–63). Relative to poor Islamist women, prosperous ones tend to wear more expensive and more stylish veils. They thus affirm their religious identity and express opposition to modern sex relations *without* rejecting the materialism of modern civilization.

Threats to the global economy

The encouragement of veiling is a shared characteristic of Islamist movements everywhere. Likewise, the promotion of Islamic banking is a standard element of every Islamist economic agenda. Notwithstanding such commonalities, the economic orientations of Islamists exhibit potentially significant variations. Most critically, Islamists, including Islamic economists, have always been divided on the merits of the market. The religious opposition that toppled the Iranian monarchy harbored several rival economic agendas. Schools led by Murteza Mutahhari and Navvab-Safavi put great faith in the market system and saw the private accumulation of capital as essential for healthy economic development. A rival school led by Ali Shariati rejected private ownership and insisted on endowing the government with vast redistributive powers (Behdad 1989; Rahnema and Nomani 1990: chap. 3). In Pakistan, Mawdudi and many of his followers have maintained that Islam is sympathetic to private property and the market mechanism. But in the 1970s, prominent Pakistani leaders interpreted Islam as favoring planned economic development and massive redistribution (Kuran 2004).

Contemporary Islamism is capable of supporting both pro- and antimarket ideologies, because this is as true of Islam itself as it is of other major religions (Kuran 1993). The fundamental sources of Islam contain justifications for respecting market outcomes along with rationales for restricting economic liberties. One also finds precepts favoring interventions on behalf of the poor along with ones that preach tolerance of inequality. Such variations provide immense flexibility to anyone who wants to have Islam serve an economic agenda or to use ostensibly Islamic economic policies for noneconomic ends. They make it possible to ground any number of arguments, strategies, and policies in venerable traditions or timeless commandments. They enable public figures whose rhetoric may make them appear traditionalist to select among various economic positions without rejecting the authority of religion. As a case in point, they allowed Ayatollah Khomeini and his associates to adapt to various exigencies without ever stepping outside Islamic discourse. Iran's theocracy continues to accommodate new needs, yield to social pressures, and make pragmatic adaptations – all while continuing to claim allegiance to a timeless, unchanging, and well-defined economic agenda (Rahnema and Nomani 1990: chap. 4).

Modern Islamist movements possess, then, the ideological capacity and flexibility to sustain a liberal economic agenda. Even if they promote illiberal policies while in opposition, they may be able to assume a liberal orientation once in power. In any case, to pursue effectively liberal policies they need not make deliberate or explicit ideological adaptations. By giving low priority to Islamist economic goals, they may end up promoting private investment, self-management, private ownership, and free trade by default. Such unintended liberalism is all the more likely where illiberal economic goals are overshadowed by objectives concerning family, sexuality, manners, and education. Though a prominent theme in Khomeini's pre-revolutionary rhetoric was the elimination of poverty and exploitation, once he rose to Iran's helm he subordinated these objectives to the general goal of restoring the centrality of Islam in public life – even to such particular objectives as eliminating the consumption of alcohol, veiling women, banning Western music, and severing Iran from its pre-Islamic heritage. After the revolution, he dismissed demands for concrete economic reforms on the ground that economic well-being is worthy of the donkey (Rahnema and Nomani 1990: 296).

The economic agendas of Islamist and Islamist-rooted political parties in Turkey have undergone an even clearer transformation. In the 1970s and 1980s Islamist parties headed by Necmettin Erbakan had promoted state-directed industrialization and heavy redistribution through wage and price controls. By the late 1990s, the Erbakan-led Virtue Party (*Fazilet Partisi*) favored "a free-market economy" and "the integration of the Turkish economy into the world economy on the basis of private ownership, free enterprise, and free competition." And the Justice and Development Party (*Adalet ve Kalkınma Partisi* or *AK Parti*), which was founded by formerly Islamist politicians, won the November 2002 elections on a platform committed to a "neo-liberal economy" in which the state provides law and order to facilitate competition. Its leaders, including Prime Minister Recep Tayyip Erdoğan, couch their arguments in pragmatic terms, without references to Islam. Although the reticence is motivated partly by a desire to retain the support of "moderate" voters, it is clear that prominent Islamists have done a lot of rethinking on economic matters (Çaha 2003: 105–9; Dai 2005).

None of this means that the Islamists' market-constraining enactments and prescriptions, whether involving interest, or planning, or redistribution, are simply gimmicks lacking long-run significance. Although there exists no necessary connection between Islamism and economic illiberalism, Islamism is capable of supporting restrictions on economic liberties. Islamist leaders who, for whatever reason, desire to restrict international trade or regulate the composition of private investment will have little difficulty justifying their actions in religious terms. Also, leaders who whip up antimarket feelings as a tactical move to gain power will not necessarily be able to control the forces they unleash.

Illiberal economic policies can harm the countries implementing them. Protectionism causes the misallocation of local resources, and it insulates inefficient firms from external competition (Bhagwati 1988). Measures to direct an economy's evolution can produce excessive bureaucratic growth, thus reorienting individual enterprise from wealth-creating economic activities to wealth-distributing political ones (Rowley *et al.* 1988). The colossal failures of the centrally planned economies and the persistent disappointments of countries that have pursued inward-oriented and highly interventionist development strategies bear testimony to these adverse consequences (Chenery 1979; Papageorgiou *et al.* 1991). Of course, the burdens of illiberal policies are not borne only by the countries pursuing them. Trade restrictions generate misallocations in countries forced to produce goods obtainable more cheaply from abroad. Likewise, excessive bureaucratic meddling in a country imposes costs on anyone who consumes its products.

When a new regime starts pursuing an antimarket agenda, the consequent costs need not catch notice immediately. Its apologists will be endeavoring to make failures look like successes. Also, hardships and inefficiencies may initially appear transitional. Even when the costs gain wide recognition, however, it will not be easy to switch gears. For one thing, certain leaders may lose authority if they repudiate the policies they have championed. For another, the government bureaucracy and protected segments of the private sector will have developed a vested interest in the status quo. As a case in point, many Iranian leaders now recognize that the statist and nationalistic measures taken after the revolution of 1978–9 have imposed great burdens on the Iranian people. Accordingly, they have begun to change course: nationalized industries are now being reprivatized, and measures have been taken to encourage foreign trade, foreign investment, and joint ventures with foreign firms. Nonetheless, the Iranian economy remains more regulated and more inward-oriented than it would have been in the absence of illiberal postrevolutionary policies (Amuzegar 1992; Behdad 1994). Even though leaders sympathetic to a radical reorientation could easily concoct an Islamic rationale for broad liberalization, they find it politically infeasible to undo all the policies they now consider unwise. The principle at work here is "path dependence": current possibilities are shaped by history. Of two societies, one market oriented and the other antimarket, the former can retain liberal policies more easily than the latter can adopt them.

Government policies influence economic performance, but they are not the sole determinant. Education, culture, expressive freedoms, and the mass media all play important roles. Islamism seeks to reshape each of these factors, mostly for reasons other than wealth creation or distribution. The relevant political efforts thus carry economic implications. A culture that insists on the inerrancy of traditional sources of wisdom, treats religious teachings as unambiguous, and considers certain issues settled may leave the societies it touches unprepared to face the challenges of a dynamic global economy. It is likely to encourage risk aversion as opposed to risk taking, cautious imitation as opposed to daring innovation, and the production of established commodities as opposed to new, and thus highly profitable, ones. In a world where some societies are inquisitive and expressively free, therefore, an Islamist-controlled society may find itself economically disadvantaged. Significantly, the Middle East's failure to match the West's economic modernization process coincided with the spread of a mindset that equates innovation with heresy and success with stability (B. Lewis 1982; Rahman 1982). Technological creativity has always been a major source of relative economic success, and creative societies are generally tolerant of political dissent, distrustful of conventional wisdom, and open to social change (Mokyr 1990, 2002).

If a society starts pursuing economically unwise policies, should outsiders raise objections? As long as they respect the society's right to make bad choices, they should not hold back. Just as an individual has a right to eat foods high in cholesterol, so a society has every right to restrict its economic growth for other objectives, be it environmental preservation, political stability, or spiritual harmony. By the same token, anyone bothered by a society's economic choices, including an outsider, is entitled to offer alternatives. There is no reason, from a liberal point of view, to prevent a society from choosing to make its economy unproductive. Nor is there a reason, however, for people disturbed by its inefficiencies to keep their misgivings hidden.

When one part of the world falls substantially behind another, there can be troubling consequences for global political stability. The economically backward societies will accumulate resentments against the global economic system, against advanced societies, and even against similarly disadvantaged others. Such resentments can become a source of international friction. Whatever their source, international conflicts threaten global trade flows and transfers of capital. They also impart uncertainty to property rights, as when an ethnic group held responsible for another's economic frustrations faces the possibility of expropriation. Hence, if a society run by Islamists performs poorly in an economic sense, other societies may also suffer.

Islamist movements need not sow social tensions only after achieving power, as a by-product of their economic failures. Because they thrive on drawing boundaries between Muslims and others, they may deliberately antagonize outsiders in the hope of benefiting from the consequent social and political polarization. Agitated outsiders may then get organized in self-defense, fueling intercommunal struggles. Such a process is under way in Egypt, where Islamic militancy has prompted Copts to organize in self-defense. The Taliban's Islamization drive in Afghanistan, coupled with the terror of September 11, 2001, provoked outside military intervention and the formation of global movements to resist militant Islamism (Calhoun *et al.* 2002). Political instability can throw property rights into jeopardy, discourage local investment, and cause capital flight, thus impairing economic growth. In the long run, of course, it may end up promoting development by destroying political coalitions responsible for entrenched inefficiencies (Olson 1982).

There is no easy answer, then, to the question of what Islamism implies for the future of the global economic order. Like other fundamentalisms, it is capable of doing economic harm, yet it can also serve as a hidden agent of economic advancement. Remember, too, that some of what passes as Islamic economics, like the establishment of Islamic enterprises, alleviates potentially explosive social problems. How, then, should policy makers committed to a liberal social order respond to Islamist economic activities and to calls for economic Islamization?

The remainder of this essay proposes three classes of responses. In the first place, one must expose the flaws and limitations of Islamic economics. Second, one needs to show that Islamist economic prescriptions have considerably less appeal than often claimed. Finally, it is essential to devise creative solutions to the festering socioeconomic problems that have fueled the rise of Islamism. The last of these policies requires efforts at understanding Islamist motivations and ideals.

A first response to Islamic economics: expose its flaws and limitations

The first response would involve disseminating information on the actual and potential effects of Islamic economics. There is a need for writings at all levels, including works that resonate with groups from which Islamist movements draw their rank and file. For all their inconsistencies and illusions, Islamist tracts have an emotional appeal often lacking in secular economic writings. They connect, therefore, with large numbers. The constituents of Islamic economics must be given exposure to counterarguments. The lion's share would have to be shouldered by non-Islamists within countries where Islamists are making credible bids for power or have already achieved control. Outsiders can help out, but in the absence of local participation, their efforts are likely to be perceived as culturally biased.

Because modern scholarship developed mostly in the West, to criticize a non-Western movement is to risk being branded a tool of Western cultural arrogance. It would be wise, therefore, to integrate evaluations of Islamic economics into discourses on the merits of competing economic approaches. If criticisms of Islamic banking come to be confused with animosity toward Islam, matters resolvable through research and debate can turn into objects of cultural confrontation, causing Islamist positions to harden. Another way to allay suspicions of cultural bias is to subject economically unsound policies issued in the name of non-Muslim faiths to exactly the same treatment as those advanced in the name of Islam. The American doctrine known as "Christian economics" has a protectionist, antimarket streak (Iannaccone 1993). If only to maintain the credibility of criticisms directed at Islamic economics, this movement should be treated no differently from the antimarket strands within Islamism. To be sure, one can strive for impartiality without avoiding the charge of bias. Fundamentalisms have a stake in perpetuating, even heightening, the perception of deep divisions between themselves and some immoral, ignorant, foreign "other." Also, it is a common rhetorical tactic to deflect criticism by attributing dark motives to its bearers. This tactic is used effectively also by diverse secular leaders.

With respect to the specifics of what needs to be disseminated, efforts are needed to enhance general knowledge on the drawbacks of nationalist and protectionist policies adopted in the name of Islam, like those of Islamic Iran. Greater awareness must be fostered of the ruses that Islamic banks employ to circumvent the prohibition of interest and of the ineffectiveness of established zakat systems. It should become better and more widely understood that the distributional consequences of Islamist-favored institutions are not necessarily equalizing. There should be greater familiarity with the unimpressive economic records of countries that have implemented Islamist-led economic reforms, like Iran and Pakistan. Finally, people who appreciate that Islamic economics is a reaction to a serious social crisis should also realize that, for all its lofty rhetoric, it fails to offer a comprehensive solution.

Much talk about Islamic economic behavior has been shallow rhetoric, for no one has come close to defining it in practical terms. The Quran has not been of much help in this regard. Of its thousands of verses, only about one-third of 1 percent provide economic directives. And these verses offer enormous choice and flexibility to anyone who wants to use them to build an economic system. Accordingly, the schools of Islamic jurisprudence have differed on numerous economic matters. Likewise, the great Muslim thinkers to whom contemporary Islamist writers commonly turn for authority and inspiration often held conflicting positions (Coulson 1969; Saleh 1986; Kuran 2004: chap. 5). The key implication that requires dissemination is that a wide variety of economic agendas admit Islamic rationales. They include economically harmful ones. Economic restrictions imposed for the sake of cultural differentiation or confrontation – an enforced ban on interest, limitations on financial dealings with non-Muslims – may weaken a country economically, keep it on the periphery of the emerging global economy, and make it vulnerable to foreign domination.

In suggesting that one publicize the economically unsound elements of Islamist agendas, I am not proposing special treatment of religion in general or of Islam in particular. On the contrary, I am insisting that economic challenges in religious garb be treated exactly like those in secular garb. To exempt Islamic economics from review or criticism would be to grant it a special privilege. When a labor union or trade association demands an anticompetitive regulation, ordinarily there are many challenges. Commentators point to the regulation's disadvantages and suggest alternative solutions to the problem that it would ostensibly solve. For a weightier example, when the young Soviet Union put its economy under central control and started to preach planning as a superior alternative to the market mechanism, its antimarket campaign met with swift intellectual opposition. Ludwig von Mises, Friedrich Hayek, and other scholars argued that central planning would prove unworkable. They showed that no government agency, however powerful, can disseminate information and coordinate individual actions as efficiently as markets operating under the rule of law. Although the antiplanning literature was initially dismissed as "reactionary," it managed to erode confidence in the Soviet economic system, thus helping to set the stage for the fall of communism.

My first policy suggestion, then, is to subject Islamist economic proposals to the same critical examination brought to bear on any ordinary economic challenge. As of the mid-1990s, it bears mention, secular intellectual communities have paid scant attention to the economic content of Islamist agendas. Part of the reason lies in the fragmentation of the social sciences. Most economists consider religion outside their professional domain, while few area specialists and students of religion have had training in economics. Another reason is that the simpleminded prescriptions of Islamic economics allow observers to dismiss all of its discourse as nonsense, even as its influence grows. Still another reason, at least in countries where Islamists have resorted to violence, is that thinkers with misgivings about the Islamist agenda are afraid to say so publicly. The assassinations of critics like Uğur Mumcu and the Egyptian thinker Faraj Foda have made many Muslim intellectuals reticent to speak honestly and openly about the goals of Islamism.[17]

Second response: establish the limits of the Islamist appeal

A second measure to mitigate the economic damage of Islamism would be to counter the Islamists' efforts to portray themselves as spokespersons for quiescent majorities. When Islamists claim to represent the authentic voice of a society long silenced by secular pressures, they are often exaggerating.

Where Islamic banks operate alongside conventional banks, their share of Muslim deposits has remained under 20 percent; in some predominantly Muslim countries, the figure is under 5 percent (Moore 1990; Kazarian 1991: 149; Ağaoğlu 1994; Hamwi and Aylward 1999; Iqbal 2001). Also, the customers of Islamic financial establishments have shown a remarkable readiness to withdraw their deposits at the first threat of insolvency.[18] By no means is it clear, therefore, that the goal of abolishing interest enjoys widespread acceptance. Nor is it clear that the goal's promoters consider themselves bound by it. An Islamic economist might reply that "genuinely Islamic" banks would be more popular than the existing "nominally Islamic" banks paying and charging interest in disguised form. Yet, if none of today's hundreds of Islamic banks is "genuinely Islamic," it behooves us to ask why. For one thing, fewer Muslims consider interest immoral than those who support the anti-interest campaign either openly or tacitly. For another, Muslims bothered by interest generally subordinate their qualms to objectives like financial security and simplicity.

It bears reemphasis that many participants in the Islamic subeconomy are skillfully using Islamic symbolism as an instrument of economic self-advancement. Not every Egyptian who keeps money in an Islamic bank or operates an Islamic grocery store is a committed Islamist. Many Muslims who pass as Islamists know almost nothing about Islamic history, philosophy, and institutions; they have little interest in developing a distinctly Islamic social system; and they have made lifestyle adaptations under modern influences. Furthermore, Muslims who have devoted considerable time to studying Islam are not all under the spell of its angry, authoritarian, and inflexible side. Some are impressed instead by its gentle, tolerant, and pragmatic side; and they are ready to allow the coexistence of multiple interpretations of Islam, even to respect the rights of unbelievers (B. Lewis 1993: chaps 8, 11).

İsmet Özel, Turkey's leading Islamist poet, readily acknowledges that few Turks are genuinely committed to the cause of creating an Islamic social order. Only 6 percent of Turkey's Muslims are true believers, he claims, though this small share is socially and politically pivotal (Özel 1989: 149–62; Meeker 1991: 215). Other leading Islamist writers take issue with the prevailing Islamist interpretation of Islam's economic mission. Suggesting that the established Islamic banks have little to do with Islam per se, they argue that some forms of interest are morally unassailable and that an effective interest ban would hamper Muslim firms in the global marketplace (Güngör 1981: 11, 150, 241; Bulaç 1990: 115–16). The proponents of prohibiting interest are out of touch with reality, they say. An Islamist regime could never achieve widespread compliance with a ban, except by force.

Claims regarding the genuine popularity of Islamist prescriptions can be tested through elections conducted by secret ballot or surveys that give respondents anonymity. This is because social pressures that regulate openly conveyed preferences are absent from settings where people's choices remain unknown to others. To my knowledge, there have been no systematic surveys to determine the true popularity of Islamic economics. But certain predominantly Muslim countries have held secret-ballot elections that gave voters the option of supporting an Islamist party. In many of these elections Islamists received far less support than is evident from the tenor of public discourse. In national elections, the Jama'at-i Islami of Pakistan never performs well. Its candidates routinely lose to rivals labeled un- or anti-Islamic. Until forced into exile through a military coup, Benazir Bhutto, whom the Jama'at-i-Islami has denounced from the day she entered politics, enjoyed far more electoral support than most Islamist politicians.[19] In Turkey, one might observe, a party with Islamist roots came to power through an election. True, but it had campaigned in favor of integration into the global economy and renounced its Islamist identity (Çaha 2003; Dai 2005).

Social pressures do not necessarily benefit Islamists. On the eve of the Algerian elections of June 1990 the Islamic Salvation Front was expected to lose decisively. It went on to win handily, suggesting that fear of government reprisals had caused many of its sympathizers to conceal their inclinations (Roberts 1994: 465–78). The point, then, is not that the publicly expressed preferences of Muslims always overstate their genuine sympathies toward Islamist causes. Rather, it is that one should never accept at face value the claim that Islamists form a silent majority.

Certain segments of the secular intellectual community are predisposed to rejecting particular Islamist claims. For instance, most economists will readily reject the assertion that people raised as Muslims consider interest unjust. This is because economists are generally trained to believe that basic economic impulses and understandings exhibit no systematic differences across societies. Other intellectuals are sympathetic to assertions of cross-national variation in values, goals, and attitudes. For instance, anthropologists and many area specialists are trained to notice, probe, and highlight differences, as opposed to similarities. Whatever their own values, many are prepared, therefore, to accept that Muslims are readier than non-Muslims to forgo the safety of fixed interest in favor of variable returns. Moreover, even if they find such a claim implausible, their professional norms may keep them from raising objections, lest they be accused of cultural bias. It so happens that interest has always played an integral role in Muslim economies (Khan 1929; Rodinson 1973: chap. 3; Mandaville 1979: 289–308; Kuran 2005). And Islamic banking is a modern creation; nothing like it existed prior to the 1970s. Scholars who teach that Islam mandates a distinct form of banking are unwitting accomplices, therefore, in myth making. In trying to respect an ostensible cultural difference, they are enhancing the credibility of Islamists posing as defenders of an endangered local practice.

A related boost to the credibility of Islamists stems from the fact that the West has lost its once-booming cultural confidence. One manifestation of this loss is the ongoing uprising in the United States against the longstanding liberal curriculum in the humanities and the social sciences, now held responsible for deficiencies in the performance of certain groups (D'Souza 1991; Schlessinger 1991). Another is the intense self-criticism occasioned by the quincentennial of Columbus' landing in America, which stood in sharp contrast to the self-congratulatory atmosphere of a century earlier. Whatever their intrinsic merits, campaigns to denigrate Western culture as inherently racist, sexist, oppressive, and inegalitarian diminish the West's confidence in its own cultural particularities. Moreover, the resulting self-doubt makes it harder for secularist Muslims to defend Westernization, and it allows Islamists to invoke Western malaise as evidence that Westernization is dangerous.

One should not seek to constrain Western self-criticism just because it yields side benefits to Islamism or, for that matter, to other fundamentalisms. Nor should one compel Islamists to refrain from cultivating the best possible image for themselves, any more than one should make Coca-Cola refrain from manipulative advertising. However, one should avoid falling for, and basing policies on, inflated claims of Islamist support. This is not a trivial point. In certain countries incumbent non-Islamist regimes are making concession after concession to the Islamists, often on the ground that Islamist demands command major support. To give one example, the Egyptian government is giving increasing coverage to religious programs on the state-controlled television network. It is also seeking the approval of religious authorities in a growing number of policy domains. Such concessions are probably shortsighted. They serve to bolster the image of Islamist strength, make non-Islamists afraid to articulate their own beliefs, and embolden the Islamist opposition even further.

Third response: listen carefully

The responses proposed thus far are confrontational. One is intended to discredit the arguments on which Islamists base their challenges to prevailing socioeconomic structures. The other calls into question the popularity of these challenges. By contrast, the final suggested response is conciliatory. It is to listen carefully to Islamist complaints about modernity, recognizing that some are motivated by tangible flaws of established social structures. Secular regimes have every right to oppose misguided challenges to their policies. By the same token, they have an obligation to hear criticism. The fact that Islamists have made some outrageous demands hardly means that their concerns are devoid of merit.

When Islamists complain about corrupt government, they are not pointing to a nonexistent problem. Government corruption is as old as government itself, yet its allocational and distributional consequences have gained importance with the state's expanding control over economic and social life. Nor are Islamists unjustified in accusing incumbent regimes of wasting human resources. Many countries feature enormous unemployment and underemployment, partly because of excessive centralization and bureaucratic inefficiency. One need not be a militant antisecularist to see that basically secular regimes in Egypt, Morocco,

Algeria, and Pakistan – to name just a few of the countries with vociferous Islamist movements – have not been entirely successful at answering the frustrations of their swelling populations. Secular elites would respond that they recognize the problems, adding that they have proposed various reforms. Yet, the measures that many of them champion would probably compound the prevailing problems. For example, Mumcu tended to support widespread economic regulation. He never quite appreciated that Turkey's huge public sector creates enormous opportunities for favoritism, influence peddling, and graft, or that various bureaucratic controls inhibit job growth. His approach to fixing the Turkish economy – tighter government controls, better planning – amounted to a more vigorous application of policies responsible for past economic disappointments.

While criticizing incumbent governments, Islamists have also been tackling certain social problems with considerable creativity. These efforts are not necessarily part of a grand plot to achieve power. Some Islamist services have emerged partly, if not mainly, to plug gaps left by poorly functioning economies. As noted earlier, Islamic clinics, dormitories, clubs, camps, and schools serve various underprivileged and disaffected groups. That these services contribute to the wider Islamist cause does not diminish their benefits to individuals who are not committed Islamists. Secular policy makers would do well, therefore, to explore how these services operate and why so many people are turning for help to Islamists.

Islamists do not necessarily offer viable solutions to problems such as unemployment and official corruption. In restricting economic freedoms, certain Islamist agendas would probably exacerbate existing problems. This is no reason, however, to dismiss all the grievances that underlie such agendas. On the contrary, the dangerous aspects of the agendas compound the urgency of lessening the grievances that account for their popularity. Unless secular authorities reduce government excesses, limit the state's economic authority, and create an economic environment conducive to free exchange under the rule of law, illiberal fundamentalist agendas will enjoy appeal. A century ago, when Engels denounced work conditions in British factories, his criticisms prompted non-Marxists to institute reforms. This was doubtless a factor in the subsequent containment of communism. In any case, some Islamists are on the right track with respect to solving critical economic problems. Those who favor regulatory reforms are not just identifying a serious source of inefficiency. They are also helping to build a consensus for a shift in direction.

Adam Smith is widely remembered for the 1776 publication of *Wealth of Nations* (1937), his treatise on the connection between market freedoms and economic prosperity. Less well known is his first major treatise, published in 1759, the *Theory of Moral Sentiments* (1976), which explores, among other matters, how social and moral norms help ensure the social stability that allows human civilization to flourish. The lesser appeal of Smith's earlier treatise epitomizes the scant attention in secular discourse to the psychological, social, and economic functions of norms. Where Islamists, like other fundamentalists, take norms very seriously, many secular intellectuals and policy makers tend either to dismiss them as unimportant or to treat them as sources of inefficiency. The study of economic development is revealing. International differences in economic growth rates are commonly attributed to differences in resource endowments, trade policies, and social stability. Economists in the mainstream generally pay little attention to cultural variables such as work habits, demand for education, attitudes toward innovation, and family structure.

Islamic economics promotes the view, we saw earlier, that behavioral norms contribute critically to economic success. However much they overrate the social virtues of altruism and underrate those of selfishness, they are right about the importance of norms (Wilson 1993; Hechter and Opp 2001). This is not to say that social definitions of right and wrong should stay fixed. Nor is it to deny the importance of laws, rules, and regulations. My point is that in vast reaches of human activity, norms remain a cheap and effective way to discipline and coordinate individual actions.

If one requirement of a free economic order is that individuals enjoy broad economic freedoms, another is that they accept responsibility for their own circumstances and take primary responsibility for improving them. Certain Islamist inclinations go against the latter requirement, for instance, the tendency to blame foreigners for domestic economic ills – a tendency evident in Mawdudi's writings on the corrupting influence of Western culture. But not all Islamists are on the look for scapegoats. In South Asia the Tablighi Jama'at encourages self-improvement and self-reliance: its members are expected to decline gifts from others and to become more generous and more honest (Metcalf 1994: 710–17).

The observed support for Islamism should never be taken at face value, I have argued, for some of it might be feigned. Islamist leaders would not necessarily object to this warning. They would quickly call, however, for equal caution with regard to the apparent support for secularist agendas and the observed opposition to public displays of religion. A prominent theme in the Turkish Islamist literature is that, since the Atatürk reforms of the 1920s, Turkish Muslims have had to keep their religious feelings private, at least in spheres officially divorced from religion. Here are a few revealing titles from Islamist presses: *The Postponed Islamic Life, Speaking in Difficult Times*, and *The Minister Who Recognized "Allah" After His Death* (Özel 1984; İ. Balcı and M. Balcı 1986–90; Yılmaz 1990).

The last title refers to Hasan Âli Yücel, Minister of Education from 1938 to 1946, a Westernizer known as a tough foe of traditional Islam. The book alleges that, contrary to his outward appearances, Yücel was deeply religious. After his retirement, it claims, he regretted his participation in the suppression of Islam, as evidenced by a long religious poem he penned. Yücel did not publish the poem during his lifetime, though he left instructions for posthumous publication. The episode testifies, the book concludes, to Yücel's fear of being denounced as a closet-obscurantist. The veracity of the account is not a matter to be settled here. What matters is the book's central message, which is that Turks have tended to be less supportive of the secularist agenda in private than they have appeared in public. An implication of the message is that efforts to eject religion from domains such as politics and economics owe their apparent support to social pressures against overt dissenters.

That certain Islamists are prepared to intimidate, censor, and silence their opponents does not refute that they, too, have had their expressive freedoms curtailed. When Islamists promote public displays of religiosity and cultivate religious symbols, this is partly, then, in reaction to past pressures that have made them lead insincere lives. The pressures could have come from official controls, established religious organizations, or simply the weight of public opinion. Whatever the cluster of sources, the pressures imply that the ongoing spread of Islamism stems from more than a rise in individual religiosity. A complementary factor is that religion is everywhere becoming more vocal, more open, and more demanding than it was, say, in the 1960s, when secularization was pushing religion progressively into the private realm.[20]

Conscious as they are of the Islamist threat to their own artistic, literary, sexual, intellectual, and political freedoms, secular intellectuals overlook that Islamists feel expressively limited and threatened. The source of this ignorance is that they rarely talk to Islamists, listen to their grievances, or read their writings. Were they to make an effort to understand Islamist concerns, they would encounter unmet spiritual needs. They would find that secular policies and pressures, like government controls on Islamic expression or the sanctions of secular public opinion, have left a huge void in some individuals. Such a realization would pave the way, perhaps, for fruitful communication between Islamists and their adversaries.

Conclusions

This essay has proposed how policy makers committed to a free economic order should respond to the rise of Islamic economics and the Islamic subeconomy. Insofar as efforts to bring Islam into economic discourse and to confer a religious identity on formerly secular economic practices are pushing long-submerged perspectives to the surface, they advance individual liberties. The spirit of the free order calls for openness about thoughts, wants, and anxieties, including religious impulses. It offers the freedom to give actions meanings of one's choice, possibly some religious interpretation. In itself, therefore, it is not a problem that certain social services are being defined as Islamic. Nor is it problematic that there now exist Islamic banks, Islamic grocery stores, and Islamic fashion shows. If Islamic economic enterprises give comfort to Muslims who consider Islam a well-defined way of life, they should be regarded as positive developments. The legitimacy of a social order is enhanced, not diminished, when a person who ascribes religious significance to a loan's form can shun interest openly, proudly, and without apology.

Yet, certain Islamist economic goals conflict with economic freedoms. Economic protectionism, which some Islamists favor, would curtail individual rights to free exchange. Likewise, forcing all Muslims to shun interest would interfere with basic economic liberties. Such moves should be opposed vigorously, regardless of their source and justification. They should be rejected because they trample on essential freedoms and also because they can be socially costly. Forcing all Muslims to shun interest would relegate Muslims to the fringes of the international economy.

The promotion and enforcement of free economic order requires, therefore, drawing a distinction between the liberty to live by Islamist economic rules and the liberty to impose such rules on others. The latter liberty clashes with the liberties of others, so it may be rejected. Thus, one may recognize the freedom to live by the rules of Islamic economics without recognizing a right to impose these rules on entire societies.

Certain Islamists might never agree to make abiding by its tenets a matter of personal choice. But there is room for optimism. The fact that they are making a primary issue out of allowing people to speak their minds, be themselves, and follow the calls of their conscience has an important implication. It means that they may be, or may eventually become, amenable to granting reciprocal rights of self-expression to others. Perhaps, then, the focus of discourse on Islamic economics should shift to matters of openness and reciprocal tolerance. A common ground could eventually emerge from an understanding that to force Islamic economic prescriptions on everyone is morally and practically equivalent to pressuring Islamists to hide their own religious identities and views.

Relative to Christianity, Islam has a good historical record with regard to religious tolerance. Historically, therefore, Muslims have felt less pressed than Christians to institute formal protections against religious tyranny. Contemporary conditions in many parts of the Islamic world are ripening, however, for a broad attempt at protecting freedom of thought and expression. With huge numbers of secularists and Islamists feeling expressively oppressed by one another, a stalemate between the two groups may set the stage for a reciprocal exchange of basic liberties.[21] The liberties might include economic freedoms, including both the right to shun interest and the right to deal in it fearlessly.

Notes

1 Here I generally use the last of these terms, mainly for simplicity. The first two are just as meaningful. As Al-Azm (1993: 97) points out, every Islamist group "is convinced that it is in the process not only of going back to the basics and fundamentals of Islam, but of reviving them as well, after a long period of, let us say, hibernation. They are reviving them as active beliefs and efficacious practices in the lives of people."

2 Mumcu (1987: 171–96), Mumcu (1988: 48–50, 151–3). A militant Islamist captured by the Turkish police in early 1996 provided evidence implicating the Iranian government. Turkish-Iranian relations worsened dramatically following the revelations, and the Turkish government considered military reprisals. See *Hürriyet*, March 12, 1996, and later dates.

3 Kuran (2004: 43–9). See, generally, Lewis and Algaoud (2001) and El-Gamal (2006).

4 Few people without training in economics worry about the financial feasibility or desirability of Islamic banking.

5 Influential contributions include Mannan (1970) and Chapra (1992). Other key contributions as well as several critiques are in an anthology of Niblock and Wilson (1999). For further references, see Kuran (2004).

6 *Economist*, January 18, 1992: 33. For a survey of these and related developments, see Kuran 1993.
7 The term refers to the practitioners of Islamic economics, who represent a small minority of all economists of the Muslim faith.
8 For related points, see Kuran (1996). Nasr (1996) examines Mawdudi's general agenda.
9 The timing of the first practical application of Islamic banking was influenced by the restructuring of the international oil market in the early 1970s. Much of the initial capital came from oil-rich Arab states seeking politically acceptable ways to recirculate their mushrooming petrodollars.
10 For several instructive case studies, see El-Ashker (1987: chap. 11). These studies provide information on the cosmetic aspects of Islamic establishments; they provide few insights into actual practices, suggesting that El-Ashker noticed nothing unusual worth reporting. Özcan and Çokgezen (2003) offer examples of corrupt practices on the part of Islamic establishments.
11 A similar argument is advanced by Baker (1990: chap. 8).
12 Based on a discussion with Mursi Saad El-Din, Cairo, August 2, 1993. For many complementary observations, see Sullivan (1994), Sullivan and Abed-Kotob (1999: chap. 2), and Singerman (1995: chap. 4).
13 Such financing occurs largely through informal channels. See Hyman (1987: 11, 19–20) and Roy (2004).
14 Such incentives arise wherever the legal system is weak. In Southern Italy, Gambetta (1993) demonstrates, they fueled the rise of the Mafia.
15 On the general phenomenon, see Elster (1983: chap. 3).
16 Information provided by Tahseen Basheer in a Cairo interview, August 3, 1993.
17 The logic that underlies this observation is developed at length in Kuran (1995).
18 For an example from Egypt, see Springborg (1989: 45–61).
19 For some figures, see Mayer (1993: 146–7, n. 31).
20 See Casanova (1992: 37–43). The religious revival of our times has also been attributed to religious deregulation. In this view, religious deregulation is fueling an explosion of new religious forms and a huge increase in public religious expression, just as industrial deregulation stimulates production by allowing firms to satisfy a greater variety of needs. On this second view, see Chaves and Cann (1992: 272–90). The two explanations are not mutually exclusive. Greater religious experimentation may go along with greater religious openness.
21 Such a stalemate lies at the origins of religious tolerance in the contemporary West. Persecutions inflicted by Christians trying to impose their own orthodoxies on other Christians convinced astute Europeans and Americans that it would be mutually beneficial to keep religion out of government affairs and grant individuals broad expressive freedoms. See Dahl (1956).

Bibliography

Ağaoğlu, E. A. (1994) "A Camel-wise Comparative Financial and Market Share Analysis of the Islamic Banks Currently Operating in Turkey," *METU Studies in Development*, 21 (4): 475–500.
Ahmad, M. (1991) "Islamic Fundamentalism in South Asia: The Jama'at-i-Islami and the Tablighi Jamaat of South Asia," in M. E. Marty and R. S. Appleby (eds) *Fundamentalisms Observed*, Chicago, IL: University of Chicago Press.
Ahmed, R. (1994) "Redefining Muslim Identity in South Asia: The Transformation of the Jama'at-i-Islami," in M. E. Marty and R. S. Appleby (eds) *Accounting for Fundamentalisms: The Dynamic Character of Movements*, Chicago, IL: University of Chicago Press.

Amuzegar, J. (1992) "The Iranian Economy before and after the Revolution," *Middle East Journal*, 46 (Summer): 413–25.

Ayubi, N. (1991) *Political Islam: Religion and Politics in the Arab World*, London: Routledge.

Al-Azm, S. J. (1993) "Islamic Fundamentalism Reconsidered: A Critical Outline of Problems, Ideas, and Approaches," *South Asia Bulletin*, 13 (1–2): 93–121.

Baker, R. W. (1990) *Sadat and After: Struggles for Egypt's Political Soul*, Cambridge, MA: Harvard University Press.

Bakhash, S. (1989) "What Khomeini Did," *New York Review of Books*, July 20: 16–19.

Balcı, İ. and Balcı, M. (1986–90) *Ertelenen İslami Hayat [The Postponed Islamic Life]*, 4 vols, Istanbul: İklim Yayınları.

Behdad, S. (1989) "Property Rights in Contemporary Islamic Thought: A Critical Perspective," *Review of Social Economy*, 47 (Summer): 185–211.

Behdad, S. (1994) "Production and Employment in Iran: Involution and De-Industrialization Thesis," in T. Coville (ed.) *The Economy of Islamic Iran: Between State and Market*, Tehran: Institut Français de Recherche en Iran.

Bhagwati, J. (1988) *Protectionism*, Cambridge, MA: MIT Press.

Buchanan, J. M. (1975) *The Limits of Liberty: Between Anarchy and Leviathan*, Chicago, IL: University of Chicago Press.

Bulaç, A. (1990/1988) *İnsanın Özgürlük Arayışı [The Human Quest for Freedom]*, Istanbul: Endülüs Yayınları.

Çaha, Ömer (2003) "Turkish Election of November 2002 and the Rise of 'Moderate' Political Islam," *Alternatives: Turkish Journal of International Relations*, 2 (Fall): 93–116.

Calhoun, C., Price P., and Timmer, A. (eds) (2002) *Understanding September 11*, New York: New Press.

Casanova, J. (1992) "Private and Public Religions," *Social Research*, 59 (Spring): 37–43.

Chapra, M. U. (1992) *Islam and the Economic Challenge*, Leicester: Islamic Foundation.

Chaves, M. and Cann, D. E. (1992) "Regulation, Pluralism, and Religious Market Structure: Explaining Religion's Vitality," *Rationality and Society*, 4 (July): 272–90.

Chenery, H. B. (1979) *Structural Change and Development Policy*, New York: Oxford University Press.

Coulson, N. J. (1969) *Conflicts and Tensions in Islamic Jurisprudence*, Chicago, IL: University of Chicago Press.

Dahl, R. A. (1956) *A Preface to Democratic Theory*, Chicago, IL: University of Chicago Press.

Dai, H. D. (2005) "Transformation of Islamic Political Identity in Turkey: Rethinking the West and Westernization," *Turkish Studies*, 6 (March): 21–37.

D'Souza, D. (1991) *Illiberal Education: The Politics of Race and Sex on Campus*, New York: Free Press.

El-Ashker, A. A. (1987) *The Islamic Business Enterprise*, London: Croom Helm.

El-Gamal, M. A. (2006) *Islamic Finance: Law, Economics, and Practice*, New York: Cambridge University Press.

Elster, J. (1983) *Sour Grapes: Studies in the Subversion of Rationality*, Cambridge: Cambridge University Press.

Gambetta, D. (1993) *The Sicilian Mafia: The Business of Protection*, Cambridge, MA: Harvard University Press.

Göle, N. (1999) *İslam'ın Yeni Kamusal Yüzleri [The New Public Faces of Islam]*, Istanbul: Metis.

Güngör, E. (1981) *İslamın Bugünkü Meseleleri [Contemporary Problems of Islam]*, Istanbul: Ötüken Neşriyat.

Gürsoy-Tezcan, A. (1991) "Mosque or Health Centre? A Dispute in a *Gecekondu*," in R. Tapper (ed.) *İslam in Modern Turkey: Religion, Politics, and Literature in a Secular State*, London: I. B. Tauris.

Al-Hamarneh, A. and Steiner, C. (2004) "Islamic Tourism: Rethinking the Strategies of Tourism Development in the Arab World After September 11, 2001," *Comparative Studies of South Asia, Africa and the Middle East*, 24 (1): 173–82.

Hamwi, B. and Aylward, A. (1999) "Islamic Finance: A Growing International Market," *Thunderbird International Business Review*, 41 (July–October): 407–20.

Hayek, F. A. (1973–9) *Law, Legislation, and Liberty*, 3 vols, Chicago, IL: University of Chicago Press.

Hechter, M. and Opp, K. (eds) (2001) *Social Norms*, New York: Russell Sage.

Hyman, A. (1987) *Muslim Fundamentalism*, London: Institute for the Study of Conflict.

Iannaccone, L. (1993) "Heirs to the Protestant Ethic? The Economics of American Fundamentalists," in M. E. Marty and R. S. Appleby (eds) *Fundamentalisms and the State: Remaking Polities, Economies, and Militance*, Chicago, IL: University of Chicago Press.

Iqbal, M. (2001) "Islamic and Conventional Banking in the Nineties: A Comparative Study," *Islamic Economic Studies*, 8 (April): 1–27.

Kazarian, E. (1991) *Islamic Banking in Egypt*, Lund, Sweden: Lund Economic Studies.

Khan, M. S. A. (1929) "The Mohammadan Laws Against Usury and How They Are Evaded," *Journal of Comparative Legislation and International Law*, 11: 233–44.

Kuran, T. (1993) "Fundamentalisms and the Economy," in M. E. Marty and R. S. Appleby (eds) *Fundamentalisms and the State: Remaking Polities, Economies, and Militance*, Chicago, IL: University of Chicago Press.

Kuran, T. (1995) *Private Truths, Public Lies: The Social Consequences of Preference Falsification*, Cambridge, MA: Harvard University Press.

Kuran, T. (1996) "The Discontents of Islamic Economic Morality," *American Economic Review*, 86 (May): 438–42.

Kuran, T. (2003) "Islamic Redistribution through Zakat: Historical Record and Modern Realities," in Michael Bonner, Mine Ener, and Amy Singer (eds) *Poverty and Charity in Middle Eastern Contexts*, Albany, NY: State University of New York Press.

Kuran, T. (2004) *Islam and Mammon: The Economic Predicaments of Islamism*, Princeton, NJ: Princeton University Press.

Kuran, T. (2005) "The Logic of Financial Westernization in the Middle East," *Journal of Economic Behavior and Organization*, 56 (April): 593–615.

Lewis, B. (1982) *The Muslim Discovery of Europe*, New York: W. W. Norton.

Lewis, B. (1993) *Islam and the West*, New York: Oxford University Press.

Lewis, M. K. and Algaoud, L. M. (2001) *Islamic Banking*, Cheltenham, UK: Edward Elgar.

Mandaville, J. E. (1979) "Usurious Piety: The Cash Waqf Controversy in the Ottoman Empire," *International Journal of Middle East Studies*, 10 (August): 289–308.

Mannan, M. A. (1970) *Islamic Economics: Theory and Practice*, Lahore: Sh. Muhammad Ashraf.

Mawdudi, S. A. A. (1985/1940) *Let Us Be Muslims*, Leicester: Islamic Foundation.

Mayer, A. E. (1993) "The Fundamentalist Impact on Law, Politics, and Constitutions in Iran, Pakistan, and the Sudan," in M. E. Marty and R. S. Appleby (eds) *Fundamentalisms and the State: Remaking Polities, Economies, and Militance*, Chicago, IL: University of Chicago Press.

Meeker, M. E. (1991) "The New Muslim Intellectuals in the Republic of Turkey," in R. Tapper (ed.) *Islam in Modern Turkey: Religion, Politics, and Literature in a Secular State*, London: I. B. Tauris.

Metcalf, B. D. (1994) " 'Remaking Ourselves': Islamic Self-Fashioning in a Global Movement of Spiritual Renewal," in M. E. Marty and R. S. Appleby (eds) *Accounting for Fundamentalisms: The Dynamic Character of Movements*, Chicago, IL: University of Chicago Press.

Mokyr, J. (1990) *The Lever of Riches: Technological Creativity and Economic Progress*, New York: Oxford University Press.

Mokyr, J. (2002) *The Gifts of Athena: Historical Origins of the Knowledge Economy*, Princeton, NJ: Princeton University Press.

Moore, C. H. (1990) "Islamic Banks and Competitive Politics in the Arab World and Turkey," *Middle East Journal*, 44 (Spring): 234–55.

Mumcu, U. (1987) *Rabıta*, Istanbul: Tekin Yayınevi.

Mumcu, U. (1988) *Tarikat, Siyaset, Ticaret [Sects, Politics, Commerce]*, Istanbul: Tekin Yayınevi.

Murphy, K. (1992) "Islamic Extremists Declaring War on Egypt's Tourist Industry," *Los Angeles Times*, October 23: A6.

Naqvi, S. N. H. (1981) *Ethics and Economics: An Islamic Synthesis*, Leicester: Islamic Foundation.

Nasr, S. V. R. (1996) *Mawdudi and the Making of Islamic Revivalism*, New York: Oxford University Press.

Nasr, S. V. R. (2004) "Regional Implications of Shi'a Revival in Iraq," *Washington Quarterly*, 27 (3): 7–24.

Niblock, T. and Wilson, R. (1999) *The Political Economy of the Middle East, vol. 3: Islamic Economics*, Cheltenham, UK: Edward Elgar.

Olson, M. (1982) *The Rise and Decline of Nations: Economic Growth, Stagflation, and Social Rigidities*, New Haven: Yale University Press.

Özcan, Gül Berna, and Murat Çokgezen (2003) "Limits to Alternative Forms of Capitalization: The Case of Anatolian Holding Companies," *World Development*, 31 (12): 2061–84.

Özel, İ. (1984) *Zor Zamanda Konuşmak [Speaking in Difficult Times]*, Istanbul: Çıdam Yayınları.

Özel, İ. (1989) *Sorulunca Söylenen [Answers to Questions One Might Be Asked]*, Istanbul: Çıdam Yayınları.

Papageorgiou, D., Michaely, M., and Choksi, A. M. (eds) (1991) *Liberalizing Foreign Trade*, 7 vols, Cambridge, MA: Basil Blackwell.

Rahman, F. (1982) *Islam and Modernity: Transformation of an Intellectual Tradition*, Chicago: University of Chicago Press.

Rahnema, A. and Nomani, F. (1990) *The Secular Miracle: Religion, Politics, and Economic Policy in Iran*, London: Zed Books.

Rashwan, D. and Gad, E. (1993) "The Marriage of Militancy and Tradition," *Al-Ahram Weekly*, July 8–14: 3.

Rauch, J. E. and Casella, A. (eds) (2001) *Networks and Markets*, New York: Russell Sage.

Reed, H. A. (1988) "Islam and Education in Turkey," *Turkish Studies Association Bulletin*, 12: 2–4.

Roberts, H. (1994) "From Radical Mission to Equivocal Ambition: The Expansion and Manipulation of Algerian Islamism, 1979–1992," in M. E. Marty and R. S. Appleby (eds) *Accounting for Fundamentalisms: The Dynamic Character of Movements*, Chicago, IL: University of Chicago Press.

Rodinson, M. (1973/1966) *Islam and Capitalism*, New York: Pantheon Books.

Rowley, C. K., Tollison, R. D., and Tullock, G. (eds) (1988) *The Political Economy of Rent-Seeking*, Boston, MA: Kluwer.

Roy, O. (2004) *Globalized Islam: The Search for a New Ummah*, New York: Columbia University Press.

Saleh, N. A. (1986) *Unlawful Gain and Legitimate Profit in Islamic Law*, Cambridge, MA: Cambridge University Press.

Saraçgil, B. (1993) "İslami Giyimde Moda ve Tüketim" *[Islamic Clothing Fashions and Consumption Patterns], Yeni Zemin*, August: 74–6.

Schlessinger, A. M., Jr (1991) *The Disuniting of America: Reflections on a Multicultural Society*, Knoxville, TN: Whittle Books.

Siddiqi, M. N. (1972) *The Economic Enterprise in Islam*, Lahore: Islamic Publications.

Singerman, D. (1995) *Avenues of Participation: Families, Politics, and Networks in Urban Quarters of Cairo*, Princeton, NJ: Princeton University Press.

Smith, A. (1937/1776) *The Wealth of Nations*, New York: Modern Library.

Smith, A. (1976/1759) *The Theory of Moral Sentiments*, Oxford: Clarendon Press.

Springborg, R. (1989) *Mubarak's Egypt: Fragmentation of the Political Orders*, Boulder, CO: Westview Press.

Sullivan, D. J. (1994) *Private Voluntary Organizations in Egypt: Islamic Development, Private Iniative, and State Control*, Gainesville, FL: University Press of Florida.

Sullivan, D. J. and Abed-Kotob, S. (1999) *Islam in Contemporary Egypt: Civil Society vs. the State*, Boulder, CO: Lynne Rienner.

Williamson, O. E. (1985) *The Economic Institutions of Capitalism: Firms, Markets, Relational Contracting*, New York: Free Press.

Wilson, J. Q. (1993) *The Moral Sense*, New York: Free Press.

Yılmaz, H. (1990) *Öldükten Sonra "Allah" Diyen Bakan [The Minister Who Recognized "Allah" after His Death]*, Istanbul: Timaş Yayınları.

3   Islam and human rights policy

Ann Elizabeth Mayer

Introduction

For some decades various institutions and ideologues have proposed that there should be a distinctive Islamic approach to human rights questions. With the founding of the Islamic Republic of Iran in 1979 and the surge in demands for Islamization of laws, how Islam should affect human rights policy ceased to be a theoretical question and became of obvious practical importance. In consequence, the relevant literature has burgeoned (An-Na'im 1990; Dwyer 1991; Mernissi 1992; Afkhami 1995; Mayer 1999; Afshari 2001; Baderin 2003; Waltz 2004). As the following review will indicate, exactly how Islam should relate to human rights policy remains a matter of deep controversy.

Background

The term human rights, *huquq al-insan* in Arabic, has only recently come into common use in discussions of Islamic principles. The ideas of rights belonging to the individual Muslim, *haqq al-'abd*, as distinguished from the right of God, *haqq allah*, were familiar to Islam's medieval jurists. However, the right to protection for private property, which could be invoked against incursions by the state, was the only right recognized by them that directly corresponds to a modern civil or political right (Coulson 1957). Islamic legal culture was traditionally more geared toward defining the believer's duties to God than toward setting forth the rights of the individual vis-à-vis the government. According to the traditional perspective, rulers had obligations to rule according to Shari'a law and to treat their subjects justly; their subjects were to obey them unless ordered to do something sinful. Legal and political institutions that could place effective curbs on rulers' despotism and injustice were not adopted till the nineteenth century, when constitutionalist movements spread. Before then, the only way that jurists envisaged of combating tyranny and oppression was through rebellion. In contrast, human rights theory presumes that governments will be bound by modern norms of constitutionalism that restrain governments and enable those whom they rule to hold them accountable.

Contentious issues in Islamic thought since the nineteenth century have been the degree to which Western-style constitutionalism and democratic freedoms are compatible with adherence to Islamic law. By the end of the twentieth century, as part of this debate, questions about whether international human rights could be accommodated in an Islamic system came to the fore. The Islamic tradition, being rich and multifaceted, contained many ideas that anticipated modern rights, as well as others that were hard to reconcile with, and contemporary Muslims may focus on the former or the latter. Given the diversity in Muslims' views on human rights issues, there is no monolithic Islam bearing on human rights policy, only a series of "islams" that accord with Muslims' varying interests and philosophies as these bear on rights.

Theoretical problems

There are thorny theoretical problems facing Muslims who want to develop public policy on human rights using Islamic standards. Some of these relate to how to define Islamic positions on issues that are already covered by international law; others relate to finding methods for extending Islamic principles to cover domains that were not treated in Islamic jurisprudence in the past, like the relationship between the modern nation state and the individual. Still others relate to the role of the nation state.

As Muslims attempt to elaborate Islamic principles on human rights, they face international human rights law in the form of numerous conventions and declarations that have been produced under the auspices of the United Nations since the Second World War. All Muslim states are United Nations members, and they are also governed by the system of international law, including a human rights system that Muslims were instrumental in building (Waltz 2004). This is acknowledged in the Charter of the Organization of the Islamic Conference (OIC), the major international organization linking Muslim countries. OIC members reaffirm "their commitment to the UN Charter and fundamental Human Rights, the purposes and principles of which provide the basis for fruitful co-operation [*sic*] amongst all people" (Moinuddin 1987: 186). However, this did not stop a later OIC initiative to chart a separate "Islamic" position on human rights.

In August 1990, a meeting of OIC foreign ministers endorsed the OIC's newly minted Cairo Declaration on Human Rights in Islam, thereby putting forward a set of supposedly Islamic rights without having first dealt with the theoretical problems that this involved – among other things, on what basis a group of nation states could control Islamic doctrine on this subject. The rights protections in the Cairo Declaration were feebler than those afforded by their international counterparts (Mayer 1994: 327–50). Therefore, the OIC initiative suggested a weakening of Muslim countries' commitments to follow international law. Various Cairo Declaration rules were also impossible to reconcile with OIC members' conflicting obligations in terms of their ratifications of international human rights conventions (Mayer 1994: 348–50).

In a resolution on the declaration issued by the Twenty First Islamic Conference of Foreign Ministers in Karachi on April 25–29, 1993, the ministers reaffirmed the OIC commitment to "the principles contained in the Charter of the OIC as well as the 'Cairo Declaration on Human Rights in Islam' as general guidelines and the Charter of the United Nations."[1] By failing to stipulate that OIC members were bound by international human rights conventions, where modern human rights norms are comprehensively set forth, the ministers seemed to be backing away from their commitments to international human rights law. Also troubling was the fact that the OIC resolution casually acknowledged the existence of certain international and regional human rights instruments, without sorting out the relationship between these and the Cairo Declaration or explaining how the OIC could expect its members to adhere simultaneously to different sets of incompatible standards. One was left to wonder: was the Cairo Declaration meant to supersede existing obligations under international law? Of course, another possibility was that the whole OIC initiative on human rights was largely devoid of input from the many Muslims who actually understood international human rights law.

The Cairo Declaration was presented to the World Conference on Human Rights that was held in Vienna in 1993 as the OIC contribution to the conference – as if it represented the views of Muslim countries. The declaration thus presupposed a consensus on Islamic rights that was belied by political realities. Not only did the principles in the declaration conflict with Muslim nations' treaty commitments, they also clashed with many rights provisions in the constitutions and domestic laws of member countries, which in turn differed from each other. Moreover, they clashed sharply with progressive ideas about how Islam could be harmonized with international law.

The issuance of the Cairo Declaration also embroiled the OIC in difficult, contested issues of Islamic law. Islamic jurists had always envisaged Islamic law as the ultimate, definitive criterion of legality. They did not contemplate today's reality, where Muslims may be simultaneously subject to two or more different, competing systems of legality, such as Islamic law, national laws, and international principles grounded on the consensus of nation states. Similarly, they also did not envisage the possibility that individual Muslims might opt to be guided by secular norms on rights issues, so that the binding force of Islamic law could be challenged by Muslims appealing to international human rights law. In actuality, international human rights principles have won a considerable following among Muslims, many of whom see in them valuable correctives to the ills afflicting Muslim countries, where human rights are routinely and often egregiously violated by undemocratic regimes. As rights-consciousness has expanded in Muslim countries and important human rights NGOs have proliferated, Muslim supporters of human rights have tended to treat the international standards as normative, even when they conflict with traditional readings of Islamic requirements, like the discriminatory features of Islamic personal status law. That is, Islamic human rights principles were being put forward by the OIC and other institutions at a time when, at the grass roots level, secular rights concepts were influencing Muslims' attitudes, prompting them to demand reforms.

Undemocratic governments perceived the growing influence of human rights ideas as a threat, which gave them an incentive to concoct new sets of Islamic rules on human rights, in which Islamic criteria could be deployed to override and circumscribe human rights and to maintain old hierarchies and forestall an expansion of freedoms. Being reactive in nature, Islamic alternatives to international human rights like the Cairo Declaration were ultimately more intelligible in terms of the politics of human rights than in terms of Islamic theology and law. That they are fraught with theoretical deficiencies should therefore come as no surprise.

What would be the basis for the authority of a document like the Cairo Declaration? It was produced via a process like the one nations use to formulate regional agreements but unlike the processes via which Islamic rules have been traditionally derived from the sources. Instead, the process mimicked the way that public international law is made, in that representatives of nation-states acted as the decision makers. That is, provisions were adopted in the Cairo Declaration simply because they had won the assent of OIC member states. The fact that governments of Muslim states endorse principles may give these principles some legal cachet among like-minded regimes, but such endorsements signify nothing in terms of the Islamic theory of sources (Mayer 1990). The OIC did not even attempt to explain how a governmental "declaration" could fit in the scheme of Islamic jurisprudence, where such state-sponsored "declarations" were unknown.

The problem of the dubious Islamic authority of the Cairo Declaration was aggravated because of the nature of the regimes involved. The states in the OIC system had, for the most part, no claim to have any Islamic character, and the pretensions of certain states like Saudi Arabia and Iran to have Islamic governments were contested by many of their own citizens as well as by other supposedly Islamic states. One would be hard-pressed to offer persuasive Islamic rationales explaining why Muslims should consider themselves religiously bound by principles agreed to by regimes as disparate as Qadhdhafi's eccentric, vaguely Maoist military dictatorship; Iran's Shi'i theocracy; Saudi Arabia's absolute monarchy with its Wahhabi orientation; Syria's rule by a clan of Alavi leaders who promote Baathist ideology; the elected government of secular Turkey; or Sudan's coalition of Sunni Islamists and the military.

Another theoretical problem afflicting the credibility of the Cairo Declaration was that the Muslim states directly involved in creating the Cairo Declaration had for the most part strikingly poor human rights records, and countries like Iran, Iraq, Libya, Saudi Arabia, Sudan, and Syria counted among the most flagrant rights violators in the world. When countries especially notorious for disregarding human rights exerted themselves on behalf of winning acceptance for the Cairo Declaration in lieu of international law, it did nothing to promote the credibility of that document. Indeed, with such regimes backing it, it was natural to assume that the declaration would strengthen the hand of governments at the expense of the rights and freedoms of their oppressed and restive citizens. In these circumstances it was no surprise to see that supposedly Islamic criteria were employed in the Cairo Declaration exclusively as a mechanism for curtailing the rights and freedoms afforded to Muslims under international law.

A list of representative provisions can illustrate the character of the declaration, which has more problematic provisions than valuable ones. Critical is the provision in Article 24 providing that all the rights and freedoms stipulated in the declaration are subject to the Shari'a, subordinating all rights and freedoms to vague Islamic derogations. In lieu of provision for equal rights for all persons regardless of sex or religion, Article 1 states that "all men are equal in terms of basic human dignity and basic obligations and responsibilities [not rights], without any discrimination on the grounds of race, colour, language, sex, religious belief, political affiliation, social status or other considerations." Article 6 provides that "woman is equal to man in human dignity," omitting to provide for equality in rights and imposing on the husband the responsibility for the support and welfare of the family, thereby accommodating discriminatory laws in the area of personal status. In contrast, in a constructive step, Article 13 provides that men and women were entitled to fair wages "without discrimination."

Article 5 provides that on the right to marry there should be "no restrictions stemming from race, color or nationality," not prohibiting restrictions based on religion, and thereby accommodating the bans on Muslim women marrying outside the faith and on Muslim men marrying others than Muslims, Christians, or Jews. International human rights are religiously neutral, but Article 10 reveals the strong Islamic bias of the OIC scheme, stating that Islam is the religion of unspoiled nature and prohibits "any form of compulsion on man or to exploit his poverty or ignorance in order to convert him to another religion or to atheism." Article 9 calls for the state to ensure the means to acquire education "so as to enable man to be acquainted with the religion of Islam," which could support mandatory instruction in Islam, even for non-Muslims. Article 2 prohibits taking away life except for a Shari'a-prescribed reason, and Article 19 states that there should be no crime or punishment except as provided for in the Shari'a.

These articles permit the death penalty to be imposed for crimes such as adultery or apostasy from Islam and would accommodate punishments like crucifixion, stoning to death, amputation, and floggings, which conflict with international law prohibiting cruel, degrading, and inhuman punishments. Obviously, these articles are meant to allow countries like Iran and Saudi Arabia to continue to apply penalties taken from the Shari'a that are banned by modern standards of humane criminal justice. Given the serious deficiencies of criminal procedural rules in the Islamic tradition, the provision in Article 19 assuring a defendant "a fair trial in which he shall be given all the guarantees of defence" combined with the assurance in Article 25 that the Shari'a "is the only source of reference or the explanation or clarification of any of the article of this Declaration," leaves open the possibility that few, if any, of the safeguards of modern criminal procedure are included. Article 20 prohibits torture without indicating how this would affect the application of Islamic criminal sanctions like amputations.

Article 18 stipulates a right to privacy in the conduct of private affairs, in the home, in the family, and regarding property and relationships, which could be used constructively to ensure a zone of privacy. Article 15 sets forth "rights of ownership" to "property acquired in a legitimate way," which is guaranteed against confiscation "except for a necessity dictated by law." Article 22 provides that freedom to express opinions is allowed in such a manner as would not be contrary to the principles of the Shari'a, thereby significantly qualifying this freedom, since how Shari'a qualifications would affect this freedom is left open to speculation. Article 14 prohibits riba, which could mean a ban on usury or on all interest charges, a precept that seems incongruous in a scheme of human rights.

Reflecting the Third World setting in which Muslim nations elaborate their positions on rights, Article 11 prohibits colonialism and states that "peoples suffering from colonialism have the full right to freedom and self-determination." Notable by their absence are provisions that would address major human rights deficits by calling for the observance of democratic principles in political systems, protecting freedom of religion, freedom of association, and freedom of the press, and guarantees of equality in rights for women and minorities.

The Cairo Declaration and other Islamic versions of human rights recognize only a small range of rights compared with the vast number established in international conventions, but the rights that they do provide are not original but are borrowed from international law and then qualified or distorted. These appropriations of ideas taken from non-Islamic sources are not acknowledged or explained, but the language used is sufficient to betray their secular origins. After selectively appropriating certain substantive rights from the international models, the authors of Islamic human rights schemes then impose on the borrowed rights vague Islamic qualifications or derogation clauses that subordinate the rights or freedoms involved to Islamic law or values. There is no established theoretical basis for saying that foreign rights concepts can be Islamized by virtue of superimposing Islamic conditions on them. International law allows certain specified curbs to be placed on rights and freedoms but does not allow any religious law to override them. This is another area where clashes with international law have been created but not acknowledged. When Article 24 of the Cairo Declaration says "All the rights and freedoms stipulated in this Declaration are subject to the Islamic *shari'a*," it leaves the governments involved free to interpret the limits that Islamic law imposes as broadly as they please, because, as is typical of Islamic versions of human rights, no attempt is made to define the scope of the Islamic limitations. Since modern civil and political rights are designed to protect the rights of the individual against infringement by the state, allowing the state complete discretion to qualify rights renders rights protections illusory.

With Islam being conceived of as a limitation on rights, the result of using Islamic human rights schemes to supplant international law is naturally that Muslims (and potentially also non-Muslims subject to the jurisdiction of Muslim states) wind up with inferior rights. No theoretical basis for assigning Muslims to an inferior standard of human rights has been offered, and candid discussion of the negative consequences for Muslims that these Islamic rights entail has been avoided by the government and institutions that promulgated them. Instead, Muslim countries like Saudi Arabia, which sponsored the OIC declaration, have claimed that Islamic human rights, because of their divine character, offer more efficacious protections for rights than does international law (Mayer 1994: 375).

One also finds academics in the West who promote the idea that better results will come from applying Islamic versions of rights than their international counterparts, seeking to refute charges that superimposing Islamic criteria on rights as the authors of the Cairo Declaration did, means degrading them (Baderin 2003).

Recognizing that they have been inspired by policies of trying to supplant international human rights and strengthening the hands of governments at the expense of rights and freedoms, persons and organizations with competence and credibility in the area of human rights have criticized the deficiencies of recent Islamic human rights schemes. For example, the retrograde character of the Cairo Declaration was roundly denounced by the International Commission of Jurists (ICJ) when it was submitted in 1992 to the UN Human Rights Commission, on which occasion Iran and Iraq both pressed for its acceptance (Vichniac 1992). Adama Dieng, the Senegalese Secretary General of the ICJ, condemned the Declaration for challenging the intercultural consensus on the international human rights standards, introducing discrimination against non-Muslims and women, deliberately restricting certain fundamental rights and liberties, and ratifying under the cover of Shari'a, the legitimacy of practices like corporal punishment (Vichniac 1992).

Around the globe, the strongest advocates of international human rights have tended to operate outside governments, and Muslim societies are no exception. Independent Muslims and human rights NGOs in Muslim countries have not been persuaded to adopt the Islamic human rights principles being purveyed by countries like Saudi Arabia and Iran. Instead, they have continued to work courageously under highly adverse conditions for the advancement of human rights according to international standards. Feminists such as the eminent Iranian human rights lawyers Shirin Ebadi and Mehrangiz Kar have stood out as particularly vigorous advocates of international norms, which guarantee women full equality. In other words, the "Islamic" rubric pasted on the human rights afforded in schemes like the Cairo Declaration has not made the emasculated rights principles that they contain more palatable to Muslims who are supportive of human rights.

All this is not to say that clashes between Islam and human rights are necessarily inevitable. Islam can be developed in an altogether more constructive way that would enhance human rights, as the work of Abdullahi An-Na'im demonstrates (An-Na'im 1990). There is ample material in the legacy of Islamic civilization for building a satisfactory system of protecting rights, but building this system is impeded by entrenched forces of reaction and a hostile climate for intellectual inquiry, factors that threaten innovative and creative thinkers in Muslim societies. Reactionary forces exploit appeals to Islamic authority to anathematize Muslims who want to experiment with new ideas that might transform Islam into an instrument of liberation. Influential clerics and Islamist leaders have attacked Muslims who dare to call for human rights and tolerance or who propose reforming Islamic thought to accommodate rights and freedoms, denouncing would-be reformers and modernizers as apostates. In the process, defending Islam has become associated with condemnations of the ideas of

Muslims like Khaled Abou El Fadl, Mohammed Arkoun, Sadiq al-'Azm, Shirin Ebadi, Fatima Mernissi, Abdullahi An-Na'im, Abdollah Nuri, Muhammad Shahrour, Abdolkarim Sorush, Said al-Ashmawi, Nasr Hamid Abu Zayd, and many others. Mahmud Muhammad Taha, a daring Sudanese reformist thinker who was supportive of human rights, was excoriated by Sudanese Islamists and was executed as an apostate in 1985 by Sudan's ruling dictatorship, which was then pursuing a reactionary version of Islamization (An-Na'im 1986). This record means that Islam has become associated with rights violations when it is actually the political systems and reactionary mentalities involved that are really to blame for Islam being used in this manner.

Not surprisingly, in a climate of fear and repression, Islamic thought has tended to be elaborated in ways that ratify existing hierarchies and legitimize repression, avoiding dealing with the actual rights problems facing Muslim societies. That is, the weakness of the theoretical literature in this area ties in with the political circumstances in which it is elaborated. Like the Muslims who live in the repressive environments of today's Muslim countries, Islam itself is a prisoner of politics.

Muslim intellectuals who want to challenge old ways of thinking about Islamic requirements are generally compelled to speak only obliquely or to go abroad to carry out their work. However, their working in exile means that they are cut off from their natural constituencies and this also attenuates the impact of their ideas in their own societies. Important figures are often obliged to seek sanctuary in the West and to write in Western languages about issues that are vital for the regeneration of Islam and for the modernization of Islamic thought, leaving young and inquiring Muslims to learn from teachers who will inculcate in them the false notions that Islam demands acquiescence in policies antithetical to human rights.

At the theoretical level, some of the most vigorous critiques of the inherited corpus of Islamic thought as it pertains to human rights issues have come from feminists, who have spoken out despite the grave risks that calling for the equality of women presents. One of the most salient features of Islamic human rights schemes is that they deny women the right to equality and nondiscriminatory treatment that is guaranteed to them under international law, and that they provide Islamic rationalizations for the legal discrimination facing Muslim women under customary and traditional mores. Islamic feminists have challenged the view that Islam mandates an inferior status for women, arguing that discriminatory elements of Islamic law are not set forth in the text of the Quran or supported by the example of the Prophet but were invented by male interpreters. Their view is that the Islamic sources, when properly understood, support the equality of the sexes.[2] Proponents of Islamic schemes of human rights that deny equality to women have to struggle to sustain retrograde interpretations of Islamic requirements in the face of feminist critiques. Islamic feminism is turning out to be a potent force for Islamic renewal and one of the most important factors contributing to the integration of human rights within a reformed Islam.

The reactions to contemporary Islamic feminism have varied. Depending on their outlook, Muslims may welcome proof that Islam can be reconceived as a progressive force that supports women's advancement and participation in society. Other Muslims may denounce Muslim women who question what Islamic jurists and clerics or fundamentalist leaders have decreed. Impeding the ability of women to carry out the mission of Islamic reform is the fact that they have long been excluded from Islamic institutions and are not recognized as members of the *ulama* (the clergy) or *fuqaha* (jurists). There is no woman Sheikh of al-Azhar, no woman mufti, no woman ayatollah. Thus, women lack some of the institutional credentials and prestigious titles that men wield when speaking on behalf of Islam and that lend authority to the positions that men articulate. The rise of militant Islamism, which has called for women to remain subordinated to male authority, menaces Islamic feminism. The results of the Islamist triumph in Afghanistan, where under the Taliban women were reduced to the status of prisoners and chattel, showed how Islamization could cancel out all the gains previously achieved by women in expanding opportunities and freedoms.

Islam and rights policies in application

Human rights policy in the Islamic Republic of Iran

Iran's policies on religion and human rights have been convoluted (Mayer 2004). In the 1960s and 1970s under the rule of the Shah, Iranians took a leadership role in the United Nations in promoting the development of international human rights law, and Iran ratified the International Covenant on Civil and Political Rights (ICCPR). However, human rights were not respected in practice under the Shah, and public anger over rights abuses was a factor leading to the 1979 Islamic Revolution. Unfortunately, human rights policy under the Islamic Republic offered changes in style and rhetoric without improving the human rights situation. Indeed, a recent study has argued that in many respects, human rights violations became worse as Islamic ideology was imposed by Iran's theocratic rulers. (Afshari 2001). Persecutions and executions of political opponents, routine recourse to cruel treatment and brutal torture of prisoners, censorship, unfair trials, and other abuses continued, to which were added aggravated forms of discrimination affecting women and religious minorities.

Since the revolution, Iran has manifested ambivalence about whether it is bound by international human rights, and it has struggled to define a tenable "Islamic" position vis-à-vis human rights. As an example of Iran's ambivalence, one could cite the fact that the Islamic Republic did not choose to terminate its status as party to the ICCPR, even though it regularly violated ICCPR principles and often issued statements at odds with those principles.

Sometimes official statements revealed hostility to human rights. In imprudent remarks that have been cited by critics of Iran's human rights policy, Iran's UN Ambassador, Sa'id Raja'i Khorasani, proclaimed that because of its Islamic values, the Islamic Republic would have no qualms about violating human rights.

According to the paraphrased record of his speech, he announced that

> conventions, declaration and resolutions or decisions of international
> organizations, which were contrary to Islam, had no validity in the Islamic
> Republic of Iran...The Universal Declaration of Human Rights, which
> represented secular understanding of the Judaeo-Christian tradition, could
> not be implemented by Muslims and did not accord with the system of values
> recognized by the Islamic Republic of Iran; his country would therefore not
> hesitate to violate its provisions, since it had to choose between violating the
> divine law of the country and violating secular conventions.[3]

Thus, Raja'i Khorasani effectively asserted that, being guided by Islamic
precepts, Iran was no longer bound by international human rights standards. The
values of the latter system derived, according to him, from an alien, Judeo-Christian
tradition, as distinguished from the Islamic tradition. He thereby implied that
Muslims, because of their religion, could only claim a standard of rights set by
Islamic law, which required violating international standards. This was tantamount
to stipulating that Muslims could only claim rights inferior to those enjoyed in the
West. However, along with his repudiation of human rights, Raja'i Khorasani
offered the inconsistent assertion that secular and non-Muslim states who could not
live up to the divine standards of Islam should at least meet the minimum requirements established by international organizations. By this he apparently meant to
convey that international rights protections, being based on secular law, should
somehow rank below the standards afforded by Islamic law. Iran's Islam, he seemed
to want to say, did protect human rights, but according to values that, due to their
divine origin, were superior to those based on mere secular authority.

Obviously, Raja'i Khorasani's alternating presentations of "Islam" as the reason
for the regime's denials of human rights and "Islam" as the guarantor of a higher
standard of rights than what was afforded by international law were contradictory.
One assumes that the contradictions came about because the regime relied on Islam
as a legitimating device in two different ways. On the one hand, Iran needed a rubric
like "Islam" to justify its rights violations. On the other hand, the regime's sole base
of legitimacy was Islam, and the more this "Islam" became associated in people's
minds with human rights violations, the more unpopular and less credible this official "Islam" became, making it less effective as a means of enhancing legitimacy. (A
similar predicament has led to similar confusion in the remarks of official Saudi
spokesmen, who have alternately appealed to Islam to justify their government's
resistance to calls for democratization and rights and extolled Islamic rights principles as affording perfect protection for rights.) Although any critical review of Iran's
human rights practice would reveal that Iran has repeatedly used "Islam" as the reason for deviating from international standards, spokespersons for the Islamic
Republic have for the most part preferred to take the route of hypocrisy, seeking to
obscure as far as possible the degree to which Iran's Islamic rights entailed deviations
from internationally protected human rights. In so doing, they have revealed that they

actually believe that international human rights are the binding standards and that Islamic rationalizations do not suffice to justify violating these in Iranians' minds.

There are reasons for saying that Iran's post-revolutionary human rights record should be seen as a reflection of political choices, not a reflection of Islamic requirements. Many of Iran's most egregious rights violations – like gross abuse of prisoners, regular recourse to severe torture, and the brutal suppression of political dissent – have had nothing to do with Islamic law. Actions by the regime had already revealed the politically contingent nature of Iran's official "Islam" well before January 1988, when Ayatollah Khomeini made his famous pronouncement that the Islamic state was entrusted with absolute power that freed it to do as it chose – even if this meant violating fundamental pillars of the Islamic religion like the pilgrimage (Mayer 1993: 193). His pronouncement meant that the government was not beholden to Islamic strictures and that Islam could be ignored whenever this was needed to serve the political interests of the regime.

The provisions of the 1979 Iranian Constitution deserve to be examined in any discussion of Islam and human rights policy. They consist of Western principles of constitutionalism upon which "Islamic" ideas have been grafted. Far from offering rights principles conceptualized *de novo* on an Islamic basis, Iran borrowed its human rights concepts from Western constitutions and from modern international law. Iran's theory that these can be somehow indigenized by imposing "Islamic" limits replicates an element commonly found in other Islamic human rights schemes.

Although the constitution is replete with Western ideas and principles, Article 4 pretends that this is not the case, providing that all laws, including the constitution itself, must be based on Islamic criteria. Moreover in the Preamble, it is stated that the constitution is based on Islamic principles. This should mean that the rights principles, being part of a constitution based on Islamic criteria, should be Islamic. However, Article 20 stipulates that human rights are to be subordinated to Islamic criteria, which seems to indicate that the rights principles are *not* deemed to be Islamic – whereas the criteria that override rights are deemed to be Islamic. That same article expressly provides that all citizens enjoy human rights (*hoquq-e ensani*) according to Islamic standards (*mavazin-e eslam*). Article 21 provides that women's rights are guaranteed in accordance with Islamic criteria (*mavazin-e eslami*). Muslims are enjoined to honor the human rights of religious minorities and to treat them according to the dictates of virtue and Islamic justice in Article 14.

It is significant that separate Islamic qualifications are specifically imposed on the rights of women and non-Muslims, without specific Islamic qualifications being imposed on the rights of male Muslims. This is tantamount to signaling that a hierarchy is being established in which Islamic criteria are being employed to ensure that male Muslims rank at the top and will be used as the pretexts for depriving women and non-Muslims of human rights. Here one sees a direct correlation between Islamic restrictions on human rights and the regime's policies, which discriminate on the basis of sex and religion in ways that violate principles of international law.

The intention to resort to Islamic law at the expense of rights can be detected in some provisions that do not specifically invoke Islamic law. Article 19 of the

Iranian Constitution provides that "[t]he people of Iran, regardless of their ethnic, family and tribal origins shall enjoy equal rights. Color, race, language and the like shall not be a cause for privilege." This formulation avoids altogether the question of whether equality can be denied on the basis of sex or religion, even though in any system based on Islamic law one would expect that the issues of equality of women and non-Muslims would be among the most sensitive. The discrimination against both women and religious minorities in the wake of the revolution indicates that the omission of protections for two categories was not accidental. One contrasts the equivocation in Iran's equality provisions with the clear statement in the UDHR, which in Article 1 provides that "all humans are born free and equal in dignity and rights," and in Article 2 provides that

> Everyone is entitled to all the rights and freedoms set forth in this Declaration, without distinction of any kind, such as race, colour, sex, language, religion, political or other opinion, national or social origin, property, birth or other status.

Paradoxically, Iran's constitution, in which Islamic criteria are used to subordinate women, includes in Article 20 an unqualified guarantee of equal protection of the law (*qanun*), the secular law, for all citizens, both men and women – without mention of any Islamic qualifications. The inclusion of a secular equal protection clause in the Iranian Constitution is perfectly emblematic of its awkward blend of Islamic rules and incongruous ideas taken from Western constitutions and international human rights law. Furthermore, the Iranian Constitution also guarantees the equality of men and women in Article 3.14 before the secular law (qanun), without imposing any express Islamic qualifications. However, referring back to other provisions like Articles 4 and 20, one is reminded that "Islamic criteria" ultimately override all other provisions in the constitution, making the guarantees of equality under the secular law nugatory. Still, their secular character is anomalous.

Article 10 does not mention women, but it calls for the family to be safeguarded according to Islamic rights and morality (*hoquq va akhlaq-e eslami*). What "Islamic rights and morality" entailed was revealed immediately after the revolution when the regime moved to abrogate the important reforms advancing women's status that had been made in the Iranian Family Protection Act of 1967, as amended in 1975, and pressured women to abandon their jobs and to return to the home, where they were expected to devote themselves to maternal and housewifely duties. Many women were removed from desirable professional and governmental positions, and their educational opportunities were sharply curtailed. (By dint of vigorous efforts they have been able to roll back some discriminatory measures and make certain improvements in their educational and professional opportunities.) Furthermore, the minimum age of marriage was lowered from eighteen to nine years for girls, and temporary marriage, an institution condemned by Iranian feminists, was promoted. Thus, after the Islamic revolution, in the guise of following Islamic requirements there were many setbacks for the progress toward equality that Iranian women had made in the 1960s and 1970s.

The Iranian Constitution in Article 13 recognizes only three religious minorities – Zoroastrians, Jews, and Christians. These three are given the right within the limits of the secular law (qanun) to perform their own religious rites and to follow their religious law in personal matters. That is, the constitution does not expressly cite the Islamic rules on *dhimmi* status to assign these minorities to the inferior position that they traditionally occupied in Iran even though these Islamic rules are behind the singling out of minorities for special treatment. Similarly, Article 144 provides that the army is to be for people who adhere to Islamic ideology and who are faithful to the goals of the Islamic Revolution, thereby revealing that non-Muslims will be excluded from the military, just as dhimmis traditionally were. Again, Islamic rules on dhimmi status that underlie this discriminatory treatment are not specifically adverted to, apparently because the regime is uncomfortable admitting that it upholds what amounts to a caste system.

Article 14, after guaranteeing the rights of non-Muslims, proceeds to warn that this guarantee protects only "those who do not become involved in conspiracies and activities which are anti-Islamic or are against the Islamic Republic of Iran." Since what activities might qualify as "anti-Islamic" is left open, this provision provides sweeping grounds for curbing the associational freedoms of members of religious minorities. This is in addition to a general provision in Article 26 that enables the government to curb the activities of groups, including "minority religious associations," if they are contrary to the principles of Islam or the Islamic Republic. Taken together, Articles 14 and 26 suggest that non-Muslims are presumed to be subversive and that their associational activities are presumed to have anti-Islamic tendencies. Of course, since Iran's official Islamic ideology legitimizes discrimination against non-Muslims, opposition on the part of non-Muslims would be natural.

The Islamic Republic has accumulated a record of exceptional religious intolerance. Iran persecutes persons who are deemed to have abandoned Islam or, in the case of Baha'is, persons who are deemed to be descended from persons who converted from Islam, who may be compelled to choose between death and returning to Islam. The historically intense antagonism toward Baha'ism in Iran accounts for why Article 13 does not recognize Baha'ism as a religion and correlates with the harsh persecution inflicted on the Baha'i minority, which has earned the Islamic Republic repeated condemnations by the international community and by independent human rights organizations.[4] Attacks on Iranians for their religious beliefs have been accompanied by official attempts to hide the religious motives behind them, which reveals Iran's lack of confidence about whether a policy of criminalizing religious belief can be justified in today's world. Iran's mistreatment of non-Muslims directly clashes with the principle of freedom of religion, an unqualified freedom in international law, which comprises the freedom to change religion.[5] With the exception of Ayatollah Khomeini's notorious death edict calling for the assassination of Salman Rushdie, the Iranian regime has sought to hide its denials of religious freedom and to disguise its policies of prosecuting converts from Islam, non-Muslims, and Muslim religious dissidents as prosecutions for other capital offenses, such as spying or treason (Mayer 1995: 178–80).

Post-revolutionary Iran has also shown considerable ambivalence about whether Islam suffices to justify treating women in ways that violate international norms. Iran wants to be perceived as a revolutionary Islamic society, and in this regard its retrograde policies affecting women alienate many observers and detract from the positive impression it wants to make. Its veiling rules have prompted international rebukes. However, since its supposedly "Islamic" standards for women's dress have become symbols of the regime's policy of reinstating authentic Islamic values, the regime cannot back away from these, no matter how reactionary they may appear. The ruling clerics have resorted to stern sermons on Islamic morality, stringent criminal laws that include flogging penalties for noncompliance with Islamic dress rules, and aggressive policing to try to cow women into submission. Despite years of vigorous propaganda and harsh repression, nonconformity with the much-resented requirements that women should wear either the *chador* or other approved versions of Islamic dress has continued to manifest itself.

Iran has been placed on the defensive when forced to explain to the international community why it needs to resort to force to compel conformity with what are supposed to be indigenous cultural norms. Women's resistance to official dress requirements has been acutely embarrassing. The more obvious the need becomes to rely on police measures to ensure compliance with what are officially described as "cultural" norms, the more Iran's pattern of repression of women begins to resemble a regime of apartheid, in which the state establishes and maintains the domination of one group and the systematic oppression of another. This suggests parallels with Saudi Arabia and its reactionary policies affecting women, which can only further damage Iran's image.

In attempts to discredit manifestations of women's dissent from the regime's policies, Iran, like Saudi Arabia, has tried to disassociate nonconforming women from the local culture, charging that their protests are products of Western conspiracies or that the women involved are "Westernized." The Islamic Republic has felt compelled to lie, denying that its Islamic dress requirements were being forcibly imposed on resisting Iranian women. In responding in February 1993 to a critical UN report on Iran's human rights record, which included negative evaluations of its discrimination against women, Iran in its defense asserted that its dress requirements and personal status laws affecting women were part of religion and, as such, were willingly accepted by Iranians. Of course, the aim was to convince the United Nations that there was no state policy of discriminating against women. The Islamic Republic's response posited the existence of uniform Islamic cultural values that were shared by all Iranians and voluntarily adhered to:

> Considering the fact that the majority of the Iranian people are Muslim, the holy Islamic codes form the basic guidelines for the laws ... [Women] freely accept regulations regarding marriage and the limitation of the rights and duties of both men and women, based on such Islamic criteria ... The legal philosophy of the observation [*sic*] of "Hijab" for women and men in an

Islamic society is fully credible and within the context of conventional international laws. Therefore, since more than 95 per cent of people in Iran are Muslim and thereby follow the laws prevailing upon [*sic*] an Islamic society, all follow and support the appropriate laws and regulations on the rights of society... Although some political groups believe that women should observe "Hijab" entirely and have criticized the Government for not responding to this matter, until now there have been no confrontations with females who do not observe the "Hijab" properly.[6]

Faced with charges that punishing women for noncompliance with Islamic dress requirements violated international rights norms, the regime felt obliged to deny its actual domestic policy of aggressive policing of women's dress. Instead of asserting that its "Islamic values" justified punishing women for not veiling, the regime argued that its Islamic dress rules applied to men, as well as women, even though the record demonstrates that the regime's preoccupation has been with forcing women, not men, to comply with Islamic dress rules. Furthermore, despite the fact that it claimed that its dress rules were based on Islamic law, by the year 1993 the regime feared that the argument that Iran's distinctive "Islamic" policies on rights justified breaching international law would not hold water. The regime's public relations strategy dictated presenting Islamic dress rules as congruent with international norms.

In the same period, the Islamic Republic decided to pose as the defender of human rights, going on the offensive to charge that it was another country, France, whose dress requirements were violating women's rights. In November 1994 Ayatollah Yazdi, the head of Iran's judiciary and human rights commission, denounced France for expelling Muslim girls from public schools if they insisted on wearing the veil. As an ayatollah, he might have been expected to attack France for cultural insensitivity or lack of respect for Islamic values. Instead, Yazdi invoked international human rights law, charging that France was violating human rights principles in the UN Charter, which, he said, emphasized the right to religious freedom.[7] This raised awkward questions. If Muslim women in France had the right to dress in accordance with their consciences and their personal religious convictions, regardless of whether this violated the long-established French policy of *laicite*, then why should not Muslim women in Iran likewise enjoy the same right? Why did Muslim women lose their freedom to dress in accordance with their own religious beliefs once they were on the territory of the Islamic Republic?

This could not be an issue according to Ayatollah Khamene'i, who supported the new line that Islamic dress was a cultural tradition: "But our women want to protect their hijab. They love chador. Chador is our national costume. Chador is an Iranian tradition before being an Islamic tradition. It belongs to our people. It is our national dress."[8] Thus, to avoid being charged with violating human rights and discriminating against women, the *faqih*, the linchpin of the Islamicity of the regime, chose to present the government-imposed uniform as a popular choice mandated by Iranian tradition, not one dictated by the commands of Islamic law – a remarkable change. In inconsistently appealing to the supremacy of Islamic criteria on rights and trying to reconcile official policies with international law, the regime was entangling itself in a web of contradictions that precluded developing a coherent policy line on human rights.

The clerical regime did not succeed in convincing the Iranian people to defer to its policies of denying freedoms. Rushdie's death edict looked different when people who had once been backers of the Islamic Revolution like the philosophy professor Abdolkarim Sorush became targeted for imprisonment or assassination after publicly criticizing governmental repression or questioning the value of clerical rule. In 1995 Foreign Minister Ali Akbar Velayati encouraged the assassination of Sorush by claiming that his expressions of opinion were harming the people's national and ideological foundations and were antagonistic to the nation and by comparing him to Ahmad Kasravi, the secular intellectual who was assassinated on March 11, 1946 by Navvab Safavi's Devotees of Islam (*Fadalian Eslam*).[9] Exposed since the 1990s to constant assaults and threats to his life, Sorush, who has become one of the most important advocates of an enlightened Islam that embraces human rights, has had to spend much of his time in havens outside Iran. In a similar vein, Ayatollah Khamene'i attacked the people in the universities who were criticizing the theocratic system, *nezam-e ruhaniyat*, condemning this as sedition. He warned those who were undermining the clergy in Iran that if "ulterior motives" or "ill-intent" were involved, the Islamic system would slap them hard in the face.[10] As the 1990s progressed, the antagonism between the ruling hardliners and university students intensified, reaching explosive dimensions that eventually culminated in violent clashes.

Meanwhile, indulging in such repression, the regime has flailed about in attempting to respond to UN and foreign criticisms, attacking the motives of its accusers and insisting that the charges that it violates human rights are lies, slanders, politically motivated, and based on misinformation and misunderstandings. Iran was obviously disturbed by the March 1995 UN Human Rights Commission condemnation of its performance. Many of the assertions of rights violations related to Iran's policy of following retrograde clerical interpretations of Islam, such as the discrimination against non-Muslim minorities, the Rushdie death sentence, the forcible imposition of Islamic dress and the sexual segregation of women, and the amputations of the fingers of thieves. Yazdi tried to make out that report was an attack on Islam. He stated that the new issue was this:

> Who says that human rights devised by the West should be applied to the whole world? Who has said such a thing? Some nations have their own cultures, some nations have their own religions, you cannot describe as human rights violations the issues which concern their religion and culture. You cannot impose the human rights as you have translated and defined them... Islamic human rights differ from the Declaration of Human Rights. Islam has its own rules and regulations.... The punishment ordained by God's law and mentioned in the Koran cannot be ignored. Human Rights must be Islamic human rights.[11]

Faced with the predicament of how to respond to UN critics of Iran's human rights record, Yazdi had felt compelled to resuscitate the idea that Islam required these human rights violations. Here, however, the defense was offered for internal consumption in an effort to discredit external critics of Iran's rights record by portraying Iran's critics as being insensitive to Iran's Islamic obligations.

The very different perspectives of the populace were expressed in the broad mandates given to Muhammad Khatami when he challenged clerical despotism and was twice elected president in 1997 and 2001 after promising to advance the causes of human rights and democracy. However, entrenched hardliners anxious to maintain their stranglehold on power were able to thwart his reform efforts and augment their repression. In 2003, clerical hardliners in the Guardian Council blocked a move by Iran's parliament to ratify the Women's Convention on the grounds that the convention contradicted Islam and the constitution.

Meanwhile, the 2003 Nobel Peace Prize was awarded to the Iranian human rights lawyer Shirin Ebadi who had insisted that support for international human rights law was compatible with Islamic beliefs, and who had fought determinedly to protect rights in a hostile environment. When she accepted her award in Oslo bare-headed, she outraged Iranian conservatives, who were at the same time protesting that the French ban on Muslim school girls wearing Islamic headscarves violated the girls' freedom of religion – paradoxically speaking as if protecting women's human rights were a concern of the Iranian regime. When in June 2005 Tehran mayor Mahmoud Ahmadinejad, an ally of the most conservative forces in the ruling establishment, won the presidency after the Guardian Council had winnowed the candidate list to preclude the election of another liberal like Khatami, it seemed to presage a clampdown on human rights in the name of respecting Islamic values. Iranian debates regarding Islam and human rights are obviously far from over.

Human rights policy in Saudi Arabia

Saudi Arabia's policy on rights has been to deny human rights in practice while giving rhetorical support to human rights – of course, only in the form of what it claims are Islamic human rights. Even this deeply reactionary regime felt compelled to respond to the mounting popular disaffection of the 1990s, when anger at the Saudi monarchy was aggravated by factors like the mismanaged and faltering economy, mounting exasperation over the corruption and arrogance of the royal family, the regime's stifling of dissent, and its arbitrary administration of justice. The Saudi alliance with the United States against Iraq in the first Gulf War intensified the restiveness of many Saudis. A secular petition was submitted to King Fahd by liberal Saudis in 1990 and another submitted by conservative ulama in 1991, both demanding reforms, the adoption of principles of constitutionalism, and respect for certain rights (Middle East Watch 1992: 6–7, 59–62). In the early 1990s, disaffected Shi'is launched campaigns to embarrass the regime over its bad human rights record in general and its mistreatment of Shi'is in particular. The restlessness of Saudi women surfaced in 1990 when a group of professional women mounted an historic driving protest in Riyadh. The protestors were punished for daring to challenge Saudi custom, and that same custom was belatedly sacralized by a *fatwa* claiming that women driving violated Islamic precepts.

Confronted with such challenges, the regime made some cosmetic concessions to popular demands for constitutionalism and human rights, such as the issuance of the 1992 Basic Law, which was composed in secret by a committee led by Prince Nayif, the Minister of the Interior. Although meant to convey the impression that certain principles of constitutionalism had been adopted, the Basic Law confirmed the right of the Saudi ruler to do as he pleased with no constraints whatsoever.

Article 7 provides that the Quran and Sunna reign supreme over the Basic Law and all other laws of the state. That is, according to this article, the Basic Law is not the supreme law of the land, but is subordinated to the Islamic sources. However, in a noteworthy omission, how the sources are to be interpreted and by whom is never precisely defined in the Basic Law. In these circumstances, what Islamic law mandated would ultimately reflect the regime's preferences, so that Saudi policy and Islamic policy would be deemed identical.

The Basic Law allows for none of the civil and political rights associated with democratic governance. All power is firmly situated in the hands of the monarch. Article 5 states unequivocally that the system of government in the Kingdom of Saudi Arabia is monarchy – that is, monarchy pure and simple, as opposed to a constitutional monarchy. Although there is mention of a consultative assembly and a judicial branch, careful appraisal of the rest of the Basic Law reveals that the system contains no checks whatsoever on the King's power. The Saudi Basic Law has no function other than placing a constitutional facade before an absolute monarchy. Article 6 includes a provision that citizens (*al-muwatinun*) are to pay allegiance to the King in accordance with the Quran and Sunna, in submission and obedience. This is a call for the kind of obedience that was in the past exacted by traditional *amirs* and sultans from their subjects and rests on a philosophy fundamentally at odds with modern constitutionalism.

Article 26 provides that the state protects human rights in accordance with the Islamic Shari'a, thereby imposing vague Islamic limitations on rights that cancel out the rights involved. Only the rudiments of a few civil and political rights provided are set forth (Mayer 1994: 348–9, 363–4). One looks in vain for a guarantee of freedom of religion, one of the most basic principles of modern human rights. This gap correlates with the Saudi disregard for the principle of freedom of religion, and it has had particularly harsh consequences for the Shi'i minority (Amnesty International 1993a,b: 6).

Heedless of the inconsistency involved, after the promulgation of the Basic Law, Prince Saud al-Faisal presented the very different set of rights provisions in the Cairo Declaration at the 1993 World Human Rights Conference as if they were definitive. The Saudis' endorsement of two disparate and inconsistent sets of "Islamic" standards on rights provides some indication of the lack of intellectual rigor with which the Saudi regime approached human rights issues. Since the ruling house had no real commitment to abiding by human rights standards, the details of the rights provisions mattered less than the main objective, which was establishing "Islamic" bases for deviating from international law. One assumes that the Saudi rulers hoped that their campaigning for the Cairo Declaration would serve to associate the regime with the cause of human rights and improve its tarnished image, while not obligating it to reform. This was possible, because, although it contained more rights than the Saudi Basic Law, the wording of the Cairo Declaration was intentionally kept vague and evasive, as the foregoing discussion of its Islamic qualifications on rights has indicated.

The contradictions in Saudi positions on rights were manifold. Article 1 of the Cairo Declaration at least pays women the compliment of recognizing that their status needs to be addressed, even though it fails to guarantee them equality in rights. The Saudi Basic Law, in contrast, completely ignores the existence of women, as if their rights were unworthy of consideration. The Cairo Declaration in Article 20 prohibits torture, but the Basic Law, in contrast, offers no prohibition of torture. Since the prohibition of torture is of vital importance in the modern human rights system, the inconsistency between the two documents on this point is significant. Many other provisions in the Cairo Declaration have no counterparts in the Basic Law, like the Article 19 affirmation that all individuals are equal before the law without distinction between ruler and ruled, the Article 9 right to education for all, the Article 11 ban on slavery, the Article 13 right to work for fair wages that do not discriminate between men and women, and the Article 23 right to participate directly or indirectly in the administration of the country's affairs.

At the 1993 Vienna Conference, Prince Saud al-Faisal asserted that the Cairo Declaration was a document that embodied "an expression of the will of over one billion people," a highly dubious claim, since the OIC and its member nations had made no effort to ascertain the views of Muslims on rights questions before issuing the declaration. He spoke as if Islam had its own efficacious scheme of rights, asserting that Islamic law was "a comprehensive system for universal human rights," meant not as moral exhortations but as "legislative orders." However, although endorsing the Cairo Declaration, Prince Saud al-Faisal did not call for rejecting the idea of universality of rights, claiming that he accepted that the principles and objectives of human rights were universal but that in their application it was necessary to show consideration "for the diversity of societies, taking into account their various historical, cultural, and religious backgrounds and legal systems."[12] That is, he seemed eager to downplay the grave conflicts with international human rights in the Cairo Declaration and to try to persuade the international community that in supporting this OIC initiative Saudi Arabia was not breaking with the international consensus on rights. Despite their efforts, the Saudis were not successful in getting the Vienna conference to endorse the Cairo Declaration as a legitimate alternative to the rights set forth in international law.

As in the case of Iran, the official endorsement of Islamic versions of human rights by Saudi Arabia in no way mitigated the pervasive rights abuses occurring in the country. By its practice, Saudi Arabia showed that, like Iran, it was as indifferent to rights that were supposedly based on Islamic principles as it was to rights established in international law. The watered-down "Islamic" human rights promoted by the Saudi regime did not persuade the long-suffering Saudi populace that meaningful improvements in their rights protections had been made.

As economic conditions dramatically soured in the 1990s and 2000s and impatience with the despotism and corruption of Saudi rulers grew, the Saudi royal family was increasingly placed on the defensive. As domestic unrest mounted and when the crisis of international terrorism grew acute after 2001, the Saudi ruling house was divided regarding what course of action to take. In Saudi society many groups mobilized to pressure the government, demanding expanded freedoms and democratic reforms, while Islamists, whose grievances mounted after the US invasions of Afghanistan and Iraq, sought to punish the royal family for its pro-Western foreign policies and carried out terrorist assaults on Saudi territory.

Under siege, the ruling house deemed it essential to offer some concessions, such as allowing municipal elections in 2005 – without, however, allowing any women to vote. The ambivalence on international human rights law continued. For example, seeking to placate critics and to convey the impression that it was not against women's rights, in 2000 Saudi Arabia ratified the Convention on the Elimination of All Forms of Discrimination Against Women, also known as Women's Convention.[13] However, in its ratification it indicated that in case of contradiction between any term of the Convention and the norms of Islamic law, the kingdom would not consider itself obliged to adhere to the convention.[14] That is, it offered a superficial indication of a willingness to follow international law but at the same time upheld the notion that its domestic version of Islamic law trumped women's human rights.

Conclusions

Muslim states have great difficulty reconciling their generally poor records on human rights with the governing international human rights standards. Against this background, various officially sponsored "Islamic" versions of human rights have been promoted that actually borrow extensively from Western rights models while imposing Islamic qualifications and converting Islam into a rationale for curbing or denying human rights that are guaranteed under international law. These Islamic versions of human rights have been developed without dealing with the theoretical problems that are entailed when a group of nations, already bound by the modern system of international law, produces nonconforming schemes of rights reshaped by religious criteria. Despite promulgating Islamic rights, in various ways regimes have continued to pay tribute to the authority and popularity enjoyed by international human rights in Muslim milieus, including trying to disguise the degree to which their policies and practices actually deviate from international norms. Meanwhile, Muslims' appreciation of the value of human rights seems to be growing, and the impetus for fusing elements of the Islamic heritage with international human rights law is likewise spreading. Unless Muslim countries democratize, this important task is likely to be accomplished by Muslims who are working in opposition to state policies on human rights.

Notes

1 See the OIC Resolution No. 41/21-P. on Coordination Among Member States in the Field of Human Rights.
2 In addition to many pertinent publications by the organization Women Living Under Muslim Laws, a variety of materials dealing with Islamic feminism has been published in other formats (Mernissi 1991; Afkhami 1995).
3 UN GAOR 3rd Commission, 39th Session, 65th mtg. at 20, UN Doc. A/C.3/39/SR.65 (1984).
4 See, for example, Final Report on the situation of human rights in the Islamic Republic of Iran by the Special Representative of the Commission on Human Rights, Mr Reynaldo Galindo Pohl, pursuant to Commission resolution 1992/67 of March 4, 1992, U.N. Doc. E/CN.4/1993/41 January 28, 1993, 54–5, and the sections on Iran in the annual reports of Amnesty International and Middle East Watch.
5 Article 18 of the Universal Declaration of Human Rights provides that "Everyone has the right to freedom of thought, conscience and religion; this right includes freedom to change his religion or belief, and freedom, either alone or in community with others and in public or private to manifest his religion or belief in teaching, practice, worship and observance." In the International Covenant on Civil and Political Rights, Article 18.1 begins "Everyone shall have the right to freedom of thought, conscience and religion."
6 Commission on Human Rights. 1993. Economic and Social Council, 49th Sess., Agenda Item 12, at 7. E/CN.4/1993/41/Add. 1: 7–8.
7 Live broadcast by Ayatollah Yazdi on March 10, 1995, Reuter Textline Monitoring Service, March 13, 1995, available in LEXIS, NEXIS Library, ALLWLD File.
8 BBC SWB, ME/2126/MED, October 14, 1994.
9 BBC SWB EE/D2510/ME, January 15, 1996.
10 BBC SWB EE/D2484/ME, December 12, 1995.
11 Reuter Textline, BBC Monitoring Service, March 13, 1995, available in LEXIS, NEXIS Library, ALLWLD File.
12 Islam Guarantees Human Rights, Says Saud, *Riyadh Daily*, June 17, 1993, available in LEXIS, Nexis Library, Saudi File.
13 For information on the UN Convention on the Elimination of All Forms of Discrimination Against Women, consult http://www.un.org/womenwatch/daw/cedaw/
14 The Saudi reservation is included in the report of reservations at http://www.un.org/womenwatch/daw/cedaw/reservations-country.htm

Bibliography

Afkhami, M. (ed.) (1995) *Faith and Freedom. Women's Human Rights in the Muslim World*, London: I.B. Tauris.
Afshari, R. (2001) *Human Rights in Iran: The Abuse of Cultural Relativism*, Philadelphia, PA: University of Pennsylvania Press.
Amnesty International. (1993a) *Saudi Arabia. Religious Intolerance: The Arrest, Detention and Torture of Christian Worshippers and Shi'i Muslims*, New York: Amnesty International USA.
Amnesty International. (1993b) *Saudi Arabia: An Upsurge in Public Executions*, New York: Amnesty International USA.
An-Na'im, A. (1986) "The Islamic Law of Apostasy and Its Modern Applicability, A Case from the Sudan," *Religion*, 16: 197–224.
An-Na'im, A. (1990) *Toward an Islamic Reformation. Civil Liberties, Human Rights and International Law*, Syracuse, NY: Syracuse University Press.
Baderin, M. A. (2003) *International Human Rights and Islamic Law*, Oxford: Oxford University Press.

Caesar, J. (1991) "Big Saudi Brother," *Christian Science Monitor*, January 4, 1991: 18.

Commission on Human Rights. (1993) "Economic and Social Council," 49th Sess., Agenda Item 12, at 7. E/CN.4/1993/41/Add. 1: 7–8.

Coulson, N. (1957) "The State and the Individual in Islamic Law," *International and Comparative Law Quarterly*, 6: 49–60.

Dwyer, K. (1991) *Arab Voices: The Human Rights Debate in the Middle East*, Berkeley, CA: University of California Press.

Mayer, A. E. (1990) "The Shari'ah: A Methodology or a Body of Substantive Rules?" in Nicholas Heer (ed.) *Islamic Law and Jurisprudence*, Seattle, WA: University of Washington Press.

Mayer, A. E. (1993) "The Fundamentalist Impact on Law, Politics, and Constitution in Iran, Pakistan, and Sudan," in M. Marty and R. S. Appleby (eds) *Fundamentalisms and the State: Remaking Polities, Economies, and Militance*, Chicago, IL: University of Chicago Press.

Mayer, A. E. (1994) "Universal versus Islamic Human Rights: A Clash of Cultures or a Clash with a Construct?" *Michigan Journal of International Law*, 15 (Winter): 303–404.

Mayer, A. E. (1995) *Islam and Human Rights: Tradition and Politics*, second edition, Boulder, CO: Westview.

Mayer, A. E. (1999) *Islam and Human Rights. Tradition and Politics*, third edn, Boulder, CO: Westview.

Mayer, A. E. (2004) "Shifting Grounds for Challenging the Authority of International Human Rights Law: Religion as a Malleable and Politicized Pretext for Governmental Noncompliance with Human Rights," in Andras Sajo (ed.) *Human Rights with Modesty: The Problem of Universalism*, Leiden: Martinus Nijhoff.

Mernissi, F. (1991) *The Veil and the Male Elite: A Feminist Interpretation of Womens' Rights in Islam*, Reading, MA: Addison-Wesley.

Mernissi, F. (1992) *Islam and Democracy. Fear of the Modern World*, Reading, MA: Addison-Wesley.

Middle East Watch. (1992) "Empty Reforms," *Saudi Arabia's New Basic Laws* (May 1992).

Moinuddin, H. (1987) *The Charter of the Islamic Conference*, Oxford: Oxford University Press.

Nazir, K. (1990) "'Women's demo was a stupid act', says Naif *Middle East News Network*," November 16, available in LEXIS, Nexis Library, ALLWLD File.

Vichniac, I. (1992) "La commission internationale de juristes denonce un projet de 'declaration des droits de l'homme en Islam," *Le Monde*, February 13: 6.

Waltz, S. E. (2004) "Universal Human Rights: The Contribution of Muslim States," *Human Rights Quarterly*, 26: 799–844.

A bibliographical note

Relevant articles can be found in journals such as a new electronic journal, *Muslim World Journal of Human Rights*, now published by the Berkeley Electronic Press, and publications of organizations like Women Living Under Muslim Laws. Pertinent material is regularly compiled and published by independent human rights groups such as Amnesty International, Human Rights First, and Middle East Watch.

4 Muslim family law

Articulating gender, class, and the state

Nahla Abdo

Introduction

Under the influence of cultural imperialism and Orientalism, Islam, in much of Western literature, has been viewed as a homogeneous and immutable entity resistant to change. Islam is often essentialized and perceived as a monolithic force residing outside of history. Global changes since September 11, 2001 have ushered in a new era when "Islam" and "Muslim" have begun to acquire new meanings. Once again and with more vengeance, Islam and Muslim are lumped together as a homogenous entity of "terrorist other" vis-à-vis "us" in the West (Abdo 2002). On the other hand, some writings by feminists, both Western and Eastern, have tended to conflate Islam and patriarchy and present the two as an inseparable phenomenon. Whereas the first approach presents Islam in a fundamentally ahistorical manner, the second approach fails to historicize and contextualize gender relations.

This chapter will argue that Islam as an ideology, Muslim laws or the Shari'a, and social customs or practices conducted in the name of Islam are not one and the same, nor are they experienced similarly in all Muslim societies. However, a strong relationship between patriarchy, cultural customs/traditions and male control over Shari'a courts' decisions, legal procedures and implementation – or lack thereof – of Shari'a laws becomes an important marker of social-gender dynamics in Muslim societies and among Muslim communities.

The historical fact is that Islam emerged and developed in already existing civilizations; that it spread into other societies already having their own social structures and ideological and cultural norms. While Islam may have influenced these societies, they, in turn, have also left their imprint on Islam. Islam, in other words, will be viewed as the changer and the changed. It will be dealt with as a force operating within history and not despite or outside of history.

This chapter will apply this historical approach to the analysis of the conditions, status, and role of women in Muslim societies and particularly within Muslim law(s). It contends that gender relations, in general, and the role, status, and position of women, in particular, are not determined by Islam alone. Without denying the role of Islam, particularly in its recent politicized form(s), this chapter maintains that women's productive and reproductive lives are largely molded, shaped, and reshaped within very real material forces of a social, economic, political, and cultural nature, and further that these forces are constantly in flux.

It is ironic that most discussions on women's issues in the Middle East and in other Muslim countries are basically confined to the contexts of the family and religion, hence, the primacy of family laws, perceived of as the only sphere for women's growth or stuntation (Hijab 1988). Muslim women's liberation, as a result, becomes predicated on their liberation from their own religion.

In contrast to this position, this chapter will examine the heterogeneity and in fact flexibility of Islam through a comparative analytical approach of the family laws in various Middle Eastern and Muslim states. It will demonstrate that a proper understanding of women in Muslim countries necessitates going beyond the sphere of ideology. One of the means of accomplishing this will entail conducting an inquiry into feminist debates within the Muslim world.

Feminist legalistic opportunism: a critique

Discussions on women in Muslim societies, not unlike general discussions and concerns regarding Islam, have been influenced by specific historical developments at both the national and international levels. For the past two decades, the Middle East has been undergoing a major identity crisis, as the region tries to come to terms with the fast changing pace of globalization and the internationalization of capital. The economic crises and political turmoil that have been gripping the region for quite some time have had major impacts on the Arab and other Muslim states in general, and on gender relations in particular. At both the national and local level, Muslim societies have also had – and continue to cope with – internal conflicts based on gender, ethnicity, religion, and nationalism. It is not surprising, therefore, that studies and debates on Muslim women have mushroomed in recent decades, nor is it unexpected to find that most discourses and debates are reactions to a perceived threat from Western culture.

It is understandable that under specific conditions, priorities, urgencies, and preferences lead to shifting emphases between and even within these contexts. This is particularly true with regard to women's participation in national liberation movements, where their primary allegiance is often focused on the wider cause. Thus, for example, during the Palestinian Intifada, women's massive political participation, especially during the first three years, was mainly geared toward resisting Israeli colonialism, therefore prioritizing national liberation over gender equality and women's own rights. On the other hand, there have also been shifts emphasizing the "internal," namely social-gender forms of oppression, and a privileging of these over "external" forms of oppression. Women of the Intifada demonstrated this shift in the last year or so of their uprising, and Algerian women's struggle is another indication of this change.

Whether the emphasis is placed on one context or the other, what needs to be asserted is that all debates on women in Islam are themselves the product of political-economic factors. Therefore, the debates on Muslim women, as well as any critical reevaluation of these debates, must be located within these broader settings worldwide. Such a contextualization (i.e. one that accounts for the particular social, economic, political, and cultural circumstances) helps to avoid an entrapment in a culturalist and ethnocentric approach, or conversely, from falling into the monolithic and homogenizing methodology or paradigm of the Orientalists (Abdo 2002). The imperative of adopting a systemic, structural, and contextualized approach to gender relations in Islam is more urgent today than ever before – partly due to the proliferation of literature on gender and Islam, and partly because of the hotly debated and quite controversial positions taken by various Muslim scholars and cultural advocates.

Since September 11, 2001 the debates and discourses about women and Islam have been raging throughout the world, including western countries governed by secular family laws. This was true for the debate about school girls' veiling in France and other issues in other European countries. But within Canada, particularly the Province of Ontario, a particularly heated debate emerged in the past three years as the Islamic Society of North America (ISNA) began advocating changing the Canadian secular family law to allow Shari'a laws to rule over Muslim women's cases of marriage, divorce, custody of children, and inheritance. With a strong and handsomely funded center in the United States, ISNA and the Canadian Islamic Congress launched a campaign, demanding that Shari'a-based family laws be included in the Ontario judicial system. This debate has outraged many human rights and Muslim women's organizations worldwide, including Amnesty International and the international organization of Women Living Under Muslim Law (WLUM). A similarly strong campaign within Canada, supported by the Canadian Council of Muslim Women, the Muslim Canadian Congress, and renowned writers like Margaret Atwood, led to the defeat of this proposal. Ontario's premier, Dalton McGuinty, asserted that secular courts cannot be used to uphold decisions on family law made through faith-based arbitration.[1]

In order to capture the diversity of debates about women and Islam, one needs to go beyond scholarly published works into the realm of popular culture, as the most controversial positions are often expressed in artifacts of popular culture. A review of two videos dealing with these issues will illuminate this point.

In a video titled *Women in Islam*, produced by the Islamic Media Service in 1991, women interviewed presented a position defending Islam and all of its assumed laws and regulations, including veiling and early marriage. An almost unanimous voice of a basically subservient position of women in most matters, including polygamy, was articulated by the heavily veiled women in this video. Most of the interviewees appeared to be of middle- and upper-class backgrounds; some were professionals, while others were students. All shared similar opinions on Islamic symbols or aspects of the family laws. Thus, for example, the veil was viewed as a symbol of purity, shielding women from objectification, while polygamy was appreciated as a form of security to women.

The discourse in this video was primarily constructed in opposition to Western values, and particularly to the notions of democracy, individual freedom, and feminism. Feminism was essentialized and homogenized to denote anything and everything immoral in women's behavior in the West. This was quite clear in the approach taken by most of the women interviewed to the issue of polygamy. Polygamy in the West, the women argued, happens in very "immoral" ways, "under the table." Islam, in contrast, has legalized and legitimized polygamy, protecting women from becoming mistresses.

The Islamic discourse presented in the previous paragraph is popular among Muslim fundamentalists or revivalists and is found in most of their popular literature (Afshar 1994). This is also true for ISNA whose representative, Kathy Bullock in a Toronto TV debate on Shari'a defended the practice of polygamy, saying "I don't see a problem with polygamy." When reminded that polygamy was a criminal offence in Canada, she simply shrugged her shoulders. Such approaches are based on the gender ideology that assumes women's minds and bodies are weakened by natural processes, and that women must accept positions in society within a very specific sphere of economic and social activity involving submission to their fathers and husbands (Maududi 1974: 114–37).

In contrast to the almost unanimous discourse mentioned earlier, a video titled *The Veiled Revolution*, produced by Elizabeth Fernea in 1992, provides a diversity of opinions on the most controversial symbol of Islam, namely, the veil (*hijab*). Here, most "newly" veiled Egyptian women see the veil as a means of protecting their place in the public sphere. Their argument suggests that the veil forces men to take women as serious partners rather than as sex symbols, and enables women to enter into the masculine world without disturbing society's order. The veil in this discourse takes on both a political and a practical meaning rather than an ideological one. Similar arguments, as shall be further discussed, are prevalent among an increasingly popular type of scholarship.

In the discourse of *The Veiled Revolution*, the veil is not unanimously embraced as a religious axiom. On the contrary, it acquires a controversial character as non-veiled Muslim women resent the interpretation of the "new Islamists." In fact, some argue that the "reinvention" of the veil is a backward phenomenon that threatens the historic achievements of Egyptian feminism.

Within Muslim feminist scholarship, writings on women and Islam fall largely into two categories: those that adopt a secular(ist) approach to women by contextualizing their lives, conditions and struggles within the wider framework of the state, class, social, gender, and cultural forces (Sa'adawi 1983, 1988; Ghossoub 1987; Hammami and Rieker 1988; Hijab 1988; Moghadam 1994; Abdo and Lentin 2002; Mojab and Abdo 2004) and those that locate their analysis within a cultural Islamic framework, suggesting that it is the misuse or misinterpretation of Islam that must be blamed for women's status (Mernissi 1988, 1992a, 1993, 1994; Ahmed 1992; Hoodfar 1993, 1996; Hessini 1994; Dirie 1996). While scholars in the first category are identified – by themselves and others – as secularists, scholars embracing the religious Islamic approach are not necessarily religious or Islamist themselves. Ironically, the most eloquently articulated studies on Muslim women's resistance within the veil or within Islam are those espoused by scholars who identify themselves as secular, modernist, or nonreligious.

The following discussion will focus on the second (i.e. religious-cultural) approach. This approach is of particular concern because of the popular appeal it claims to command, and also because of what I suggest is the problematic nature of its current argumentation. Scholars in this category may adopt different social science approaches and may focus on different points in explaining issues of women in Islam. For example, Leila Ahmed (1992) takes an interesting historical approach in order to revisit the role of Muslim women since the inception of Islam. Hoodfar (1991, 1993, 1996), on the other hand, takes an anthropological ethnographic approach, focusing on daily life experiences and forms of resistance espoused by Muslim women. Whether the case study is Iran or Egypt, Hoodfar's conclusions appear to describe a particular trend: veiled women, even if veiling was imposed, do not see themselves as victims. To the contrary, Hoodfar identifies "Islamic feminists" as women who are active, conscious, and capable of resistance and self-empowerment.

Authors in this category deal with various aspects of Islamic laws, such as polygamy and divorce; nonetheless, veiling remains on the top of their agenda. Feminists subscribing to this approach unfalteringly consider the veil a tool of patriarchy. However, this tool is presented as a double-edge sword; while imposed as a patriarchal and oppressive tool, the veil, these authors insist, can also be used by women to "subvert patriarchy." Leila Hessini's description of how Moroccan *Muhajjabat* (i.e. veiled women) utilize the veil speaks well to this issue. According to Hessini, "by wearing the Hijab women can enter into traditional spaces without disturbing society's equilibrium; this also demonstrates a woman's choice to belong to a group which professes ethical standards in tune with Muslim values" (Hessini 1994: 51).

"Subverting patriarchy" or changing women's position, in this literature, is believed to be possible either through female interpretation of the Muslim family laws (e.g. Mernissi's position), or through incremental gains achieved by women who challenge patriarchy through their own daily life experiences (e.g. Hoodfar's analysis). The latter position does not offer any definition to these gains, which can refer to anything from using the veil as a coping mechanism to a much more subtle and passive mode of resistance in the street or in the bus (Hoodfar 1993, 1996).

Common to scholars adopting this position is what I refer to as Feminist legalistic opportunism. Feminist legalistic opportunism refers to the feminist position (implicitly or explicitly made) that women's problems, oppression, and victimization, as well as their solutions and emancipation, can primarily be attained within the confines of the Muslim laws and the boundaries of the legal system. In other words, this approach entrusts all discussions of women's problems and prospects to the legal system, trusting the latter to be the ultimate savior or champion of women's emancipation. Additionally, this approach confines women's rights to religious jurisprudence, albeit with a call to reinterpret the Shari'a.

Fixation on the legal sphere is quite characteristic of the work of the prolific scholar Fatima Mernissi, particularly in her book, *The Veil and the Male Elite: A Feminist Interpretation of Women's Rights in Islam* (1992b). While Mernissi's approach is more of a social-psychological one that, among other things, is heavily concerned with men's or the masculine perception of women's bodies, her solution to women's oppression within Muslim laws is similar to that adopted by other scholars in this approach. For Mernissi, the main problem for Muslim women is that the Quran, the Shari'a, and the Hadith have been interpreted by men in order to serve their own interests. To change their conditions, Muslim women must engage in the work of reinterpreting the Family Laws, diverting it from a male-centered into a female-centered interpretation.

The ethnographic or micro-level analyses characteristic of this literature can be interesting and illuminating, particularly as this approach tries to challenge Orientalist perspectives by restoring a human face onto veiled, "faceless" women. Equally illuminating and quite important is the work of Mernissi when she challenges Islamic laws as immutable. For Mernissi, the power of these laws comes from the male and patriarchal character of their inventors or interpreters, and not from a divine unchallenged source. Nevertheless, I believe that the approach of feminist legalistic opportunism remains highly problematic and, sometimes even dangerous.

This approach gains its strength and perhaps even popularity mainly through the strong claim made by its propagators who identify themselves as secular and present a religious (Islamic) thesis based on their claim that "you need to speak the language of the masses in order to reach them." This position presents an ethical problem, namely, that of accepting secular life for oneself while advocating a religious one for the other. A more important issue here is that the scholarly or scientific community has yet to demonstrate that the masses of Muslim women do indeed prefer an Islamic solution over other forms of solutions. Moreover, from a tactical perspective, it is difficult to maintain that an Islamic solution will lead to women's liberation (and more generally to human liberation). In the absence of any research on the true needs or wishes of the masses, the basis of such popularity becomes difficult to sustain. In reference to the Pakistani case, for instance, Fauzia Gardezi (1990: 21) warned against applying ideal factors to explain women's oppression, while ignoring, in the process, the real material life conditions and experiences of women. It is important to note that a new genre of scholarly work on women and Islam has emerged since the late 1990s focusing more on Muslim women's realistic situation and the impact of Shari'a laws, customary practices, and patriarchy in their lives (An-Na'im 2002; Welchman 2003; Welchman and Hussain 2004).

It is interesting to note here that privately, among political grassroots activists, another discourse is taking shape. Here, Islam, reinterpreted and employed by women to achieve certain (particularly political) gains, becomes a tactical device. It is, as one Sudanese activist confided: "fighting men in power with the very same weapon they use against us." In this discourse the Islamic shield is used as a temporary working device to politicize the "poor, the illiterate and the disempowered." However, the ultimate goal or long-term strategy is articulated in terms of the separation between religion and state. Intellectualizing for public (and mainly Western) consumption is not a concern for these activists. Their concern is with effecting political changes in their daily lives. As much as one can appreciate such an experiential and activist position, the privacy surrounding what is tactical and what is strategic makes it difficult to engage in any discourse or debate.

Confining one's analysis to the legal sphere leaves room for other lacunae. Various women's organizations in the Muslim countries, including the Center for Women's Counseling and Legal Aid in the West Bank, and WLUML, with its two branches in Lahore and Paris, have been working for several years to reform the family laws. These women's organizations work to empower women living within Muslim laws, by raising their awareness about their rights, and overcome the misconceptions about the laws. However, these organizations are coming to the realization that there is a limit to reform within the status quo. Short of rejecting the divinity of the Quran, how can, for example, any feminist analysis feminize the following verses – let alone convert them into emancipatory principles?

> If you fear that you cannot treat orphans with fairness, then you may marry other women who seem good to you: two, three or four of them. But if you fear that you cannot maintain equality among them, marry one only, or any slave girls you may own. This will make it easier for you to avoid injustice.
>
> (IV: 2)[2]

Or, consider the following verses from the same sura (chapter) of the Quran:

> Men have authority over women because God has made the one superior to the other, and because they spend their wealth to maintain them. Good women are obedient. They guard their unseen parts because God has guarded them. As for those from whom you fear disobedience, admonish them and send them to beds apart and beat them. Then if they obey you, take no further action against them.
>
> (IV: 34)

Feminist legalistic opportunism, as this discussion reveals, faces problems at various levels. Take for example the Muslim inheritance law that affords women the right to inheritance – albeit a lesser portion than that of the male. In practice, women have not benefited from this law. Historically, most women have been deprived of their right to property. Even if activists or feminists strive for, and succeed in, reforming this law to give women, in theory, an equal share as that of the men, there is no guarantee that women will, in practice, inherit property. Customarily, inheritance has been tied to traditional cultural norms of landed and other forms of property, around which the whole unit of the family, clan, or tribe have been maintained and reproduced. Challenging the inheritance law would necessitate challenging the traditional cultural norms and not only the letter of the law. Having said this, however, this argument should not be construed as an antireform position. Quite to the contrary, legal reforms are necessary, particularly in the face of the fast changing material life that all Muslim societies have been undergoing. The point here is that confining women's emancipation primarily to the legalistic sphere is no guarantee for a real change.

Clearly, a one dimensional, single sphere (legalistic) analysis is too narrow an approach. Among other things, it fails to account for the role of culture and tradition. This is evident in the way scholars tend to conflate Islam with patriarchy. Islam is often essentialized and discussed as a monolith rather than as an ideological force that is often sustained and reproduced under particular social, economic, and political conditions. Islam is frequently used interchangeably with culture, thus masking the differences between, for instance, Arab, Iranian, and Indian or Pakistani cultures.

Furthermore, there is a potential danger in adopting such approaches. Such peril lies in the failure of these approaches to demonstrate the connection between women's conditions and the wider context within which these conditions arise, develop, and are reproduced, namely, the nature and character of the state and the class structure. Few and far between are the studies that attempt to perceive social-gender problems as institutionalized systemic problems that are the product of the specific historical junctures of patriarchy, the religious elite, and the state. In fact, any form of state criticism in almost all of this literature is surprisingly and shockingly absent, as if the state does not matter. Yet, as will be shown shortly, the relevance of the state is central to any analysis or understanding of women's conditions. It is not incidental, one may note, that throughout the Middle Eastern region only Tunisian and Turkish women currently enjoy the abolition of polygamy. Such legal transformation could not have been possible had it not been for the direct intervention of the state. Short of abolishing such a law, it is difficult to imagine what type of gender equality any reform or feminist interpretation could bring about.

Finally, considering the multiplicity of male hegemonies reinforced by the recent tide of Islamization, such scholarship – appearing even implicitly to condone acts restricting women's movement – might feed into the already existing patriarchal systems of the religio-political parties.

These discourses and debates, despite their problematic nature have mushroomed during the 1990s, as the world witnessed a transitional epoch; the end of the bipolar world and the beginning of the single-polar imperial power of the United States. The entrenchment of the latter with the accompanying hegemonic imperialist discourse in the late 1990s and the early twenty-first century has produced new ideological discourses based on a sharpened sense of white exclusivism (read, national racism), racism and disdain toward the Muslim "other." Without the historical contextualization which seemed to at least partially characterize the debates on the 1990s and away from the heterogeneity which marked debates on Muslim women, the new hegemonic discourse has largely tied itself to the state and its interest. Without going into any details here, suffice it to mention that renowned radical feminists such as the late Andrea Dworkin (2002) have targeted Palestinian women "suicide bombers" as a means to demonize and dehumanize the whole Palestinian society, its culture, religion, and modes of life.[3]

Islam, patriarchy, and the state: an alternative approach

An alternative approach to studying women and Islam, or women and family law, must be contextualized within the specific history of the particular region or geographical locality under investigation. The merit of such an approach is that it avoids a monolithic essentialist approach to Islam. Moreover, by contextualizing Islam within the history of a particular culture, such an approach can show the relationship between culture, patriarchy, the state, and Islam as an ideology and practice.

Whether one employs the concept of "classical patriarchy" (Kandiyoti 1991) or "neo-patriarchy" (Sharabi 1988) to describe the male nature of power and control that characterizes most states and institutions throughout the Middle East, it remains pertinent to realize that this maleness or patriarchy is not a purely abstract ideological construct. Rather, it is the product of very specific historical junctures of socioeconomic and political configurations, with deep roots in real historical material culture. It is within this material base of the modes or forms of production of class structures and states that women's conditions must be understood.

When first introduced in the Hijaz, Islam encountered a highly patriarchal structure on which it built its main tenets. In pre-Islamic Arab (tribal) society, a marriage contract strongly resembled a bill of sale according to which the woman became the husband's possession. Esposito describes some characteristics of pre-Islamic law. First, the woman's tribe received the dower (*mahr*) from the husband for the bride; in return, the tribe relinquished all claims to the woman and to her future children. Esposito notes that the woman's worth at that time was deemed to be her dower and that in her life, chastity and fidelity were encouraged and emphasized. Further, women were denied any rights to inheritance because this would mean the transfer of property from one tribe to another, which was inconceivable. Women had no say whatsoever in the contracting of the marriage, nor in its dissolution; upon marriage, the woman became subject to her husband's control. It was also a common, legitimate practice for girl children to be buried at birth because they were devalued to such a large degree (Esposito 1982).

It is not surprising therefore that Islam retained some aspects of the already existing gender practices, while abolishing some, such as the "wa'd" (burying of female children at birth) and altering others, such as including women in inheritance. More research is needed to illustrate how Islam was received or changed by cultures that practiced matrilineal, rather than patrilineal or even patriarchal forms of relations. There are some indications suggesting that the introduction and imposition of Islam in, for example, parts of Kerala in India and among the Qabyle Berbers in Algeria, where matrilineal practices predominated, took different forms than in the overwhelmingly patriarchal societies of the Muslim world. In some parts of Muslim India, such as Kerala, it was not until the state (both the British colonial and the Indian) enforced Islamic laws that a patriarchal system began to dominate.

Control over private property and inheritance are basic mechanisms of power used by all states. Such control, as Souad Joseph (1996) has correctly observed, is a fundamental element in the reproduction of gendered citizenship throughout the Middle East. Yet, in order to understand this aspect of Muslim family laws, one cannot resort to ideological interpretations alone. It is historically plausible and logically conceivable that inheritance acquires an important status in the transition to private property. In order, for example, to comprehend why some Muslim women did historically inherit property (i.e. among upper-class women in late nineteenth-century Egypt (Tucker 1985)), and why others did not, one must look at, among other things, pre-capitalist class structures and forms of marriages. One may note here that inheritance or lack of it varies not only between countries but within the same country among regions. In tribal, often exogamous marriages, the value placed on property is different from when landed property is at stake. Peasant societies place a special value on landed property, since land is their primary means of survival, as well as their major source of wealth and social prestige. It is not incidental, for example, that in pre-capitalist Palestine endogamous marriages, particularly among first cousins, were encouraged as such marriages were expected to keep property within the family, Hamula, or clan (Abdo 2006).

One may ask, why, despite the destruction and disappearance of most pre-capitalist forms of production and social life, ideological forms of social-gender organizations continue to survive. What contributes to the longevity of traditional forms of marriage and inheritance despite the destruction of the material basis that gave rise to them in the first place? To simply state that an ideology expressing the articulation of traditional customs and religious beliefs dies hard is not sufficient. Other factors are equally, if not more, important. These include political and economic forces, such as the level of economic development or the state of economic dependency under which most previously colonized countries found themselves after independence. Another important factor lies in the role of the state in maintaining and reproducing various forms of gender inequality. As demonstrated elsewhere (Abdo 1987), both the British and the Israeli colonial states have played a crucial role in fostering and further reproducing gender inequality among the Palestinians. "The different political projects of modern nation-states," as Kandiyoti observes, "account for deep and significant variations in policies and legislation affecting women. These variations find concrete expression in the degree of access that women have to education, paid employment, social benefits, and political participation" (Kandiyoti 1991: 38).

The analysis in this chapter focuses primarily on the level of the canon versus reality/experience. There is, however, another important level of analysis, the inclusion of which improves our understanding of Islam. That is religion versus politics, or the distinction between Islam the religion (i.e. the relationship between the individual and God) and Islamization as a political movement. The latter, whether referred to as fundamentalism or revivalism, represents a political movement based on existing or reinvented religious codes. Political Islam, expressed in the various Islamicist movements and operating in almost all Muslim countries, seeks state power with a somewhat common agenda. This is a highly conservative, patriarchal agenda which, in terms of its social-gender implications, is also reactionary.

It is in this context, namely, when Islam acquires a basically political face, that one begins to comprehend how the state in the Middle East walks a tightrope between secular nationalism and Islamism. This is particularly so in the context of international/global capitalism.

Globalization often pushes the state toward further Westernization and modernization. In this regard, the state can be viewed – particularly by its female citizens – as the site for their protection and, perhaps, even emancipation. However, when faced with internal resistance by Islamists (political Islam) and in a bid to control and maintain the status quo, the state does not hesitate to abandon its "secular" outlook, adopting more rigid and often oppressive measures, particularly in the domestic, private sphere. The role of the Algerian state throughout the past two decades provides an example: on the one hand, the state has tried to pacify the FIS (*Front islamique de salut*), while on the other, under economic pressures and a strong women's resistance, it has also attempted to not alienate the secular "modern" forces. The state's ambivalent role was most obvious during the introduction of the controversial Family Code of 1984, which instead of addressing the injustices against women in Algeria, reinforced the existing patriarchal grip over them.

During nation-state building, particularly in periods of economic and political crises, the state often seeks alliances with different ideological-political movements. Such alliances, particularly with political Islam, often work to the detriment of women's equality and against improving their status. In a study of the Indian state, Amrita Chhachhi cites examples of how the state, at different points during its nation building, aligned itself both officially and unofficially with Hinduism, thus alienating Muslims. She also explains how in the 1950s, the government sought to convince Muslims within India that it was committed to creating a nation-state that would grant all religions the same rights, by allowing the continuation of Muslim personal law rather than pushing for equality of all women before the state law. Muslim women in India, as Chhachhi concludes, became twice oppressed by virtue of their religion and their sex (Chhachhi 1991). Racism against Indian women of Muslim background, particularly in the state of Gujarat, gained more momentum with the emergence of the BJP – Bharatiya Janata Party (Bannerji 2003).

A similar situation was observed in Malaysia where Malay women and men continued for centuries to follow the Law of Adat (customary laws). Both sexes enjoyed "equal rights to property (including land) and divorce, and were subject to the same codes of sexual behaviour, promiscuity being condemned in both sexes" (Agarwal 1988: 17). Yet, as in the Indian and other experiences, the intervention of the state, influenced by increasing Islamization, has begun to threaten the customary non-Islamic cultural traditions, particularly as they relate to gender-sex relations.

The states in predominantly Muslim countries have taken a vacillating position between the secular and the religious, depending on the priority of the state, often dictated by an outside force. The secular position (in support of women's rights) gets chosen over the religious (Islamicist movements) when advantageous to the state's interest. The ambivalent role of the Egyptian government is a case in point. On the one hand, fearing a tide of Muslim Brotherhood (al-Ikhwan), a recent law was issued banning school girls from wearing the hijab. Yet a contradictory position is demonstrated through the widely publicized case of the two Cairo University scholars who were forced to divorce each other because of the Azhar's verdict of alleged blasphemy committed by the husband. In fact, even the most secular state in the region, Turkey, could not escape such dualism. Since the military intervention in 1980, the Turkish state has increasingly been struggling to maintain a balance between its nationalist secular legacy and the pressure of Islamization that threatens the country's political stability from within.

In its constant effort to balance the major contending tendencies, the state often places women in an equally ambivalent position with a penchant for viewing the state as both the protector and the oppressor, depending on the particular configuration of alliances struck during any particular period. However, what women often tend to forget is that secularism, particularly in the national(ist) context of the Middle East, is not necessarily emancipatory or libratory, especially when issues of gender equality are at stake. The ideology of nationalism is a patriarchal, gendered ideology based on the assumption that women are (or should be) primarily mothers and housewives and secondarily workers. As history has shown, women's mass public participation and political activism during the upsurge of national movements have yet to be translated into change in the movements' gender ideology. Addressing this dilemma within the Iranian context, Afsaneh Najmabadi notes that "with the consolidation of the Pahlavi state, women became objects of contestation of loyalty, as they became crucial to the state's project of social transformation, while remaining central to the Islamic claims of moral community" (Najmabadi 1991: 70).

The complex, multifarious and often pernicious role played by the state, to use Agarwal's words, is not confined to the Middle East. It is also evident throughout the countries of Asia where political Islam is gaining increasing momentum. In these countries the role of the state, similar to that in the Middle East, has been extended into the spheres of people's reproductive choices, religious beliefs, and even interpersonal relationships, dress, and behavior patterns (Agarwal 1988: 1).

Women and family laws in Islam

The articulation of traditional culture, the role of the state (whether colonial or nation-state), class structure, and women's organized resistance are crucial to understanding the gendered Muslim family laws. Three areas in the Personal Status Law, also known as the Family Code, will be traced in the following section. These are marriage, polygamy, and divorce.

At the outset of this discussion on family laws it is important to point out that there are different schools in Islam that provide varying interpretations of the laws. While the scope of this chapter inhibits any detailed account on these schools, changes espoused by the four schools of Sunni jurisprudence, as al-Hibri affirms (1992), are minor as the differences between the schools are more cosmetic than fundamental.

Marriage

Traditionally, marriage is considered one of the most important, if not the most important, event in the life of the community in Muslim Middle East. Children, mainly girls, are often prepared at a young age for such an event. Because of the transitional form it takes, namely, between the extended family and the smaller, more nuclear living arrangement, marriage is assumed to be the road toward asserting individuality and even securing a level of freedom. This individuality, however, does not translate itself into individual freedom at the legal level of state and citizenship. Throughout the Muslim countries of the Middle East, citizenship is the prerogative of the man/father/husband and not the woman/mother/wife. Children are typically included in the passport of the father, consequently depriving the mother of the right to travel with her children if she chooses to do so. Women cannot give citizenship to their children; only men, even if married to non-Muslims, can confer citizenship on their children. The alliance constructed here between state and religion enforces the exclusion of women from true citizenship in the nation-state. In the Middle East, the woman, viewed as an appendage or dependent, derives her citizenship through her relation to the man, be he father or husband (Joseph 1996; Abu Hassan 2005; Azzouni 2005).

The institution of marriage in most Muslim countries in the Middle East has undoubtedly undergone major changes due to increased urbanization, proletarianization, and the nuclearization-individualization of the traditional extended family. Exogamous marriages, particularly in urban areas, are increasingly replacing endogamous marriages. Also changing in urban areas, particularly among middle-class people, is the concept and practice of arranged marriage which is being gradually replaced with love marriage or marriage of the choice of the couple. Despite these changes, traditional forms of marriages remain the norm.

One area in which traditional Muslim marriage is slow to change is in mixed or interfaith marriages. This phenomenon to which I refer as "female religious endogamy versus male exogamous rights," remains a point of contestation for scholarship on women and Islam. Al-Hibri (1992) takes up this point by showing how the Hanafi school, considered by her as the more lenient school, deviates on the issue of mixed marriage from the Sunna. The Sunna, according to al-Hibri, indicates that marriage should be based on piety as the preferable reference point. However, the Hanafi school of jurisprudence has established that sex, rather than piety, be the basis of its jurisprudence on mixed or intrareligious marriages, therefore making sameness in religion the basic condition for Muslim women's marriages. This restriction is imposed on women only; Muslim men in all schools of jurisprudence are allowed to marry outside of Islam (al-Hibri 1992: 3; Azzouni 2005). Nevertheless, the assertion made by al-Hibri by no means suggests that restrictions on mixed marriages are limited to the Hanafi school. In fact, all Muslim schools of jurisprudence share these constraints. Such restrictions make it very difficult even for a Sunni Muslim to marry a Shi'i Muslim.

Mixed marriage is an issue in the various urban centers of the Middle East, yet very little attention has been paid to it. Scholars who write about countries having a predominant Muslim presence, such as Pakistan, the Gulf states, and Morocco, tend to treat this as a non-issue. In other parts of the Arab Middle East, such as Tunisia, Palestine, Lebanon, and Jordan, women appear to be more interested in discussing and debating this form of inequality, partly because of the principle of injustice involved in this "law" and partly because of the prevalence of such practices. In most of these countries, mixed marriages have been enacted not only among lay women and men but also among the political-national elite. While in most of the elite practices marriages have been conducted between Muslim men and non-Muslim (mainly Christian) women, mixed marriages involving Muslim women and non-Muslim men are not unheard of.

Although Islam prohibits Muslim female mixed marriages, it is interesting to note that class does often mediate such a prohibition. Muslim women who can afford to choose their partners often have a particular class backing that allows them to engage in such relations. The presence of such a class background is crucial for providing some social, moral, and economic security for the woman who finds herself isolated and, in many cases, shunned by the community. The class backing in such relations is all the more important when one considers the role of the state or lack thereof. No religious state in the Middle East (including Israel) has any mechanism to support such choices by its citizens. In fact, mixed marriages, like other gender issues vaguely and arbitrarily assumed to be in the realm of "family honor," are areas where the state refuses to interfere. Secular Muslims who choose such marriages can place their lives at risk while the state turns deaf ears and blind eyes. There is no legal means to formalize or legitimize interfaith marriages. Except on Turkey, where family laws have been secularized, civil marriages are virtually nonexistent throughout the Middle East. Even Israel, a country that prides itself on having a strong civil society, confines all family matters within the boundaries of religious courts and rules (Jewish, Muslim, and Christian jurisprudence). Among Palestinians, for example, a couple wishing to engage in a mixed marriage would have to leave Palestine/Israel, obtain civil marriage outside and return home. Civil marriages, while not performed in Israel, are still accepted as legal marriages.

Marriage restrictions imposed on Muslim women have far-reaching gender implications, particularly in the area of citizenship. Muslim countries will have to eventually deal with the thousands of women who, while living in their home countries, cannot give their nationality to their children because they are either married to foreigners, divorced, abandoned, or widowed. In many cases, as Nahid Toubia observes, the children become stateless persons with no educational, health, or employment rights. This situation occurs even if the father is from another Muslim country – an increasingly common occurrence with the expansion in labor migration to the Gulf countries (Toubia 1994: 56). On the other hand, the phenomenon of immigration and labor migration that characterizes many Muslim countries does not seem to be abating. Quite to the contrary, further globalization and integration within international capitalism will most likely reinforce and strengthen Muslim migration to the West. Consequently, it is expected that mixed marriages may become more of a reality in the new living conditions for both sexes in Muslim communities. Such a reality, for example, was crucial in the Tunisian government's decision to abolish restrictions on inter-faith marriages. It was also a major consideration in the Lebanese government's decision in 1994 to pass a nationality law that would give a woman the right to grant her nationality to her children as well as to her foreign-born husband.

A related issue is the age of marriage, which represents a clear testimony to the diversity of rules and practices among different Muslim communities. It is generally held that according to the Shari'a, the age of marriage for the woman is when she reaches puberty or once menstruation begins. This can be as low as 11 years of age. In Iran, for example, prior to the 1979 Revolution, the age of marriage was set at 13 for women. The Islamic Republic changed the rules and decreed the legal age of marriage to be 9 for girls. After some dissent and debate, the Revolutionary Council brought back the old rule and accepted marriage for girls at the age of 13. The declaration of the new age of marriage, however, did not cancel the existing rule (Hoodfar 1996). In practice, parents can still marry off their daughters at the age of 9 without facing any legal repercussions.

In most Arab countries, a minimum age of marriage has been set at 16 for girls and 18 for boys. Yet, in many rural and poor urban communities girls are still married off under the legal age (Toubia 1994: 24). Some countries, such as the Sudan, Yemen, and Bahrain have no standard age of marriage (al-Najjar 2005; Basha 2005). Reaching puberty or menstruation is considered legitimate. Except for Egypt, which considers marriage under the age of 16 as illegal (El-Azhary Sonbol 2005), most Arab countries sanctify marriages under the minimum age as long as a court order is obtained. Obtaining a court order, as studies have revealed, is not difficult: all that is needed is a physician's certificate asserting that the girl has reached puberty.

Marriage age is heavily influenced by economic conditions, levels of literacy, and cultural traditions or customary laws. For example, in rich Arab countries, such as the United Arab Emirates, the rate of adolescent or minor marriages is estimated to account for 55 percent of all marriages. In this case tribal cultural norms, rather than economic well-being, appear to predominate. High rates of minor or adolescent marriages have also been reported in some of the very poor countries; Sudan has a rate of 41 percent of minor marriages. In this case it is more likely that economic conditions along with a high rate of illiteracy are the major contributors to the phenomenon of early marriages (Toubia 1994: 25). A combination of poverty with illiteracy or constrained access to education, together with social and political repression can have regressive effects on the age of marriage. In the Gaza Strip, for example, although the Egyptian law has been followed – where marriages are set at the age of 16 for the girl and underage mar-riages are declared illegal – during the Intifada (which produced harsh economic and political realities, and a consequent high dropout rate from school), girls as young as 13 were reportedly pulled out of schools and forced into arranged marriages (Hammami 1993; Azzoni 2005; Shalhoub-Kevorkian and Abdo 2005).

Another contested issue in Muslim marriages is that of the *wali* (the male guardian), where consent is a precondition for a marriage contract. The idea of having a wali is based on the gender ideology that assumes the inferior status of women, depicting them as weak, emotional, and incapable of making rational decisions on their own (Agarwal 1988; al-Hibri 1992; Mernissi 1992b; Abdo 2006). Despite slight differences between different schools of Islamic jurisprudence on the role of the wali, most Muslim countries follow similar policies of requiring the wali.

The only exception is, once again, Tunisia, which abandoned *wilaya* (male guardianship) as a condition for marriage and gave mature women the right to choose whether they want to contract their marriages by themselves or relegate it to a wali (Perkins 1986; al-Hibri 1992). In various countries, such as Syria, Egypt, and Algeria, reforms to the role of the wali have been attempted at various times. However, as al-Hibri points out, such changes were of hardly any significance. The wali continues to have the right to prevent marriage if he finds it "not in the interest" of the girl who is often his daughter or blood relative. For example, in Egypt, where women can marry without the consent of the guardian, the father/guardian can request the annulment through court on the basis of incompatibility (Toubia 1994: 57; Bellafronto 2005). The negligible change in the Algerian Code on this matter was from its "not profitable" form as it existed in the 1981 Code, to "not in the interest of the daughter" as expressed in the 1984 Family Code (al-Hibri 1992: 235).

The role of the guardian, however, goes beyond issues of marriage. Whether a father, a husband, or a brother, the guardian often controls women's movement. Sudan, for example, commands the most restrictive measures on women's movement by the wali based on an administrative regulation. The Numeiri regime and all governments that followed it enforced the law that requires a woman, regardless of her age or marital status, to have the consent of her male guardian if she wishes to obtain a passport. A guardian can be a teenage boy who is given authority over mature older sisters. In both Egypt and Morocco, married women need the consent of their husbands to obtain a passport. In many Muslim countries women also need the consent of the husband to take a job. As Toubia indicates, Syria, Tunisia, and Bahrain have the least restrictive laws, but they still discriminate according to marital status:

> Unmarried women must have the consent of their fathers if they want a passport, but a wife who applies for a passport does not need her husband's consent, and he cannot stop her from traveling unless he secures a court order.
>
> (Toubia 1994: 50)

With a slight difference in details, the situation is similar in other Arab countries (Deeb 2005; Pargeter 2005).

Polygamy

Polygamy, or the right to marry more than one person, is the prerogative of men throughout the Muslim Middle East, with the exception of Turkey and Tunisia where polygamy was abolished in the 1956 Personal Status Code. Muslim jurists have different opinions on this issue. Some jurists, particularly among the new Islamists, defend polygamy as an indisputable Muslim rule that, among other things, is seen as necessary for the propagation of the Muslim *Umma* (nation). Other jurists differ slightly, arguing that polygamy does not have to be an absolute right; the prospective wife has the right to place a condition in the marriage contract to prohibit her husband from taking another wife. In cases where some reform has occurred, such as in Libya, Syria, and Morocco, polygamy, while still sanctioned by the law, is permitted only in court. In these countries the husband must inform or obtain the approval of the existing wife before marrying another (Toubia 1994: 60). Al-Hibri (1992) observes that many Muslim countries, particularly Arab countries, have recognized women's right to intervene in the marriage contract around the issue of polygamy. Such intervention (real or potential), however, must be understood within the context of power relations between husbands and wives.

The poignant reality for most Muslim women is the fact that for traditional and customary reasons, women are often a marginalized party in the marriage contract, leading, in most cases, to women forfeiting their rights of negotiation. Numerous reasons may account for this, ranging from the relatively high rate of illiteracy among women, particularly rural, poor, and young women who are forced into arranged marriages, or by women unwilling to take the risk of being rendered socially outcast, or to others who realize the futility of challenging male hegemony in the overwhelmingly male-dominated structures and institutions (Abu Hassan 2005; Azzouni 2005; Abdo 2006).

Women's education and their awareness about their right to interfere in, and perhaps shape, their marriage contract, while necessary, are not sufficient. Raising women's consciousness about their legal rights in marriage has become an integral part of women's activities in many Muslim countries. For instance, the Women's Legal and Counselling Center in Jordan, the Lahore-based Women Living Under Muslim Law (WLUML), and the Center for Legal Aid and Counselling for Women in the West Bank have all been involved in education and consciousness raising. Yet, for consciousness-raising efforts to work, there needs to be not only mass-scale grassroots organized work, but also legal mechanisms and enforcement policies. In the absence of enforcement laws, of legal and institutional recourse and state commitment to enforce stipulations in the contract, this exercise and the efforts of many women's organizations remain futile.[4] The reluctance of the state to intervene in the issue of polygamy, or for that matter, in other aspects of family laws, leaves the Islamic/Shari'a courts in a position of full control over the lives of women.

Polygamy, like other forms of religiously based legal measures used to control women's bodies, has more symbolic meaning at the national-political level than it does in terms of its practical relevance. As noted by Perkins, the abolition of polygamy in Tunisia had no major implications for the conditions of women, since less than 3 percent of the Tunisian population was involved in multiple marriages at the time (Perkins 1986: 124). In Iraq, on the other hand, after the Iraq-Iran war,

Saddam Hussein encouraged polygamy and prohibited the use of contraceptives in order to meet the regime's insatiable need for soldiers (Helow 1996: 18).

Encouraging polygamy as a means of controlling women's reproductive activities by confining them to the domestic sphere was the basis for the uproar in the Algerian political quarters in 1984. Despite the fact that multiple marriages as a practice was far from being widespread among the increasingly individualized and urbanized Algerian family, the state's attempt at restricting polygamy was met with fierce resistance from the religious elite. Thus, according to Article 8 of the Family Code of 1984,

> It is permitted to contract marriage with more than one wife within the limits of Shari'a if the motive is justified, the conditions and intentions of equality provided, and after the consultation of the preceding and future wife. Either wife may take judicial action against the husband or request divorce should he ignore her refusal to consent.
>
> (Cheriet 1996: 24)

However, as Cheriet observed, "conservative delegates swiftly and violently denounced the Article as 'heretic'...Out of 60 interventions reported...45 opposed placing conditions on polygamy" (1996: 25). While reasons for such opposition varied, the most startling, according to the author, is the one which held that

> Polygamy is not to be disputed, whatever the case, for a Muslim state is one based on Jihad, and this calls for the involvement of men alone. To whom will women be left in the case of Jihad, and how will society be protected from subsequent depravity, if widows cannot find parties to marry? Polygamy is therefore a must.
>
> (Cheriet 1996: 25)

Divorce

Not unlike other aspects of the Shari'a that pertain to women's status, the issue of divorce is contested among various schools of jurisprudence. All Muslim jurisprudence, while not questioning the right of the man to divorce his wife or wives, accepts the view that the woman may have the right to divorce her husband if, and only if, this right is clearly established as a condition in the marriage contract. However, as al-Hibri points out, this condition can be violated and even nullified through other legal and extralegal recourse reserved for men. According to the Hanafi school, a limited monetary payment to the wife can revoke the significance of such a condition, while in the Maliki jurisprudence if a judge learns about the existence of a stipulation granting women the right to divorce, he can annul the whole marriage (al-Hibri 1992: 235). In other words, the liberal appearance of the Hanafi school over the Maliki on this issue is only in form, or in theory, with little practical or real significance.

There appears to be a uniformity in rule over the issue of marriage by all schools. This uniformity stands against the intent of the Sunna. "The Prophet," al-Hibri asserts, "regarded conditions in the marriage contract as most worthy of satisfaction" (al-Hibri 1992: 235). In fact in many Arab countries, the husband still has repudiation rights over his wife. The extent to which the Shari'a rules, despite attempts at reform by some of the more liberal countries, is evident. Egypt, Lebanon (the Sunni population), and Syria, countries that accept the right of the wife to initiate divorce – albeit under strict conditions – nevertheless continue to uphold the husband's right to repudiation (Toubia 1994).

In a situation where the wife is able to initiate her own divorce, provided this condition is included in the marriage contract, divorce for her is neither necessarily a gain, nor does it indicate an improved status. Quite to the contrary, she frequently remains the main victim. A divorced woman in a traditional patriarchal society is, to say the least, a missfit. In a society where the discourse on women is framed either in the context of "Woman as sexual being" or in the context of "Woman as male/family honor," virginity remains the most sacred quality imposed on women; a nonvirgin is less than desirable.

Although variations in divorce experiences exist, in many Muslim societies a divorced woman has little, if any, choices to make. In some Arab countries, for example, if she remarries she knows she is entering into a new contract with inferior status. If she remains single, which is often the case as society constructs her fate, her new status will be that of an unfavored member of the community. No matter how mistreated, abused, or victimized she was during marriage, the woman is often blamed for the breakdown of marriage. It is not incidental that popular culture, at least in several Arab countries, has constructed fixed images of the divorced woman. It is perceived that a woman who "breaks" the first marriage is capable of breaking the second; or, had she been fit for marriage she would have not been divorced in the first place!

Breaking up marriages in cultural contexts where dowry or bride price (*mahr*) is a significant part of the contract, renders women not only socially undesirable, but perhaps in danger of being abused or even, in some cases, killed. Pakistan provides a case in point. Various reports indicate that a woman suffering sexual abuse by her husband or a member of her marital family rarely finds support from her own family. As one report states,

> Marrying a woman off involves a significant financial commitment which makes her relatives committed to making sure that she remains with her husband. Furthermore, a woman's leaving her husband's house or exposing what is seen as a private matter between husband and wife is seen as a source of shame to her family...A common social response to a woman who leaves her husband's home is that she is a bad, incapable or dangerous woman and that other women related to her must have the same qualities.
>
> (Special Bulletin 1995: 47–8)

Moreover, divorce becomes particularly poignant in Muslim countries because of the role, or rather, the absence of the role of the state in this arena. The inability of the state to act in favor of divorced women, by devising certain mechanisms, such as shelters, protection rights and means of survival for women on their own or when with children, may be interpreted as a result of the power of the religious institutions. However, there is evidence that supports the claim that the state can, under specific conditions, curb the power of the religious institutions. The Egyptian crackdown on al-Azhar is just one example. The state's reluctance to take responsibility for family or domestic issues that have implications on gender relations can be better explained in the patriarchal or neo-patriarchal nature of most of these states. Lack of interference, which in this case means keeping a tight lid on a potentially revolutionary force – the women – helps maintain the status quo. It is not incidental that so far no Muslim country has had the courage to officially and legally deal with issues of domestic sexual abuse, incest, or rape. To date, while some Muslim states, such as Pakistan, sanction "killings for honor," known otherwise as *karo kari* crimes, many Muslim states are complacent when it comes to "honor killings."

Changes in family codes or personal status laws and the consequent changes in women's status in the family and in society, must simultaneously occur in both the structural and cultural realms. While structural changes can lead to legal changes, ideological and legal changes can also influence social relations. Changes to the Divorce Act in India provide a case in point. Pressured by women's demands and the concern that Muslim women were converting to other religions in order to attain the divorces denied them under the existing Muslim personal laws, the ulema in India pushed for the passing of the Dissolution of Marriages Act (Chhachhi 1991: 160). Similarly, the firm stand on family or personal status laws adopted by the consecutive Tunisian governments, no doubt, has had an empowering effect on the improved status of women in this country.

Conclusion

The above analysis on family laws in Muslim countries has demonstrated that a diversity of Islams and a multiplicity of laws, regulations, and rules prevail throughout the predominately Muslim countries. This chapter has argued that despite attempts at homogenizing Islam by both the outside forces of the Orientalists and the inside forces of the fundamentalists, Islam is a diverse and complex ideology.

Specifically, this chapter has undertaken a critique of feminist legalistic opportunism as a means to analyze the complexity of family laws in the Middle East. It has attempted to expose the potential dangers of employing this approach, arguing that while its emphasis on legalities provides an important and useful tool for analysis, it risks an overemphasis on the legal aspect while neglecting other important issues. Rather, this chapter has contended that state initiated laws, as well as Islamic or Shari'a laws, are heavily influenced by social, economic, political, and cultural factors. The state can play a crucial role in maintaining, reproducing, or even abolishing repressive laws against women. The reluctance of most Muslim states to do so must be located in the ability or inability of the state to represent its citizens as a sovereign state. The background of patriarchy together with the economic and political dependency of most of these states on the West, further combined with their ineffective ways of dealing with internal class contradictions, the urban-rural divide, ethnic and religious problems, as well as the increasing danger of political destabilization they face from the Islamist movements, render most Middle Eastern states incapable of protecting even the simplest human rights of their female citizens.

Under relatively stable economic and political situations – very rare in today's Muslim countries – a commitment on the part of the state to liberalize or Westernize the economy can simultaneously lead to openness around social-gender relations through legal changes. Turkey and Tunisia have been clear examples. Yet, when economic crisis and political instability are the lot of a country, neither liberalization, nor attempts at progressive changes can survive – as witnessed, for example, in the unsuccessful attempts at liberalization of economy and laws in the late 1970s by Sadat in Egypt.

It is not insignificant that in the cases of both Turkey's secular laws and Tunisia's most progressive laws affecting women, the personal intervention and commitment of the head of state was involved. Ataturk and Bourguiba were personally involved in encouraging women's rights. While the issue of personality, particularly at the level of leadership, might play a role, the true measure for the success of social-gender changes must be located elsewhere, namely, in the realms of structural and cultural changes. For, despite the success of both Turkey and Tunisia in promoting progressive legal structures, one cannot but observe the vulnerability of both systems in today's international context. Such vulnerability is not the sole work of "outside" forces such as the emergence of strong Islamicist movements. It is also the result of the failure of both governments to accompany the legal changes with concrete structural changes to sustain their economies: rural populations in both countries remained largely removed from the process of change.

Finally, this chapter has asserted that Muslim women must not be seen as passive recipients of their victimization. Through personal agency and organized forms of resistance, women throughout the Muslim Middle East have and continue to resist their subjugation. Women's organizations and feminist activism in the form of centers for women and feminist studies, legal aid to women, counseling on women's legal rights, and a multiplicity of other activities, have mushroomed in the past decade and a half. In addition to local and national organizations, a number of international Muslim women's solidarity organizations and networks have also emerged in the past decade. The Lahore and Paris based network of WLUML is one such organization. Among its aims, WLUML seeks to provide information for women and women's groups from Muslim countries and communities, support women's struggles from within the Muslim countries and communities and make them known outside, and provide channels of communication among women from Muslim countries and communities (Helie-Lucas 1990: 73).

It is nevertheless important to remember that women are not of one class, nor is the concept of gender of a unitary or homogeneous character. While most women may agree on the fact of their lower status in the family and society, they disagree on the means to achieve progress or gender equality. As part of the real world in which they live and work, Muslim women's political activism is influenced by the class and political ideological movements to which they belong. Moreover, family, clan and tribal allegiances can also influence women's activism or lack thereof. Finally, not unlike the heterogeneous movement of feminism in the West, feminism in Muslim countries is also heterogeneous. The two most influential groups are those who struggle for the secularization of family laws, the separation of state and religion, and the eventual democratization of the state, on the one hand, and those who choose the Canon (Quran and Sunna) as their point of reference and orient their struggles and energies toward a reinterpretation of the text, on the other. In either case women's resistance efforts must be accompanied with changes at both the structural-institutional as well as the cultural levels.

Notes

1 For more on the debate about Shari'a courts in Ontario, see http://www.muslimchronicle. blogspot.com/. Last accessed on November 17, 2005. See also "Ontario Bill Bans Faith-Based Tribunals," in Globeandmail.com, November 15, 2005 (http://www. theglobeandmail.com/servlet/story/RTGAM.20051115.wshari1115/BNStory/National/).
2 Translations of the Quran from Dawood (1993).
3 For more on the arguments and rebuttal of this issue see Abdo and Lentin (2002: 1–36).
4 For more on these two organizations see, Women Center for Legal Aid and counseling at http://www.wclac.org. For more on WLUM see http://www.wluml.org/english/ index.shtml

Bibliography

Abdo, N. (1987) *Family, Women and Social Change in the Middle East: The Palestinian Case*, Toronto: Canadian Scholars' Press.

Abdo, N. (1991) "Women of the Intifada: Gender, Class and National Liberation," *Race and Class*, 32 (4): 19–35.

Abdo, N. (1993) "Race, Gender and Politics: The Struggle of Arab Women in Canada," in L. Carty (ed.) *And Still We Rise, Feminist Political Mobilizing in Contemporary Canada*, Toronto: Women's Press.

Abdo, N. (2002) "Eurocentrism, Orientalism and Essentialism: Some Reflections on September 11 and Beyond," in S. Hawthorne and B. Winter (eds) *September 11, 2001: Feminist Perspectives*, Melbourne, Australia: Spinifex Press.

Abdo, N. (2006, forthcoming) *Sexuality, Citizenship and the Nation State*, Syracuse University press.

Abdo, N. and Lentin, R. (2002) *Women and the Politics of Military Confrontation: Palestinian and Israeli Gendered Narratives of Dislocation*, New York: Berghahn.

Abu Hassan, R. (2005) "Jordan," in S. Nazir and L. Tomppert (eds) *Women's Rights in the Middle East and North Africa: Citizenship and Justice*, New York: Freedom House.

Afshar, H. (1994) "Why Fundamentalism? Iranian Women and Their Support For Islam," University of York, Department of Politics, Working Paper No. 2.

Agarwal, B. (1988) *Structures of Patriarchy: The State, the Community and the Household*, London: Zed Books.

Ahmed, L. (1992) *Women and Gender in Islam: Historical Roots of a Modern Debate*, New Haven, CT: Yale University Press.

Al-Hibri, A. (1992) "Marriage Laws in Muslim Countries: A Comparative Study of certain Egyptian, Syrian, Moroccan, and Tunisian Marriage Laws," *International Review of Comparative Public Policy*, 4: 227–44.

Al-Najjar, S. (2005) "Bahrain," in S. Nazir and L. Tomppert (eds) *Women's Rights in the Middle East and North Africa: Citizenship and Justice*, New York: Freedom House.

An-Na'im, A. A (ed.) (2002) *Islamic Family Law in a Changing World: A Global Resource Book*, London: Zed Books.

Azzouni, S. (2005) "Palestine," in S. Nazir and L. Tomppert (eds) *Women's Rights in the Middle East and North Africa: Citizenship and Justice*, New York: Freedom House.

Bannerji, H. (2003) "Demography and Democracy: Reflections on Violence Against Women in Genocide or Ethnic Cleansing," *Resources for Feminist Research (RFR)*, 30 (3–4).

Basha, A. (2005) "Yemen," in S. Nazir and L. Tomppert (eds) *Women's Rights in the Middle East and North Africa: Citizenship and Justice*, New York: Freedom House.

Bellafronto, C. (2005) "Syria," in S. Nazir and L. Tomppert (eds) *Women's Rights in the Middle East and North Africa: Citizenship and Justice*, New York: Freedom House.

Cheriet, B. (1996) "Gender Civil Society and Citizenship in Algeria," *Middle East Report*, No. 198 (January–March): 22–6.

Chhachhi, A. (1991) "Forced Identities: The State, Communalism, Fundamentalism and Women in India," in D. Kandiyoti (ed.)*Women, Islam and the State*, London: Macmillan.

Dawood, N. J. (1993) *The Koran: With a Parallel Arabic Text Translated with Notes*, New York: Penguin.

Deeb, M. (2005) "Oman," in S. Nazir and L. Tomppert (eds) *Women's Rights in the Middle East and North Africa: Citizenship and Justice*, New York: Freedom House.

Dirie, F. (1996) "Female Circumcision and Islam," Seminar presented at the Canadian Arab Women's conference, Toronto, March 1st.

Dworkin, A. (2002) "The Women Suicide Bombers," *Feminista! The Online Journal of Feminist Construction*, http://www.feminista.com/archives/v5n1/dworkin.html (accessed June 15, 2006).

El-Azhary Sonbol, A. (2005) "Egypt," in S. Nazir and L. Tomppert (eds) *Women's Rights in the Middle East and North Africa: Citizenship and Justice*, New York: Freedom House.

Esposito, J. (1982) *Women in Muslim Family Law*, Syracuse, NY: Syracuse University Press.

Gardezi, F. (1990) "Women's Movement in Pakistan," *South Asian Bulletin*, 10 (2): 18–24.

Ghossoub, M. (1987) "Feminism – Or the Eternal Masculine – in the Arab World," *New Left Review*, 161: 3–18.

Hammami, R. (1993) "Women in Palestinian Society," in M. Heiberg and G. Ovensen (ed.) *Palestinian Society: A Survey of Living Conditions*, Oslo: FAFO.

Hammami, R. and Rieker, M. (1988) "Feminist Orientalism and Orientalist Marxis," *New Left Review*, 120: 93–106.

Helie-Lucas, M. A. (1990) "Report: Women Living Under Muslim Law," *South Asia Bulletin*, 10 (January): 73.

Helow, J. (1996) "Women's Court in Beirut," *Middle East Report*, No. 198 (January–March): 18.

Hessini, L. (1994) "Wearing the Hijab in Contemporary Morocco: Choice and Identity," in F. M. Goecek and S. Balaghi (eds) *Reconstructing Gender in the Middle East: Tradition, Identity and Power*, New York: Columbia University Press.

Hijab, N. (1988) *Womanpower: The Arab Debate on Women at Work*, London: Cambridge University Press.

Hoodfar, H. (1991) "Return to the Veil: Personal Strategy and Public Participation in Egypt," in N. Redclift and M. T. Sinclair (eds) *Working Women: International Perspectives on Labour and Gender Ideology*, London and New York: Routledge.

Hoodfar, H. (1993) "The Veil in Their Minds and On Our Heads: The Persistence of Colonial Images of Muslim Women," *Resources for Feminist Research (RFR)*, 22 (Fall/ Winter): 5–18.

Hoodfar, H. (1996) "Reflections on Gender and Religion in the Middle East: Can Muslim Women Be Feminists?" Lecture, Carleton University, March 15.

Hussain, S. and Lyn, W. (eds) (2004) *Honour Crimes, Paradigms, and Violence Against Women*, London: Zed Books.

Joseph, S. (1996) "Gender and Citizenship in the Middle East," *Middle East Report*, No. 198 (January–March): 4–10.

Kandiyoti, D. (1991) "Islam and Patriarchy: A Comparative Perspective," in N. Keddie and B. Baron (eds) *Women in Middle Eastern History: Shifting Boundaries in Sex and Gender*, New Haven, CT: Yale University Press.

Maududi, A. A. (1974) *Purdah and the Status of Women in Islam*, Delhi: Markazi Maktaba Islami.

Mernissi, F. (1986) *Beyond The Veil: Male–Female Dynamics* in *Modern Muslim Society*, London: al-Saqi.

Mernissi, F. (1988) "Muslim Women and Fundamentalism," *Middle East Report*, No. 153 (July–August): 8–11.

Mernissi, F. (1992a) *Islam and Democracy: Fear of the Western World*, Reading, MA: Addison-Wesley.

Mernissi, F. (1992b) *The Veil and the Male Elite: A Feminist Interpretation of Women's Rights in Islam*, Reading, MA: Addison-Wesley.

Mernissi, F. (1993) *The Forgotten Queens of Islam*, Minneapolis, MN: University of Minnesota Press.

Mernissi, F. (1994) *Dreams of Trespass: Tales of a Harem Girlhood*, Reading, MA: Addison-Wesley.

Moghadam, V. (ed.) (1994) *Gender and National Identity: Women and Politics in Muslim Societies*, London: Zed Books.

Mojab, S. and Abdo, N. (eds) (2004) *Violence in the Name of Honour: Theoretical and Political Challenges*, Istanbul: Bilgi University Press.

Najmabadi, A. (1991) "Hazards of Modernity and Morality: Women, State and Ideology in Contemporary Iran," in D. Kandiyoti (ed.) *Women, Islam and the State*, London: Macmillan.

Pargeter, A. (2005) "Libya," in S. Nazir and L. Tomppert (eds) *Women's Rights in the Middle East and North Africa: Citizenship and Justice*, New York: Freedom House.

Perkins, K. J. (1986) *Tunisia: Crossroads of the Islamic and European Worlds*, Boulder, CO: Westview Press.

Sa'adawi, N. (1983) *Women at Point Zero*, London: Zed Press.

Sa'adawi, N. (1988) "The Political Challenges Facing Arab Women at the End of the 20th Century," in N. Toubia (ed.) *Women of the Arab World*, London: Zed Books.

Shalhoub-Kevorkian, N. and Abdo, N. (2005) *The Ordeals of Palestinian women in East Jerusalem*, Women Studies Centre, Jerusalem: Palestine.

Sharabi, H. (1988) *Neopatriarchy: A Theory of Distorted Change in Arab Society*, New York: Oxford.

Special Bulletin (1995) *Women Living Under Muslim Law*, Lahore: Shirkat Ghah.

Toubia, N. (ed.) (1994) *Arab Women: A Profile of Diversity and Change*, New York: The Population Council.

Tucker, J. (1985) *Women in Nineteenth-Century Egypt*, Cambridge: Cambridge University Press.

Veiled Revolution, The (1993) A video produced by Elizabeth Fernea.

Welchman, L. (2003) "In the Interim: Civil Society, the Shari'a Judiciary and Palestinian Personal Status Law in the Transitional Period," *Islamic Law and Society*, 10 (1): 34–70.

Welchman, L. and Hossain, S. (2005) *"Honour": Crimes, Paradigms and Violence Against Women*, London: Zed Books.

Women in Islam (1991) A video, directed by Ahmad Abdul-Rahman, produced by the Islamic Media Services in two parts.

5 Islam and labor law

Some precepts and examples

Karen Pfeifer[1]

Introduction

Labor law officially defines relationships between employers and employees and the formal constraints under which each group operates, such as how much leeway managers have in hiring and firing employees, and how much freedom workers have to organize collectively. These relations are at the core of the productive processes that sustain society. Further, through the presence or absence of specific codes regulating the employment of women and children, labor legislation provides clues to the economic underpinnings of gender and family relations within a country. In reality, the codes may not be fully enforced, or may be enforced selectively by sector or firm size. By the same token, certain unmodified "laws" may operate in practice. However, the formal legislation serves as an indication of the image a government seeks to project to its own citizens and to the international community.

This chapter explores the range of ways in which Islamists define the capital-labor relationship, how those interpretations have influenced the prevailing labor legislation in countries ruled by explicitly "Islamic" regimes, and what influence Islamist movements might have on labor law in predominantly Muslim countries where secular governments now rule.

Islamic precepts about labor relations

Most writing on Islamic doctrine pertaining to labor relations has been generated by adherents of "Islamic economics," in the belief that Islam constitutes a "third path" between capitalism and socialism (Behdad 1992: 77; Pfeifer 1997). By organizing society according to Islamic precepts of fairness and justice, they argue, Islamic economics will avoid the degradation and exploitation of workers, and the vast gaps in wealth that they associate with capitalism, as well as the denial of individual talent and creativity that they ascribe to the communist countries (Mannan 1986: 80–8).

Beyond this general premise, there are considerable differences among "Islamic economists" in their policy prescriptions. In part, this stems from the fact that the texts used to derive their interpretations date from the seventh century and cannot directly address the complex labor issues that arise from contemporary productive processes. In interpreting these texts for the present day, moreover, Islamic economists evidence the same broad range of political points of view, from right to left, and theoretical disagreements, from neoclassical to historical materialist, familiar to western economics regarding property rights, market-based relations, and the capital/labor relationship (Behdad 1994). They contend among themselves over what constitutes an Islamic view of work, how it confers rights and imposes obligations on employers and employees, and on the role of the state in managing these relationships.

Islamic views of work

Anticipating "the Protestant work ethic," Muslims can trace the association between labor and godliness to their own scriptures from several centuries before the Protestant Reformation. In these texts, the sanctity of labor is derived from the belief that all of the earth is God's property, entrusted to mankind to be used for the prosperity and enjoyment of human society (Said 1972: 61). God endowed humanity with creativity in order to extract the fruits of the earth, and, although labor is not one of the five pillars of Islam, work is a duty of all able-bodied citizens and an expression of obeisance to God (Al-Faruqi 1980: 79–80; Abd al-Salam 1992/93: 25–6).

Sloth is frowned upon, and, while Muslims are enjoined to give charity to the poor, Islam discourages begging by those who are able to work (Said 1972: 64; Cummings *et al.* 1980: 42, 229). Furthermore, those capable of working are instructed to seek employment at a distance if none is available locally (Said 1972: 101).

In contrast to the Protestant work ethic, however, which regards work as a religious duty and promotes laborers who "work with the interest of over-satisfying their daily needs for moral, material, and social reasons," Islam encourages moderation in working because it is a mundane concern rather than a spiritual enterprise. It may even be that the Islamic texts meant to ascribe holiness to "*amal*" as good deeds, not "*amal*" as literal work (Bayat 1991: 6, 18–22).

Islam expects employers and employees to treat each other with respect. While capitalism denigrates workers as lacking in intellect and/or initiative, Islam holds that mistreatment of employees will be judged harshly by God, as reflected in the saying of the Prophet (*hadith*), "The owners who mete out evil treatment toward their servants shall find the gateway to Paradise shut in their faces" (Shabon 1981: 274; Moore and Delener 1986: 75). By the same token, employers are not viewed as less productive than, or morally inferior to, workers. Marxism portrays employers as owners of capital who exploit labor while performing no productive work of their own, but Islamist thinkers see employers as managers who contribute special organizational and intellectual skills (Al-Faruqi 1980: 79–81; Moore and Delener 1986: 75; Yusuf 1988: 74–5).

Employers' and employees' rights and responsibilities

Once hired, workers are expected to perform their jobs faithfully and honestly, without stealing from their employers or damaging their property, because *tatfif*, or shirking, as well as theft are moral transgressions. Furthermore, faithful performance will benefit not only their employers, but also society as a whole (Said 1972: 58–61; Mannan 1986: 88–91; Afzal-ur-Rahman 1990: 150–1, 168).

In exchange for workers' diligent labor, Islam imposes obligations on their employers. It prohibits them from forcing their employees to undertake labor against their will, or punishing the workers for equipment damages that are not their fault. Employers may not overtax their employees by extending the working day or requiring labor that exhausts the worker. Workers are entitled to periods of rest during the day, on the weekly Sabbath, and on vacation. Working conditions should be safe from accidents and should not damage the employee's health (Said 1972: 100–2; Chapra 1979: 17; Mannan 1986: 89; Moore and Delener 1986: 75–6; Afzal-ur-Rahman 1990: 151; Abd al-Salam 1992/93: 32; Aziz 1992: 54). Some scholars go further, finding in the Shari'a an obligation for employers to provide their workers with housing, medical facilities, transportation, education, and meals (Said 1972: 85), or to sell them the products of their labor at subsidized prices (Khan 1983: 108). Some consider vocational education to be an employer's obligation, because it enhances the individual's productivity and society's productive capacity overall, and because it connotes a form of respect to the laborer from the employer (Aziz 1992: 48–9; Chapra 1992: 253).

The Islamic texts prohibit the economic exploitation of workers, as Muhammad said that the employer who fails to pay workers their due shall meet the displeasure of God (Chapra 1979: 17; Abd al-Salam 1992/93: 33). However, most Islamic economists reject, implicitly or explicitly, the notion that exploitation is inherent in capitalist labor relations. If the employers pay workers a "just" or "fair" wage, set by mutual agreement through written or oral contract before the work is undertaken, there is no exploitation. It is ambiguous, however, whether a fair wage is equivalent to the average product of labor (Choudhury 1989: 8) or the equilibrium wage that results when demand equals supply, that is the value of the marginal product of labor (Abd al-Salam 1992/93: 33; Aziz 1992: 51–2), or a legally specified price floor.

Yusuf argues that it is the private ownership of natural resources by some which compels others to undersell their labor. Given that the earth's resources belong only to God, all agricultural land, pasture, standing timber, and mineral deposits should be public property, and all individuals would earn a "just wage" if they were able to live from their own labor. A person would agree to be employed by someone else only if the wage offered were greater than what he could earn from his own labor using free resources. The state would not have to impose a minimum wage so long as it ensures equal access to productive resources, and employers would not have to be concerned about the subsistence or comfort of their employees (Yusuf 1988: 74–9).

There is a clear basis in Islam for the promotion of profit sharing. Its roots lie in the ancient system of *mudaraba*, in which one individual supplies the financing for a venture, while the other performs the work, dividing the profits according to prior agreement. Muhammad himself is said to have participated in such arrangements. Islamic economists disagree, however, on how widespread these profit sharing systems should be and on the method of dividing profits. At a minimum, any division of proceeds between owners and workers, even if unequal, would qualify as mudaraba (Afzal-ur-Rahman 1990: 230–3). Or perhaps profits should be divided equally between owners and employees (Said 1972: 68). At a maximum, every firm would be required to share profits, distributing part to workers as a cash supplement to wages, and part to finance workers' necessities such as housing, daycare, and medical expenses (Chapra 1992: 254–5). Indeed, the modern day equivalent of mudaraba might be the cash distribution of profits or employee stock ownership plans, perhaps combined with worker representation in management decision making (Choudhury 1989: 321–4; Aziz 1992: 52–3).

There is no explicit prohibition on the employment of women. On the one hand, Aziz argues, the Quran specifically enjoins employers to hire the person best suited for the job, eschewing discrimination based on gender, race, religion, or national origin. On the other hand, he suggests, women should dress modestly and men should lower their gaze when approaching women (Aziz 1992: 50–1). Furthermore, a woman should obtain permission from her husband or any other male guardian to work, and, Abd al-Salam maintains, Islam proscribes the intermingling of male and female employees and prohibits women from working at night (Abd al-Salam 1992/93: 41).

The role of the state

In Islamic economic theory, the government is charged at minimum with enforcing the rights and responsibilities of employees and employers, however defined. There is debate, though, around whether the state has additional obligations to workers and whether government should regulate collective action by employees.

For example, some scholars suggest that workers may be unable on their own to negotiate a "fair" wage. Employers might voluntarily raise wages in accordance with workers' experience, the cost of living, and the company's profits, through contractual negotiations based on religious precepts (Abd al-Salam 1992/93: 35). Acknowledging that labor market forces might depress wages below subsistence level, both Mannan and Abd al-Salam support government intervention to elevate them, and Chapra and Said explicitly endorse minimum wage laws (Said 1972: 98, 109; Chapra 1979: 17; Abd al-Salam 1992/93: 31, 42–3).

According to Khan, the first four caliphs believed it to be incumbent upon the state to provide a minimum standard of living, including food, clothing, and shelter, for all citizens. By the same principle, a contemporary government must provide medical care and education as well as, in essence, the modern welfare state (Khan 1983: 108). Likewise, Abd al-Salam holds that "the Islamic society is responsible for filling the gaps between workers' wages and the [costs of the] necessities of life" (Abd al-Salam 1992/93: 35) and this was also the position of the Muslim Brotherhood in pre-1952 Egypt (Beinin and Lockman 1987: 377).

The proponents of minimum wage laws generally call for additional forms of government intervention as well. If an individual's duty is to be productive, then it is up to the state to find employment for those unable to do so on their own, or provide them with unemployment benefits and/or vocational training (Said 1972: 75, 103; Chapra 1979: 1, 12, 18; Abd al-Salam 1992/93: 23–7; Aziz 1992: 49–52). Al-Faruqi argues further that Islam's emphasis on production obligates the state to ensure that all necessary work be done. This entails planning, including assigning people in their adolescence to different career tracks, and training them properly for the functions they will ultimately fulfill. As individuals have different talents, an Islamic society should seek to channel individuals into the careers for which they are best suited. Ideally, the faithful would do this willingly, but "the state is empowered to coerce its citizens to undertake the jobs which are necessary for its welfare, just as it is entitled to conscript them into the military for its defense" (Al-Faruqi 1980: 83).

The Shari'a seems to specify that employment be undertaken by contract, with a wage agreed upon in advance, assuming a situation where an individual worker negotiates with a lone employer, typical of the master/servant relations of ancient times. The rub is in translating such precepts into the modern day, where hundreds, sometimes thousands, of workers can perform similar jobs in the same establishment. Perhaps the logical extension of such precepts is to endorse labor unions and collective bargaining. Although some countries claiming to apply the Shari'a, such as Saudi Arabia, outlawed trade unions, the works reviewed here present no textual basis for this prohibition. Muhammad Akram Khan implicitly assumes unions' existence, and both Mannan and Abd al-Salam specify that there is no Islamic injunction against them. Said concurs that Islam does not explicitly prohibit either strikes or lockouts, but argues that, whether initiated by employers or workers, work stoppages impede production and thereby harm society (Said 1972: 106–9; Khan 1983: *passim*; Mannan 1986: 92–4; Abd al-Salam 1992/93: 32).

More generally, clashes between workers and employers are viewed as injurious to the fabric of society, so both parties are expected to strive for amicable relationships and, in upholding Islamic principles, to minimize industrial conflict. This belief led the Muslim Brotherhood in pre-1952 Egypt to actively discourage labor militancy (Beinin and Lockman 1987: 383–4). Where disputes do arise, adherents of this position expect the state to resolve them fairly (Shabon 1981: 275–6). Thus, Mannan maintains that in an Islamic world workers would have no need of or desire for unions (Mannan 1986: 94).

This review of Islamic precepts indicates that there is no uniquely "Islamic" system of labor/state and labor/business relations. Islam clearly promotes the idea that workers be treated "fairly," but the concepts of fairness and justice are so vague, and the modern work environment so different from what was prevalent in Muhammad's time, that there is room for a wide range of diverse and sometimes contradictory interpretations of how the basic texts of Islamic jurisprudence apply to contemporary society. The range is so wide that either a minimalist state or one that intervenes extensively in labor markets can be construed equally well as "Islamic."

Islamic regimes and labor law

Saudi Arabia, Pakistan, and the Islamic Republic of Iran provide three examples of predominantly Muslim states that claim to be organized on Islamic legal principles. They share a worldview that conceives of society as one giant enterprise in which the state, business, and labor cooperate harmoniously to produce the national product, to reproduce the citizenry, and to maintain and enhance social well-being. As in other contemporary "welfare states" at the turn of the twenty-first century, the arrangement often entails programs such as public education that benefit labor and other parts of the citizenry and comprise a kind of "social contract" or "moral economy."

While labor is usually a junior partner, not privy to decision making by the powerful, the state provides these functions not simply to serve capital in an instrumental way (capital using the state to promote its own narrow interests), but rather to promote and protect the system as an integrated structure. In contrast to a developed capitalist economy in which capital can usually control labor through production technologies and labor market mechanisms in order to achieve this, the government in a developing state may have to perform two seemingly contradictory tasks. On the one hand, the state presumes to regulate labor on capital's behalf with a labor code it can enforce through its judicial and policing functions. On the other hand, the state claims to provide protections for workers from the worst vagaries of the labor market, protections like unemployment compensation and social security insurance. These institutions serve to promote social and political quiescence in the short run and to ensure the reproduction of the workforce, and thereby the economy and society, over the long run.

Islamism does not present any specific or consistent agenda for labor policy. Saudi Arabia, Pakistan, and Iran illustrate that an Islamic state can use labor law to tightly restrict the rights of workers to organize their own unions and to exercise forms of protest like the strike. However, Islamism is not synonymous with either etatist economic policies or authoritarian controls on societal groups. There have been periods when Islamism has been associated with more democratic or labor-friendly policies, namely, in Saudi Arabia in the decade after King Faisal came to power, in Pakistan in the years immediately following independence and the first few years under Zulfiqar Ali Bhutto, and in Iran during and immediately after the 1979 revolution. These periods provided broader scope for workers to openly and successfully exercise their organizing and bargaining rights. In general, workers cannot predict whether Islamism will deliver them from their prior oppressors or impose a different oppression.

Similarly, in other countries of the Persian Gulf and Arabian Peninsula, labor organizations and strikes were generally illegal in the late twentieth century. Even where unions were technically legal, namely Kuwait and Yemen (before and after unification), the unions were closely controlled and often suppressed by the government, and strike activity was tightly regulated or even prohibited (Shabon 1981). This did not prevent workers from organizing and even striking illegally, often over political as well as economic issues, but such activity usually called down a harsh and repressive governmental response. In the early twenty-first century, however, as we will see in the following pages, pressures for change, and perhaps some actual changes, seemed to be underway.

The case of Saudi Arabia

In Saudi Arabia, the Hanbali interpretation of the Shari'a is the law of the land, supplemented in the twentieth century by a growing body of legally binding royal decrees to handle those areas of modern life not covered by the Shari'a. The Hanbali school of Islamic thought is relatively laissez-faire in economic policy, allowing wide latitude to private business. However, in Saudi Arabia it was tempered with a paternalistic expectation regarding the government's responsibility toward its citizens' welfare, *maslaha* (Nomani and Rahnema 1994: 150). It assumes that an Islamic economic system is "based on a one-class society rejecting any kind of class struggle or class distinction," where the government is charged with responsibility for warding off class conflict (Shabon 1981: 273–6; Moore and Delener 1986: 76).

In reality, class conflict surfaced quickly in this "classless" society as it was steered by a consortium of international oil firms from a pastoral, agrarian, and trading economy toward contemporary capitalism. The first of a long series of oil-worker strikes took place in 1935. Soon after, the government instituted mechanisms for managing industrial and class relations, and the first formal law governing compensation of workers in the technical (oil-related) sector was decreed in 1937. After many more strikes, the government outlawed both strikes and unions in 1956.

The Saudi Islamic conception of the classless society shapes social relationships between employers and employees and also affects family life directly and indirectly. Religious injunctions about work, the worker's relation to God, and the employer's obligations to the employee are frequently intoned in everyday work life (Moore and Delener 1986: 75–9). Shaw quotes Saudi labor regulations as enjoining "the employer to 'treat his workmen with due respect and refrain from any work or deed that may affect their dignity or religion'" (Shaw 1986: 98). More concretely, in Saudi Arabia it is common for employers to provide nonmandatory benefits to employees, such as payment of bonuses just before the major Islamic holidays, cash loans to workers for a wedding or other special event, and shortened workdays during the month of Ramadan (Shabon 1981: 71).

King Faisal, the oil-cartel-backed "rational reformer," decreed a full-fledged labor code dealing with contemporary capital/labor issues in 1969. The code provided for such modern features as formal labor contracts, paid vacations, regulation of working hours and overtime, safety standards and medical treatment on the job (Shabon 1981: 68; Nomani and Rahnema 1994: 142–3, 151). The code made it legal for women to work, and mandated accommodations for pregnant and breastfeeding women, including medical care, maternity leave, shortened hours of work and time off from work to feed the child during the day. However the same code restricted the hours that women could work, segregated them from men on the job, and ruled them out of some occupations entirely (Council of Ministers 1970: 35–7; Shabon 1981: 74).

The legacy of this Islamic regime for women's participation in society is mixed. Saudi women's educational status improved significantly over subsequent years, with an adult literacy rate of 68.2 percent in 2001 (77.1 percent for all adults), and an enrollment rate of 57 percent in the three levels of school combined (58 percent for the whole of the eligible population). Women's employment also rose to an index of 145 in 2001 from a base of 100 in 1990. However, that absolute 1990 employment base was very small by world standards, so that, even with the seemingly large leap, the female labor force participation rate was just 21.6 percent in 2001, equivalent to 28 percent of the male rate, significantly below Pakistan, Iran, and most other predominantly Muslim countries (UNDP 2003).

At the same time that the labor code was promulgated in 1969, the regime expanded the welfare state and created a social insurance system for its citizens. The high volume of oil revenues in the 1970s and early 1980s provided the largesse with which to fund these benefits, among the most generous of such programs in the Arab World. They were expected to play an important part in further averting labor conflict, providing an additional economic inducement for workers to rely on the government rather than on their own organizations for their welfare (Shabon 1981: 74).

The 1969 labor code specified the mechanisms for adjudication of disputes between employers and employees, giving the edge to employers. One procedure was for binding arbitration by a mediator chosen by the disputants and approved by the ministry of labor. Alternatively, a hearing could be conducted by one of three lower ("preliminary") three-person panels appointed by the ministry of labor, in which two out of the three members had a law degree in Shari'a. After closed deliberations, the announced ruling could be appealed to a High Commission at the national level, made up of appointees of the ministries of labor, commerce and industry, and petroleum and mineral resources. In either procedure, the ministry of labor enforced the ruling. While all these adjudicating bodies were enjoined to make their judgments in accordance with the Shari'a, there was no role for advocates of labor at any point in these proceedings (Shabon 1981: 78–80; Lerrick and Mian 1987: 316–29; Nomani and Rahnema 1994: 151).

The lesser power of labor was also made clear in the code's onerous penalties for union and strike activity. The monetary penalties imposed on *employees* for violations of the labor code ranged from 1000 to 10,000 rials (in the mid-1970s, 3.5 to the US dollar) and possible jail terms ranged from one month to six years. In contrast, the code did not threaten incarceration for *employers* and specified monetary fines ranging from just 100 to 1000 rials for each violation (Council of Ministers 1970: 39–40).

A similar top-down decision-making process governed the determination of the wage structure. There was no advocate of labor, save a representative appointed by the ministry of labor, on the committee that recommended changes in the minimum wage to the Council of Ministers (Shabon 1981: 70). This may explain why the minimum wage was not systematically enforced and why the labor code did not apply to those sectors where it could have made the biggest difference, that is, for low-wage, often casual, workers, mainly in domestic service and agriculture (Shaw 1986: 101; Nomani and Rahnema 1994: 150–1). These two sectors have a high representation of women and foreign workers.

In 1990, about 60 percent of the labor force in Saudi Arabia was non-Saudi (Abdel Jaber 1993: 149). As the 1969 labor code was updated, it did not exclude foreign workers from any of its provisions, except to define what permits and qualifications they needed and to stipulate preference for hiring Saudis whenever possible. The code specified that employees of contractors working under concession (i.e. foreign-owned companies) be treated in the same way as employees of other firms (Council of Ministers 1970: 12, 30).

The situation of expatriate workers was not otherwise highlighted in the labor code, although code violations by employers against them were routine both before and after the code was promulgated. Some discrimination became tied directly to citizenship, such as prohibiting foreign workers from owning real estate, corporate stock, or other commercial property without a Saudi partner, and preventing them from bringing their families to live in Saudi Arabia. Occupational segregation by ethnic group became common, concentrating non-Yemeni Arabs in the professions, Yemenis in the commercial and artisanal trades, and Asians in construction, domestic service, health service work, and other less desirable posts. Even controlling for occupation, however, there emerged a discriminatory sliding scale of wage payments based on national origin: in the late 1980s, a Saudi professional or technical worker was paid 1.4 times as much as a non-Saudi Arab for the same work, or 3.6 times as much as an Asian worker. The ease with which Saudi Arabia expelled up to one million Yemenis and Jordanians during the 1990–1 Gulf crisis, often with great financial hardship to the deportees, bespeaks the insecurity experienced by even the Arab foreign workers (Abdel Jaber 1993: 150–7; Stevenson 1993: 15).

At the turn of the twenty-first century, international groups such as Human Rights Watch continued to criticize Saudi Arabia for the abuse and inhumane treatment of foreign workers, women in particular (Sherry 2004a,b). The reported violations included beatings and rape, forced confinement, sexual slavery, severe overwork, denial of rights to seek legal help from the workers' home consulates, and expropriation of passports, visas, and return-trip plane tickets. Some workers accused of crimes were tried without access to legal defense and were subjected to forced confessions and harsh penalties, including beheading.

After the year 2000, public sentiment in Saudi Arabia began to condemn openly the oppression and abuse of migrant workers, partially on grounds that it is contrary to Islam. As reported by Human Rights Watch, Middle East,

> the kingdom's highest Muslim religious authority, Grand Mufti Sheikh Abdul Aziz Al Sheikh, has already acknowledged that migrants suffer "exploitation and oppression." His comments, published in 2002 in the Saudi daily *Al Madinah*, included the observation that "Islam does not permit oppressing

workers, regardless of religion... As we ask them to perform their duty, we must fulfill our duty and comply with the terms of the contract..." [It is] "illegal and a form of dishonesty" to withhold their salaries or delay payment of wages under threat of deportation. He counseled that Islam prohibits "blackmailing and threatening [foreign] laborers with deportation if they refuse the employers' terms which breach the contract."

(HRW ME, No. E1605, 7/14/04)

Increased recognition of labor rights appeared on the agenda of several Middle Eastern states after the year 2000. Saudi Arabia went so far as to legitimate labor "associations" in 2002, apparently, in part, to improve its relations with the United States. Perhaps Saudi Arabia was also influenced by the example of its close neighbor, Bahrain. In the process of reinventing itself as an international financial and service economy, Bahrain's 2002 labor code fully legalized unions and the right to strike and added protections regarding wages, hours of work, and working conditions. Unlike many other countries in the region, Bahrain had little apparent problem with child labor, and also took active steps to promote the employment of women and reduce discrimination against them. Furthermore, the nongovernmental Bahrain Center for Human Rights had mounted a well-publicized campaign to provide protection to mostly foreign female domestic workers, leading to improved living and working conditions for "the most abused of the work force" (Posusney 2005).

The case of Pakistan

For much of its post-Second World War history, Pakistan's leaders cast its labor policy as "Islamic" and benevolent. Labor organizations had played an important part in the independence movement, and the issue of "Islamic labor policy" was explicitly addressed in the formative years of the Pakistani state from 1947 to 1958. In 1949, the first Pakistani labor conference was opened by Prime Minister Liaquat Ali Khan with a statement proclaiming that the founding Islamic principles of Pakistan impelled the abolition of exploitation and the guarantee of justice to labor. Labor policy in this initial phase officially assured freedom of association for workers and for employers, freedom to "negotiate the terms and conditions of employment," and the right to strike and to lock out, respectively. It also stressed that the main aim of labor policy should be to raise living standards via economic growth and, to that aim, to promote industrial peace (Khan 1994: 55–65, 74). In a speech to the International Labor Organization Conference in Geneva in June 1954, the leader of the Pakistani delegation proclaimed that his country was building a society "where there is [the] widest possible distribution of property and income, where there is no hoarding or usury, and, above all, where duties and responsibilities are taken as a moral trust" (Khan 1994: 79).

The military-led regimes of Ayub Khan and then Yahya Khan, from 1958 to 1971, however, promoted a more pro-business program, stressing economic growth and industrial peace at the expense of the rights and needs of workers. Labor policy was used to suppress "industrial conflict so much that in 1968 it erupted to shake the very foundation of the socio-economic order" (Khan 1994: 56). Militant unionism, strike activity, and political opposition reached a crescendo in 1968. In response, the regime enunciated a "New Labor Policy" in 1969, granting concessions to labor and promising fewer restrictions.

Martial law was ended in 1971 and the election of Zulfiqar Ali Bhutto and his Pakistani People's Party (PPP) to office ushered in a new era ostensibly more favorable to labor. Like his predecessors, Bhutto laid claim to the Islamic tradition as the framework of his "socialistic" policies (Khan 1994: 58). Recognizing that "industrial conflict is inherent in the factory [capitalist] way of production," he posited that the level of conflict could be lowered if the rights of workers to organize and bargain collectively were respected. The emphasis in labor policy shifted back from industrial peace toward "distributive justice," the latter both for its own sake and as a stimulus to productivity growth. Collective bargaining was seen as "a modus operandi of the industrial relations system" and simultaneously "a problem-solving institution" for society (Khan 1994: 56–8).

The Bhutto government's labor policies expressly claimed the objectives of establishing a just social order and giving workers a role in participatory management. To that end, the regime promoted profit sharing and worker participation programs, and saw to it that workers' bargaining power, wages, benefits, and job security improved. However, Bhutto's regime maintained at best a patronizing, and at worst an authoritarian, relationship to labor. The PPP forcibly took over the leadership of unions, while the state security service repressed those labor leaders who resisted, leaving a confused legacy of "Islamic," "socialistic," and repressive labor policy (Nomani and Rahnema 1994: 122).

Another military regime headed by General Zia-ul-Haq came to power in 1977. Reclaiming the mantle of Islam, this regime promoted economic reforms such as the abolition of interest, the introduction of mandatory *zakat* and a land tax, and the establishment of profit-and-loss-sharing procedures in banking. The regime also introduced a more "Islamic" educational system, enforced bans on drinking of alcohol and gambling, imposed the classical punishments for theft, robbery and adultery, and promoted fasting during Ramadan, observance of daily prayers, and modest dress for women (Esposito 1980: 152–5).

Leaving the official labor policy of the Bhutto era on the books, the regime downplayed the "Islamic right" of all participants in an economic activity to be treated justly and paid fairly and emphasized the "Islamic obligation" of all parties, employers and employees alike, to promote the objective of economic growth, based on "the right Islamic attitude to work and property" (Kennedy 1990: 63; Khan 1994: 57–9). During the period of martial law from 1977 to1985, "Islamism" was then used to justify circumvention of those features of the labor law favorable to labor, especially the ability of unions to be recognized and to bargain collectively. Some employers successfully refused to recognize union agency, and others persuaded the government to restrain or forbid strike activity and even to ban unions altogether, such as in television and radio broadcasting. There were mass firings in some public sector companies such as Pakistan International Airlines (*Far Eastern Economic Review* 1986: 63–4).

By 1990, Pakistan had a relatively well-developed and well-organized workforce by developing world standards. About 2.5 million people, or 20 percent of the labor force, worked in industry, and 40 percent of industrial workers belonged to unions (United Nations 1994: 162). The strongest unions were in the public sector, particularly in textiles. However, this potentially great strength was diluted by the anarchic structure of the union system. Unions were organized by enterprise, not by industry, there was often more than one union per enterprise, and bargaining was conducted locally between a union and its individual enterprise. The individual unions (8,300 of them in 1986) were grouped into a large number of federations. The eight largest federations encompassed about two-thirds of total union membership, but competed fiercely among themselves. The union movement seemed to have no clear political strategy, as evidenced by their member unions' complex alliances with right, left, Islamic, or mixed political formations (*Far Eastern Economic Review* 1986: 63–4).

Observers expected a return to the more pro-labor practices of the earlier years after the lifting of martial law and restoration of elections in the late 1980s (*Far Eastern Economic Review* 1986: 64). Benazir Bhutto's first electoral success promised an "Islamic welfare state." This promise was repeated by her successor, the business leader Nawaz Sharif, and then again by Benazir Bhutto in her second term, even as their administrations directed resources toward promoting private enterprise rather than a new labor policy or new welfare initiatives (Khan 1994: 59). Furthermore, the beneficial aspects of the labor-policy legacy from earlier regimes came under attack from the world financial community during the structural adjustment program of the 1990s, similar to the experience of many other countries in Asia, Africa, Latin America, and the Middle East in that era (Nomani and Rahnema 1994: 121–34). Measures such as privatization of public enterprises, for example, threatened to abrogate job security provisions in the Pakistani labor law by lifting restrictions on the employer's ability to fire workers.

Pakistan's record on human development and human rights undermines its claim to a moral economy based on Islamic principles. Although the economy of Pakistan had grown at a relatively fast pace until 1990, and its basic structure had shifted toward industrialization, it did so with a slower-than-average improvement in human development, a pattern that may explain the sharp decline in growth after 1990 (Easterly 2003). Pakistan's real income per capita rose by a total of 41 percent in the decade 1980–90 but by just 15 percent from 1990 to 2000, while its score on the human development index (HDI) rose from 0.372 in 1980 to 0.453 in 1990 to 0.499 in 2001, scores consistently below those of India and Sri Lanka, and slightly above those of Bangladesh. In 2002, however, even Bangladesh pulled ahead of Pakistan in HDI scores (0.509 vs. 0.497, respectively), as Bangladesh' school enrollment improved while Pakistan's actually fell from 41 percent of eligible population in 1995 to 37 percent in 2002 (UNDP 1992, 1997, 2002, 2004). In 2002, Pakistan remained the only country in South Asia, and one of only a handful of developing countries, where education was not compulsory.

The legacy of "Islamic" regime policy toward women was mixed. Women's educational status was still low in 2001, with female adult literacy at just 28.8 percent (as compared to 44 percent for all adults) and 27 percent of females (36 percent overall) enrolled in school, all levels combined. However, women's labor force participation rate was 35.8 percent, with an index of female employment at 125 in that year (up from the base of 100 in 1990), equivalent to 43 percent of the male rate (UNDP 2003). These literacy and education figures are much below those of Saudi Arabia, Iran, and the other countries discussed in the last section of this chapter, but the labor force participation figures are significantly above those of Saudi Arabia and Iran, and about equivalent to those of Egypt.

This seemingly anomalous pattern – a rise in women's employment combined with a fall in society-wide educational attainment – may be explained by the partial liberalization of the economy in the 1990s during structural adjustment. With liberalization, the key textile industry shifted from import-substitution to export-promotion, and unorganized low-paid female workers replaced the organized male workforce previously covered by the labor code. One of the consequences appears to have been exacerbation of the apparently severe and widespread employment of un- and undereducated children.

Pakistan was criticized by human rights organizations in the 1990s for its continued oppression of workers and its widespread use of child labor, a problem that certainly exists elsewhere (see the section on Iran), but that seems to be more acute, enduring, and politically intractable in Pakistan. Children are often sold into bondage by their impoverished parents, and work for low pay in occupations as dangerous as welding, scrubbing the inside of oil tank trucks, and sewing leather products like footballs. A "strike against privatization, for a minimum wage, and for the abolition of contract and child labor" in early 1995 was followed a few months later by the murders, in rapid succession, of the president of the union federation that organized the strike, a 12-year-old leading children's rights activist, and a union organizer in the Muslim Commercial Bank Ltd. (Jabeen 1995; Bokhari 1996).

Despite laws regulating child labor (1991) and outlawing bonded labor (1992), plus pressure from western purchasers of Pakistani products and government investigations of these murders, child labor remained widespread in 2002, especially in the brick-making and carpet-weaving industries. One hopeful response was a transition program undertaken by the government with foreign aid to take children out of work for five to six hours per day to attend nearby informal schools (Garrels 2002). If successful and universal, such programs would serve to promote both human and labor rights, although they still would not end child labor.

The case of Pakistan illustrates the flexibility of Islam in serving as the framework for various, and sometimes contradictory, socioeconomic or labor policies. Zulfiqar Ali Bhutto was a modern secular social democratic politician until he came to power in 1971. Then he began advocating the "Islamisation of the country" in order to promote his "socialistic" economic and political agenda.

While Bhutto was criticized for using and abusing Islam to these ends (Esposito 1980: 160), so too was General Zia-ul-Haq criticized for using and abusing Islam to promote a pro-business social and economic agenda unfavorable to many other groups in Pakistan.

At of the turn of the twenty-first century, Pakistan had failed to furnish an example of an Islamic system that consistently provides for "the abolition of exploitation and the guarantee of justice to labor" as promised at the first labor conference of independent Pakistan in 1949. It continued to struggle to provide a clear sense of what constitutes a contemporary "Islamic" state (Khan 1994: 70–9). As Esposito summed it up for an earlier period, so it still was in 2002 that "beneath Pakistan's Islamic and nationalist rhetoric and terminology is a vacuum, an unresolved identity crisis which promises to be a source of continued unrest" (Esposito 1980: 160).

The case of Iran

Prior to 1979, Iran was ruled by an authoritarian monarchy, which, as in Saudi Arabia, exercised close control over labor and industrial relations. However, the Pahlavi monarchs, first Reza Shah and then his son Mohammed Reza Shah, were more secular in orientation than the monarchs in Saudi Arabia and used the state more actively to lead industrial development. After the restoration of the Shah to power in the 1953 coup d'etat following a two-year period of nationalist rule, his regime promoted rapid industrial development with the participation of direct foreign investment (Bayat 1987: 22–4). The majority of manufacturing firms remained very small, but by 1979 state-run enterprises were responsible for more than 70 percent of employment in large industrial firms (those having ten or more workers) and 79 percent of industrial output (Rahnema 1992: 74).

The working class, though fragmented by ethnic and other fissures, grew in tandem with industry, so that by 1978 more than half of the economically active population had become wage workers and one-third of the total labor force were working in industry (Bayat 1987: 25–6; Rahnema 1992: 75–81). Workers and their organizations seem to have played a major role in all the political transformations of Iran in the twentieth century and were just as frequently curbed or outlawed. As early as 1921, for example, workers organized a trade union federation that was soon suppressed. A similar and larger federation emerged in the 1940s, was suppressed, and then resurged under the nationalist government, only to be banned again when the Shah was reinstated. With the promulgation of a new labor code in 1959, unions were made legal again, but were kept tightly under the regime's control (Rahnema 1992: 71).

The Shah's regime sought simultaneously to win workers over with a paternalistic provision of benefits and to intimidate workers who might challenge its authority. In the 1960s and early 1970s, the Shah offered grand promises of much higher wages for everyone, universal employer-provided housing, profit sharing, and employee-stock-ownership schemes (Ladjevardi 1985: 237–46). While secular, the regime's conception of the relationship between workers and employers was reminiscent of Saudi Arabia's. It held up "the idea of a community founded upon the cooperation of all its members (workers, bosses, state agents)," with the addition, when ideology did not suffice, of manipulation of union leadership and the threat of dismissal (or worse) to keep workers cooperating with the management (Bayat 1987: 60). This labor policy was consistently similar to its Saudi counterpart in strictly prohibiting both political and strike activity (Bayat 1987: 59–60).

Despite an oppressive legal apparatus, Iranian workers engaged in both political and strike activity against the Shah's regime, and mounted a successful general strike in 1978 (Moghadam 1996: 81–4). During the emergence of the revolutionary movement in the late 1970s, and especially in the fall of 1978, local strike committees evolved into a new form of labor organization, the *showra* or workers' council. The councils became an important vehicle at the production site for mounting economic resistance and fomenting the political struggle for the overthrow of the Shah (Bayat 1987: 77–81; S. Rahnema 1992: 71–2).

In the period immediately following the revolution of February 1979, the councils restored production in those firms where the owners or managers had fled and pressed their demands for improved conditions and worker control in those firms where management remained (Bayat 1987: 100–7). Even though the economy contracted between 1979 and 1980 and production fell, wages continued to rise. Leftist organizations and intellectuals played an important role in this process, and May Day of 1979 represented the pinnacle of their influence, a grand celebration of the breadth and strength of the council movement and the unity of the workers in their contribution to the revolution (Moghadam 1996: 82–7).

However, as the Islamic regime consolidated its control of the new republican state, the secular and left-wing leaders of the councils were removed, at first by political means and later by more violent methods, and the councils became Islamicized, that is, taken over by Islamic Republican Party (IRP) operatives (Moghadam 1996: 86–7). With the purging of the left-wing and liberal secular allies of the IRP from the national political structures in the summer of 1981, independent workers' organizations were crushed and the workers' councils were replaced by "Islamic Associations" composed of management, selected workers' representatives, and appointees of the government (Ladjevardi 1985: 246–54). This represented effectively an "Islamic" reincarnation of the authoritarian approach to managing labor prevalent under the erstwhile Shah's regime. Once again, labor policy was to be enforced by a combination of Islamic ideology, paternalistic promises of benefits, and suppression of dissent (Bayat 1987: 183–90, 1991: 72–88).

In the national political sphere, especially in the new parliament of the Islamic Republic, the first few years evidenced a tendency for the alleged "Third Way" of an Islamic economy to dissolve into the left-right debates common to virtually all contemporary societies regarding capital-labor relations and the role of the government in the economy (Zubaida 1989; Valibeigi 1993; Behdad 1994). In the context of the war with Iraq, 1980–8, with its great loss of life and social wealth, this debate resulted in a stalemate that crippled the economy. Economic stagnation and the weakening of labor's bargaining power were exacerbated by the regime's shifting of resources out of modern industry. The 1986 census indicated that the industrial labor force had declined as a proportion of the total labor force, while unemployment, self-employment, the share of the informal economy, and income inequality all rose (Moghadam 1996: 88–92).

The debate over a new labor law, first proposed in 1982, did not escape the class conflict implicit in the larger debate over the direction of the economy. The core argument focused on whether Islam allows only a one-to-one contractual relationship between an employer and an employee, in which no government intervention is needed because the former is simply renting something from the latter, or whether Islam enjoins the government to intervene in this relationship to set the minimum conditions for the contract and to protect the employee (Bayat 1987: 185, 192).

The proposed labor code included the standard interventionist clauses on working age, working hours, social insurance, and paid leave, and included some improvements, like a limited unemployment compensation provision and a modest social security system. But this code placed new restraints on female employees, and prohibited labor's right to form independent unions or to strike. Under this code, all non-Islamic labor organizations from the pre- and post-revolutionary era were to be dissolved and "state-run Islamic labor councils and Islamic societies [associations] constitute the only legal labor organizations" (Nomani and Rahnema 1994: 174–5).

The new labor code was finally enacted in 1990. It conformed in important ways to ILO recommendations regarding employment contracts, working conditions, occupational safety and health, wages and benefits, and mechanisms for settling disputes. It also recognized workers' right to organize, but only in the form of "Islamic associations" and "Islamic labor councils" supervized by the Ministers of Interior and of Labor and Social Affairs (Islamic Republic of Iran 1990; Moghadam 1996: 88).

Some students of contemporary Iran have argued that not only had the "Third Way" of the Islamic economy disintegrated into the same old two-way, capital/labor class struggle, but also that the predominant power for the foreseeable future had shifted to capital, that in this case Islamism did not end class exploitation but came to legitimize it (Moore 1992; Vakili-Zad 1992; Parvin 1993). In the context of global pressures for economic liberalization in the 1990s, which even Iran could not escape, the laissez-faire policy advocates appeared to gain traction (Nomani and Rahnema 1994: 169–72, 182–4).

The legacy of the Islamic Republic's policy toward women was mixed. In the early 1990s, Iran passed legislation entitling women to wages for labor in the home and requiring husbands to pay them prior to a divorce. Though derived from the Islamic texts and consistent with the Islamic Republic's civil and constitutional codes, the law was controversial within the religious community (Kar 1996: 37). Women's educational status improved under the Islamic regime, with female adult literacy at 70.2 percent in 2001 (compared to an overall adult literacy rate of 77.1 percent) and 63 percent of women (64 percent overall) enrolled in school, all levels combined. Women's employment index rose to 137 in 2001 (from a base of 100 in 1990), but the female labor force participation rate was just 29.5 percent, equivalent to somewhat more than one-third of the male rate (UNDP 2003).

As in Pakistan, Iranian and international human rights organizations continued to struggle with issues of child labor into the twenty-first century. The 1990 labor code raised the minimum age for employment to 15 years (up from the 12 years decreed in the 1958 code), and restricted access to the more dangerous and unhealthful jobs for 15–18-year-old workers. However, like earlier codes, it exempted children who work in their own ("first class") family workshops or in other domestic labor, and had no enforcement mechanism to curb routine abuse by informal employers of bonded child laborers. As of 2002, these children were working in activities as diverse as shoemaking, tailoring, garment sewing, glassware manufacturing, food packaging, and construction (*Andisheye Jameah* 1999: 4).

Working children were typically from "refugee" families who recently migrated to Tehran from the rural areas and provincial towns, and who were taken out of school in order to supplement the family's income. In running away from impoverished families and abusive employers, these children often took to living in the city streets. Because of their own desperation, or because of what they were "taught" in their workplaces (where narcotics were commonly used to keep them awake at their jobs during the night), they would become criminals and drug addicts too socially disabled to return to school even if they were caught and placed in rehabilitation centers. As the (female) psychiatrist at one of these centers put it, "it seems that leaving school is one of the main factors that encourages children to work ... (and) it seems that there is [a] relation between nature of profession and crime in children" (*Andisheye Jameah* 1999: 5).

Some nongovernmental organizations attempting to help the street children estimated that there were 35,000 in Tehran alone in 2005. A director (also a woman) of one such organization, The House of Children, argued that if the NGOs did not do this work, the government's efforts would be totally unsuccessful. Government officials claimed that they were supporting the work of these NGOs, but agreed that the Islamic Republic needed to do much more to solve this deep social problem (Unger 2005).

Islamic movements and labor law changes

Saudi Arabia, Pakistan, and Iran illustrate that what might be labeled as "Islamic" labor law can vary widely from country to country and from era to era, subject to the particular constellation of Islamic and other forces in, or contesting for, power. The cases that follow involve countries in which Islamist movements had a powerful political presence by the turn of the twenty-first century, having developed significant, if not lasting, alliances with their respective labor movements in the process. While none of them had come to power as of 2005, they too provide evidence that there is little consistency in the relationship between political

Islamism and the promotion or protection of the interests of labor. Egypt will be described in some detail because of the explicit and high profile political alliance between the Islamist movement and the socialist labor party there.

The case of Egypt

As of the year 2000, Egypt's labor law, Law 137 of 1981, was predicated on the notion of a benign, interventionist, welfare state like that established by the regime of Gamal Abdel Nasser in the 1950s and 1960s. It was supplemented by special codes that privileged workers in the public sector, where the laws were more consistently enforced than in the private sector. Taken together, these laws constrained employers' ability to fire individual full-time, permanent workers, and prohibited mass workforce reductions without the express permission of the government. Public sector workers enjoyed other privileges as well, most notably access to public housing in the large industrial centers, and women found better opportunities and conditions in the public sector than in the private sector.

The status of women had improved significantly in Egypt in the 1980s and 1990s, albeit from a very low base. Female literacy in 2001 was just 45 percent (as compared to 56 percent for all adults), but female gross school enrollment was 72 percent in that year (76 percent overall), ahead of Saudi Arabia, Pakistan, Iran, and Morocco, but still behind Tunisia and Jordan (UNDP 2003). Women workers had fared relatively well in the public sector, where there was no formal discrimination and no wage disparity by gender, until structural adjustment led to the shrinking of government employment. While more than a third of women were in the labor force in 2001 (45 percent of the male rate), and their employment level had increased by 17 percent in the previous decade (UNDP 2003), the female unemployment rate was four times that of men by 2004 (Posusney 2005).

Organized labor, with its core strength in the public sector, successfully staved off several efforts by the regimes of Anwar Sadat and Hosni Mubarak to liberalize the economy and privatize the public sector in the 1970s and 1980s. Egypt's trade unions finally agreed to support the privatization legislation designed by the regime in 1991 (law 203) with the proviso that all firms sold under the auspices of this law continue to abide by the existing labor legislation, and subsequent sales agreements contained clauses guaranteeing that the firms' workforces would not be reduced (Posusney 1992, 1995a).

However, economists and the multilateral lenders promoting Egypt's structural reform, mainly the International Monetary Fund and the World Bank, objected that these restrictions undermined the privatization program, in particular, by making public enterprises less desirable for purchase, and were a general obstacle to private sector development (Posusney 1995b). Within a few months, the government responded to these pressures by commissioning another body to secretly renegotiate the labor law. The participants included representatives of the Egyptian Trade Union Federation (ETUF), business organizations, the Ministry of Labor, the legal community, and the International Labour Organization (ILO), which provided funding for the endeavor (Freeman 1992; al-Hilali 1994: 10–11).

Proposed changes to labor law

The proposed new law was typical of the "flexibilization" of labor markets being promoted throughout the Middle East and North Africa (MENA) region, especially in countries undergoing structural adjustment programs supervized by the IMF and the World Bank (Posusney 1995b). It proposed to give employers far greater leeway in hiring and firing, changing job assignments, using "temporary" labor, and downsizing the workforce according to "economic conditions." It gave managers greater leeway to set lower wages and cut benefits for new hires, and undermined the annual cost of living adjustment to the national minimum wage.

The 1981 legislation had required that employers consult a tripartite committee representing management, unions, and the Ministry of Labor before firing a worker and allowed dismissed employees to appeal its rulings and still be paid. The new legislation changed the composition of the committee to include judges who were more likely to side with employers and eliminated ongoing salary payments (Al-Muhami 1994: 20). Finally, in an explicit quid pro quo for the "right to fire," the draft law recognized labor's right to strike for the first time since 1952, but only under restrictive and tightly controlled conditions.

The alliance between the Islamists and the socialists

The changes proposed to labor law in the 1990s engendered widespread and sustained public criticism of the Mubarak regime, including from the Islamist movement. This marked the first time since the 1940s that Islamist forces had played a significant and public role in the dialogue about labor law. Some Muslim Brothers had been involved in the labor controversies that developed during the initial year of Free Officers rule in 1952–3, but, after their widespread arrest and imprisonment in the 1950s, they laid themselves low for several decades, and, in fact, appeared to ignore workers as an organizational category (Posusney 1997: chaps 1, 2).

In the 1980s and 1990s, the Islamists concentrated their organizing efforts among the well-educated urban professional middle class. The base of the mainstream "Islamist trend" became the doctors, dentists, engineers, lawyers, pharmacists, and university students, among others of the "young professional underclass," or "lumpenelite," who were disenchanted by the forced contraction of the welfare state, disappointed by the decline of employment opportunities, and alienated by the corruption and authoritarianism of the Mubarak government (Wickham 1997: 122–3). To this base, the Islamist trend offered alternative institutions for the essentials of contemporary middle-class life: housing, healthcare, life insurance, libraries, business training, kindergartens, and after-school programs. The Islamists presented "a new sense of civic obligation and a new perspective on their own capacity to effect social change" (Wickham 1997: 124). Without confronting the state directly, the Islamists offered a more egalitarian and democratic model of leadership, raised the call for "civil liberties" and the "rule of law," and worked to build a constituency for evolutionary political change, but all under the umbrella of an Islam that harked back to the ideal society of the "four rightly guided caliphs" (Wickham 1997: 130–2).

The election of Islamists to leadership positions in the professional syndicates allowed them to function like a political party in the 1980s, but they did not yet serve as proactive organizers of labor unions or advocates for labor vis-à-vis employers and the state. However, in 1987 the Muslim Brotherhood (*al-ikhwan al-muslimin*), or at least its left-leaning wing, broadened its strategic objectives to reach out to organized labor and the working class in general. The Islamists entered into an alliance (*tahaluf*) with the Socialist Labor Party (SLP – *hizb al-amal al-ishtiraki*, hereafter SLP), and contested both parliamentary and trade union elections. By April of 1994, the party's newspaper (*al-Sha'b*) and its other propaganda came to reflect the views of these "mainstream" Islamist forces.

The SLP publications criticized the authoritarianism of the state and its failures to meet the needs of the Egyptian people. The alliance did not have a full and clear alternative program for economic reform, but it was effective in challenging the program required of the government as part of its structural adjustment compact with the international financial institutions in the 1990s. When the alliance learned of the existence of the clandestine labor law commission, the SLP exposed details of the secret negotiations, formed "committees for the defense of workers' rights" in industrial areas, convened a labor conference to denounce the draft law, and then published a thorough critique, entitled *la li-qanun al-amal al-muwahhid* ("No to the Unified Labor Law") (Al-Sakhawa 1994).

The alliance's critique was similar in logic to that of the more left-leaning Islamist thinkers discussed in the first section of this chapter, supporting an interventionist state that takes primary responsibility for preserving social peace, regulating the private sector in the interests of society, and providing protection for labor against unemployment, illness, and industrial injuries. The alliance opposed those features of the draft law that would cause unemployment, treat labor as a commodity, favor employers' interests over those of employees in hiring and retention of workers, and give a "free hand to exploitative capitalists." Contrary to the notion that trade union activity is "un-Islamic," the alliance objected to provisions in the labor law restricting the right to strike, and denounced the president of the trade union federation for his corruption and malfeasance for his role in the clandestine labor law meetings (Al-Sakhawa 1994).

Beyond opposing the flexibilizing provisions in the proposed law, the alliance argued for extending protections for workers in the existing law, such as those that made firing more difficult for employers. Arguing that an Islamic society must ensure that workers' take home pay is sufficient to support their families, the alliance not only opposed provisions that allowed employers to lower workers' wages because of "economic circumstances," and that let the real value of wages, including the minimum wage, shrink due to inflation, but also called for the application of international standards for overtime pay (Al-Sakhawa 1994).

Despite this common rhetoric, significant differences remained between the secular socialists and the Islamists in the alliance. The socialists were angered that Islamist allies elected to union office neither initiated mass struggle around labor issues nor supported labor protest generated by others. In one dramatic example, the Muslim Brotherhood condemned a 1989 occupation by workers at the Helwan Iron and Steel plant that was brutally suppressed by the Egyptian government. Their magazine, The *Banner of Islam* (*luwa' al-islam*) warned of the social dangers of labor militancy and praised the role of the police in suppressing the protest. This was the main reason why numerous Islamists who had captured union office in 1987 lost their seats in the 1991 elections (Al-Shafi'i 1994: 203, 206–9). Furthermore, while the two movements seemed to share a belief in an interventionist welfare state, the Islamists did not share the socialists' fundamental hostility to capitalism. Whereas the socialists were opposed in principle to the privatization of public enterprises, the Islamists argued only for the imposition of certain conditions on the sales (Posusney 1995a, 1995a,b).

The alliance between the secular left and the Islamists served both parties' strategic goals in the 1990s. On one side, the socialists were defending the status quo ante that had been molded by Gamal Abdel Nasser into a moral economy, especially for workers in the public sector. The attraction of the alliance for the SLP was that Nasser's emphasis on reciprocal rights and responsibilities between workers and the state seemed to have underpinnings in Islamic notions of fairness and justice, which had lent his heritage legitimacy and broad popular appeal. On the other side, it was not politically feasible for the Islamists to gain credibility among Egyptian workers by going with the flow of liberalization and challenging the established Nasserist understanding while the latter were enduring the pain of structural adjustment. Rather, their recasting of Islamic precepts about labor relations to conform to the Nasserist moral economy lent them legitimacy, in turn, as a coherent opposition force.

However, the alliance withered as both the Muslim Brothers and the SLP suffered the full blast of the government's power in the late 1990s. Dozens of Muslim Brothers were arrested in those years, while the SLP was subjected to a blistering government-initiated media campaign. In the year 2000, the government's Political Parties Committee "froze" all of the SLP's activities, including the publication of its newspaper (Stacher 2001; Brownlee 2005). The new "flexibilized" labor law, encompassing most of the provisions the alliance had contested, was then passed in 2003 without much opposition. Neither the Islamists nor the socialists achieved their strategic goals in the 1990s, as their opposition was outmaneuvered by the ruling party and overwhelmed by the institutional power of the authoritarian state under Hosni Mubarak. Their alliance had been one of strategic opportunity, not of common principle.

Other cases from the Arab world

In other countries, as in Egypt, it was the increasing pressure for flexibilization in the labor market by authoritarian governments pushing "economic reform" that occasioned the strategic drawing together of the Islamist movement and organized labor. In no case did the Islamists actively mobilize to help protect organized labor from flexibilization or to defend the right to bargain collectively. As in other cases examined earlier, the outcomes of these alliances and struggles were due largely to the political dynamics internal to each country (Alexander 2000), not to Islamist leadership or to pressures from "globalizing" processes such as free-trade agreements or signing on to the conventions of the International Labor Organization. In fact, in all the countries that have undergone flexibilization so far, including Egypt, Jordan, Tunisia, and Morocco, violations of these conventions, and even of the countries' own constitutions regarding civil, human, and labor rights, remain routine (Posusney 2005). Islamic morality and politics seem irrelevant to these practices.

The case of Jordan is similar to Egypt in so far as the Islamist movement focused on penetrating the professional syndicates, not the labor unions, and appealed to the educated middle class as opposed to the working class. The most vocal political work of the Islamist-led syndicates was not to promote an alternative economic agenda, but to criticize the authoritarianism of the state and its acquiescence in the US-supported Israeli military occupation of the Palestinian Territories. In March 2002, during the Israeli takeover of Jenin on the West Bank, the Islamists organized large and well-publicized demonstrations by the syndicates and university students, surrounded by riot police who used water cannon on the student demonstrators spilling over campus boundaries.

Jordan was also similar to Egypt in having made a peace treaty with neighboring Israel in 1994. It was rewarded with a free-trade agreement with the United States that allowed products from Jordan's special enterprise zones along the border to be exported to the United States duty-free as long as they could be labeled with a minimum of "Israeli content." A flexibilized labor law accompanied the free-trade agreement in 1996, formally entailing a "right to strike, right to fire" trade-off similar to Egypt's. But the flexibility went to the employers, while labor's rights to organize remained tightly controlled, along with civil liberties and freedom of expression (Posusney 2005).

Jordan had one of the best records in the Middle East on human development, with an HDI rank of 90 in 2001. Women have a literacy rate of 85.1 percent (compared to 90.3 percent of all adults) and a gross school enrolment rate of 78 percent (77 percent overall) (UNDP 2003). However, one of the government's responses to political pressure from the Islamist movement was to adopt Shari'a as the shaping force for the law of the land. This has not been to women's advantage, as it has been interpreted to mean that women need their husband's approval to work outside the home. Despite Jordan's well-educated female population, the female labor force participation rate was just 21.7 percent in 2001 (about one-third that of males), partly due to women being squeezed out of employment in the shrinking public sector. In 2002, female unemployment was 22 percent, as compared to 14 percent for the men, and women made up a large majority of those working for subminimum wages, for example in the enterprise zones (Posusney 2005), all too reminiscent of the situation in Morocco.

Labor law was made more flexible in Morocco in 2003, and the outcome of the negotiations around the law's provisions led to better results for organized labor than elsewhere. The new law prohibits antiunion discrimination, and, uniquely among Arab countries, allows competitive unionism. This outcome seems to be related to Morocco's peculiar political history, in which the state never provided the "moral economy" bargain with labor or developed the institutions that tightly governed labor and the workplace under a Nasserist regime such as in Egypt. This left the labor movement more independent and even attracted Islamist tactical penetration and influence in the late 1980s and early 1990s (Alexander 2000: 485).

The new Moroccan law did not, however, improve the situation of female workers. Their labor force participation rate is the highest in the Arab World, at 41.6 percent (52 percent of the male rate) (UNDP 2003). However, they are concentrated in industries, especially in production for export, where discrimination is the rule. Women make up 95 percent of the workforce in the textile industry, where most are paid less than minimum wage, forced to work overtime for no pay, and provided with no maternity leave or social security benefits (Posusney 2005). Women's situation is worsened by Morocco's poor record on human development, among the worst in the Arab World, although not as poor as Pakistan's. Only 37.2 percent of Moroccan adult females were literate in 2001 (as compared to 49.8 percent of all adults), and female gross school enrollment was 46 percent (as compared to 51 percent overall) (UNDP 2003).

In Tunisia and Algeria, Islamist alliances with organized labor were based on strategic assessments of opportunities for challenging the state's authority in the 1980s and early 1990s (Alexander 2000: 468). Aiming not for fundamental economic transformation, but rather for evolutionary change that would allow them to enter the political power structure as partners with the existing elite, the Islamists had no truck with socialist ideas of classes or class struggle, or with the working class as an actor in the historical transformation of society (Alexander 2000: 468–9). During certain periods, the Islamists allied with the labor movement briefly and superficially, to "use labor as a bargaining tool" in the Islamist strategy to be recognized by the state. For example, it was rare for the Islamists and the labor movement to coordinate their political actions, such as strikes, in order to achieve economic ends. But for their part, workers would vote for Islamists if they were convinced that the Islamists would protect their interests and promote greater distributive justice, that is, if they would promote the material and secular interests of the working class (Alexander 2000: 486–7). This is reminiscent of the relation between the Islamists and organized labor in Iran in the aftermath of the 1979 revolution.

As in Egypt, the alliances between the Islamists and organized labor in Tunisia and Algeria soon faded. Tunisia adopted its flexibilized labor code in 1996, similar to the case of Jordan, with enhanced employer rights to hire and fire at will, but with continued state controls on the right of workers to organize and strike. As of 2002, most of the benefits promised to labor, such as unemployment insurance, had not yet been implemented. Tunisia had long been a leader in human development in the Arab World. In 2001, it ranked ninety-first on the human development index, just behind Jordan. For women, there was still a long distance to go, as female literacy in 2001 was 62 percent (compared to 72 percent for all adults), but female gross school enrolment had reached a par with that of males at 76 percent. As women crowded into growing labor-intensive export industries, the female labor force participation rate rose to 37 percent in 2001 (almost half of the male rate), lower than Morocco's but higher than that of Egypt and Pakistan and other countries in our sample (UNDP 2003).

As of 2004, Algeria was still resisting the tide of "flexibilization" and had made a formal commitment to gender equality in employment. However the female labor force participation rate in 2001, at 30 percent (40 percent of the male rate), was much lower than those of Tunisia and Morocco. Its record on human development was weaker than Tunisia but much better than Morocco. Female literacy was 58 percent (as compared to 68 percent of all adults), but gross female school enrollment had improved to 69 percent in 2001 (71 percent overall) (UNDP 2003). Algeria, like all other countries under pressure to continue liberalization and flexibilization, must soon endure a shrinking of public sector employment, where women workers had fared best, and a loosening of labor protections that these "adjustments" regularly entail. As elsewhere, the government is also under pressure from the Islamist movement to adopt Islamic law. If it does so, probably more in regime self-defense than by religious principle, as in Jordan, this in turn may mean the overriding of its legal commitment to non-discrimination by gender (Posusney 2005).

Conclusions

Islamist movements and governments claiming an Islamic mantle have left an inconsistent legacy in regard to labor rights. In the cases examined here, Islamic precepts regarding labor are open to competing interpretations. Some offer workers little or no protection from the vagaries of the capitalist labor market, while others support a high degree of government regulation of business, guaranteeing employment with at least a minimum living wage, protection from overwork and/or arbitrary dismissals, and the provision of basic social services. Yet others offer pro-labor laws on the books but do not enforce them. The rights of female labor, child laborers, and foreign workers are the least well-respected in many cases, and the rights of women workers seem to be more threatened, and in new ways, as they get squeezed between "economic reform," on the one hand, and the political influence of certain Islamist movements, on the other.

An abstract Islamic framework does not provide clear and consistent rules for constructing labor law or building a successful labor movement. Nor can labor rely on paternalistic politicians, no matter how well intentioned or how imbued with moral or religious precepts, to protect their interests for them. The way for workers to assure that labor law effectively promotes their welfare is to be organized in independent unions, Islamist or not, with an overarching political strategy and economic agenda appropriate to their specific conditions in a particular society at a given time in history. Their struggles against employers and/or the state help to shape the overall political/ideological environment in which Islamist forces operate. When Islamist forces come to power, a labor movement can effectively influence the direction of social change only if it retains its own organizational integrity and only when its alliances with those forces have embodied an explicit mutual commitment to a coherent common agenda. Labor cannot rely on faith alone.

Note

1 The author would like to acknowledge the original contributions of Marsha Pripstein Posusney as coauthor of "Islam, Islamists, and Labor Law," in Sohrab Behdad and Farhad Nomani (eds) *Islam and Public Policy, International Review of Comparative Public Policy* 9 (1997: 195–223), and in providing unpublished information for this paper on changes in labor law in the Arab World in the early years of the twenty-first century.

Bibliography

Abd al-Salam, J. (1992/93–H. 1413) "Haqq al-Amal fi al-Islam," *Majallat al-Mu'amalat al-Islamiyya*, 1: 13–45.

Abdel Jaber, T. (1993) "Inter-Arab Labor Movements: Problems and Prospects," in S. El-Naggar (ed.) *Economic Development of the Arab Countries*, Washington, DC: International Monetary Fund.

Afzal-ur-Rahman, M. A. (1990) *Economic Doctrines of Islam*, volume 1, 3rd edn, Lahore: Islamic Publications Ltd.

Alexander, C. (2000) "Opportunities, Organizations, and Ideas: Islamists and Workers in Tunisia and Algeria," *International Journal of Middle East Studies*, 32 (4): 465–90.

Al-Faruqi, I. R. (1980) "Islam and Labour," in I. R. Al-Faruqi (ed.) *Islam and a New International Economic Order: The Social Dimension*, Geneva: International Institute for Labour Studies.

Al-Hilali, A. N. (1994) *Hatha al-Mashru' Lan Yamirr*, Helwan, Egypt: Dar al-Khidamat al-Niqabiyya Bihilwan.

Al-Muhami, S. S. A. (1994) "Al Harika al-'Ummaliyya wi al-Nidal al-Qanuni," *Al-Badil*, August: 20.

Al-Sakhawa, M. (1994) *La li-Qanun al-'Amal al-Muwahhid*, Cairo: n.p.

Al-Shafi'i, U. (1994) "Al-Quwa al-Siyasiyya w'al-Intikhabat al-Niqabiyya al-Ummaliyya," *Al-Harika al-Ummaliyya fi Ma'rakat al-Tahawwul*, Helwan: Trade Union Services Center.

Andisheye Jameah (a monthly magazine) (1999) "Labor Law and Child Rights in Iran" 7, December: 3–21, http://www.netiran.com/php/artp.php?id=947

Aziz, A. (1992) "Firm Level Decisions and Human Resource Development in an Islamic Economy," in E. Ahmed (ed.) *Economic Growth and Human Development in an Islamic Perspective: Proceedings of the Fourth International Islamic Economics Seminar, Issues in Contemporary Islamic Thought*, Herndon, VA: The International Institute of Islamic Thought.

Bayat, A. (1987) *Workers and Revolution in Iran*, London: Zed Books.

Bayat, A. (1991) *Work, Politics, and Power: An International Perspective on Workers' Control and Self-Management*, New York: Monthly Review Press.

Bayat, A. (1992) "The Work Ethic in Islam: A Comparison with Protestantism," *Islamic Quarterly*, 36 (1): 5–27.

Behdad, S. (1992) "Property Rights and Islamic Economic Approaches," in Jomo K. S. (ed.) *Islamic Economic Alternatives*, London: Macmillan.

Behdad, S. (1994) "A Disputed Utopia: Islamic Economics in Revolutionary Iran," *Comparative Studies in Society and History*, 36 (4): 775–813.

Beinin, J. and Lockman, Z. (1987) *Workers on the Nile: Nationalism, Communism, Islam, and the Egyptian Working Class, 1882–1954*, Princeton, NJ: Princeton University Press.

Bokhari, F. (1996) "Pakistan to Crack Down on Child Labor," Institute for Global Communications," July 26, http:// www.hartford-hwp.com/archives/52/013.html

Brownlee, J. (2005) Private communication with Karen Pfeifer.

Chapra, M. U. (1979) *The Islamic Welfare State and its Role in the Economy*, Leicester, UK: The Islamic Foundation.

Chapra, M. U. (1992) *Islam and the Economic Challenge*, Herndon, VA: The International Institute of Islamic Thought, Islamic Economics Series, 17.

Choudhury, M. A. (1989) *Islamic Economic Co-operation*, New York: St. Martin's Press.

Council of Ministers, Kingdom of Saudi Arabia (1970) *Labor and Workmen Regulations*, Dhahran: Arabian American Oil Company.

Cummings, J. T., Askari, H., and Mustafa, A. (1980) "Islam and Modern Economic Change," in J. Esposito (ed.) *Islam and Development: Religion and Socio-Political Change*, Syracuse, NY: Syracuse University Press.

Easterly, W. (2003) "The Political Economy of Growth without Development: A Case Study of Pakistan," in D. Rodrik (ed.) *In Search of Prosperity, Analytic Narratives on Economic Growth,* Princeton NJ: Princeton University Press, 2003.

Esposito, J. (1980) "Pakistan: Quest for Islamic Identity," in J. Esposito (ed.) *Islam and Development, Religion and Sociopolitical Change*, Syracuse, NY: Syracuse University Press.

Far Eastern Economic Review (1986) April 3: 63–4.

Freeman, R. B. (1992) "Labor Market Institutions and Policies: Help or Hindrance to Economic Development?" *Proceedings of the World Bank Annual Conference on Development Economics*, Washington, DC: World Bank.

Garrels, A. (2002) "Report on Child Labor in Pakistan," National Public Radio, *Morning Edition*, Febuary 13.

Islamic Republic of Iran (1990) *Labour Code*, November 20, in ILO, *National Laws on Labour, Social Security and Human Rights*, http://www.ilo.org/dyn/natlex/docs/ WEBTEXT/ 21843/64830/E901IRN01.html

Jabeen, S. (1995) "Child Labour, in Human Bondage," *Pakistan Trade Union Defence Campaign Bulletin*, 1 (November 17), http://www.hartford-hwp.com/archives/52/015.html

Kar, M. (1996) "Interview," *Middle East Report*, No. 198, January–March: 37.

Kennedy, C. H. (1990) "Islamization and Legal Reform in Pakistan, 1979–1989," *Pacific Affairs* 63 (1) (Spring): 62–77.

Khan, A. H. (1994) "Pakistan," *International Encyclopedia of Labor Law*, Supplement 159 (June): 46–281.

Khan, M. A. (1983) *Issues in Islamic Economics*. Lahore, Pakistan: Islamic Publications Ltd.

Ladjevardi, H. (1985) *Labor Unions and Autocracy in Iran*, Syracuse, NY: Syracuse University Press.

Lerrick, A. and Mian, Q. J. (1987) *Saudi Business and Labor Law*, 2nd edn, London: Graham and Trotman.

Mannan, M. A. (1986) *Islamic Economics: Theory and Practice*, Cambridge, UK: Hodden and Stoughton.

Moghadam, V. (1996) "Making History, But Not of Their Own Choosing: Workers and the Labor Movement in Iran," in E. J. Goldberg (ed.) *The Social History of Labor in the Middle East*, Boulder, CO: Westview Press.

Moore, J. M. (1992) "The Iranian Revolution Revisited," in C. Bina and H. Zangeneh (eds) *Modern Capitalism and Islamic Ideology in Iran*, New York: St. Martin's Press.

Moore, R. M. and Delener, N. (1986) "Islam and Work," in G. S. Roukis and P. J. Montana (eds) *Workforce Management in the Arabian Peninsula: Forces Affecting Development*, New York: Greenwood Press.

Nomani, F. and Rahnema, A. (1994) *Islamic Economic Systems*, Atlantic Highlands, NJ: Zed Books.

Parvin, M. (1993) "On the Synergism of Gender and Class Exploitation: Theory and Practice Under Islamic Rule," *Review of Social Economy*, LI (2): 201–16.

Pfeifer, K. (1997) "Is There an 'Islamic Economics'?" in J. Stork and J. Beinin (eds) *Political Islam*, Berkeley, CA: University of California Press.

Posusney, M. P. (1992) "Labor as an Obstacle to Privatization: The Case of Egypt, 1974–87," in I. Harik (ed.) *Privatization and Liberalization in the Middle East*, Bloomington, IN: University of Indiana Press.

Posusney, M. P. (1993) "Irrational Workers: The Moral Economy of Labor Protest in Egypt," *World Politics*, 46 (1) (October): 83–120.

Posusney, M. P. (1995a) "The Political Environment of Economic Reform in Egypt: The Labor Movement vs. Privatization Revisited," *Amsterdam Middle East Papers*, No. 2, September.

Posusney, M. P. (1995b) "Egypt's New Labor Law Removes Worker Provisions," *Middle East Report*, no. 194/5 (May–August): 52–3, 64.

Posusney, M. P. (1997) *Labor and the State in Egypt: Workers, Unions, and Economic Restructuring*, New York: Columbia University Press.

Posusney, M. P. (2005) Private communication with Karen Pfeifer.

Rahnema, S. (1992) "Work Councils in Iran: the Illusion of Worker Control," *Economic and Industrial Democracy*, 13 (1): 69–94.

Said, H. M. (1972) *The Employer and the Employee: Islamic Concept*, Karachi: Dar Al-Fikr Al-Islami.

Shabon, A. (1981) *The Political, Economic and Labor Climate in the Countries of the Arabian Peninsula*, Philadelphia, PA: Wharton School.

Shaw, P. F. (1986) "Saudi Arabian Manpower Requirements," in G. S. Roukis and P. J. Montana (eds) *Workforce Management in the Arabian Peninsula*, New York: Greenwood Press.

Sherry, V. (2004a) "Bad Dreams: Exploitation and Abuse of Migrant Workers in Saudi Arabia," Human Rights Watch: Middle East, HRW Index No.: E1605, July 14: http://hrw.org/doc?t=mideast&c=saudia "Bad Dreams": Exploitation and Abuse of Migrant Workers in Saudi Arabia

Sherry, V. (2004b) "Workers' Hell in Saudia Arabia," *The South China Morning Post*, Human Rights Watch: Middle East, July 24: http://hrw.org/doc?t=mideast&c=saudia Workers' Hell in Saudi Arabia

Stacher, J. A. (2001) "A Democracy with Fangs and Claws and its Effects on Egyptian Political Culture," *Arab Studies Quarterly*, 23 (3): 83–100.

Stevenson, T. B. (1993) "Yemeni Workers Come Home: Reabsorbing One Million Migrants," *Middle East Report*, no. 181 (March/April): 15–24.

Unger, B. (2005) "Iranian Streets Are Full of Children Working Illegally," *Voice of America News*, 7/8/05. http://www.vianews.com/english/2005–07–08-voa22.cf

United Nations Development Program. UNDP (Annual). *Human Development Report*, New York: Oxford University Press.

Vakili-Zad, C. (1992) "Continuity and Change: the Structure of Power in Iran," in C. Bina and H. Zangeneh (eds) *Modern Capitalism and Islamic Ideology in Iran*, New York: St. Martin's Press.

Valibeigi, M. (1993) "Islamic Economics and Economic Policy Formation in Post Revolutionary Iran: A Critique," *Journal of Economic Issues*, XXVII (3): 793–812.

Wickham, C. R. (1997) "Islamic Mobilization and Political Change: The Islamist Trend in Egypt's Professional Associations," in J. Stork and J. Beinin (eds) *Political Islam*, Berkeley, CA: University of California Press.

Yusuf, S. M. (1988) *Economic Justice in Islam*, New Delhi: Kitab Bhavan.

Zubaida, S. (1989) *Islam, the People and the State*, London: Routledge.

6 Commercial law
The conflict in Shari'a and secular law public policy

William Ballantyne

Commercial law is, strictly speaking, merely one aspect of the law of contract, but its volume and the importance of its subject-matter, have elevated it to the rank of an independent branch of the law in general.

(Gutteridge 1949: 34)

A legal tenet is considered to go to 'public policy' (Ordre public: An-nitham Al'Aam) if its purport is to establish a public benefit, be it political or social or economic, touching upon the highest order of society, thus taking precedence over individual benefit...
There is no firm tenet absolutely defining 'public policy' applicable to every age and place, because public policy is a relative matter, thus it is only possible to set a flexible yardstick, viz 'the public weal, going to the highest regulation of society. The application of such yardstick in one civilisation leads to results different from those which we may find in another civilization'.

(Al Sanhuri 1953, Vol. III: 81)

In this particular context of his brilliant comparative jurisprudential study, Al Sanhuri was dealing with the subject under the general heading of 'Validity of the object (objet: Mahall) of the (commercial) transaction in western jurisprudence'. He then went on to consider the position at the Shari'a. It is as well to appreciate at the outset of this chapter, a fundamental difference.

Where, in most Western systems, the law may be refashioned as a result of political considerations, this can never, in theory at any rate, be the case in Islam. For here the law is the eternal blueprint to which the structure of state and political policy must, ideally, conform. As a matter of abstract principle, therefore, Islamic political theory represents the rule of law in its most absolute form. From the provisions of the rigid and immutable Shari's no one, neither the ruler himself nor any official of state, is by privilege exempt.

(Anderson and Coulson 1958: 929)

Thus, in essence, while that essential flexibility to which Al Sanhuri refers may be said to exist in secular legal systems, the same cannot be said of the Shari'a itself where, if any such flexibility is to be found, it must, in view of the religious origin of the Shari'a, be strictly circumscribed; indeed, it may be said that, in regard to immutable basic tenets of the Shari's which stem from the Quran and Sunna, it does not exist at all, other than by recourse to often contentious differentiations of definition. To anticipate what follows, for example, that riba is forbidden, is indeed a great sin is unarguable; however, what riba *is*, has been debated by jurists at great length.

In dealing with public policy in Islam as affecting commercial law, there were, it seems, two possible approaches. The first, and perhaps most obvious, was to examine the matter on an academic or historical basis, by reference to the essential attitude of the ideal Islamic state, or Caliphate as going to public or state policy in the matter of commercial law. The second approach was to treat the subject in the context of the modern world, with examples from contemporary legal systems, their constitution and their codes. As essentially a practicing lawyer, I have without hesitation chosen the second option, although in effect there is little difference between the two, where consideration of the immutable tenets of the Shari'a is in issue. Public policy imposed upon a state, whether the ideal Islamic state as originally envisaged or a modern Islamic state, by the tenets of Islam, hence the Shari'a, necessarily extends to the legislation of such a state and to commercial contracts. Thus, under the Shari'a, we cannot differentiate between public policy, meaning state policy, and public policy or public order (ordre public: *An-nitham Al'Aam*) in commercial contract. The principles are the same.

I shall, in this chapter, use the term 'public policy' to denote those principles of law which go to 'ordre public' or An-nitham Al'Aam and which, being mandatory at the Shari'a, must be applied by a judge applying the law of Islam and cannot be avoided by contract.

Modern Islamic states have had to deal with the very difficult situation of trying to reconcile their religious and, usually, constitutional obligations with the practices of modern commerce. It is here that conflict arises.

It would, of course, be impossible to cover the whole complex of Islamic states world wide. I have thus taken my examples largely from the jurisprudence of the states of the Gulf Cooperation Council (Kuwait, Saudi Arabia, Bahrain, Qatar, the United Arab Emirates – UAE and Oman) with, inevitably, references to Egypt from whose codes and doctrine much that is relevant in the Gulf systems derives. Those states provide an excellent study in microcosm and this is largely due to historical circumstance. All were precipitated with startling rapidity from a condition of virtual tranquility into one where they have been obliged to adapt to and participate in the contemporary commercial and economic world, due, of course, to the sudden cataclysmic creation of wealth derived from oil. These states, and others with them, are all Islamic states whose very constitutions provide for the Shari'a as the, or one of the, principal sources of legislation. At the Shari'a, many of the usual provisions in a modern commercial contract are anathema; at the Shari'a, they offend principles of 'public policy' and, thus, would lead to nullity. Therein lies the conflict. Does an Islamic state, at one end of the scale, pass secular legislation in defiance, or defeasance of the Shari'a; or does it at the other end, continue to pay lip service to the Shari'a whilst in practice ignoring it; or does it adopt a grey middle position and endeavour to make its codes comply as far as possible with Shari'a principles, in a new *ijtihad*?

Therein lies a real and increasing crisis of conscience. Dealing with this problem by reference to the Arab states,

> The problem is that the Arabs have, to a greater or less degree, in wishing to adopt the existing international world of commerce, come face to face with the classic situation: an irresistible force against an immovable object.
>
> As it is not uncommon in these circumstances (not by any means only in the Arab world) the question has been begged on all sides. It will be, to say the least, interesting to see for how long and to what extent this apparent anomaly can continue.
>
> (Ballantyne 1980: 121)

The difficulty was propounded with his customary lucidity by Sir Norman Anderson:

> the Shari'a, or 'canon' law, of Al Islam...still – officially, at least – reigns supreme in Saudi Arabia; that it constitutes only one among severally mutually conflicting sources from which the comprehensive and progressive Kuwaiti codes have been derived; that it still prevails throughout the whole area, largely unchanged, insofar as the 'personal' or family law of Muslims is concerned; and that it is difficult to say whether Saudi Arabia, on the one hand, and Kuwait and Bahrain on the other, will continue to pursue their present line of policy. In all probability, they will; but it is far more difficult to foresee whether the references to the Shari'a which are included in almost all the constitutional enactments in the other States in the peninsular will prove to have been pointers to the law which will actually be applied in matters which are still wholly uncovered by legislation – or, indeed to the way in which the courts will interpret, or fill the lacunae, in those enactments which have already been, or will soon be, promulgated – or whether, instead they will turn out to have been little more than pious acknowledgements of an undoubted religious allegiance.
>
> (Anderson 1980: viii)

Al Sanhuri's general definition of public policy retains validity, but there is a world of difference between what constitutes public policy at the Shari'a and at secular law. Modern commerce, in the secular non-Islamic sense, demands of its laws concepts of public policy different from those enjoined by the Shari'a. It is those differences that must be examined, together with the difficulties caused by them in theory and in practice and how modern legislators have sought to deal with the problem. Commercial law is predominantly a matter of contract. Thus, we examine at the outset the question of the sanctity of contract, the theory that '*pacta sunt servanda*'. Here the path is clear. At the Shari'a, as in secular systems, the binding force of contract is a basic precept. At the Shari'a this emanates from the highest authority. Sura V of the Quran reveals: 'Oh yet who believe, fulfil your contracts (bonds).' Another revelation equally implores the Muslim to observe his obligations: 'Nay, but (the chosen of Allah) is he who fulfils his covenant' (Sura III: 76). There are countless further injunctions as to the fulfillment of obligations, and the Prophet himself commented thereon: 'Muslims are bound by their stipulations/agreements' (Schacht 1959: 139).

All authority emphasises that

> A party to an agreement cannot free himself from his obligations thereunder by his will alone, even if he had resolved such faculty for himself at the time the contract was concluded, unless such stipulation is specifically authorised by the Divine Legislator.
>
> (Abu Zahrah 1938: 218; Mahmasani 1955: 79;
> Al Sanhuri 1953: 50, et seq.; see also *Majallat
> al-Ahkam al-Shari'a* – Definition, Articles 162–5)

Further, the great Hanbali jurist Ibn Taimiyya, in propounding the theory of the sanctity of contracts, opined that transactions not expressly forbidden at the Shari'a are permissible: 'The following rule shall be obeyed: men shall be permitted to make all the transactions they need, unless those transactions are forbidden by the Book or by the Sunna' (Laoust 1948: 167).

It may be fairly submitted that in modern circumstances, this is a view which would be generally accepted. However, even in this light, there are, as will be seen, prohibitions at the Shari'a which affect public policy and would cause severe embarrassment to, or indeed defeat, many modern commercial contracts.

At the Shari'a, therefore, contracts must be performed under Divine sanction; but of what may such contracts consist?

The problem reared its head, inevitably, early in the history of modern international commercial arbitration. In the Aramco Arbitration (*Arabian American Oil Company (Aramco) v Kingdom of Saudi Arabia*, ILR 1958: 27), the arbitrators had no difficulty in holding that the proper law of the concession agreement was the law of Saudi Arabia, which they found to be the Shari'a in the Hanbali school; they had, correspondingly, no difficulty in finding that the rule of *pacta sunt servanda* was strictly applied at the Shari'a. However, when they came to consider the substance of the particular concession contract, they ran into the brick wall of public policy at the Shari'a – had the contract to be interpreted strictly at the Shari'a, many of its provisions must be held to be void. They thus found it necessary to hold that the regime of oil concessions had remained embryonic in Muslim law, and to 'fill the gaps in the law of Saudi Arabia' by resorting to 'world-wide custom and practice in the oil business and industry, world case law and doctrine and pure jurisprudence'. They also managed to hold that all the circumstances of the case demanded that the *lex arbitri* be public international law.

Similarly, in the earlier case of *Petroleum Development (Trucial Coast) Limited v the Shaikh of Abu Dhabi*, Lord Asquith rejected the Islamic law as applied in

Abu Dhabi as not being competent to regulate a modern commercial instrument and, accordingly, applied 'principles rooted in good sense and common practice of the generality of civilised nations – a sort of modern law of nature'.[1]

Further, in *Ruler of Qatar v International Marine Oil Company Limited*,[2] the arbitrator, again, found the law of Qatar to be the proper law of the concession, and to be the Shari'a, Hanbali school, but also found that the latter was inappropriate to govern a modern oil concession. To quote from the Award,

> There are at least two weighty considerations against that view (i.e. the adoption of Islamic law). One is that, in my opinion, after hearing the evidence of the two experts in Islamic law, Professor Anderson and Professor Milliot, there is no settled body of legal principles in Qatar applicable to the construction of modern commercial instruments...I have no reason to suppose that Islamic law is not administered there (Qatar) strictly, but I am satisfied that the law does not contain any principles which would be sufficient to interpret this particular contract...Both experts agreed that certain parts of the contract, if Islamic law were applicable, would be open to the grave criticism of being invalid. According to Professor Milliot, the Principal Agreement was full of irregularities from end to end according to Islamic law applied in Qatar. This is a cogent reason for saying that such law does not contain a body of legal principles applicable to a modern commercial contract of this kind.

In effect, therefore, the Arbitrators in all three of these early arbitrations, faced with the situation that the proper law of the contract, the Shari'a, contained provisions according to which the contract was void – rendering themselves, presumably, *ab initio ex officio* (!) – chose not to apply the proper law. Instead, they invoked outside principles: where provisions of the proper law going to public policy are such as to avoid the contract, substitute another proper law, to avoid a situation of *non licet*! A strange solution, but perhaps inevitable as the only alternative to their packing their bags at the outset, with the dispute between the parties unresolved.

It should be said that were these cases to be adjudicated upon today, the arbitrators would find in both Qatar and Abu Dhabi (now a constituent Emirate of the UAE) modern codes based upon the civil system. Saudi Arabia, however, on the other hand remains in much the same position as before.[3]

The problem inherent in the earlier examples was dealt with by Sir Norman Anderson and Professor Coulson in the following terms, referring to the Shari'a as

> a system of law which attained its formal perfection centuries before the demands of modern technology, finance and marketing were dreamed of...But as we see it, it is preferable to recognise the typical economic development agreement (such as an oil concession) of today, with the detailed terms which the exigencies of the trade and the needs of the two contracting parties commonly dictate, as *sui generis*.
>
> (Anderson and Coulson 1958)

It may be submitted that however much the inherent flexibility of an international arbitration may admit of such solutions, it would be very difficult, to say the least, for a judge in a forum, whose conflict rules dictated the Shari'a as the proper law, to ignore its provisions in this way.

It is now necessary to examine, albeit briefly, provisions of the Shari'a which may be said to be mandatory or going to public policy, after which some practical examples may be examined as to how some states have dealt with the undoubted difficulties.

Overall, there is an ostensible difficulty in that the classical *fuqaha* (jurists) did not endeavour to elicit in the *fiqh* any overall theory of contract; rather, they expounded on the basis of a series of nominate contracts representing those in most common usage. The first difficulty might be, therefore, whether the commercial lawyer is obliged to fit his transaction into one of these categories. We have referred to the opinion of Ibn Taimiyya in this respect. Al Sanhuri wrote

> Thus, what the fuqaha (jurisprudents) maintained of nominate contracts, were only those contracts which formed the majority of transactions during the era, and if civilisation develops other contracts in accord with established principles of fiqh (jurisprudence), such contracts are lawful. The new Iraqi Civil Code is based upon this policy of the Shari'a. Article 74 thereof enumerates the types of contracts in accordance with their objects as set out in Murshid Al Hairan. That is then followed by a general provision, Article 75, as follows:
>
> The contract may deal with any other thing wherein the obligation is not forbidden by law or contrary to public policy or morals.

This principle is generally adopted by other Civil Codes of the Arab countries, and it may be confidently stated that it would now be unlikely that an Arab civil or commercial forum, called upon to apply the Shari'a, would take the restricted view that only if a transaction fell within one of the classes of contract dealt with by the classical jurists, would it be entertainable.[4] Rather, an attempt would be made to extract a basic theory of contractual obligations and apply it to the contract in question. Herein, however, as we have seen, lies the difficulty. Al Sanhuri continues the earlier passage:

> However, the scope of public policy in the Islamic jurisprudence is wider than in western jurisprudence. The prohibition of contracts involving riba, and contracts of qarar greatly broaden such scope in the Islamic jurisprudence and similarly the theory of the associated condition in contract increases the widening of such scope to a great extent. Thus the basic principle in the Islamic jurisprudence is *freedom of contract within the limits of public policy, but the multiplicity of the principles which are considered as going to public policy narrow such freedom.*
>
> (Al Sanhuri 1953, Vol. III: 81,
> emphasis added)

Al Sanhuri then narrowed the main difficulty to the three aspects: riba, *gharar* (risk or uncertainty) and associated conditions. These are difficult to define succinctly in English but may be broadly described as any unjustified accretion and upsetting of the equivalence of the contract – the obvious and most contentious example being the ban on interest on monies lent (riba), the element of uncertainty (gharar) and, where you have extraneous conditions, a multifarity of transactions within one contract.

> You will observe that each of these three matters had a profound effect on detailed provisions to the extent that, in many such, the Islamic jurisprudence distanced itself from the requirements of the transaction. If it were possible to clarify our understanding of these three matters in accordance with the development of civilisation, then much of the reasoning which prevents the Islamic jurisprudence from going along with the requirements of such development would disappear.
>
> (Al Sanhuri 1953, Vol. III: 14)

While it cannot be said that reference to these three matters alone suffices to include all the difficulties inherent in the application of the Shari'a in commercial law, Al Sanhuri's condensation continues to have considerable relevance.[5] The concept of riba alone, embracing as it does in any acceptable definition an absolute embargo on interest on monies lent, or owing, is enough to constitute an insuperable obstacle to modern commercial transactions.

It is not possible in this chapter to analyse in detail the extent of the difficulties imposed even by the three main obstacles mentioned by Al Sanhuri. To highlight their main purport suffices to demonstrate the difficulties, going in effect to invalidity of the object in a commercial contract.

It may be submitted that the main element is that of uncertainty. A judge called upon to apply the Shari'a, would be obliged to listen to considerable argument as to the actual meaning of gharar, riba and extraneous conditions. For the purposes of this chapter, we shall accept that all of these considerations contain severe obstacles to commercial contract. Riba is the one most commonly encountered, having been identified loosely with the prohibition on interest (although it goes much further than that – see Chapter 8 in this volume) and, indeed, being the principle which, bracketed with gharar, has led to the creation of the whole structure of Islamic banking. As the early cases quoted earlier show, it is virtually impossible to envisage a modern commercial agreement which would not contain serious illegalities if construed in the light of Shari'a tenets which are mandatory, under Divine sanction leading to inevitable temporal observance. Can one envisage, for example, any loan agreement which did not contain provisions for interest, or a complicated contract for the supply of weapons, linked to the most complex and diverse financing provisions and with several volumes of conditions, which was limited to one transaction, containing equivalence of prestation (offering)? Such contracts make the early oil concessions look simple indeed. It must be accepted that the uncertainties, difficulties and illegalities exist.

Thus, modern commerce and modern economics are irreconcilable with many mandatory provisions of the Shari'a, much of such policy being of Divine origin. This has inevitably led to a crisis which is not only juridical, but for Muslims, one of conscience. Al Sanhuri's avowed object of drafting the 1948 Civil Code of Egypt with due regard to the requirements of the Shari'a in the hope that gradually the principles of the Shari'a would predominate has been submerged in the sea of conventional economics.

It is now necessary to consider how in practice some of the Arab states have sought to deal with the situation of the 'irresistible force against an irremovable object'. The example of riba will be taken as that most commonly occurring and as constituting, in the context of conventional financing, the most obvious obstacle. Such a study, however superficial, reveals, in the undoubted reassertion of Islamic principles now taking place, the inevitable crisis of conscience.

We first consider the relevance of the Shari'a in the modern commercial laws of the Arab states, which consist, from Morocco in the West to Oman in the East, of 18 jurisdictions. All of them, with the strict exception of Lebanon, are Islamic states whose constitutions provide that Islam is the religion of the state with the Shari'a, in varying degree, as a source of legislation.

Due largely to the genius of Al Sanhuri, who drafted not only the Civil Code of Egypt of 1948 but also subsequently the Codes of Syria, Libya, Iraq and Kuwait,[6] and also provided the monumental civil commentary 'Al Wasit', Egypt has provided the source of codes and doctrines for many of the Arab jurisdictions, and continues to do so. In 1980, the constitution of Egypt, which until then had provided for the Shari'a as *a* principal source of legislation was amended to make it *the* principal source of legislation.[7] This change led to a furor among the judiciary, puzzled as to whether its effect must be to oblige them to apply immediately the strict provisions of the Shari'a, in defiance of the modern commercial legislation and practices prevalent in Egypt. The Egyptian Court of Cassation took the unusual step of circularizing the courts to the effect that no change should be given effect pending clarification (Ballantyne 1986c: 50; Appendix XV). Clarification finally came in the guise of the decision of the Constitutional Court discussed later.

A similar reference to the Shari'a as *the* principal source of legislation is to be found in the Constitution of Qatar. In Bahrain, Kuwait and the UAE it is *a* principal source.[8]

In 1992, Saudi Arabia promulgated its new Constitution, providing in Article I

> The Kingdom of Saudi Arabia is an Arab Islamic state, having full sovereignty: its religion is Al Islam and its constitution is the Book of God Almighty and the Sunna of his Apostle (God's prayers and peace be upon him); its language is Arabic and its capital Riyadh.
>
> (*Umm al Qura*, Official Gazette,
> No. 3397, March 6, 1992)

The sole source of law continues to be Shari'a. Article 45 provides:

> The source from which a *fatwa* [official religious decree] is to be derived in the Kingdom of Saudi Arabia is the Book of God Almighty and the Sunna of his Apostle (God's prayers and peace be upon him): the law shall provide for the set up and powers of the Body of Senior Ulema (jurists) and the Directorate of Scientific Research and *Ifta* [source of fatwa].

And Article 46, 'The judiciary is an independent authority; there is no authority to impose on them, when adjudicating, other than that of the Islamic Shari'a.' And Article 48,

> The Courts shall apply, to matters brought before them, the provisions of the Islamic Shari'a in accordance with the precepts of the Book of God and the Sunna and the laws that are enacted by the Kingdom which are not inconsistent with the Book and/or the Sunna.
>
> (Al Mehaimeed 1993: 30)

Thus, in Saudi Arabia the law paramount remains the Shari'a. 'Regulations' (not 'laws' which are of Divine origin) must confirm to the Shari'a to avoid nullity.

The constitution of the Yemen Republic provides the following:

> *Article 2*: Islam is the religion of the state and Arabic is its official language.
>
> *Article 3*: The Islamic Shari'a is the principal source of legislation.

In Oman, the 'Basic Regulation of the State' (in effect the constitution) provides the following:

> 2 The religion of the state is Al Islam and the Islamic Shari'a is the basis of legislation (Asās Uttashri') (Sultani Decree – 101/96).

This formula is in its choice of wording (Asās) unusual, and, semble could lead to interesting conflicts where, as evidenced by the Egyptian and Kuwaiti cases cited, infra provisions of secular legislation which contravened the Shari'a were challenged as unconstitutional.

We thus find a broad spread of constitutional provisions, ranging from where, as in Saudi Arabia, the Shari'a remains the sole source of legislation and Regulations are valid only insofar as they do not infringe the Shari'a, to where the prescription is of the Shari'a as *the* principal source of legislation (Egypt, Qatar, Yemen), to where it is *a* principal source of legislation (Bahrain, Kuwait, UAE), to where the constitution is silent (Jordan), to where it is the *basis* of legislation (Oman).

The basic question for determination is to what extent can a state, within the ambit of its constitution as the paramount law, legislate in defeasance or defiance of Shari'a principles? In particular, to what extent may a given state legislate to replace those aspects of the Shari'a which are mandatory or go to public policy but which are found to be incompatible, nay irreconcilable, with the commercial and economic interests of the state?

At one end of the scale, in Saudi Arabia, where the Shari'a reigns supreme, the answer is simple. In many cases, notably where riba is involved, commercial necessity turns a blind eye to the difficulty, but this gives no satisfaction to the commercial lawyer required, for example, to give a clearing Opinion on a syndicated loan Agreement. Where such an Agreement was expressed to be subject to Saudi law, it would be 'as full of irregularities from end to end' as were the old Concession Agreements (see earlier) – the solution being, of course, to provide, where possible, for another proper law for the contract, with jurisdiction vested in the courts of the lender and, in addition, assets outside the Kingdom against which any judgment may be enforced (Mallat 1988; Ballantyne 1995).

In other Islamic jurisdictions, the matter must be individually considered in each case by reference to the Constitution in the first place, and then by reference to legislation promulgated downstream from the Constitution. To the Western lawyer – in particular, the Common lawyer – the necessity to go behind the laws 'on the statute book' to look at the constitution appears strange. It is not, however, so strange in jurisdictions where there are Constitutional Courts and where the actions of the executive and even the constitutionality of legislation can be, and are, challenged.[9] Two examples suffice to illustrate this.

We have referred to the furor caused by the change in the constitution of Egypt in 1980. The question that immediately arose was whether such a deliberate change in the prescription of the Shari'a from '*a*' to '*the*' principal source of legislation, immediately obliged the judiciary to have regard to the Shari'a, in defeasance of existing provisions in the laws which were contrary to the Shari'a. Here, our prime example of *ribawi* (based on riba) transactions provides a convenient yardstick.

The matter came to a head in 1985 in *Rector of Al Azhar University v The President of the Republic, The President of the Council of Ministers, The President of the Legislative Committee of the People's Assembly, and Atef Fouad Goudah* before the Supreme Constitutional Court of Egypt.[10]

The essence of the dispute went to the constitutionality of Article 226 of Al Sanhuri's Civil Code of 1949. That Article provides that

> If the object of the obligation is a sum of money of a known quantity, and if the debtor is late in repaying it, then the debtor is obligated to pay the creditor interest at the rate of 4 percent in civil matters and 5 percent in commercial matters by way of compensation for the delay.

The Plaintiff pleaded that this text was contrary to the absolute prohibition of interest in the Shari'a, which prohibition must be immediately applied having regard to the change in the Constitution.

The lower court of Egypt, in application of that Article, had ordered Al Azhar to pay an amount of 592 Egyptian pounds *plus interest*, at the rate of 4 per cent until date of payment, pursuant to Article 226. The Plaintiff argued that although the jurists differed in some details, they were practically unanimous in condemning interest as riba.[11] Thus, in the light of the change in the constitution, Article 226, which offended against the Shari'a in this respect, was now unconstitutional.

It will be appreciated that the significance of this case went far beyond its immediate substance. Had the Court agreed with the basic proposition of the Plaintiff, this would not only have rendered Article 226 unconstitutional but would also have had the same effect upon many further provisions of the Civil Code, the Commercial Code and generally the secular commercial laws (in particular, the banking laws) of Egypt. It would, in effect, have decreed the paramountcy of the Shari'a and the illegality of interest, with corresponding repercussions through the Islamic world. There can be little doubt that the Constitutional Court adverted to such weighty considerations in formulating its judgement.

In any event, the Court found no need to contribute to the great debate on riba. The Court based its judgement upon the principle of non-retroactivity, deciding that the amendment to the Constitution should not be given retroactive effect.

In its judgement, the Court referred to the 1979 Report of the Committee on the amendment to the Constitution:

> It enjoins on the Legislature to have recourse to the rules of the Shari'a in its quest for the rule of law which it is seeking, to the exclusion of any other system of law and in case it does not find in the Shari'a a clear ruling, then it should apply the approved methods of deducing legal rules from the authorised sources of endeavour in Islamic jurisprudence. These may help the Legislator in making a ruling which does not contradict the principles and general framework of the Shari'a.

The Court found that this principle was to be followed in future legislation but that the change in the constitution did not cover former legislative enactments. The Court quoted with approval further extracts from the Report, which are worth quoting here in full:

> The Constitution of 1971 was the first constitution in our modern history which explicitly provided that the Shari'a is *a* principal source of legislation. Then later on, the Constitution was amended in 1980 so that the Shari'a becomes *the principal source of legislation. This amendment* means that *it is no longer possible in future to enact any legislation which contradicts the rulings of Islamic law. It also means that it is imperative to review the laws which were in effect before the application of the Constitution of 1971 and to amend these laws, in such a manner as to make them conform to the principles of Islamic law.*

(Emphasis added, see Note 10)

The Report of the General Committee goes on to say that

> The departure from the present legal institutions of Egypt, which go back more than one hundred years, and their replacement in their entirety by Islamic law require patient efforts and careful practical consideration. Hence, legislation for changing economic and social conditions which were not familiar and were not even known before, together with the innovations in our contemporary world and the requirements of our membership in the international community, as well as the evolution of our relationships and dealings with other nations – all these call for careful consideration and deserve special endeavours. Consequently, the change of the whole legal organisation should not be contemplated without giving the law-makers a chance and a reasonable period of time to collect all legal materials and amalgamate them into a complete system within the framework of the Quran and the Sunna, and the opinions of learned Muslim jurists and Imams...

Thus, the Court decided that

1   The change to the constitution did not affect existing legislation; however
2   All legislation enacted thereafter must conform to Shari'a principles, otherwise it would infringe the constitution; and furthermore
3   Such finding did not free the Legislature from responsibility with regard to existing enactments, but imposes on it the duty of purifying them of principles which infringe the Shari'a.

If anything, therefore, this important judgement highlighted the dilemma of the 'irresistible force against the irremovable object', without suggesting any compromise solution: the existing social and *a fortiori* commercial and economic structure in Egypt requires ratione materiae, secular laws which offend against the Shari'a; public policy at the Shari'a, reflected *a fortiori* since 1980 in the Constitution, requires the abrogation of such laws. The conflict continues.

The Constitutional Court of Kuwait, at its session on 28 November 1992, issued an important judgement touching upon Article II of the Kuwaiti Constitution of 1962, which provides that the Shari'a is *a* major source of legislation. The point at issue was the legality under the Constitution of Articles 110 and 113 of the Kuwaiti Commercial Code which provide for the charging of interest. The Court, after reciting the paramount nature of the Constitution and the necessity for ensuring always that the legislation had complied therewith said

> The second Article of the constitution provides: The religion of the State is al Islam and the Islamic Shari'a is a principal source of legislation and the passage in the Explanatory Memorandum to such provision reads: This Article does not limit itself in its limitation that the religion of the state is al Islam, but also that the Islamic Shari'a – meaning the Islamic fiqh – is a principal source of legislation, and in thus providing and directing the legislator to a basic Islamic approach without precluding him from giving effect

to principles and other sources in matters in which the Islamic fiqh does not lay down any provisions, or where it is approved to develop such provisions with regard to giving effect to the necessities of natural development with the passage of time: in the provision, for example, which permits the adoption of modern penal laws together with the *hadd* punishments of the Islamic Shari'a, all of which would not be acceptable if it were said 'and the Islamic Shari'a is *the* principal source of legislation' in that *the requirement of such a provision would also make it illegal to take from any other source on any matter dealt in by the Shari'a*, which subjects the legislator to an extreme dilemma where practical necessities move him to pause before accepting as obligatory the view of the Shari'a fiqh in some matters, in particular e.g. regulations going to companies, insurance and banks and loans and Islamic punishments etc... It should also be noted in this connection that provisions set out in the Constitution, that 'The Islamic Shari'a is *a* principal source of legislation' *only imposes upon the legislator a trust to adopt the Islamic Shari'a to the extent possible* and summons him expressly and clearly to such a path, thus the said provision does not preclude the adoption, sooner or later, of Shari'a provisions in toto in all matters if the legislator is of such opinion: this indicates that the constitutional directive to the legislator in the second Article aforesaid, in the light of its constitutional interpretation, is a political directive to the legislator to adopt the provisions of the Shari'a as far as possible for him to do so, considering them as a substantive source from which to deduce the legal principles to be applied by him in matters put to him and further, that they are not an official source for the law – otherwise there would have been an express provision to that effect. Furthermore, *the provision of the aforesaid Article in the form which provides 'a principal source' without providing that it be 'the principal source' has the effect of making the Islamic Shari'a a material source from among other sources of legislation without being the sole source*: thus, this effect of the constitutional provision is not to oblige the legislator to be limited in his choice of principles of legislation to the Islamic Shari'a alone, so that there is nothing which prevents him from drawing such principles from sources other than the Islamic Shari'a which he deems suitable for the requirements of the moment, without thereby falling into the position of contravening the Constitution, whereby the judge thus becomes obliged to apply it.

The Court accordingly gave judgement:

As a result of the foregoing, whereas the foundation of this appeal is contravention by Articles 110 and 113 of the Commercial Code of Article 2 of the Constitution, based on the contention that the provisions of these two Articles contravene the Islamic Shari'a, which is created by Article II of the Constitution as *a* principal source of legislation – in that the said Article, as explained above, does not preclude the adoption of principles of legislation from sources other than the Islamic Shari'a., so as to nullify them because their provisions are in conflict with the Islamic fiqh – *whatever may be the opinion of the Islamic fiqh*, it is not acceptable. Thus judgment must issue not to accept the constitutional argument put forward.

(Ballantyne 1986c: 50 et seq.
Emphasis added throughout)

Here the Court, in a very tautologous judgement, virtually adopted the official commentary to the Constitution: the Shari'a was merely prescribed as *a* principal source; thus, the legislator has considerable freedom. If, however, the provisions were for the Shari'a as *the* principal source, the result would be otherwise. This reasoning would seem to be at variance with that of the Supreme Constitutional Court of Egypt. Although the reasons for not upsetting existing legislation were very different in both cases, the effect of the more restrictive wording of the Constitution was given virtually the same construction. (See, for example, the position in Saudi Arabia and the constitutions of Qatar and Yemen.)

It is interesting to compare here that part of the Commentary to the Civil Code which deals with Custom, as another prescribed source of law in Kuwait:

Customs (*aadat*) which contradict the social, political, economic or moral principles upon which the community rests, can never be elevated to Custom (*urf*) even if of long duration: *in a country such as Kuwait, whose religion is by the Constitution Al Islam it is not possible that anything which contravenes one of the bases or established precepts of Islam should constitute Customs.*

(Ballantyne 1986c: 52 et seq.
Emphasis added)

Thus, semble, express legislation may contravene the Shari'a; Custom may not. What, then, of Custom which becomes codified in legislation?

Against the foregoing constitutional backdrop, it remains to consider some of the formulae adopted by states in prescribing their sources of law, with examples of how these mandatory provisions of the Shari'a have been dealt with in legislation. In so doing, we shall continue to concentrate upon riba as constituting perhaps the most intractable of the Shari'a principles in this respect, while again recognizing that even riba, wide ranging as it is in its effect, does not have a monopoly of difficult in this context.

Downstream from the Constitutions, we find prescriptions in the various codes of the sources of law upon which the judge is to rely in formulating his judgement.

In Egypt, the Civil Code provides the following:

Provisions of law govern all matters to which these provisions apply in letter or in spirit.

In the absence of a provision of law which is applicable, the judge will decide according to custom and in the absence of custom in accordance with the principles of Moslem law. In the absence of such principles, the judge will apply the principles of natural justice and the rules of equity.

In Kuwait, the Civil Code gives preference to express legislation, failing which 'the judge gives judgment in accordance with the dictates of the Islamic Jurisprudence (fiqh) most in accord with the morality and interests of the country in the absence of which according to custom.'[12]

In Oman, there is as yet no Civil Code; however, the Authority for the Settlement of Commercial Disputes is referred to:

> clauses and laws in force in the Sultanate: contracts between the litigants provided that such do not conflict with the laws, public order or morals; established and observed customs in the field of commercial activity; and that which will achieve justice between the adversaries and lead to stability in commercial transactions.

Further, the provisions of the Omani Banking Law appear to confer upon contracting parties the right to choose both jurisdiction and law (Omani Banking Law 1974 – Ballantyne 1986c: 50, 163).

The Omani Commercial Code (Sultani Decree 55/1990) provides the following:

> *Article 1*   The provisions of this law apply to merchants and all commercial matters engaged in by any person even if not a merchant.

> *Article 2*   In specifying the principles which apply to merchants and to commercial matters regard shall be had to contracts recognised at law. The contracts referred to shall take effect by the mere consensus of offer and acceptance unless the provisions of this law otherwise provide:

> *Article 3*   The basis of commercial contracts is that they may be proved by all methods of proof whatever their value unless the provisions of this law otherwise provide.

> *Article 4*   If there is no contract, or if there is and it is silent or the provision in the contract is void, the legislative provisions contained in this law and other laws apply to all matters covered by such provisions expressly or impliedly.

> *Article 5*   If there is no legislative provision the principles of custom apply, special custom or local custom taking precedence over general custom and if there is no custom then the provisions of the Islamic Shari'a shall apply, then the precepts of justice.

The Code continues by defining 'the Court' when referred to in the Code, as the committee for hearing of commercial disputes, or any other court which may be subsequently formed by law. The Code makes reference to special laws governing companies, agency, property and so on.

In the light of the prescription of the Shari'a as 'the basis of legislation' in the Omani 'constitution' of 1996 (supra), interesting points would arise were challenges to be made to the constitutionality of laws which offend the Shari'a.

In Saudi Arabia, it is not surprising to find that Regulations which derogate from the Shari'a as the law paramount can be attacked as unconstitutional.

In Bahrain,

Article 1

(a) Legislative provisions apply to all matters governed by such provisions expressly or impliedly

(b) If there be no legislative provision whereby the judge may adjudicate, he shall do so in accordance with custom; and if there be none, he shall adjudicate in accordance with the Islamic Shari'a taking guidance from the best opinions (Ara') thereof having regard to the status of the country and its circumstances, and if there be none, he shall adjudicate in accordance with the principles of natural law and precepts of justice.'

(Decree Law 19/2001
Issuing the Civil Code)

The Commercial Code (Law 7/1987) not only defines the sources of Bahraini law in Commercial matters but also, as we shall see, effectively grasps the nettle of riba. Article 2 of the code provides the following:

1 There shall apply to commercial matters that upon which the two contracting parties have agreed provided that such agreement does not conflict with mandatory legislative provisions.

2 If there is no special agreement the principles of commercial custom shall apply insofar as there is no relevant provision in this or any other law relating to commercial matters. Special Custom shall be preferred over general Custom.

3 If there is no commercial Custom the laws relating to civil matters shall be applied, in the absence of which the judge shall deduce the bases of his judgment from the principles of the Islamic Shari'a then the principles of natural law and justice.

It may be doubted whether these provisions have done much to clarify the jurisprudential position in Bahrain (Ballantyne 1987: 354 et seq.) In view, however, of the provisions in the Commercial Code referred to, it may be submitted with some confidence that the Shari'a should not now be regarded as having an overriding mandatory effect in a commercial matter.

In the United Arab Emirates, against the constitutional backdrop of the Shari'a as a principal source of legislation, we find that the law setting up the Union Supreme Court provides the following:

The Supreme Court shall apply the provisions of the Islamic Shari'a, Union laws and other laws in force in the member Emirates of the Union *conforming to the Islamic Shari'a*. Likewise it shall apply those rules of custom and those principles of natural and comparative law *which do not conflict with the principles of the Shari'a*.

(Law 10/1973, Article 75.
Emphasis added)

Further, the Union Law which set up the Union Courts in the first instance provided

> The Union Courts shall apply the provisions of the Islamic Shari'a, Union laws, and other laws in force, just as they shall apply those rules of custom and general legal principles which do not conflict with the provisions of the Shari'a.
>
> (Union Law 6/1978, Article 7; see also
> Law 17/1978 and Ballantyne
> 1986c: 57 et seq.)

The Code of Civil Transaction (the Civil Code) (Union Law 5/1985) prescribes the sources of law to be applied as follows:

> *Article 1* Legislative provisions apply to all matters governed by such provisions expressly and impliedly. There is no place for elucidation (Ijtihad) in case of a provision of clear meaning (Dalala). If the judge finds no provision in this law he shall adjudicate in accordance with the Islamic Shari'a provided that he shall select the most suitable solutions from the two schools of the Imam Malik and the Imam Ahmad Bin Hanbal and if he finds none then from the other reliable schools as benefit dictates.
>
> If he (still) finds none then the judge shall adjudicate in accordance with custom provided it is not in conflict in with public order (nitham) or morals and if the custom be peculiar to a specific emirate, then his judgment shall apply to such emirate.

The wording of Article 1 seems to envisage that legislative provisions in the Code should be applied by the judge even if they contravene the Shari'a.

Further, the Civil Code contains in Article 10 et seq. basic principles of private international law (conflict) (Ballantyne 1986b: 245 et seq.; Union Law 5/1985). In contract, the principle of *automomie de la volonte*, the right of the parties to choose the law which is to govern a commercial contract, is enacted (Law 5/1985, Article 19). However, a sweeping up provision at the end of this conflict section of the Code provides,

> It shall not be lawful to apply principles of law designated by the foregoing provisions if such principles are contrary to the Islamic Shari'a or public policy or morals in the UAE.
>
> (Law 5/1985, Article 27)

Thus again the predominance of the Shari'a appears to be preserved in Union Law. By reference to Article 27, those mandatory provisions of the Shari'a which form an essential embarrassment to a commercial contract cannot, in the Union forum, be avoided by the choice of a foreign law to govern the contract. This raises further the extent to which a non-Union forum would apply the chosen law, in a contract of which the *lex loci solutionis* were entirely Union law, in defeasance of public policy provisions of Union law.

The UAE Law of Commercial Transactions (the Commercial Code: Law 18/1993) provides the following:

> *Article I*   The provisions of this law shall apply to merchants and to all commercial matters engaged in by any person even if not a merchant.
>
> *Article II*
> (1) There shall apply to merchants and commercial matters that upon which the contacting parties have agreed provided their agreement be not in conflict with a mandatory commercial provision.
> (2) If no special agreement be found the principles of commercial custom shall apply where no provision in respect thereof appears in this law or in other laws relating to commercial matters and special or local custom shall have priority over general custom and if no commercial custom be found then the provisions particular to civil matters must be applied where there is no conflict with the general principles of commercial activity.
> (3) Special agreements or principles of commercial custom shall not be applied if in conflict with public policy or morals.

A final example may be taken from another Gulf State, Qatar, where the Civil and Commercial Code (Law 16/1971) provides the following:

> *Article 2*   In prescribing principles which apply to merchants and commercial acts regard shall be had to contracts recognised by law, which constitute the law of the contracting parties.
>
> *Article 3*   If there is no contract or if there is but it is silent as to (a particular) provision or the provision set out in the contract is void, the legislative provisions set out in this law shall apply.
>
> *Article 4*   In the absence of a legislative provision which can be applied, the judge shall adjudicate in accordance with custom, special or local custom taking precedence over general custom, and in the absence of custom the principles of the Islamic Shari'a shall be applied.

The foregoing provisions must of course be viewed against a constitution which provides for the Shari'a as *the* principal source of legislation. As to whether the Shari'a must in such circumstances be regarded as paramount, I have expressed the view that as the Shari'a is not expressed by the Constitution of Qatar to be the *sole* source of legislation, it might not be regarded as paramount, in defeasance of the other specified sources of law. However, a contrary view has been expressed in two constitutional court cases of Egypt and Kuwait (Ballantyne 1986c: 56).

With the foregoing examples in mind, we turn to consider how these Shari'a difficulties going to public policy, best typified in, although not monopolized by, riba, have been dealt with in the contemporary legislation.

In the Kuwait Civil Code, loans are dealt with in Articles 543 to 551 inclusive. Article 547 provides the following:

1   Loans shall be without interest. Any condition to the contrary is void, without prejudice to the loan agreement itself.
2   Any benefit stipulated by the lender shall be considered interest.

The Explanatory Memorandum to the Code declares that

> Islam allows loans on the basis of human co-operation and brotherliness and the relieving of worries and the reverses of fate. It vehemently denounced those who practise usury, and threatened them with the severest kinds of threats and menaces. It was accordingly forbidden in Islamic jurisprudence that loans should include a provision granting a benefit to the lender. Otherwise, the contract is void as to such provision.
>
> (Kuwaiti Law 67/1980)

Such elevated sentiments were not, however, adverted to in framing the Kuwaiti Commercial Code, passed contemporaneously with the Civil Code (Law 68/80; see also Ballantyne 1986c: 128 et seq.):

Article 102
(1)   The creditor has the right to interest in a commercial loan unless the contrary is agreed. If this rate of interest is not specified in the contract, the interest due shall be the legal interest of 7 per cent.
(2)   If the contract contains agreement on the rate of interest and the debtor delays in payment then interest for delay shall be calculated on the basis of the agreed rate.

Article 104 of the Code provides that there can be no prepayment of a loan unless by express agreement, unless the interest for the whole period is paid to the creditor. Article 110 provides that where there is delay in payment of a commercial loan in a liquidated amount, interest shall be paid at the legal rate. Article 111 limits the rate of interest to that set from time to time by the Central Bank.

Despite some attempts at justification in the commentary to the Commercial Code, it cannot be contended that these provisions of the Code do not offend against the Shari'a. Thus, the strategy of paying lip service to the Shari'a in the Civil Code while legislating to the contrary in the Commercial Code, is in contravention to the Shari'a – hence, the application to the Kuwaiti Constitutional Court referred to above (Ballantyne 1986c: 103).

This strategy has, *faute de mieux*, been adopted by other Islamic jurisdictions under consideration, of which the following can serve as examples.[13]

Again the Civil code of the UAE (Law 5/1985) pays lip service to the Shari'a in many of its Articles, following in many respects the Civil Code of Jordan. Article 714 stipulates that

> If there be stipulated in the loan Agreement any benefit additional to the requirement of the contract other than security to the lender, the condition is void and the contract valid.
>
> (CP Jordanian Code 640)

This at least makes clear that the principle of severance applies. However, the UAE code of Commercial transactions (Union Law 18/1993) provides for bank loans in Articles 409 et seq.

Article 409
(3)   The borrower is obligated to discharge the loan with interest to the bank at the times and on the conditions agreed upon.

Article 441 deals with the calculation of interest in cases of discounting; Articles 450 et seq. with loans secured by commercial paper; Article 457 with interest charged; and Article 475 et seq. cover negotiable instruments. Interest may be stipulated in bills payable at sight or a fixed period after sight; promissory notes are similarly treated (Article 594).

We may therefore highlight, within the constraints of this article, the essential difficulties which would inevitably arise were the Shari'a to be applied per se to a modern commercial transaction. The position in that respect remains basically as it was at the time of the early arbitrations referred to earlier.

The veto on riba alone, viewed even in its narrow sense as interest on money, ostensibly constitutes a direct opposition to the economic system of the capitalist world. Our world today is ruled by economics and finance. It is virtually impossible to contemplate a contemporary commercial contract in the international sector, which does not contain complex financing arrangements involving not only interest, but also broad elements involving gharar, and multifarious and complex conditions. The basic clash of ideologies inherent in this situation points up the dangers, along with the need to consider those ideological problems which are quickly becoming identified with the political aspects of confrontation.

The rationale of the Islamic position on interest was well summed up by the great Hanbali jurist, Ibn al Qayyim, who, following Shafi'i's doctrine, wrote

> Dirhams and dinars are the units of valuation of articles sold, and constitute the standard by which the evaluation of property is recognised. It must therefore be fixed and regulated so that it does not go up or down, since were the price (of currency) to go up or down like commodities we would not have a standard with which to value the articles sold. Indeed, everything is commodity,

and the people's need for a price by which to value articles sold is a general and compelling one. Such valuing is not possible, save on the basis of a rate by which to know value. This requires a standard on the basis of which things are assessed, which continues upon one state of affairs, and which is not itself assessed by reference to anything else. If it becomes a commodity which goes up and down, then the transactions of people will be impaired.

(Ballantyne 1988b: 1)

It is basically for these reasons, and because of the uncertainty (gharar) inherent in the conventional system, that 'in Islam the relationship between work and capital has been based on a just partnership of the two factors in the profit and loss accrued, and the payment of a pre-determined profit has been forbidden' (Shirazi 1990: 10).

From these principles stems of course the whole still emerging system of Islamic Banking,[14] a system based essentially upon such partnership, to the exclusion of riba. It cannot be denied that it is in the banking and financial sector that the conflict between conventional Western methods and the public policy provisions of the Shari'a is most glaringly apparent. Further, in looking at the contemporary macroeconomic scene today, with its conventional banking system, it seems difficult to dismiss the Islamic precepts, which involve in essence equity rather than lending at interest, as inappropriate. *The Economist*, in 'A Survey of Islam' (1994: 10) observes that

Despite this (i.e. the disadvantages) some people in the West have begun to find the idea attractive. It gives the provider of money a strong incentive to be sure he is doing something sensible with it. What a pity the West's banks did not have the incentive in so many of their lending decisions in the 1970s and 1980s. It also emphasises the sharing of responsibility of all users of money. That helps to make the free market system more open: you might say more democratic.

In conclusion, the following propositions may be offered by way of summary.

1 Overriding considerations of public policy in al Islam as propounded in the Shari'a are incompatible with what man has made of international commerce.
2 Thus, contemporary commercial laws contain much that would be illegal if adjudged at the Shari'a.
3 Islamic states have dealt with this dilemma in a variety of ways but only effectively in legislation in defiance or defeasance of the Shari'a. With the reassertion of the Shari'a, the latter solution may not be tenable for much longer.
4 It is incumbent upon the Western lawyers, advising their clients with regard to an Islamic jurisdiction, to consider from the beginning whether the Shari'a does or could apply, and if so, of the difficulties inherent in such an application and how, with reference to the particular jurisdiction concerned, it may be dealt with.

As to any overall solution, it may be restated: what, if anything, can be done by the Western lawyer, other than to sit back and wait for an inevitable crash application of the Shari'a? First of all, realise the existence of the problem, and problem it is! Second, Western lawyers must show a great sympathy and understanding for this powerful religious and cultural background, and we have to devise where necessary (not as yet in all jurisdictions), our bridges – if indeed these can be built. There are many ifs. The Shari'a is a sacred subject and, apart from understanding on the Western side, any dialogue requires the co-operation of the Muslim side in what, in many quarters, is regarded as a forbidden subject. Certainly, let us never underestimate the importance of this subject at this time – a classical and rigid application of the Shari'a to modern economic agreements could be catastrophic, and it is sobering to reflect that this could occur in most of the Arab jurisdictions with no need for prior legislation. Let it not be thought either that such application is relevant only within a Muslim jurisdiction. What of the situation in a Western court directed by its conflict rules to apply to a contract the Shari'a law, proved by expert evidence to be the law applicable as the proper law of contract? Also, what of the enforcement of foreign judgments in the Muslim jurisdictions? These are grave matters. Perhaps what is required in today's climate is not just a restructuring of the Shari'a to fit Western economic concepts, but some restructuring of those concepts in order to meet the Shari'a – a study of just how far Western and Shari'a concepts are incompatible in the light of a new ijtihad. Insofar as dialogue is possible, let us pursue it. We must take the opportunity for discussion while wise and moderate men are available to participate in it. Really, this can only be done by lawyers and, in the final analysis Muslim lawyers at that – such is the difficulty where the law is identified with religion. The political implications are, of course, obvious. But for the issue to become an international political issue, or to be overtly treated as such, is, I hope, unthinkable – to say that doing so would be counterproductive is to understate the obvious. We are too apt to write learned memoranda based upon the material pros and cons of a situation. Despite the obvious difficulties, I am optimistic enough to believe that something may be achieved (Ballantyne 1988a: 317 et seq.).

Notes

1 *International Law Reports* (ILR) 1951: Case No. 37; *International Common Law Quarterly* (ICLQ) 1951. It may be noted that in so deciding, Lord Asquith entirely overlooked, or ignored, the fact that at the time the British Crown exercised extraterritorial jurisdiction in Abu Dhabi, with laws prescribed by Order in Council based upon the Anglo Indian law.

2 ILR (20, 1953: 543: Once again the arbitrator (Lord Radcliffe) failed to advert to the extraterritorial position in Qatar.

3 As to Qatar, Law No. 16/171: Civil & Commercial Code. As to UAE, see the Code of Civil Transactions, Law 5/1985, and Ballantyne (1986b: 245 et seq.). See also in UAE Commercial Code, Law 18/1993. As to Saudi Arabia, see Al Mehaimeed (1993: 30).

4 Refer to the Codes of, for example, Syria, Jordon, Kuwait, Qatar and UAE.

5 A broad definition of the incidents of the Shari'a going to public policy and morals may be found in the distinction between Haqq Allah (the law of God) and haqqal'abd (the law of the slave). recepts of the former are immutable, mandatory and unavoidable by contract (Al Sanhuri 1953, Vol. III: 101 et seq.).

6 The 1961 Commercial Code of Kuwait, done by Al Sanhury, has now been replaced by the Civil & Commercial Codes of 1981, Laws 67/1980 and 68/1980 respectively. For the index to both Codes, see Ballantyne (1986c: Appendix XV).
7 Constitutional amendment dated May 1980. As to the predominance of the constitution as the law paramount, see Badawi (1971) and Barthelemy and Duez (1933: 183).
8 As to the constitutional position in the Gulf states, see Ballantyne (1986c: Appendix XI).
9 In Kuwait, for example, there is an active Constitutional Court, which has issued numerous judgments – see Ballantyne (1986c, Appendix XIII).
10 Case No. 20 of Judicial year 1. For an extract (translated into English) from this judgment and a Note thereon, see Ballantyne (1986a).
11 The great debate as to what constitutes riba in this context has filled, and will continue to fill, many volumes (Al Sanhuri 1953, Vol. III: 176 et seq.; Ballantyne 1986c: 121; Mallat 1988). For modern authority on the principles involved see Nabil Saleh (1992), Al Sanhuri (1953, Vol. III: 196 et seq.), Mallat (1988: 69) and Ballantyne (1986c: 121 et seq.).
12 Kuwaiti Civil Code Law 67/80 Article 1(2) as amended by Law 15/96. As to 'custom' see earlier, and generally see Ballantyne (1986c: 52 et seq.).
13 The great importance of ensuring that a loan is 'commercial' within the definition in the applicable code, as distinct from 'civil', will be apparent.
14 Also see Shirazi (1990), Ray (1995) and the collection of articles in Mallat (1988).

Bibliography

Abu Zahrah, M. (1938) *Property and Contract in Muslin Law*, n.p.
Al Mehaimeed, A. (1993) 'The Constitutional System of Saudi Arabia: A Conspectus', *Arab Law Quarterly*, 8 (1): 30–6.
Al Sanhuri. A. (1953) *Masadir al-Haqq fi al-Fiqh al-Islami*. Beirut: Manshurat Mohammad Addaiyat.
Anderson, J. N. D. and Coulson, N. J. (1958) 'The Moslem Ruler and Contractual Obligations', *New York University Law Review* 33 (4): 917–33.
Anderson, N. (1980) 'Foreword', in W. Ballantyne (ed.) *Legal Development in Arabia*, London: Graham and Trotman.
Arabian American Oil Company [ARAMCO] v Kingdom of Saudi Arabia (1958), *International Law Reports*, 27.
Badawi, Th. (1971) *Al-Qanan al-Dusturi*, Cairo: n.p.
Bahraini Commercial Code (1987) *Decree Law* 7/1987.
Ballantyne, W. (1980) *Legal Development in Arabia*, London: Graham and Trotman.
Ballantyne, W. (1986a) 'The Constitution of the Gulf States: A Comparative Study', *Arab Law Quarterly*, 1 (2): 158–76.
Ballantyne, W. (1986b) 'The New Civil Code of the United Arab Emirates: A Further Reassertion of the Shari'a', *Arab Law Quarterly*, 1 (3): 245–64.
Ballantyne, W. (1986c) *Commercial Law in the Arab Middle East: The Gulf States*, London: Kluwer Law.
Ballantyne, W. (1987) 'Index to the Commercial Code of Bahrain', *Arab Law Quarterly*, 2 (4): 352–6.
Ballantyne, W. (1988a) 'Coulson Memorial Lecture', *Arab Law Quarterly*, 3: 317.
Ballantyne, W. (1988b) 'Islamic Law and Financial Transactions in Contemporary Perspective', in C. Mallat (ed.) *Islamic Law and Finance*, London: Graham and Trotman.
Ballantyne, W. (1994) 'The Shari'a: Bridges or Conflict?' A Foreword to *The Newsletter of The Arab Regional Forum of the IBA*, 1 (1).

Ballantyne, W. (1995) 'Syndicated Loan Agreements', in C. Mallat (ed.) *Commercial Law in the Middle East*, London: Graham and Trotman.

Barthelemy, J. and Duez, P. (1933) *Traite de droit constitutionnel*, Paris: Dalloz.

Gutteridge, H. C. (1949) *Comparative Law*, Cambridge: Cambridge University Press.

Laoust, H. (1948) *Le traité de droit public d'Ibn Taimiya* (Translation of *Siyasa Shar'iya*) Beirut: n.p.

Mahmasani, S. (1955) 'Transactions in the Shari'a', in M. Khaddouri and H. Liebesny (eds) *Law in the Middle East*, Washington, DC: The Middle East Institute.

Majallat al-Ahkam al-Shari'a (1981) (Definition, Articles 162–5), Jeddah: Al Tuhama Press.

Mallat, C. (ed.) (1988) *Islamic Law and Finance*, London: Graham and Trotman.

Petroleum Development (Trucial Coast) Limited v The Shaikh of Abu Dhabi. (1951) International Law Reports, Case Number 37, *International Common Law Quarterly*.

Qatar Civil and Commercial Code (1971) Law 16/1971.

Ray, N. D. (1995) *Arab Islamic Banking and the Renewal of Islamic Law*. London: Graham and Trotman.

Rector of Al Azhar University v The President of the Republic, the President of the Council of Ministers, The President of the Legislative Committee of the People's Assembly, and Atef Fouad Goudah. Supreme Constitutional Court of Egypt; Case No. 20 of Judicial Year 1. [Extracted and translation into English, with a note in W. Ballantyne (1985a).]

Rule of Qatar v International Marine Oil Company Limited (1953) *International Law Reports* 20.

Saleh, N. A. (1992) *Unlawful Gain and Legitimate Profit in Islamic Law*, Cambridge: Cambridge University Press.

Schacht J. (1959) 'Islamic Law in Contemporary States', *American Journal of Comparative Law* 8 (2): 133–47.

Shirazi, H. (ed.) (1990) *Islamic Banking*, London: Butterworths.

UAE Code of Civil Transactions (1985) *Law* 5.

UAE Commercial Code (1993) *Law* 28.

Wilson, R. and Baldwin, D. (1988) 'Islamic Finance in Principle and Practice', in C. Mallat (ed.) *Islamic Law and Finance*, London: Graham and Trotman.

7 Zakat, taxes, and public finance in Islam

Volker Nienhaus

In an Islamic state, legislation and policy must not fall into conflict with general rules and specific regulations of the Quran and the Sunna. General rules have to be applied to specific cases, and specific regulations of the past may no longer be applicable under changed socioeconomic circumstances today. Islamic economics is the perception and application of economic theories with an explicit consideration of the value system of Islam. Jurists (theologians, *fuqaha*) have been, for centuries, the experts for the interpretation and application of Islamic values and norms. But today, the monopoly of Islamic jurists to apply Islamic values and to give guidance in all aspects of economic, social, and political life has been challenged by Muslim social scientists and economists. They are familiar with contemporary theories and can claim a higher competence for the explanation of complex economic and social relations. Since understanding is the precondition for judging, the recommendations and assessments of Islamic economists should be taken seriously if they are explicitly based on the Islamic value system. Islamic economists have come up with proposals for the design of a system of taxation and public finance in a modern Islamic state which differ from the traditional views of Islamic jurists.

This chapter will comment on the quality of the new contributions and point to some implications which have not yet attracted due attention. Although the basic principles of taxation and public finance in Islam will be presented, the chapter is not meant to be encyclopedic but interpretive. Further, it is mainly based on contributions of authors belonging to Sunni Islam. A basic difference between Sunni and Shi'i Muslims is that the latter do not recognize the right of an Islamic state to organize the compulsory levy of *zakat* which is often considered the core element of the Sunni system of taxation. Therefore the Shi'i concept of public finance and its contemporary implementation in the Islamic Republic of Iran differ in several respects from the Sunni model which is discussed in this chapter.

Methodology for an "Islamic system"

For economics in general and taxation and public finance in particular, the Quran contains no technically clear instructions but only some principles and rules which need an interpretation before they can be applied in practice. What the

Prophet began in this respect was continued by the four Rightly Guided Caliphs. The policies and regulations they implemented during the "Golden Age" of Islam became the prime reference for all later jurists.

Three decades after the Prophet began the rule of an Islamic state, approximately fifteen different types of compulsory levies and sources of public funds were known. It is neither possible nor necessary to deal with all in this chapter. A considerable number of revenue categories were related to the conquest of new territories which is no longer relevant today. The most important conceptual and practical problems of taxation and public finance in a contemporary Islamic state will be covered by an analysis of four major compulsory levies, namely zakat ("poor tax" on wealth and agricultural produce), *jizya* (poll tax on non-Muslims), *kharaj* (land tax), and *ushur* (import tax).

The early Islamic state as the period of reference

The socioeconomic conditions today differ fundamentally from those of the early Islamic period. In contemporary society, interdependent anonymous markets are crucial for the coordination of individual production and consumption decisions, technological progress enhances productivity and causes far-reaching structural changes, the importance of agriculture is decreasing and that of industry and services is increasing, and the majority of people work on a contractual basis for a fixed income. In the early Islamic period, however, economic transactions were largely based on personal relations. Dynamic changes were rare and the economy was basically static: agriculture and trade were dominant, self-employment and slave work were the rule, and hired labor was the exception.

But in spite of fundamental changes, Islamic economists, to be Islamic, must rely on or at least reckon with the past developments and the methodology of Islamic law.[1] Whenever clear instructions for a specific issue exist in the Quran (which is the primary source of knowledge and guidance) they must be implemented. If only related rules and principles can be found, they must be considered for application in analogy. When nothing particular can be found, general Quranic principles related to goals and functions of an Islamic state must be consulted. For implementing regulations, the practice of the Prophet is crucial because he was the explicitly authorized interpreter of the Quran. In addition, the practices of the rightly guided caliphs must be considered carefully because of their outstanding reputation and closeness to the Prophet.

Taxation and public finance were developed on a case by case basis which led to a considerable diversity of practices from the early period onward. For example, only two of the four most important compulsory levies have an explicit Quranic base and were applied systematically by the Prophet (zakat and jizya). Of the other two, the Prophet had applied only one tax (kharaj), but merely in a single case and not systematically. In particular the second caliph Umar changed the tax system in many respects.[2] He systematically applied kharaj, amended zakat by including additional items to the tax base, and introduced ushur (import tax). Later caliphs continued with this, but they also reversed some decisions of their predecessors.

The "divine" character of zakat

"In *Shari'ah* the word *zakah* refers to the determined share of wealth prescribed by God to be distributed among deserving categories. It is also used to mean the action of payment of this share" (Al Qaradawi 1973/I: xxxix). Being one of the "five pillars of Islam," the payment of zakat is one of the highest religious duties of Muslims. The individual Muslim can fulfill this obligation by direct payments to deserving individuals or to institutions recognized to collect and distribute zakat (such as mosques, religious schools or – recently – specialized agencies). The Quran stipulates the individual zakat obligation, but it does not prescribe that the state should organize the collection and distribution of zakat. This was done in the second year after Hijra by the Prophet who thus made zakat a compulsory levy (Kahf 1999).

Islamic economists often create the impression that the Quran and the Prophet established – at least for zakat as the most important compulsory levy – a detailed and conclusive system with a definite tax basis and tax rates which cannot be changed by any individual or state authority.[3] Although this opinion is widely held, it is nevertheless faulty. Contrary to what is often maintained, the Quran does not describe the zakat system in full. The Quran is explicit only with respect to the groups of beneficiaries. The sources and rates of zakat were specified by the Prophet. To declare them immutable by any individual or state authority gives them the same divine epistemological status as the Quran. Seemingly, this position was not shared by the companions of the Prophet and by the early caliphs who have changed sources as well as rates only a few years after the death of the Prophet (details later). Most of these changes were sanctioned later by Muslim jurists who themselves proposed further modifications of the zakat system.

It seems that the early jurists had a perception of the methodological status of the zakat regulations of the Prophet which differs substantially from that of many contemporary writers. Because the Prophet received revelations from God, his zakat regulations could have the same epistemological status as the Quran. They could be the word of God which is eternal and cannot be modified by human beings. But there is no tradition that the Prophet himself held this view, and the conduct of the companions also does not indicate that they treated the details of the worldly zakat regulations as being divine revelations. If the regulations are not divine or revealed, then they can only be of human origin. They are the result of the Prophet's efforts to exercise *ijtihad*, that is to interpret and apply Quranic principles (M. A. S. Siddiqi 1983: 54–62). The ijtihad of the Prophet is different from that of any other human being in one important respect. In several cases God has corrected the Prophet through a special type of revelation when he made a mistake in his ijtihad, and the Prophet changed his position afterwards. Faulty ijtihad is irreconcilable with the religious and political role of the Prophet. This implies that any noncorrected ijtihad of the Prophet has an implicit divine sanction and approval. It is the best possible interpretation and implementation of Quranic principles and can claim validity and obedience – but not for all times to come.

Only a word of God is eternal truth, but a word of man (even if he is the Prophet) can claim truth at best for a certain place in time and space.

Because of the outstanding epistemological qualities of the ijtihad of the Prophet, his zakat regulations must be carefully studied and evaluated. If circumstances change, amendments and adjustments may become not only permissible but even necessary in order to serve best the eternal objects of the Quran. However, even if today's socioeconomic situation were totally different from that in the days of the Prophet, a completely free reconstruction of zakat only "inspired by the Quran" but without any explicit reference to historical practices cannot be reconciled with the elaborate methodological concepts of the institutionalized Islam.

Case law instead of general principles

The zakat regulations of the Prophet were meant for an unspecified time but not for eternity. They are examples for the application of the principle of "realism" in legislation which "was meant to deal with actual events only. Presupposition, speculation and hypothetical issues were excluded from the philosophy of legislation" (M. A. S. Siddiqi 1983: 67). Unfortunately, the explication of principles was also excluded because this was not necessary. The detailed regulations covered all actual cases; an explication of principles would have been necessary only when the legislation was meant to deal with presently unknown (future) cases.

The early caliphs have amended the zakat regulations of the Prophet.[4] They did not only include items into the zakat base which were not included by the Prophet, but they also excluded an item on which zakat was levied under the Prophet, and they changed the rate in one case (see later). For none of these modifications are the reasons explicitly reported.

It was not before the last quarter of the first Islamic century that Muslim jurists became more systematic, began to develop legal theories, and made efforts to identify principles for the implementation and modification of zakat regulations. The problem with these legal theories is that none of them can explain all modifications with only one single principle. All theories have to combine several principles. This reduces the precision and informative value of each theory, and it allows several theories to coexist.

The traditional theories developed by jurists of past centuries discuss at great length cases which today are at best of minor importance. The "modernization" of the legal theories and the integration of knowledge and insights of modern social sciences and economics has just begun (Kahf 1999), and apparently this is an arduous undertaking. Many economists seem to be more interested in propagating what they as trained economists believe zakat should be than in a dispute on, and an advancement of, legal theories. But on the other hand, many Muslim jurists are also reluctant to enter into a dialogue with social scientists and economists: the result of such a dialogue could be a confirmation of the devaluation of their conventional wisdom for the adaptation of Islamic institutions to the modern world.

Taxation

Zakat

Zakat is the most prominent and most elaborate element of an Islamic system of compulsory levies. These levies must not be taxes in the modern sense because – as in the case of zakat – the proceeds may be earmarked for particular purposes and cannot be spent by the state at its own discretion. Zakat is mentioned several times in the Quran (e.g. II: 177, IX: 60)[5], and the beneficiaries of the poor due are listed. However, nothing detailed can be found in the Quran regarding the base for the levy, the rate(s), the methods of payment, and the exemptions. This was not a serious problem as long as zakat was a voluntary payment, but particulars had to be fixed when it was transformed into a compulsory levy collected by the state.

The Prophet enumerated items on which zakat had to be paid (zakat base), namely (1) animal properties (camels, sheep, cows), (2) gold, silver, and coins, (3) agricultural produce (wheat, barley, dates, and grapes), and (4) buried treasures. It is doubtful whether zakat was also levied on merchandise and honey. The Prophet specified for each item a minimum quantity below which no zakat was due (*nisab*), and the rates for quantities above that minimum. From today's perspective, the most important rates are 2.5 percent for gold, silver, and coins, 5 percent for agricultural produce from irrigated land and 10 percent from rainfed land. The Prophet also determined the timing for the zakat payment, namely, for animal properties and gold, silver, and coins once a year, for agricultural produce at the time of harvest, for buried treasures at the time of extraction.

It is important to note that the Prophet did not give a general definition of the items subject to zakat. Such a definition could have been used after his death when new items emerged or known items changed their character. The early caliphs continued with his "pragmatic legislation." When they were confronted with a specific new case – for example whether zakat should be paid on horses or not – they decided this case only. They did not establish principles reaching beyond the particular case. It were the jurists who later, approximately since the end of the first century, evaluated the practice and the case law of the Prophet and the early caliphs by applying rational arguments (analogy) to formulate more general principles (ijtihad). The problem is that the legal principles are not sufficiently general and abstract and that different principles conform with the practices of the Prophet (and the early caliphs). These different principles (must) coincide for past cases, but they often come to different conclusions for new cases. Further, the principles of the early jurists do not cover all issues dealt with by contemporary economists. For example, no clear principle was established to decide whether assets or income were or should become the tax base for zakat, and what the appropriate rates were for the zakat levy. This is of particular significance today where a large variety of assets (in particular financial assets and ownership rights) and forms of income (in particular contractual income) exist which were unknown in the early Islamic period.

Tax base

There is a considerable diversity of views – if not a confusion – regarding the nature and scope of the tax base of zakat. It is neither clear whether it is primarily a kind of wealth or income tax, nor is it established what types of wealth or income exactly are to be included in the tax base. The state administers zakat as a compulsory levy today only in relatively few Muslim countries, but even there the calculation of zakat for specific items (such as cash and precious metals, merchandise or commercial papers, and shares) must be done by self-assessment. In Muslim countries where zakat is not state-administered and in non-Muslim countries, the whole calculation of zakat is based on self-assessment. For this purpose various guide books, online instructions, questionnaires, and calculators have been produced by individuals and private and public organizations.[6]

IS ZAKAT A WEALTH OR AN INCOME TAX?

From many texts of Islamic economists, one gets the impression that zakat is basically a kind of wealth tax with the addition of ushr as a levy on agricultural produce. A reservation is that not all categories of wealth are subject to zakat but only those which are actually or potentially productive.[7]

The items on which the Prophet charged zakat have been enumerated in the earlier paragraphs. There is no doubt that gold, silver, coins, and buried treasures are forms of wealth which economists would classify as "stock variables." This is also the case for animal properties. But it is doubtful with respect to agricultural produce. Agricultural produce is more income (in economic terminology: a "flow variable") than wealth, and it is often argued that the difference in the zakat rate for rainfed and irrigated land reflects (in a rudimentary way) the difference in the production costs. From this some jurists and economists conclude that zakat was levied not only on wealth but also on income – at least on income from agriculture. This view is sometimes supported by reference to the practice established under the early caliphs to subtract zakat at source from (annually paid) state pensions. In a rather straightforward manner, several present-day zakat regulations and recommendations include the (net) income of salaried persons as well as the (net) profit of self-employed people and companies. From an academic point, however, the issue of wealth or income levy is not yet settled because for the historical examples of agricultural produce and pensions a more "wealth-oriented" interpretation can be given.

To argue that the final base for zakat is not the (flow variable) agricultural produce but the (stock variable) land, it must be realized that basically the land brings out the agricultural produce and that the actual value of the wealth category "land" is approximated by the agricultural produce. In the case of rainfed land, the whole produce is attributed to the land which is fertile by itself. In contrast to this, irrigated land becomes fertile only when combined with considerable human efforts. The value of the asset "irrigated land" is only half the value of rainfed land. Under this perspective, the charge of 10 percent or 5 percent of the produce of land is not an income but a special way to calculate and collect a wealth tax.

A similar argument applies to the state pensions. The pension payment is based on an individual's claim against the state which economically is a valuable asset (because it entitles to annual payments). As such it is part of the individual wealth. Therefore, not the current income but the possession of the right or claim, that is the underlying wealth category constitutes the zakat duty, and the deduction of zakat at source is again a special way to administer a wealth tax.

For the modernization of the traditional zakat system, a clarification of the character of the tax is of high importance and has far-reaching consequences for the fiscal potential and its allocative and distributive effects. A compulsory levy also on salaries and profits would yield much higher proceeds than a mere tax on a limited list of wealth items. Estimates of zakat proceeds based on specific wealth items and agricultural produce reach a magnitude of up to 2 percent of GDP while the inclusion of some types of income triple the proceeds to 6 percent of the GDP (Kahf 1999: 23). Despite this background, opinions and actual practices are still very divergent. This is probably due to the vagueness of the crucial Quranic verses and the ambiguity of the historical practice of the Prophet and the early caliphs. Nevertheless, most of the actual regulations and recommendations include some income elements into the zakat base.

IS ZAKAT ON PRODUCTIVE OR UNPRODUCTIVE WEALTH?

There is a broad consensus on the inclusion of productive and exclusion of unproductive forms of wealth. However, in a developed market economy this distinction does not make much sense. Any type of wealth can be transformed into any other type, for example from "unproductive" jewelry into "productive" agricultural land. This does not even necessitate a sale of wealth items: "Unproductive" assets can be used as collateral for the financing of productive assets. Suppose persons A and B both own jewelry worth 100,000 Dinar. As long as they keep their wealth in this form, it is "unproductive" and exempt from zakat. If person A sells his jewelry and buys agricultural land, his new wealth will become subject to zakat. Person B keeps his jewelry and obtains a bank credit backed by the jewelry as collateral to purchase agricultural land. He will not pay zakat because the debt can be subtracted from the value of the purchased land so that his productive net wealth is zero. The result is very unsatisfactory: two people with the same wealth do not pay the same zakat.

THE PROBLEM WITH ONE FULL YEAR OF OWNERSHIP

The first caliph Abu Bakr gave a very specific interpretation of the practice of the Prophet to collect zakat on properties only once a year, namely that no zakat was due before a full (lunar) year of ownership had passed. Some Islamic economists emphasize this principle again today.[8] Its far-reaching implications are rarely discussed in the academic literature. If the principle of one full year of ownership is applied for each asset separately, it becomes very easy to avoid compulsory zakat payments: the respective asset is sold before the full year of ownership is completed (i.e. transformed into a different type of wealth such as cash), and it is repurchased after a short while. A pragmatic solution would be to aggregate all types of assets (at least those assets for which no specific zakat rates had been fixed) and to calculate the net wealth a person has owned for one year.

Zakat should be charged for the minimum value the net wealth has reached during the year. Because it is hardly possible and certainly very costly to calculate the value of the net wealth for every day in order to find out the minimum during the year, the practice is much cruder, namely to calculate only the net value at the end of the zakat year. This is compared to the net value at the beginning of the year (= the net value of the end of the previous year), and the smaller of these two figures is taken as the basis to which the zakat rate is applied (e.g. Rahman 2003). Only in some countries and for some wealth items, the calculation is more precise: for example, in Malaysia (where daily stock exchange quotations are at hand) the lowest value of the year is taken as the basis for zakat on shares (Pusat Pungutan Zakat 2004: 103).

Immutable rates?

The rates of zakat were fixed by the Prophet. This alone is a sufficient justification for most authors to maintain these rates for all times. They discuss rates only when new items of wealth or income have to be included in the zakat base. The question then is which of the established rates should be applied in analogy. But such a restrictive stance with regard to modifications of rates is not very convincing. Although the rates set by the Prophet have a divine sanction, they are not of divine origin. They were the best possible rates for achieving the aims and objectives of zakat at the time of the Prophet, but this does not mean that they are the best rates for all times under all conceivable circumstances.

The Prophet did not establish principles but implemented solutions for practical problems. With respect to zakat, the Quran enumerates the categories of beneficiaries for whom the zakat proceeds have to be spent. It is consistent with the approach of pragmatic legislation to assume that the Prophet determined the basis and the rates of zakat in such a way that the proceeds were sufficient to allow a financial support for the beneficiaries which was held adequate at that time. This was the main problem which had to be solved by his pragmatic legislation. Compared to tax rates (compulsory levies) of 50 percent and more for agricultural produce which were not uncommon at that time, a zakat rate of 5 or 10 percent is very moderate.

Empirical data on the level of support per capita for each category of beneficiaries relative to the income of the "average man" of the early Islamic period are not available. A very rough mark is offered by nisab, that is the minimum of wealth or agricultural produce exempted from zakat. If people with less wealth (or income) cannot maintain a reasonable standard of living from their own resources, zakat should fill the gap between the actual wealth (or income) and the minimum. Today, absolute amounts set by the Prophet may no longer be sufficient to secure a reasonable standard of living or the minimum necessary for mere survival. The socially accepted minimum or reasonable standard of living differs in time and place. Therefore, all figures of the early Islamic period should be translated into relative terms – for example compared to the standard of living of a small trader, craftsman, or farmer – before implementations in modern societies are considered. Since it is implausible to assume that the rates set by the Prophet are appropriate for all times and under all conceivable socioeconomic circumstances, zakat rates should be reconsidered today. Methodologically, the modification of zakat rates is not different from a modification of the zakat base. Both are based on the ijtihad of the Prophet and are economically interchangeable: to include an item into the zakat base with a specified rate means to change its zakat rate from zero to a positive value. Considerable deviations from the Prophetic tradition are widely accepted only for modifications of the zakat base but strangely not for modifications of zakat rates.

A conclusive determination of zakat rates under fundamentally changed socioeconomic conditions requires further research. For example, by his fixing of individual rates the Prophet defined a specific structure of zakat rates. The rate for irrigated land was numerically double the rate for gold, silver, and coins, and the rate for rainfed land was double the rate for irrigated land. It is not obvious why he determined such a structure, and it needs more reflections whether only the level or also the structure of zakat rates could be adjusted to modern circumstances, and what should be the guiding rules for a restructuring.

Contemporary practice: confusion and deficiencies

Zakat is – besides the prohibition of riba (interest) – the second most constitutive element of an Islamic economic system. Compared to the vast amount of literature on interest-free banking, the conceptualization and especially the practice of zakat have attracted far less attention of researchers. Empirical studies are limited in number and coverage. There are, however, a number of recent contributions. Al-Omar (1995) examines administrative and organizational aspects of zakat in thirteen Muslim countries (most of which do not claim to be "Islamic states"). El-Ashker and Haq (1995) study a number of cases based on 1980s data, and Kahf (1999) presents a survey of previous studies and some recent quantitative findings. Shirazi (1996) has examined the practice of zakat in Pakistan and Khan (2003) adds important observations on zakat auditing. Attitudes of zakat payers in four Gulf countries are analyzed by Guermat, Al-Utaibi and Tucker (2003). Weiss (2002) reviews social welfare in general and zakat in particular in Nigeria and other West African countries. Basic data for Malaysia are published regularly by Pusat Pungutan Zakat (2004).

A comparative study by Al-Omar (1995) discloses a wide variety of practical arrangements. For example, the payment of zakat is voluntary in seven countries (Bahrain, Bangladesh, Egypt, Iran, Iraq, Jordan – compulsory from 1944 to 1953, and Kuwait) and compulsory in six (Libya, Malaysia, Pakistan, Saudi Arabia, Sudan, and A. R. Yemen). The zakat base for the compulsory levy differs substantially among the respective countries. All six countries which have zakat compulsory do charge it on agricultural produce. But in Malaysia only rice is subject to zakat. Livestock is subject to zakat in five countries (Libya, Malaysia, Saudi Arabia, Sudan, Yemen); only one country (Libya) includes camels and cows used for agricultural work (ploughing, irrigation, etc.). Zakat on gold, silver, cash, and other forms of invisible wealth is collected in four countries, but they assess these assets differently. Three countries (Libya, Saudi Arabia, and Sudan) collect zakat for treasures buried in the earth. Only one country (Sudan) imposes zakat "on wealth that yields income, such as rented property, factories, farms, etc.," and in two countries (Sudan and Saudi Arabia) "regulations provide for the collection of zakah in respect of factories, hotels, art producing companies, taxi owners and offices of real estate agents" (Al-Omar 1995: 39). Income is subject to zakat in two countries: "The Saudi and Malaysian regulations are...the same as to the imposition of the zakah in respect of free vocational jobs and employees' salaries" (Al-Omar 1995: 39). Kahf (1999: 27–8) explicates that the income of certain professionals (physicians, engineers, lawyers, etc.) is subject to zakat in Saudi Arabia only if they work independently but not if they are salaried persons, while professional incomes are generally not included in zakat in Yemen but always – whether independent or salaried – in Sudan. A further study of academic literature and of numerous guidebooks in print and increasingly online will add to this picture of minimal consent and vast diversity.[9]

The empirical data on zakat proceeds are incomplete and not always reliable. But even in those two countries whose governments tried to Islamize their economies in the second half of the 1980s and the early 1990s – Sudan and Pakistan – the zakat proceeds ranged only between 0.3 and 0.5 percent of GDP (Kahf 1999: 28). In Malaysia the zakat collected amounted to just 0.5 percent of government revenues (Pusat Pungutan Zakat 2004: 104) or approximately 0.1 percent of GDP. Such quantities are far away from what was expected, and they are obviously much too small for any sizeable macroeconomic effect on the overall allocation, the general stabilization, or the redistribution of income and wealth. Kahf concedes that the amount of zakat proceeds

> that can realistically be made available for redistribution is very humble indeed. ... All the effects of Zakah on the aggregate variables of the economy becomes negligible if all we can mobilize is a maximum of one half percent of GDP, and thinking of marginal variations in the allocation of disbursement of Zakah becomes a mere mystic wishful ritual!
>
> (1999: 30)

It may be that figures on official zakat collections underestimate the actual zakat yields and distributions somewhat because a considerable number of Muslims accept their individual duty to pay zakat but deny a right of the state to levy zakat (Guermat *et al.* 2003). Thus they may evade the official collection but pay zakat voluntarily. Such a behavior may exist, but its quantitative effects are most probably marginal at best. The aim of zakat evasion practices of wealthy Muslims in countries such as Pakistan is not to shift from compulsory to voluntary zakat payments but to reduce the zakat burden finally (Shirazi 1996). The case of Pakistan also illustrates that legal obligations are not effectively implemented. The zakat administration of Pakistan is chronically understaffed and uses anti-quated accounting and auditing techniques which cannot generate the information needed for an effective monitoring of the zakat system. But seemingly the government and the parliament do not worry too much. The achievements and the deficiencies and shortcomings of the zakat system are documented in annual zakat audit reports. "Although the zakah law says that the audit reports would be placed before the parliament, yet, these reports have never been submitted to the parliament so far. During the last 15 years, a backlog of over 8400 audit observations had already accumulated and was in the pipeline" (Khan 2003: 40).

Zakat and redistribution

Suppose there is a consensus in each Muslim country on the exact definition of the groups of zakat beneficiaries and on the reasonable level of support. Then the funds for the beneficiaries could be raised through an adapted zakat system with a "modernized" zakat base and modified zakat rates. The base and rates could be optimized (for each country) in such a way that the desirable level of support can be granted to the beneficiaries. Alternatively, a traditional zakat system with an old, relatively narrow zakat base and rigid rates could be implemented. In this case zakat revenues will most probably not suffice to satisfy all reasonable claims of the beneficiaries. Then either claims can be satisfied only partially, or the traditional zakat system has to be supplemented by "secular" taxes or compulsory social security contributions. Both cases do not throw a favorable light on the genuine Islamic institution of zakat. It can ensure by itself merely an insufficient support for the beneficiaries, and a satisfactory support level is achieved only by the superimposition of secular elements.

The risk of insufficient revenues is minimized (but not excluded) if a broad zakat base (e.g. productive wealth plus all types of income) is applied. A broad zakat base could also prevent injustices which may occur if zakat is levied on a limited number of items only. According to Muslim jurists, the category of agricultural produce does not include items such as tea or rubber. The application of a narrow and rigid interpretation then leads to the strange situation that small farmers who produce wheat or barley have to pay zakat while rich landlords who own large plantations and produce tea or rubber are exempted from zakat. In this case zakat does not allow the poor a share in wealth of the rich but facilitates a redistribution from low to the lowest income groups or from the poor to the poorest sections of the society. It is obvious that such an implementation of zakat neither complies with ideological claims nor contributes to a popularization of a genuine Islamic concept.

It seems that a thorough revision of traditional Islamic concepts and institutions is needed whereby the opinions of traditional jurists should be considered seriously but not taken as the final word. Economic and political consequences of alternative implementations must be studied in a more comprehensive, systematic, and maybe also radical manner than in "mainstream Islamic economics" today. Both proponents (e.g. Kahf 1999) and critics (e.g. Kuran 2004) agree that zakat as it is practiced today cannot deliver what Islamic economists had promised in the 1970s and 1980s. If zakat is levied on traditional items of wealth and forms of income only while modern variants which are dominant in industrializing and service based economies are exempted, redistribution may take place only amongst the poor and the very poor: The poorer segments of the population – including most of the legitimate recipients of zakat – are typically concentrated in the traditional sectors (especially agriculture) with property and income subject to zakat. The better-off segments in the "modern sectors" (industry, services) will neither receive zakat nor contribute to the zakat proceeds. Thus, there may be only a modest redistribution within a certain segment of the populations whereas the inequalities between the segments are not reduced but maybe even reinforced.

But even if the redistributive effects of zakat may be minimal, it seems that zakat has contributed to a reduction of absolute poverty. Figures for Pakistan (Shirazi 1996), as well as some observations for Arab countries (Brahimi 2002: 105), point to this direction. A systematic empirical analysis of this issue, however, is still lacking.

Other taxes of the early Islamic period

The tax system of the early Islamic state was not confined to zakat. For the state budget, other compulsory levies were even more important than zakat. Their revenues were considerably higher, and the use of the tax receipts was not restricted to specific beneficiaries.

Kharaj

Kharaj was a land tax levied on conquered land. It had no explicit Quranic foundation, and the Prophet did not apply kharaj systematically (Chaudhry 1992: 70). Kharaj was introduced as a systematic land tax by the second caliph Umar after the conquest of Iraq. Instead of distributing the conquered land among his officers, the former non-Muslim owners could keep their land against the payment of a tax. Initially, kharaj was determined as a fixed amount of money per acre land, and it was differentiated according to the type of produce of the land. By relating the fixed amounts to the average total produce, one can calculate implicit tax rates which increase when yields decrease. In such cases they could reach excessive dimensions. Therefore, seemingly, the system of fixed amounts was moderated by the introduction of an upper limit at half of the produce (Mannan 1986: 248).

Later the system was changed to proportionate rates where the farmers had to pay a specified percentage of the harvest. This proportionate rate was determined by the ruler in view of the financial needs of the state (Salama 1983: 44). The tax rate was differentiated with respect to the type of produce, the method of irrigation, and the proximity to the market in the case of orchards. The rates ranged from 20 to 50 percent or sometimes even more.

In terms of receipts, kharaj was the most important tax, and its revenues could be used by the ruler to his discretion. Kharaj was considerably higher than zakat on agricultural produce. Since initially Muslims were obliged to pay zakat only, many land owners in conquered territories converted to Islam in order to reduce their tax burden. The loss of disposable tax revenues in noticeable amounts as a consequence of conversions led to an important modification of the tax. It was no longer tied to the status of the owner of conquered land but to the status of the land itself; all conquered land became kharaj land, and Muslim owners of kharaj land had to pay this tax, too.

Without a substantial modernization, kharaj being a land tax suffers nowadays from a deterioration of the macroeconomic significance of its tax base: the agricultural sector shrinks while industry and services expand. Income from the industrial and service sector gains rapidly in importance. Further, if the growing nonagricultural income categories are tax exempt, this leads to a strong tax discrimination against the farmers which can hardly be justified by any Islamic rule or principle.

While the vast majority of Islamic economists simply recapitulate the historical kharaj without reflections on the problems of its application today, Kahf (1983, 1999) has proposed that in cases where kharaj land is no longer used for agriculture but for other commercial purposes such as the construction of a factory, a warehouse, or a shopping center, the nonagricultural users of the land should become subject to kharaj. An implementation of such a proposal requires the determination of an adequate tax base (e.g. profit or turnover) and of corresponding tax rates. This cannot be done without (very) free analogies interspersed with speculative elements.

Although Kharaj is an early Islamic tax, it has neither a Quranic origin nor a firm foundation in the Sunna. Today it is outdated and can be modernized only with the help of excessive analogies. The prime aim of kharaj, to provide the (Islamic) state with revenues, can be achieved much better, for example, by implementing a secular income tax. A modern income tax is much better suited to prevent injustices than an artificially "upgraded" land tax. The clear consequence would be to give up kharaj altogether. Such an obvious conclusion, however, is not drawn or discussed by Islamic economists. The reason may be that they hardly analyze kharaj under contemporary conditions but refer to early Islamic practices and repeat old legal doctrines without much reflection. To the contrary, a very old and somewhat strange version of kharaj as a tax on non-Muslim businesses was proposed by the newly elected state government of Terengganu in Malaysia in 1999 (Kamali 2000: 283–303). Its weak Islamic foundations as well as its strongly discriminating effects attracted much criticism.

Jizya

Jizya was a poll tax for non-Muslims living in an Islamic state. It was based on the Quran (IX: 29) and applied by the Prophet. He charged one Dinar on every male adult non-Muslim; women and children and old men were exempted from jizya. Umar differentiated the rate according to the income of the taxpayer. He charged one Dinar from poor, two Dinars from middle, and four Dinars from rich non-Muslims. The reasons for this tax structure are not known (Oran and Rashid 1989: 88; Chaudhry 1992: 59).

The discriminating character of the poll tax for non-Muslims has been criticized in the West, but Muslim jurists and economists point out that jizya was introduced as a modest compensation for privileges granted and services provided by the Islamic state to the non-Muslims. For example, they were exempted from military services, they were not subject to zakat, and they were entitled to the same public goods and social services of the Islamic state (including support from zakat funds) as the Muslims. Further it is argued that jizya was not a heavy financial burden but more a symbol of the recognition of the supremacy of the Islamic state.

Contrary to what is maintained by some Islamic economists (e.g. Kahf 1983; Oran and Rashid 1989), jizya can hardly be considered an equivalent of zakat for the non-Muslims in the early Islamic period. It was charged on a totally different base and with different rates, namely as a fixed amount per capita instead of a percentage of wealth and agricultural produce. Thus, the relative tax burden of jizya was inversely related to wealth, while zakat increases roughly proportionate with wealth. But even if the historical jizya was not an economic equivalent of zakat for non-Muslims, the contemporary proponents of jizya argue in favor of such an equivalent because otherwise non-Muslims would have a tax advantage over Muslims. This goal, however, could be achieved simply by abolishing the old jizya rules and applying the techniques of zakat to non-Muslims too. Then all residents of a country (irrespective of their religion) would become subject to the same nondiscriminatory compulsory levy. This levy may be called zakat for Muslims (for whom it has an additional religious dimension) and jizya for non-Muslims, but only the name would be left from the original poll tax.

Ushur

The last of the taxes of the early Islamic state is ushur. The term "ushur" or "ushr" has different meanings. First, it is used for the zakat levy of 5 or 10 percent on agricultural produce. Second, it stands for a foreign trade tax. This tax had neither a Quranic basis nor was it applied by the Prophet. Ushur was introduced by Umar in response to similar taxes imposed by other countries on Muslim traders. Non-Muslim traders from abroad had to pay a tax of 10 percent on the value of their merchandise when they entered the Islamic state, that is, for imports. According to some authors, 10 percent was also charged from nonresident non-Muslim traders for exports. Later ushur was charged on imports (and exports) of non-Muslim residents of the Islamic state at a rate of 5 percent and of Muslim residents at a rate of 2.5 percent. "[I]t turned out to be a particularly important source of revenue for the Islamic State after its introduction by the Caliph Umar" (Oran and Rashid 1989: 89).

Seemingly there was a considerable difference between the treatment of non-Muslim and Muslim traders: the former had to pay ushur for each cross-border transaction, while the Muslims had to pay ushur only once a year. The payment once a year and the tax rate of 2.5 percent indicate that for Muslim traders ushur was not really meant as an import duty but as a special form of the collection of zakat on merchandise. In the early Islamic period, the levy of ushur from Muslim traders might have been justified by technical reasons regarding the tax collection, but today, no serious argument is given why zakat on merchandise could not be fully integrated into the general zakat system.

The higher ushur rates for non-Muslim traders are an obstacle to the "modernization" of ushur. Today nowhere in the world are import duties differentiated with reference to the religion of the trader; any attempts in this direction conflict with existing international trade agreements. Further, if the trader is not a natural but a legal person, the trader does not have a religion. If the religions of the owners of a legal person (e.g. the shareholders of a joint stock company) are taken instead, this may be a mix if Muslims and non-Muslims jointly own a company. Finally in the case of companies whose shares are traded on anonymous stock exchanges, it is nearly impossible to identify the religions of the owners. For all these reasons the traditional ushur should not be revived in a modern Islamic state.

Additional secular taxes?

There is an ongoing debate among Muslim jurists and economists whether an Islamic state has the right to impose taxes in addition to zakat. In this formulation the question seems to be exaggerated because the Prophet himself and the Rightly Guided Caliphs – in particular Umar – have imposed additional taxes, namely jizya, kharaj, and ushur. Thus, the real question is not whether but under what conditions additional taxes can be imposed. To raise this question implies that the legislative body of an Islamic state is not free to impose new taxes as it deems suitable.

The Islamic legislation and government is limited by rules and principles laid down in the Quran, applied by the Prophet, and explicated and developed further by the early caliphs and the Muslim jurists. Authors who are reluctant regarding new taxes emphasize the importance of the traditional Islamic wisdom. They warn against ignoring the body of knowledge accumulated over the centuries and to rush to conclusions based on nothing but "Islamically inspired" individual reasoning of modern economists. For them, a Quranic verse, a Prophetic hadith, or a legal opinion of an eminent jurist is more than just a decoration or "fashionable" dress (or disguise?) for long-held personal sentiments based on conventional economics.

Kahf (1983: 119) points out that jurists have allowed additional taxes only "in cases of defence needs, assurance of a subsistent living of the poor and the indispensable expenses that safeguard the collective interests of Muslims." "Specifically, purposes of welfare, development, and/or economic equilibrium have no references in texts of Quran or Sunnah whether explicit or implicit." This is a strong position against a large number (if not the majority) of Islamic economists. They base their proposals for additional secular taxes on exactly such purposes and aims of an Islamic state, which they deduce from the Quran and Sunna. Because Kahf is strict on the justification of additional taxes, his criteria could constitute a kind of lowest common denominator for additional secular taxes.

In his view, the imposition of additional taxes could be justified if the revenues from zakat and alternative sources of finance are not sufficient for the following purposes (Kahf 1983: 119–20): provision of internal and external security; financing the political, legal, and administrative apparatus of the state; relief in cases of emergencies; maintenance of a minimum standard of living for all; and development of a production capacity adequate to provide the subsistence living if the private sector is not providing such production. For Kahf, the alternative sources of finance are kharaj, jizya, revenues of public enterprises utilizing the public ownership of natural resources, interest-free borrowings from domestic and international sources, revenues from equity financing of income generating development projects, fees for government services, and voluntary contributions.

Kahf's concept of public finance limits the state to core functions, but he does not advocate a "minimal state" in the Western libertarian sense. He excludes subsidies for producers, but most other activities of modern governments are covered (although they are not explicitly listed as purposes of an Islamic state): A large variety of "social goods" provided by modern states can be financed from different sources, including even zakat, as long as the goods fall into the category of "minimum standard of living." This comprises, inter alia, minimum education, transportation, and health care; the state must also look after housing for the poor. Other activities should not be financed from zakat, but they nevertheless could be accepted tasks of the state. Infrastructure and development projects are the most important cases here. It follows that a restriction of the power to impose additional taxes besides zakat makes an Islamic state neither a minimal nor a poor state.

The Islamic state can legitimately perform most of the tasks of contemporary secular states, and the financial resources at its disposal may be plentiful if zakat is levied on all modern forms of wealth (including, in particular, financial assets and fixed capital of companies) and income (including contractual income), if jizya is transformed into an equivalent of zakat for non-Muslims, if kharaj is charged not only for agricultural but for any use of land at relatively high rates, and if infrastructure and development projects are financed by borrowing or equity participation.

Other Islamic economists do not ignore the nontax revenues emphasized by Kahf, but it seems that they are more skeptical regarding the revenue capacity of the non-tax sources. They usually start from a discussion of necessary or legitimate expenditures of an Islamic state and concede the power to introduce additional taxes if needed to cover the necessary or legitimate expenses. This approach is exemplified in the following section.

Public expenditures

There are two types of public expenditures in an Islamic state. First, the Quran enumerates the groups of people for whom proceeds from the compulsory levy zakat have to be spent. Second, the Quran and the Sunna require certain tasks (such as defense, civil administration, the propagation of Islam) to be fulfilled by the Islamic state. In this case, the legitimacy of public expenditures follows from the legitimacy of the tasks themselves.

Beneficiaries of zakat

The Quran (IX: 60) lays down that zakat is "for the poor and the needy, and those employed to administer the (funds); for those whose hearts have been (recently) reconciled (to Truth), for those in bondage and in debt; in the cause of Allah; and for the wayfarer." Discussions are mainly on the exact historical and contemporary definition and demarcation of these groups, on their relative share in the zakat revenues (equal or with priorities), and on the level and form of support that should be given (in cash or in kind, only direct and personal or also indirect for larger groups).

Definitions and demarcations

Without going into details, the following definitions can be given (A. A. Muhammad 1993: 80–5; Al Qaradawi 2000/II): the poor are those who do not possess any properties and do not have an income from employment. The "needy" are those who have some possession or income, but not enough for their sustenance.

- "Those employed to administer zakat" were employees of public zakat institutions, but today this category would also include employees of private zakat organizations in particular in countries where no public zakat systems have been established.
- "Those whose hearts have been reconciled" means converts to Islam. The Prophet paid generous amounts to tribal leaders who converted to Islam, but this type of spending was reduced under the first and terminated under the second caliph.
- "Those in bondage" were the slaves, and zakat was used to purchase their freedom. In our times this category has lost its literal relevance, but some authors suggest – in a rather "free" interpretation – that today zakat should be used to free the Muslim world from "mental slavery" (e.g. intellectual and cultural domination by the West). Such a view is not strongly rejected but also not enthusiastically supported by the majority of Islamic economists.
- "Those in debt" are people who are unable to repay a debt which they incurred either to help others (e.g. as a guarantor) or because they had no other possibility to secure their own survival. Debts incurred to finance a "luxurious lifestyle" should not be included in this category, while some authors suggest that commercial debts caused by a bankruptcy should be.

- "In the cause of Allah" is a very comprehensive and vague category. Initially under this head compensations were given to people who (voluntarily) fought for Islam in a war and were not paid by the state. But literally the meaning of "in the cause of Allah" is much wider and not confined to military struggle. It covers all efforts to seek the pleasure of Allah and to establish truth and justice. Muslim jurists have included the propagation of Islam as well as salaries for teachers and scholarships for students or even health facilities. "[T]he zakat share here is allocated in the general welfare, just like any modern state which uses taxes for the same purpose" (Oran and Rashid 1989: 93).
- The "wayfarer" means a person stranded on a journey which he or she under-took for a respectable cause, in particular to perform *hajj*, to earn a living, or to seek knowledge. A support from zakat funds should enable travelers either to return home or to reach their destination. Some contemporary authors have widened this category vastly and include transport and communication facilities in general. This, however, has not found a broader consent.

The debate on a "wide" or "narrow" interpretation of the beneficiary cate-gories has lost its acuteness when it became generally accepted that an Islamic state can levy secular taxes besides zakat. If this would not be permissible, most Islamic economists favor an extensive interpretation of the categories of benefi-ciaries so that most if not all public expenditures of a secular state would be cov-ered by them. A problem with such an extensive interpretation of zakat beneficiaries is that zakat revenues would in most cases be totally insufficient to cover all proposed expenses if the traditional base and rates were maintained. Since the rates are not put into question by most Muslim jurists and economists, it is consequent that proponents of a broad definition of beneficiaries favor a wide zakat base which includes all forms of wealth and – more important – income. But with an average wealth tax rate of roughly 2.5 percent and an average income tax rate around 10 percent, the allocative and distributive potentials of the budgets of Islamic states would in general be far more limited than the present potentials of governments in Muslim as well as Western countries.

Allocation and level of support

Neither the Quran nor the Prophet gave an explicit ranking of the eight categories of zakat beneficiaries. But this does not mean that they all should receive equal amounts. It seems that the Prophet did not treat all categories equally; he spent relatively large amounts of zakat for converts and warfare. The companions also did not treat all categories as equally important. For example, Umar stopped the payment of zakat for converts. The concept of pragmatic legislation suggests that the allocation of zakat was in such a way that it contributed best to the solution of actual problems. When problems changed, the allocation of funds changed too. In the light of widespread poverty in most of the densely populated Muslim countries today, it would be reasonable to give priority to the poor and the needy.

With respect to the level of support for the poor and the needy, it is argued that the maximum benefit is the Zakat-free minimum (nisab) of twenty Dinars per year, which may be too little to survive in some countries today; Oran and Rashid (1989) calculated that the nisab would amount, annually, to US$1400 in 1984. While some assert that zakat should secure the mere survival, others are far more generous and maintain that "the Shari'ah does not only advocate the provision of the bare necessities of life to the poor and the needy, but goes much further and advocates that they should enjoy what is now termed as a reasonable 'standard of living'" (Muhammad 1993: 81).

It should be noted that twenty Dinars is the nisab for wealth in gold, silver, and coins only. For each category of wealth a separate nisab is defined. The question arises as to why not all nisab values are added up to define one nisab for total wealth.

Public expenditures and goals of an Islamic state

Zakat transfers to beneficiaries are public expenditures in countries where the state made the payment of zakat mandatory. Zakat expenditures are financed from compulsory levies, and the care for the poor and the needy is a recognized public duty. Besides this, the state has to finance other expenditures. Islamic economists have dealt at length with the question of what are necessary or legitimate or permissible tasks for which an Islamic state can rightly incur public expenditures and charge taxes. A typical Islamic theory of public expenditures starts with need fulfillment, reduction of inequality, security, and development as the main goals of an Islamic state. Subsidiary goals are employment, stability, and scientific progress (M. N. Siddiqi 1987: 149 and Kuran 2004).

Mandatory functions and expenditures

Islamic economists can provide convincing evidence from the Quran, the Sunna, the early caliphs and the Muslim jurists that need fulfillment or the guarantee of a minimum standard of living and internal and external security are main goals of an Islamic state. For "distribution" and "development," however, the foundations in the Quran and Sunna are considerably weaker. Goals which are anchored in the Quran and Sunna lead to permanent functions of an Islamic state and corresponding heads of expenditures are also permanent. They can be specified as expenditures for defense, law and order, justice, civil administration, need fulfillment (support of the poor), and the propagation of Islam.

Some authors (e.g. M. N. Siddiqi 1987) add regulations and guidance, and the fulfillment of socially obligatory duties if the private sector fails to fulfill. Regulations and guidance are "a wide category including market regulation, supervision of the common man's behavior in public places and enforcing Islamic practices in general" (M. N. Siddiqi 1987: 157). The fulfillment of socially obligatory duties by the state if the private sector fails to honor this duty is the essence of *fard kifaya*. "A fard kifaya is a duty ... [that] is not addressed to individual persons but to the community. The Law-Giver wants the duty done, irrespective of who does it" (M. N. Siddiqi 1987: 155). The scope for fard kifaya is very wide. It ranges from prayers for the deceased to the establishment of essential industries. Only some socially obligatory duties were specified in the Quran and the Sunna while most others were later added by Muslim jurists. This raises doubts whether all socially obligatory duties should be considered in the category of mandatory and permanent expenses. Functions mandated by the Quran and Sunna express the explicit will of Allah and lead to permanent heads of expenditure with highest priority ("mandatory expenditures").

Necessary functions and circumstantial expenditures

A second category of public expenditures comprises those expenditures which experts deem necessary for realizing the objectives of Shari'a under the present socioeconomic circumstances. This category comprises in particular expenditures for the protection of the environment, for public goods in addition to those included in mandatory expenditures, for scientific research, capital formation and infrastructure, for economic development, for subsidies for private activities, and for stabilization policies (M. N. Siddiqi 1987: 158). It is maintained that each of these heads of expenditure is related to a duty of the Islamic state derived from objectives of the Shari'a such as preservation of lives, need fulfillment, and strengthening the Muslim community. In contrast to the mandatory functions which express the "will of Allah," the necessary functions express the "will of experts" and lead to temporary heads of expenditure which can vary in importance with changing circumstances ("circumstantial expenditures").

Assigned functions and expenditures

To extend the scope of legitimate expenditures of an Islamic state even further, Muslim economists introduce a third category of "assigned functions" which should be based on the "will of the people" (M. N. Siddiqi 1987). The corresponding "assigned expenditures" are revocable if the people so decide.

Theoretically, it is an idealistic belief that the people assign tasks to the state. The logic of collective action explains why one should not expect that "the people" as a very large group will organize themselves and assign well-defined activities to the state. Those who "assign" tasks to the state are much smaller groups looking for exemptions from general rules, for privileges and support. The most efficiently organized groups in Western democracies are producers (capital owners and workers) in ailing industries who approach politicians for subsidies, protection against external competitors, and preferences in government procurement programs. Politicians (have to) take up such demand if the lobby groups can mobilize considerable support or opposition at the next election. The costs of a privileged treatment of producers are dispersed widely and borne mainly by consumers and taxpayers.

Usually the privileged treatment of well-organized lobby groups is justified by politicians with (vague) references to the general welfare, to employment, or to a mandate given by the voters. But factually "the voters" never gave a specific mandate, and "the people" never assigned a specific task to the government. Another set of problems is caused by the fact that circumstantial and assigned functions can come into conflict with each other. For example, experts could argue that the state should not protect jobs in ailing industries which have lost their markets to foreign competitors. Instead the state should use funds to accelerate the development of industries with good growth prospects and job potentials. But the people may give more importance to the conservation of existing jobs than to the creation of new jobs. Therefore, they assign the function "conservation of traditional jobs" to the state while economists are opposed to this. In such a case, a political decision is necessary; the classification of public expenditures in mandatory, circumstantial, and assigned categories does not solve the problem.

Practical significance of a categorization of public expenditures

The value of classification and categorization of public expenditures for the development of a coherent Islamic concept of public finance is not questioned here, but doubts arise concerning its practical significance. It would be significant if the Islamic concept would call for expenditures which a secular state would not commence by itself or prevent expenditures which a secular state would have made. It seems, however, that practical differences in this sense are marginal.

RELEVANCE OF CLASSIFICATIONS

It is obvious that a secular state will not spend money on the propagation of Islam. Moreover, every item of expenditures listed can be found in contemporary secular states. Further, the classifications of the Islamic theory do not prescribe the instruments with which the goals of public expenditures shall be achieved. For example, need fulfillment could be achieved, in the short run, by direct public transfers to the poor or, in the long run, by their gainful employment in expanding industries. The latter requires private and public investment. However, resources spent for capital formation and development (classified as "circumstantial expenditures") cannot be used for direct transfers to the poor (classified as "mandatory expenditures"). Thus, a government which spends large amounts on development projects and subsidies for industries but little on direct transfers may argue that it is best serving the long-term need fulfillment although it allocates much less resources to mandatory than to circumstantial expenditures. In addition, if the government spends enough to secure the survival of all although it could spend much more on welfare if it reduces defense or investment expenditures, it can point out that public funds have been allocated to all mandated heads of expenditure and that there is no rule determining the proportion in which the funds have to be allocated.

In sum, the practical significance of a categorization of public expenditures is very limited. Either a government does already allocate public funds to mandatory and circumstantial functions – then the categorization is redundant. Or a government has neglected mandatory functions and is not really willing to change its pattern of expenditures – then it can find many excuses or justifications for its practice and the categorization remains ineffective.

It seems that Islamic economists are more concerned with the inclusion of items of expenditure in, than with their exclusion from, the categories of permissible expenditures. Muslim economists claim that an Islamic economic system is superior to any secular system in terms of allocation, distribution, and stability. Everything which is not explicitly forbidden is allowed in Islam, so all except a few types of public expenditures (e.g. interest payments or subsidies for prohibited productions such as wine or pork) must be permissible. The superiority was deduced from the Islamic value orientation and from the replacement of interest-based financing by profit and loss sharing techniques. However, the realities of Islamic states such as Pakistan and Iran and of Islamic banks in many Muslim countries have revealed a multitude of reasons why the ideal of the Islamic economists could not be realized in practice. A convincing theory on how to achieve a (gradual or evolutionary and not enforced or revolutionary) transformation from the status quo to the Islamic ideal is still missing.

There is a remarkable contrast between the efforts of Muslim economists to show the modernity of an Islamic economic system and modern developments in the Western theory of public finance. First, many Muslim economists with a preference for a Keynesian type of stabilization policy tried to expound why a countercyclical fiscal policy would not contradict the concept of public finance in Islam. In contrast to this, Western mainstream economics turned away from macroeconomic fine tuning and favored a noninterventionist type of monetary and fiscal policy. Second, Muslim economists are factually rather permissive with respect to public expenditures, while Western economist become increasingly worried about the factually unlimited power of the state to raise taxes and to spend public money according to political preferences.

Contrary to most Muslim economists who still consider state interventions a solution for social and economic problems, many Western economists consider interventions and regulations the origin of the problems. State interventions, government regulations, and rent-seeking negatively affect allocation, growth, stability, and distribution. For an increasing number of Western economists not the inclusion but the exclusion or limitation of heads of expenditure from the state budget has priority, and not the further extension but the limitation of the state's power to tax and to spend are of main concern.

Financing of budget deficits

There was an extensive debate in the 1980s and early 1990s on the possibilities and qualities of budget deficits in an Islamic state (Ahmad 1980; Ahmed *et al.* 1983;

Gulaid and Abdullah 1995). When budgets of Western states run into deficit, governments usually issue interest-bearing bonds to finance the deficit by borrowing from the capital market. Because of the prohibition of interest (*riba*) this is not possible in an Islamic state (unless this prohibition is simply ignored as it was the case in the Islamic Republic of Pakistan). Starting from here, or taking this as a background, the academic contributions have gone – roughly speaking – in two directions.

The first direction is questioning whether budget deficits (except in emergency situations) are of any social benefit. With reference to the dangers of excessive public expenditures (inflation, "creeping socialization," burdening of future generations, etc.) the answer is generally negative. However, because deficits do more harm than good, the proponents of this line of thinking argue that the technical impossibility to finance budget deficits would be an advantage of an Islamic system: it prevents governments from implementing harmful policies.

The second line of reasoning is directed toward the design of interest-free bonds, that is, commercial papers issued by the government and promising subscribers a competitive noninterest return. For example, some propose papers whose subscribers participate in the profits of state-owned enterprises (e.g. power stations) or revenue generating infrastructure objects (e.g. toll bridges). However, in market economies the state is not expected to act as an entrepreneur. Therefore, the number of profitable enterprises would be very small, and only small amounts could be mobilized. Some Islamic economists have proposed government papers with a rate of return proportional to the growth rate of the economy. Their rationale is that the subscribers of these papers enable the government to facilitate growth of the economy. This entitles the subscribers to receive a share from the economic growth. This is a fallacious argument. The growth of an economy depends on many factors – including the state's policies. Sometimes, the policies of government may even hinder economic growth. One cannot establish an unambiguous or quantifiable link between the subscription of a government paper and the overall growth of the economy.

The Islamic sanction of interest-free bonds of the "first generation" was rather weak. The financial engineers could neither point to similar constructions in the formative years of Islamic law, nor did they pay much attention to traditional forms of Islamic contracts. Thus, there was no consensus on the various types of interest-free government papers, and most of the proposals were never applied in practice.

The situation changed substantially only in recent years. A new financial product is gaining rapidly in popularity amongst Islamic banks in the Arab world and Islamic departments of Western financial institutions. It is called *sukuk*. Sukuks are supposed to be standardized asset-backed securities with predictable nominal returns to be issued by private or public entities and traded on a secondary market. Obviously there is a need for a Shari'a compliant substitute for interest-bearing bonds (Al-Amine 2001). In an extreme form – as applied in principle for the sukuk issue of a highly indebted German state government of Saxony-Anhalt in August 2004[10] – the construction could be explained as follows: (1) The government

G sets up a legally independent but wholly owned business unit B (for tax reasons in a tax haven abroad). There are no Shari'a objections against this transaction. (2) G concludes a Shari'a compliant sales contract with deferred payment for office buildings with B. (3) The office buildings are rented by G from B on the basis of a long-term lease contract with a fixed rental income for B. Leasing (ijara) has become a preferred mode for the Shari'a compliant long-term financing of fixed assets. (4) B will issue commercial papers which document a standardized (temporary) partial ownership of the office buildings purchased from and rented to G. From the Shari'a point of view there are no objections against this type of securitization if the market value of the papers is due to the participation in a rental income. This rental income is nominally fixed and predictable for a specified period which factually gives the sukuk the economic characteristics of an interest-bearing bond. (5) Since sukuks represent partial ownership of real assets, they can be traded legitimately on a secondary market at prices determined by supply and demand.[11]

The approval and acceptance of the sukuk model by Shari'a experts has far-reaching consequences for the further development of Islamic finance. With this model, Islamic financial institutions as well as private companies and indebted governments can replicate a large variety of interest-based financing techniques and securities. The basic ploy is that the bank, company, or government creates a legally independent but wholly owned business unit as a partner for legally effective but commercially fictitious sale and lease transactions. By this technique all types of productive and unproductive assets can be mobilized. Nonmarketable assets can be marketed and generate a "market income" where no market exists. To illustrate this with an extreme example, consider the following. The government could create the "Public Defense Ltd.," sell to it all its defense assets and lease them back at fixed rates. The issue of sukuks by the Public Defense Ltd. allows the government to finance budget deficits of nearly any size at fixed costs. The calculation of leasing rates and issue prices will tie the Islamic sector to the interest-based economy.

Conclusions

Islamic economics is defined by an explicit value orientation and a particular methodology for legitimizing legal systems and policies. Not the technicalities but the underlying principles and the method of legitimization constitute the Islamic substance of institutional arrangements. Against this background, the evaluation of the literature on taxation and public finance exposed a surprisingly large number of methodological inaccuracies, free interpretations of the Shari'a, and even conceptual errors. Much of the literature lacks analytical depth. Neither unreflected quotations of traditional legal texts nor mere classifications would replace economic theories. They are not helpful in the development of a consistent Islamic worldview. But a more convincing case for an Islamic system of taxation and public finance could be made if the real behavior of people and politicians in the contemporary Muslim world were taken into consideration. The low level of zakat proceeds and the seemingly widespread practice of zakat evasion have discredited all models which assume a world populated by "ideal Muslims." It cannot be taken for granted that even the highest religious duties are fulfilled voluntarily. Therefore, the proposed Islamic transformation from the present to the ideal conditions becomes highly problematic: how to reach an ideal from a reality that differs in fundamental behavioral respects. Empirical analyses of the realities in Muslim countries and transformation strategies toward an Islamic ideal based thereon should become a major topic in Islamic economics. The value of the so far dominant abstract or axiomatic and prescriptive models is quite limited for the explanation of observable phenomena (the "real world") and for policy design.

Notes

1 See for example, Siddiqi (1980), Zarqa (1992), Behdad (1993), Haneef (1995), Kuran (1992) and (2004), Nomani and Rahnema (1994), and Chapra (1992 and 2000).
2 See in particular Qureshi (1978), Ra'ana (1970), Siddiqi (1983), Shirazi (1996), Kahf (1995).
3 See Afzal-ur-Rahman (1976), Metwally (1983), El-Din (1986), Salama (1983, 1995).
4 See in general, H. S. M. Zaman (1991), Duri (1985), Salama (1983), and Kahf (1999).
5 Translation of the Quran by A. Y. Ali (1983).
6 See as examples Rahman (2003), Ministry of Islamic Affairs, Endowments, Da'wah and Guidance of the Kingdom of Saudi Arabia (2005), and Pusat Pungutan Zakat (2004), www.zakat.com.my
7 See in particular Afzal-ur-Rahman (1976), Shaik (1980: 19–20), Chaudhry (1992: 25), Abdullah (1995: 18–19).
8 See, among others, Chaudhry (1992: 25), Abdullah (1995: 19), El-Badawi, and Al-Sultan (1992: 70–1).
9 See for example, www.islamicity.com/mosque/Zakat/, and www.zakat.com.my,http://zakat.al-islam.com/eng/
10 For further information see: http://www.thebanker.com/news/fullstory.php/aid/1910/Germany_launches_Europe%92s_first_Sukuk.html and http://www.bankerme.com/bme/2005/feb/how_to_structure_sukuk.asp
11 For a detailed presentation see Adam and Thomas (2004). Information on recent activities in the sukuk market can be found on various websites, for example www.bma.gov.bh (Bahrain Monetary Agency), www.bankerme.com (Banker Middle East), or www.securities.com/ifis/ (Islamic Finance Information Service).

Bibliography

Abdullah, M. A. (1995) "Introduction," in M. A. Gulaid and M. A. Abdullah (eds) *Readings in Public Finance in Islam*, Jeddah: Islamic Development Bank, Islamic Research and Training Institute.
Adam, N. J. and Thomas, A. (2004) *Islamic Bonds*, London: Euromoney Books.
Afzal-ur-Rahman (1976) *Economic Doctrines of Islam*, vol. III, Lahore: Islamic Publications.
Ahmad, K. (ed.) (1980) *Studies in Islamic Economics*, Jeddah and Leicester: International Center for Research in Islamic Economics and The Islamic Foundation.
Ahmed, Z., Iqbal, M., and Khan, M. F. (eds) (1983) *Fiscal Policy and Resource Allocation in Islam*, Islamabad: Institute of Policy Studies.

Al-Amine, M. A. M. (2001) "The Islamic Bonds Market – Possibilities and Challenges," *International Journal of Islamic Financial Services*, 3(1), http://islamic-finance.net/journals/journal9/albashir.pdf

Ali, A. Y. (1983/1934) *The Holy Quran – Text, Translation and Commentary*, Brentwood: Amana Corp.

Al-Omar, F. A. (1995) "General, Administrative and Organizational Aspects," in A. A. El-Ashker and M. S. Haq (eds) *Institutional Framework of Zakah: Dimensions and Implications* (Proceedings of the Third Zakah Conference, Kula Lumpur 1990), Jeddah: Islamic Development Bank, Islamic Research and Training Institute.

Al Qaradawi, Y. (2000/1973) *Fiqh Al Zakah: A Comparative Study of Zakah, Regulations and Philosophy in the Light of Quran and Sunnah* (2 volumes) translated by M. Kahf (original: Fiqh al-Zakat. Beirut 1973), Jeddah: King Abdulaziz University.

Behdad, S. (1993) "Appendix: Fundamentals of Islamic Jurisprudence," in K. S. Jomo (ed.) *Islamic Economic Alternatives – Critical Perspectives and New Directions*, Kuala Lumpur: Ikraq.

Brahimi, A. H. (2002) "Poverty Eradication and Development from an Islamic Perspective: The Case of the Arab World," in United Nations Development Programme (ed.) *Arab Human Development Report 2002*, 105, New York: UNDP.

Chapra, M. U. (1992) *Islam and the Economic Challenge*, Leicester: The Islamic Foundation.

Chapra, M. U. (2000) *The Future of Economics: An Islamic Perspective*, Markfield: The Islamic Foundation.

Chaudhry, M. S. (1992) *Taxation in Islam and Modern Taxes*, Lahore: Impact Publications International.

Duri, A. A. (1985) "Taxation in Early Islam," *Journal of Islamic Banking and Finance*, 2 (April–June): 61–70.

El-Ashker, A. A. and Haq, M. S. (eds) (1995) *Institutional Framework of Zakah: Dimensions and Implications* (Proceedings of the Third Zakah Conference, Kuala Lumpur 1990), Jeddah: Islamic Development Bank, Islamic Research and Training Institute.

El-Badawi, M. A. and Al-Sultan S. M. (1992) "Net Working Capital versus Net Owner's Equity Approaches to Computing Zakatable Amount: A Conceptual Comparison and Application," *The American Journal of Islamic Social Sciences*, 9: 69–85.

El-Din, S. T. (1986) "Allocative and Stabilizing Functions of Zakat in an Islamic Economy," in M. A. Gulaid and M. A. Abdullah (eds) *Readings in Public Finance in Islam*, Jeddah: Islamic Development Bank, Islamic Research and Training Institute.

Guermat, C., Al-Utaibi, A. T., and Tucker, J. P. (2003) "The Practice of Zakat: An Empirical Examination of Four Gulf Countries," University of Exeter, Discussion Papers in Economics, 03/02. http://www.ex.ac.uk/sobeinternal/Research/DiscussionPapersEcon/Econ2003/Econ0302.pdf

Gulaid, M. A. and Abdullah, M. A. (eds) (1995) *Readings in Public Finance in Islam*, Jeddah: Islamic Development Bank, Islamic Research and Training Institute.

Haneef, M. A. (1995) *Contemporary Islamic Economic Thought: A Selected Comparative Analysis*, Kuala Lumpur: Ikraq.

Jomo, K. S. (ed.) (1993) *Islamic Economic Alternatives – Critical Perspectives and New Directions*, Kuala Lumpur: Ikraq.

Kahf, M. (1995/1983) "Taxation Policy in an Islamic Economy," in Z. Ahmed, M. Iqbal, and M. F. Khan (eds) *Fiscal Policy and Resource Allocation in Islam*, Islamabad: Institute of Policy Studies; quoted from the reprint, in M. A. Gulaid and M. A. Abdullah (eds) *Readings in Public Finance in Islam*, 105–27, Jeddah: Islamic Development Bank, Islamic Research and Training Institute.

Kahf, M. (1999) "The Performance of the Institution of Zakah in Theory and Practice," Paper prepared for the International Conference on Islamic Economics Towards the 21st Century, Kuala Lumpur, April 26–30, 1999; for download: http://monzer.kahf.com/papers/english/performance of zakah malaysia 1999.pdf

Kamali, M. H. (2000) *Islamic Law in Malaysia: Issues and Developments*, Kuala Lumpur: Ilmiah Publishers.

Khan, M. A. (2003) "Zakah Accounting and Auditing: Principles and Experiences in Pakistan," *Islamic Economic Studies*, 10 (2): 29–43.

Kuran, T. (1992) "The Economic System in Contemporary Islamic Thought," in K. S. Jomo (ed.) *Islamic Economic Alternatives – Critical Perspectives and New Directions*, 9–47, Kuala Lumpur: Ikraq.

Kuran, T. (2004) *Islam and Mammon: The Economic Predicaments of Islamism*, Princeton, NJ and Oxford: Princeton University Press.

Mannan, M. A. (1986) *Islamic Economics: Theory and Practice*, Sevenoaks: Hodder and Stoughton.

Metwally, M. M. (1983) "Fiscal Policy in an Islamic Economy," in Z. Ahmed, M. Iqbal, and M. F. Khan (eds) *Fiscal Policy and Resource Allocation in Islam*, 59–81, Islamabad: Institute of Policy Studies.

Ministry of Islamic Affairs, Endowments, Da'wah and Guidance (Kingdom of Saudi Arabia) (2005) *How to Calculate Your Zakah?* http://zakat.al-islam.com/eng/

Muhammad, A. A. (1993) *Zakat and Rural Development in Malaysia*, Kuala Lumpur: Berita Publishing.

Nomani, F. and Rahnema, A. (1994) *Islamic Economic Systems*, London and New Jersey: Zed Books.

Oran, A. and Rashid, S. (1989) "Fiscal Policy in Early Islam," *Public Finance*, 44 (1): 75–101.

Pusat Pungutan Zakat (2004) *Laporan Zakat 2003 [Zakat Report 2003]*, Kuala Lumpur, http://www.zakat.com.my/download/laporan2003.pdf

Qureshi, A. I. (1978) *Fiscal System of Islam*, Lahore: Institute of Islamic Culture.

Ra'ana, I. M. (1970) *Economic System under Umar the Great*, Lahore: Sh. Muhammad Ashraf.

Rahman, M. (2003) *Zakat Calculation*, Markfield: The Islamic Foundation.

Salama, A. A. (1983) "Fiscal Policy in an Islamic State," in Z. Ahmed, M. Iqbal, and M. F. Khan (eds) *Fiscal Policy and Resource Allocation in Islam*, Islamabad: Institute of Policy Studies.

Salama, A. A. (1995) "Empirical Economic Effects of Obligatory and Non-Obligatory Payment of Zakah to the State," in A. A. El-Ashker and M. S. Haq (eds) *Institutional Framework of Zakah: Dimensions and Implications* (Proceedings of the Third Zakah Conference, Kuala Lumpur 1990), Jeddah: Islamic Development Bank, Islamic Research and Training Institute.

Shaik, A. A. (1980) "Concept of Zakah: A Survey of Quranic Texts and their Explanations in Shariah and Contemporary Economics," in M. R. Zaman (ed.) *Some Aspects of the Economics of Zakah*, 2–65, Plainfield, IN: The Association of Muslim Social Scientists.

Shirazi, N. S. (1996) *System of Zakat in Pakistan: An Appraisal*, Islamabad: International Institute of Islamic Economics.

Siddiqi, M. A. S. (1983) *Early Development of Zakat Law and Ijtihad*, Karachi: Islamic Research Academy.

Siddiqi, M. N. (1980) "Muslim Economic Thinking – A Survey of Contemporary Literature," in K, Ahmad (ed.) *Studies in Islamic Economics*, Jeddah and Leicester: International Center for Research in Islamic Economics and The Islamic Foundation.

Siddiqi, M. N. (1987) "Public Expenditure in an Islamic State," *Journal of Islamic Banking and Finance*, 4 (October–December): 7–34.

Weiss, H. (2002) "Zakat and the Question of Social Welfare: An Introductory Essay on Islamic Economics and Its Implications for Social Welfare," in H. Weiss (ed.) *Social Welfare in Muslim Societies in Africa*, Stockholm: Nordic Africa Institute.

Zaman, H. S. M. (1991) *Economic Functions of an Islamic State – The Early Experience*, Leicester: The Islamic Foundation.

Zarqa, M. A. (1992) "Methodology of Islamic Economics," in A. Ahmad and K. R. Awan (eds) *Lectures on Islamic Economics* (Papers and Proceedings of a Seminar on Teaching Islamic Economics for University Teachers, Islamabad 1987), 49–58, Jeddah: Islamic Development Bank, Islamic Research and Training Institute.

8 The dilemma of riba-free banking in Islamic public policy

Farhad Nomani

Introduction

The juridical meaning of *riba* (literally, an excess or increase) and its application in interest-free Islamic banking have always been controversial in contemporary Islamic public policy. The controversy is about the Quranic prohibition of riba and, to a lesser degree, its related Shari'a concept, *gharar* (literally, hazard). The practical side of this debate is the elimination of riba from financial transactions, and the establishment of a banking system based on legally recognized Islamic contracts.

Despite the consensus among Muslims that riba is explicitly prohibited in the Quran and the Tradition of the Prophet (*Sunna*), the meaning of riba, gharar, and acceptable Islamic banking has always been subject to diverse interpretations. For some contemporary Muslims riba signifies only usury and "excessive" interest, and for some others, simply interest or even any other gains. Since the 1980s, governments in Muslim countries have had different approaches to Islamic banking. Despite their differences in the interpretation of the Shari'a, the Shi'i Iranian and Sunni Sudanese governments claim that their banking law and banking system are totally Islamic. Other countries, notably Pakistan, Egypt, and Saudi Arabia have gradually, and in practice, adopted dual banking systems. In these countries, Islamic banking operates under the laws for conventional banking. Pakistan has followed this path since the 1970s because of continued politico-religious debates concerning "Islamic banking" and conventional banking laws. Saudi Arabia claims that it does not have to change its banking law because it has always been Islamic. So far, Egypt and Saudi Arabia have been able to avoid any formal legal and administrative changes. Malaysia is the only country that officially has separate and parallel legal and regulatory systems for Islamic and conventional banks in a systematic and planned manner in an open economy.[1]

This chapter identifies difficulties in drawing, based on the Shari'a, a unanimously agreed upon policy for the elimination of riba and gharar, and for establishing a viable Islamic banking. The first section of this chapter summarizes the debate on riba, gharar, and Islamic partnership contracts among classical jurists of major schools of Islamic law, Hanafi, Shafi'i, Maliki, Hanbali, and the Ja'fari Shi'i. The second section reviews the contemporary debates on riba-free banking in general, and in Egypt, Iran, and Pakistan in particular. This chapter demonstrates that differences of opinions on interest-free banking exist not only between policy makers and Islamic scholars in different countries, or between those belonging to different schools, but also among those in the same country or school. The persistence of these controversies is a source of rent and segmentation for Islamic banks in national and international financial markets.

Classical views on riba, gharar, and financial contracts

Riba

Riba was a common practice in the Arabian Peninsula at the advent of Islam.[2] It was mainly an extra amount of an article in case of delay in its delivery. Thus, the failure to fulfill a sale contract or a loan in kind at the time of maturity led to the continuous multiplication of the obligation. The Quran explicitly prohibits this practice, which in this chapter will be called the Quranic riba, or simply riba.[3]

The Traditions of the Prophet are also explicit about the injunction against riba. Yet, according to classical jurists, not all of the reports of the sayings of the Prophet (*hadith*) are equally reliable or are unanimous about what constitutes riba and what forms of contracts come under the Quranic prohibition.[4] One of the most accepted or relevant sayings of the Prophet about riba, reported in most compilations of the sayings of the Prophet, asserts that riba exists when six articles of the same kind are either bartered unequally or not delivered immediately. These articles were identified as gold, silver, dates, salt, barley, and wheat (Saleh 1992: 24–33).

According to the Quran and the Tradition of the Prophet, unlike the corporal punishment for theft and other illicit acts, there is no specific punishment for the practice of riba among Muslims except the loss of God's blessing in this world and the torture of hell in the next. Moreover, both sources leave the question of whether Muslims may or may not practice riba with people of another religion entirely open.

All schools of Islamic law condemn riba and prohibit transactions that are susceptible to riba. Nevertheless, classical books on fiqh repeatedly state that the Second Caliph, Umar, had doubts about the clarity of the application of riba in practice, and that a respected Companion of the Prophet, Ibn Abbas, could only recognize riba in sales with deferred delivery (Nomani 2002).

Classical jurists were interested in the concept of riba within the framework of the Islamic law of contract. They categorized various type of contracts as sales and asserted that the Quran and the Sunna had permitted *bay'* (selling or exchange, trading) and prohibited riba. They did this because they believed that in the Quranic verse on riba (II: 275), which states that sale is licit and riba is illicit, riba was either an ambiguous (*mujmal*) or a speculative general (*amm*) term that had to be specified by the Sunna.[5] By asserting that riba is an ambiguous or a general term, and not a specific concept that would be free from interpretation, all the classical jurists prevented the application of the prohibition of riba to all "increases" or "excesses" and limited its interdiction to only certain objects of sale.[6] They confined riba to sale contracts because the authentic hadith that could clarify and specify it, limited riba only to sales. In this endeavor, they gradually classified riba into two categories: *riba al-fadl* (riba of increase or riba by way of excess) and *riba al-nasia* (riba of delayed payment or riba by way of deferment).

Riba al-fadl is the unlawful excess of the counter-values in a "hand-to-hand" barter transaction and all jurists prohibit it because it does not realize the balance of the exchanged counter-values. However, early jurists differ from each other in detail concerning the conditions of sale and the articles the exchange of which were susceptible to riba. Riba al-nasia arises when the exchange of counter-values is delayed, since a deferred exchange could produce a gain in one of the counter-values. Nevertheless, such an exchange was unlawful whether or not it gave rise to a gain (Saleh 1992: 24–33, 204–5). The notion of the interdiction of deferred delivery is closely related to the concept of gharar, and for this reason the idea in prohibition of riba al-nasia is to make the transfer of ownership when the contract is drawn up.

Thus, the early dominant trend among the jurists of all Islamic schools of law considered riba as a prohibition affecting sales. This view ignored the discussion of loans based on riba in which an advantage or an increase was stipulated for the lender. Early jurists recognized a loan mainly as a gratuitous transaction that excludes riba. Consequently, these jurists accepted the validity of giving a premium or an "increase" to a lender, but condemned it if such premium was a requisite (Homoud 1985: 54–5). Only the contemporary jurists explicitly categorize riba differently and recognize riba in both sales and debts on equal footing.

Moreover, some classical jurists, mostly Hanafis, Shafi'is, and Shi'is, allow legal tricks that would circumvent the prohibition against riba, provided such tricks and conditions are possible, reasonable, and lawful (Homoud 1985: 100–10; Saleh 1992: 44–61). There are several devices for the evasion of the prohibition of riba. One of these tricks is the use of a pledge (*rahn*), such as the use of a real estate to secure the repayment of a debt. Such a device enabled the lender to derive some advantage from the pledge during the period of the loan. Riba in debts could be legalized by different kinds of double sale contracts. One of these double sales enables a prospective debtor to sell to a creditor something for cash, and buy the article back from the lender for a greater price payable at a future date. To avoid the prohibition of riba by the sale of one money for another money on credit, the legal trick would be that one buys an article from a seller and pays in one money; then the seller shall purchase back the article on credit.[7] Such multiple transactions, each of which valid by itself, together can realize the objective of the contractors. In fact, many practical contracts that facilitate Islamic banking in modern economies, such as resale with a stated profit (*murabaha*) or demanding a pledge to secure the repayment of a loan, are all legal devices.

Gharar

Islamic law considers all sale or hire contracts that involve speculative risk (gharar) invalid. To avoid gharar in a sale contract the following must be known: the object and its quantities, the price or the counter-value, the time of delivery, and sale condition of payment (Doi 1984: 399). The requirement that the object and its quantity in a contract must be known is very sensitive for articles that can be measured or weighed (Schacht 1964: 147; El-Gamal 2001: 2–10).

Classical jurists approve of future sale contracts only when such contracts are "free" from riba or gharar. For example, sale of most foodstuffs, but not of gold or silver (as money), for future delivery with prepayment in cash (*salam* or *salaf*), delayed payment for goods delivered at once (*nasia*), and hire and lease (*ijara*) of services of human beings, lands, or buildings are authorized. In general, such sales are valid if they are sales of a known benefit in return for its known equivalent (Saleh 1992: 62–105; El-Gamal 2001: 3–7). In other words, most Islamic schools of law do not permit contracts with an unspecified price which will be determined in the future by the market or by another person. However, some jurists have allowed a "small" element of risk (gharar) and uncertainty (*juhala*) if a greater part of the contracted goods is delivered. Contracts that are not free from the element of riba and gharar but are allowed by many jurists are agricultural share-cropping (*mudara'a*), share-cropping in the case of orchards and gardening (*musaqat*), fixed land rent and fixed wages in return for unspecified work or unrelated to profit and loss of the enterprise. The contract is valid in the first two cases simply because the Prophet explicitly allowed them and himself had entered into such a contract.

The last case is, however, a matter of controversy in Islamic law (Afzal-ur Rahman 1982). In contrast to the views of the classical jurists of the Hanbali, Shafi'i, and Hanafi schools, some jurists like Ibn Taimiyah, approve of transactions based on gharar and *maisir* (gambling or speculation) if their prohibitions lead to hardship for people (Islahi 1988: 166–8).

Mudaraba and musharaka

Laws that are based on ethical constraints of transactions, including Islamic law, do not recognize the liberty of contracts in general, and contracts of association in particular. In the operational framework of currently functioning Islamic banks, the relevant and most recognized forms of associations are *musharaka* (or *shirka*, partnership), especially the limited type, and *mudaraba* (or *qirad*, dormant or sleeping partnership). These are transactions through partnership rather than through exchange of goods.[8]

The Quran does not refer to mudaraba, although the contract was used before the advent of Islam. However, the Tradition is explicit about the approval of the Prophet and his companions in such a contract (Udovitch 1986: 132). For this reason, all Islamic schools of law permit the use of mudaraba and some other forms of partnership.

Inasmuch as mudaraba combines the advantages of partnership and loan contracts, it can be used as a device for avoiding the prohibition of riba. In fact, jurists identify mudaraba only as a special form of partnership. In general, partnership involves participation of at least two persons with defined amount of capital for jointly running a business and for sharing profit and loss in predetermined proportions. Mudaraba is not a partnership proper since it consists of a fiduciary relationship and a procuration. It is similar to partnership because the profit is to be shared between partners, although only the dormant partner or the owner of the capital, and not the agent (or active partner) bears the loss; the agent looses only his time and effort after the deduction of all expenses. Like a loan contract, the investor in a mudaraba agreement is not directly in association with the agent who is responsible for the management of the capital, but is entitled to a certain proportion of profit of the enterprise. In practice, this predetermined share of profit could correspond to interest. It is for this reason that classical jurists have been careful defining the nature and terms of the legality of the contract.

In any case, the application of medieval mudaraba and musharaka contracts to modern banking in the form of two-tier mudaraba (or mudaraba under mudaraba) is an innovation in fiqh. Despite their differences on the form of capital involved, that is, cash or in kind, the distribution of profit and financial liabilities of partners, and the duration of mudaraba and musharaka contracts, classical Sunni and Shi'i fiqh restricted the use of mudaraba to only short-term trade. The reasoning was that only in commerce the result of the activity is unpredictable or unknown, and hence riba is absent (Abu Saud 1981: 70; Siddiqi 1987). However, contemporary jurists have gradually accepted the idea of the application of mudaraba in different kinds of economic activities. They have accepted the two-tier mudaraba contract in banking.

In the case of two-tier mudaraba, which is the only form of mudaraba that would suit modern banking, the active partner (i.e. the bank) receives capital from a dormant partner (i.e. the bank's client), and, in turn engages in another mudaraba contract with another active partner (i.e. an entrepreneur). Related to this case is the use of mudaraba capital for a musharaka contract with another active partner.

In short, the literal application of the rulings of the classical Islamic schools of law to modern socioeconomic conditions, including modern civil and commercial laws, in general, and financial markets, including Islamic banking, in particular, is not easy without the introduction of innovation in fiqh. This is due to the historical specificity of the law and the fact that the definition and scope of contracts and injunctions are not always clear or unanimous.

In developed market systems barter, sales in which currency is not one of the counter-values (riba al-fadl) and barter sales by way of deferment (riba al-nasia) are rare and hardly relevant. Financial markets and their products such as stocks, bonds, and insurance commodities in which the object of transaction and the price or both are not determined and fixed in advance, could not be in the jurists' list of various cases of gharar. Besides, the confinement of mudaraba to short-run trade and the application of classical requisites for similar partnerships are not reasonable and practical at present. Nevertheless, the Shari'a, interpreted differently in different regions and even within the same region, has always been part of the social consciousness of Muslim communities, and in the modern times, Muslim countries. Therefore, historically the contradiction between theory and practice has given rise to Islamic legal devices, Western-inspired rules and devices, legal innovations and new interpretations, all of which have incited religious and popular criticism and disapproval (Nomani 2003: 59–64).

Modern interpretation of riba

The limited and broader definition of riba

The debate on the interpretation of riba among Islamist scholars, and to a lesser degree among ulama, was intensified in the early twentieth century at the advent of modern Western banking in Muslim countries. These banks that mainly served the governments and the trade with the European countries, were eventually replaced by state or privately owned national banks and savings institutions. All these banks paid interest on savings accounts and charged interest on their loans. This practice led to dissatisfaction among ulama and Islamic intellectuals. However, it is interesting to note that anti-riba slogans have never mobilized Muslim masses, despite fierce rhetoric of the majority of ulama and Islamic intellectuals in condemnation of riba.

From the beginning, two major views have been shaped concerning the legal meaning of riba. One has argued for a limited definition, and the other has insisted on a broader meaning of riba. The former view defines riba as usury, and, there-fore, asks only for the prohibition of excessive interest. Proponents of this view argue that riba leads to exploitation of the poor by means of usurious consumption loans. Despite differences in detail, the views of advocates of a limited definition of riba have influenced and shaped public-civil laws, codes, and policies of almost all Muslim countries in the twentieth century, especially until the 1980s. Thus, the Iranian civil code that was adopted in 1927–32, and the civil codes of the majority of Arab countries, adopted in 1930–60, all recognize riba implicitly or explicitly as usury or excessive interest. All the other Muslim countries that became independent during the first two decades after the Second World War have also opted for a tacit recognition of "reasonable" interest as lawful.

The civil codes of all Arab countries, especially those adopted by the help of the Egyptian lawyer Abd al-Razzaq Sanhuri, except Lebanon, forbid compound interest on the ground that this rate is close to the Quranic riba, that is doubling and redoubling of the principal. Many of these countries, including Egypt, deter-mine maximum contractual rates that are normally lower for civil compared to commercial matters. However, a separate law governs banks that charge higher rates. Besides, commercial laws permit interest not only in contracts of loan but also of pledges in addition to the expenses relating to both contracts, the cost of enforcement and compensation for losses resulting from defects in the thing pledged. Yet, in some of the Persian Gulf states such as Kuwait and Bahrain interest is authorized in commercial codes but forbidden in civil codes. Thus, such countries officially restrict interest payment to commercial debts.

In Libya where the state banks pay interest on the savings accounts, interest on a loan is allowed only between legal entities. Algerian law is silent on the issue of interest, but interest is charged and paid and the central bank sets the rate of the banks.[9] The Saudi Arabian "Commercial Regulations" avoids the use of the word "interest" and replaces it with "profit" and "commission" for all commercial transactions including loans. The banking (or Monetary Agency) law of Saudi Arabia explicitly bars the central bank from charging interest. However, alternative solutions exist, for example, by paying "commissions" on savings accounts (Kay 1979: 34–6, 74–80). Iran and Pakistan's banking laws prohibit riba defined as all forms of interest, but many legal tricks soften the prohibition (Nomani and Rahnema 1994: 129–36, 177–82). In Southeast Asian Muslim countries, the law is secular and there is no substantive law against interest. However, some of these countries, for example Malaysia, have introduced legislation for Islamic banking that are regulatory and operate along interest-based banking system (Connors 1986: 57–66).

Since the 1970s, the supporters of the limited definition of riba have been on the defensive and their views were eclipsed by the rise of the Islamic resurgence movement. This movement has been associated with the extended view of riba, espoused either by pure traditionalist or modern radical Muslims.

The traditionalist and modern advocates of a broader definition of riba assert that any interest is riba, and is, therefore, forbidden by the Shari'a (Qureshi 1970: 113). The traditionalists, including the majority of Sunni and Shi'i ulama accept legal tricks from a juristic point of view, while, modern revivalist Muslims deny the legitimacy of such devices on ethical grounds. In addition, with the expansion of Islamic banking in small, but rich, Persian Gulf countries, under the pressure of practical solutions to modern financial contracts and international financial competition, some of the Shari'a supervisory boards of Islamic banks have had a more innovative approach to Islamic banking (DeLorenzo 1997: x, 100–1). However, still a minority of ulama and Islamic intellectuals define riba as any monopolistic profit, speculation, and hoarding, and reject the use of legal tricks (see Choudhury 1986: 130; Khan 1987: 19). There is also a very small group of Islamic intellectuals who reject capitalism because of its exploitative characteristic that is explained by the concept of riba.[10]

Since the 1970s, the supporters of the extended definition of riba have had an effective mobilizing influence in many Muslim countries, effectuating minor or drastic changes in the codes related to riba and banking rules and institutions. The relationship of the majority of ulama with this trend has been influenced by the strength and the radicalism of the Islamic movement. In general, the enthusiasm of the majority of ulama for a complete Islamization of the commercial laws and the banking sector, in glaring contrast to their insistence on Islamic personal and criminal rules, has been lukewarm. It seems that unlike some of the Islamic intellectuals, the majority of ulama are satisfied with a formalistic introduction of Islamic banking nomenclature, and, therefore, are not enthusiastic about radical demands for a strict interpretation of transactions that are capable of riba. However, this does not mean that when riba is explicitly defined in a limited manner, the majority of ulama have kept quiet and that they have not attacked the innovatory interpretations; riba is still for them a key symbol in religious and political discourses for an Islamic economy.

The debate on riba in Egypt

The problem of riba has been part of a broader problem of the application of the Shari'a in Egypt since the latter part of the 1970s. With the amendment in 1980 of the 1971 Constitution, the Shari'a is the principal source of legislation in Egypt (Skovgaard-Petersen 1997: 200–2). Therefore, it is mandatory that all laws, including the banking law of Egypt, be in conformity with Islamic principles and rules. To the present, no major banking legislation has been enacted, partly because the public, the government and ulama are divided on the issue.

However, the issue of riba in banking was raised in the early years of the twentieth century. In those years, many of the owners of the savings accounts of the newly established Postal Savings Fund refused to receive interest from the Fund. The new grand mufti of Egypt (chief jurisprudent), Muhammad Abduh, one of the most influential leaders of Shari'a reform movement and modernist approach to Islamic law, was put in a delicate position when he was asked to present his legal opinion on the matter (Homoud 1985: 122). He was confronted with a choice between his deep loyalty to the authority of Islam and his desire to modernize Islamic teaching (Haddad 1994: 30–63; Cragg 1995: 11–12). Abduh identified the interest paid by the Postal Fund as riba, and argued against the use of money, not as a means of exchange, but as a means to unfair increase of wealth by riba. He also asserted that the Postal Fund was not borrowing money from the public (depositors) out of necessity, and, therefore, the prohibition of the payment of interest could not be lifted. However, in order to facilitate economic activities, Abduh proposed the replacement of the savings accounts by mudaraba contracts in order to avoid riba.

Even though the role of mudaraba in banking practices was not further elaborated by Abduh and the Fund's operation continued as before, his reasoning and the idea of the use of mudaraba have inspired Muslims who favored a broader definition of riba. At the same time, in line with his Salafi's approach, Abduh's emphasis on the division of Islamic prohibitions into absolute and "adjustable" or less rigid injunctions that could be lifted under certain conditions due to "necessity" (*darura*), was utilized by later modernists who advocated a limited definition of riba.

Yet, it is important to note that the views of Muslim scholars concerning Abduh's position on riba are not unanimous. Some like Rashid Reza and Saleh insist that Abduh considered only the pre-Islamic riba, and, therefore, compound interest as the absolutely forbidden riba (Saleh 1992: 35–6). Others, such as Homoud and Mallat find this view as an uncritical acceptance of Rashid Reza's interpretation of Abduh's position and assert that the Grand Mufti identified the interest received by the Postal Fund depositors as riba (Homoud 1985: 115–26; Mallat 1986: 72–4).

The second important debate over the meaning of riba took place around the draft of the new civil code of Egypt in the 1930s and 1940s. At this time, A. R. Sanhury, a prominent member of the Association of Lawyers and an Islamic reformist was in the center of the debate. Lawyers related to the cause of reform expressed their views in articles in *Dar al-Ifta* (published under the auspices of Mufti A. M. Salim). These lawyers had a more technocratic interpretation of Islamic law, and despite their insistence on the idea that Islam is both religion and state, argued that modern legislation should be based on a proper and modernized interpretation of the rulings of fiqh (Skovgaard-Petersen 1997: 165–6). Thus, the civil code that was drafted by a commission led by A. R. Sanhuri, declared any predetermined and fixed return on money as permissible. Precisely, the debate focused on articles of the code related to the payment of interest in case of delay of payment and the ceiling on interest rate beyond which the rate was considered as usury or riba. These articles aroused a politically calm, yet analytically forceful, opposition among the traditional jurists. After all, in the introductory articles of the code, Shari'a was considered as a major source of the law, and its interpretation was the responsibility of the muftis (Ziadeh 1968: 141–7; Hill 1989: 163–79).

Abu Zahra, a leading jurist of Egypt in that period questioned the validity of the articles of the civil code on interest payment by the following argument. He stated that it is wrong to rely on a limited definition of riba on the principles of "necessity" and "public interest" (*maslaha*) to justify the payment of interest. He argued that these principles cannot be used in the case of riba because "necessity" applies only at the level of individuals, and in the case of loans with interest, it is relevant only for a single borrower and not lenders of money. In addition, in his view, since the Islamic principle of necessity is applicable to individual cases and not to the society in general, the principle of the public interest cannot be invoked in defense of interest rate for the whole society (Kamali 1991: 273–80). According to Abu Zahra, it is true that the act of borrowing for riba is not absolutely forbidden as a "first-degree sin." However, loans based on riba are forbidden per se. In his opinion, this is because the Quranic riba is riba al-nasia (riba by way of deferment), which is like a modern loan. Therefore, all kinds of interest are riba and forbidden. To avoid the prohibition of riba, mudaraba can be used in the banking system (Homoud 1985: 62, 121–2; Mallat 1986: 70–7).

In reaction to this argument, Ibrahim Zaki al-Badawi, who was working on the draft of the code in relation to Islamic law, presented the following rebuttal. He asserted that riba al-nasia based on a continuous multiplication of the principal, is the only absolutely prohibited Quranic riba. However, he insisted that riba al-fadl (riba of increase) was forbidden by the Prophet in order to prevent the circumvention of the Quranic prohibition of riba. Echoing the views of Ibn Taimiyah and Ibn Qayyim on the degrees of prohibition in Islam, Badawi states that the prohibition of riba al-fadl is lighter. This riba is allowed in case of need (*haja*), while the Quranic riba can be permitted only in cases of absolute necessity.

Besides, a loan based on interest for productive purposes that eventually creates benefit is valid. According to Badawi, this is because unlike the "excess" or increase in the Quranic riba that periodically grows at the time of maturity, the principal of the loan increases with interest at the moment of contracting based on mutual consent (and not compulsion). Most financial transactions and instruments (e.g. bonds, debts, stocks, and insurance) are beneficial and facilitate economic activities of Muslims, and, therefore, should be considered as necessity in Islamic public policy and codification. In Islam nothing is forbidden unless the Shari'a has explicitly prohibited it. Thus, Badawi concludes that by allowing simple interest rates and forbidding compound interest rates, the proposed civil code of Egypt is in conformity with the Shari'a (Mallat 1986: 79–81).

In the 1950s, Sanhuri elaborated the argument presented by Badawi. He argues that riba has been forbidden in Islam for public policy considerations, that is, preventing hoarding of necessities, speculation on currency, and unfair sale transactions. However, he asserts that there is a difference between the riba al-fadl and riba al-nasia of the Tradition on the one hand, and the Quranic riba; the latter is forbidden per se, while the first two are only forbidden to close the roads which might lead to pre-Islamic riba. As a result of such degrees of prohibition, the ban on the Quranic riba can be lifted only in case of pressing necessity, while the riba of the Tradition can be permitted in case of need (haja) for public policy purposes.

Therefore, Sanhuri believes that jurists like Ibn Qayyim erred by not differentiating between the Quranic riba and riba al-nasia. The Quranic riba was based on compound interest and assigned equal importance to the original capital and the interest received. Besides, modern loans are not the same as the aforementioned prohibited ribas, and could not lead to riba. Modern loans with interest, not being the aim of the ban on riba, cannot be forbidden per se, and, therefore, the principle of "need" can be invoked in their favor, enabling the law to lift the ban. In a market system, the need for loans is natural and common. Therefore, as long as loans based on simple interest are not changed into loans based on compound interest, they would be acceptable and are in conformity with the Shari'a (Homoud 1985: 58–63, 120–2; El-Ahdab 1992: 48–9; Saleh 1992: 36–7)

Ironically, Badawi presented a rebuttal to Sanhuri's analysis in 1964 and denounced his former position on simple interest. In his self-criticism, Badawi took side with the traditional ulama and claimed that any kind of interest is riba. His criticism of Sanhuri's argument is methodological. Badawi implicitly opposes not only Sanhuri's eclectic method, but also that of Abduh's. According to Badawi, Abduh and Sanhuri's reformist methodology calls for returning to the primary sources, especially the Quran. This methodology emphasizes the time-specificity of the rulings and prohibitions of Islam, and divides them into absolute and more flexible rules.

Badawi insists that Abduh and Sanhuri introduce the principle of necessity and public interest in order to justify the lifting of some of the prohibitions and orthodox rulings. This approach is eclectic, in Badawi's view, because it arbitrarily disregards the rulings of the classical jurists. The method is based on rationalism and innovates legal solutions or reinterprets the old ones by using a comparative evaluation and selection of rules of the doctrines of four Sunni schools of law. In this effort, in Badawi's opinion, Abduh and Sanhuri were particularly inspired by Ibn Taimiyah, Ibn Qayyim, Wahhab, and one of the companions of the Prophet, that is, Ibn Abbas. What Badawi insinuates is that Abduh and Sanhuri rely on the principle of necessity and public interest of Ibn Taimiyah and Ibn Qayyim and their independent and interpretative spirit (Mallat 1986: 81–2; Islahi 1988: 57–74), that they are reiterating the call of Wahhab for the return to the Quran and the Tradition of the Prophet (see Islahi 1988: 57–74); and that they are influenced by Ibn Abbas' emphasis on the importance of knowing the circumstances in which Quranic prohibitions were revealed in order to avoid misunderstanding and his erroneous interpretation of the Quranic riba (Kamali 1991: 40, 43).

Since 1970, several attempts to change the Egyptian Civil Code in relation to interest charges have not been successful. One such attempt was made in 1985. Based on the fact that the amended constitution of 1980 identifies the Shari'a as "the" principal source of legislation, the Rector of the al-Azhar brought a suit before the High Constitutional Court, demanding the prohibition of the payment of interest on delay of loan repayments. The Court dismissed the case, arguing that the Shari'a rulings cannot be applicable to the already existing legislation retroactively without creating confusion and instability for the commercial and judicial process (Edge 1986: 45). According to the Court's decision, the constitutional amendment did not mean that the Shari'a had become positive law in Egypt, but only a guiding principle for future legislation (Skovgaard-Petersen 1997: 204–5).

The next important round of the debate on riba was ignited by a public fatwa issued in September 1989, by Tantawi Mufti of Egypt. In this fatwa, he asserted that predetermined returns, as simple interest, and bonuses on saving certificates are beneficial to individuals and the public alike, and are licit (something that Sanhuri had insisted on in the 1950s).

Tantawi's fatwa was criticized by the advocates of a broader definition of riba. These critics who were not satisfied with the government's treatment of the financial problem of Islamic investment companies in 1988, claimed that the mufti was legalizing what God had prohibited. However, the Central Bank of Egypt, encouraged by the fatwa, allowed banks to raise interest rates to encourage savings in the local currency and attract funds to the banking system. The central bank's concern was that private Islamic investment companies were paying a much higher rate of profit to depositors than banks before the change of their status into shareholding companies. The central banks argument for this change was that Islamic companies were giving savers only a receipt in exchange for deposits and not share certificates. Apparently, this practice was not in conformity with the Shari'a, as interpreted by legal advisors of the central bank (Najjar 1992: 65–8; Galloux 1993: 56–61; Skovgaard-Petersen 1997: 301–14). Surprisingly, in the 1990s there has not been a major debate over Islamic banking in Egypt. Tantawi's views on the legitimacy of interest on productive loans has gained the support of a former grand mufti and three other jurists from Al Azhar, while other jurists still insist that all kinds of interest are riba (*Business Recorder* June 20, 2002).

Nowadays, the Egyptian government permits conventional banks to maintain Islamic banking windows, even though the accounts of these operations in conventional banks are maintained separately. According to the Institute of Islamic Banking and Insurance, as of 2002 there are eight Islamic banks and financial firms coexisting with conventional banks in Egypt.[11] However, the preoccupation of the government is the reform in the banking system within a more competitive and semi-open economy.

The debate on riba in Pakistan

Before the 1980s, the problem of riba in Pakistan was overshadowed by a more crucial constitutional debate over the role of the Shari'a as the source of public and private laws. When in 1956 the first constitution was approved, the state was to be the Islamic Republic of Pakistan and no law was to be promulgated contrary to the Quran and the Tradition of the Prophet. Naturally, there were also clauses in the constitution for the removal of riba and the establishment of Islamic tax, *zakat*. However, Pakistan was not transformed into an "Islamic state" and, in fact, in 1962, there was even an unsuccessful attempt to drop the word "Islamic" from the official name of the republic and eliminate the clauses requiring laws to conform with the Shari'a. Subsequently, bowing to public pressure, the Council of Islamic Ideology (CII) was formally given the function of bringing existing laws into conformity with the Shari'a (Mahmood 1973: 25–31).

The Council's most important concern in the second half of the 1960s and in the 1970s was the problem of the ban on riba. In 1964 the government raised the issue of the interest in the banking system with the CII, and the response of the Council in 1966 and 1969, despite the lack of participation of the ulama in the decisions, was clear. The Council asserted that riba is forbidden in Islam and Pakistan should have an interest-free banking system (Malik 1989: 253–4). In the meantime, there was an attempt to eliminate riba from the banking system, but the problem was ignored due to political upheavals and the constitutional question of the early 1970s.

The debate on riba in Pakistan was shaped by traditionalist and modernist views, presented principally by Abdul Ala Mawdudi and Fazlur Rahman, respectively. Mawdudi views all kinds of interest as riba and criticizes the modern economic theories on interest in the West. He argues that riba is a predetermined fixed rate on the use of money, claimed by any lender. A guaranteed and fixed positive return on money is unjust in contrast to entrepreneurial profit which is subject to uncertainty. Mawdudi argues that the modern loan based on interest is just like the riba al-nasia or the Quranic riba. In his view, risk taken by the lender of money cannot justify interest since risk can lead to positive or negative return. Abstinence and waiting do not justify interest unless money is used for productive activities that can lead to a profit or a loss. The lender cannot be rewarded for time, because time cannot be owned. Interest is not like rent, because the concept of rent applies to durable goods and it is a return for the depreciation of these goods. However, in his opinion, a reward for the owner of money is justified only when the owner is ready to enter in a mudaraba contract and share the risk of the enterprise with the agents or partners (M. N. Siddiqi 1981: 237–8, 253–8; Pal 1994: 65–7).

This view was left theoretically uncontested in Pakistan until 1963, when Fazlur Rahman expressed views similar to those of the Egyptian modernist Muslim scholars. As a liberal reformer, Rahman's analysis of riba is only an integral part of his general view on Islam. He is against literal interpretation of the Quran that, according to him, prevented the adaptation of Islam to modern circumstances. Like Abduh, he believes that Muslim scholars must study the historical circumstances of the Quranic verses, the specificity and the requirements of the modern era in order to be able to apply the principles behind the revelations (Sonn 1995: 408). Accordingly, he questions the reliability and the importance of the hadith, emphasizing the understanding of the spirit of the Quran (Commins 1995: 119–22). In his lengthy argument on riba in 1963 and his study of the Quran, Rahman asserts that the Quranic riba is the continuous multiplication of the sum of capital "against a fixed extension of the term of payment of debt" following a default (Rahman 1964: 5). He finds the division of riba into riba al-fadl and riba al-nasia in the hadith unreliable, and he insists that only the Quranic riba is prohibited per se. In his view the prohibition of the Quranic riba is essential for the public welfare; however, the medieval jurists wrongly drew the conclusion "that all forms of interest are banned" (Rahman 1980: 41).

Rahman asserts that the market determines the rate of return to modern loans. In his view, interest in modern economics is just like any other price, and it is determined by demand and supply for loans. Yet, Rahman suggests, an Islamic economic policy must be based on the establishment of the spirit of cooperation and solidarity demanded by the Quran. Therefore, the Islamic government should regulate the market forces against excesses because the elimination of interest in modern economies is theoretically possible only if the supply of money is infinite at any level of demand (Rahman 1964: 1–43, 1980: 34–41).

In 1973, Pakistan had a third constitution in which ulama and Islamic political parties, including Mawdudi's Jama'at-i-Islami, limited the legislative power of the parliament. The new constitution granted the Council of Islamic Ideology the function of providing legal Islamic opinions (fatwas) when necessary. At the same time the CII was asked to prepare a report for the elimination of Islamic prohibitions, including recommendations for bringing all laws in conformity with the Shari'a (Nomani and Rahnema 1994: 134–6). However, Islamization of the economy was initiated seriously only under the presidency of General Zia in 1977. Accordingly, the CII that by then had changed the composition of its membership to reflect the views of the new government, was made responsible for a report on an Islamic restructuring of the economy (Malik 1989: 257–9).

In 1980, the report of the CII demanded the restructuring of the banking sector and taxation. This voluminous report, which was first prepared by economists and experts of the Central Bank and the Ministry of Finance and was then approved by the CII for conformity with the Shari'a, was a blueprint for the reorganization of banking practices and procedures on the basis of Islamic legal concepts (Wohlers-Scharf 1983: 72; Gieraths 1990: 173–5). This document relied on an earlier attempt by Sunni religious scholars and economists from Muslim countries who in 1977 started the preparation of a Handbook of Islamic Banking (HIB) in Arabic. The HIB was published with the technical advice and "financial assistance recommended or channeled through" the International Association of Islamic Banks (Malik 1989: 257–9; Kazarian 1993: 5–6, 246). In addition, the CII report benefited from the discussion of religious scholars who worked out the operational framework and banking instruments of two Egyptian Islamic banks in 1979 and 1980 (Algabid 1990: 88–112).

The importance and the scope of the issue of Islamization inevitably gave rise to disagreements among Sunnis, Shi'is and even "secularists" of the Council of Islamic Ideology who advocated traditional, moderate, and sectarian Islamic views. The Shi'i ulama were particularly concerned with the dominance of the Sunnis in the CII, eventually leaving the Council over the problem of zakat and the Sunni-Shi'i interpretation of the tax (Malik 1989: 264–5). In fact, the ideological and Islamic disagreements among the members of the CII can partially explain the inability of the council to become a political platform for the traditionalists in the past twenty years. In any case, as regards riba and Islamic banking, the CII report reflected the opinion of Muslim economists who, following Mawdudi and other Islamic intellectuals, advocated a broader definition of riba (Z. Ahmed *et al.* 1983: 103–257).

In fact, in a seminar on the subject of monetary and fiscal economics of Islam in Pakistan in 1981, the participants overwhelmingly supported the views expressed in the report. They emphasized that all kinds of interest charged on consumption, as well as investment loans, are riba, and, therefore, are normally and legally invalid. The general line of the reasoning and the rationality of this position were very similar to the opinion of Mawdudi on riba expressed in the 1930–70 period (Z. Ahmed *et al.* 1983: 2–14, 103–11).

Since the Islamization of the banking system in Pakistan, the debate on riba has focused on the "impurity" of the interest-free banking practices and its formalistic aspect. In fact the CII report itself anticipated the debate by explicitly frowning upon the potential widespread use of legal tricks in Islamic banking, despite their acceptability in most Islamic schools of law (Z. Ahmed *et al.* 1983: 118–19). Many Muslim intellectuals, economists, judges, and Islamist political parties were not at ease with the institution and publicly expressed their dissatisfaction.[12] One view argued for a much broader definition of riba, demanding the elimination of all kinds of injustice and exploitations that prevails in Pakistan or other Muslim countries. According to this view, the CII report only took position against riba al-nasia, ignoring the prohibition of riba al-fadl.[13] In the meantime, advocates of the limited view of riba did not present a comprehensive opinion on the CII report, despite their occasional, timid, and theoretical criticism of the elimination of interest in a defensive manner (Pal 1994: 73–6).

Since 1990, the traditionalist view and supporters of a broad definition of riba have continued their pressure for a "complete" end to interest-based banking by demanding the application of the Shari'a to different spheres of life. In fact,

Khurshid Ahmad, a writer and political activist of Jama'at-i-Islami, insisted that "99 percent" of Islamic banking in Pakistan is based on interest (Kuran 1993: 315). In the summer of 1990, Islamic parties sponsored a bill in the Senate where they had majority, demanding the re-imposition of the amputation of hands as a criminal punishment, the elimination of interest rates, and the subservience of the Assembly to the Shari'a court. In 1991 their candidate for premiership modified the bill, emphasizing generalities such as Islamization of education and guaranteeing the validity of all existing contracts until the development of an alternative Islamic system. The bill also envisioned the abolition of riba in three years, with a possibility of the extension of the period by the Assembly. In the meantime an advisory Commission for the Islamization of the Economy (CIE) was to define usury and pass judgment over all the existing banking instruments with regard to riba (S. Ali 1991a: 20–1).

In 1991, independently, the supreme religious court, the Federal Shari'a Court (FSC) of Pakistan, working on 119 cases that challenged various economic legislative enactments and statuary provisions as un-Islamic, conducted an extensive survey and a study on different economic topics such as the Islamic nature of the banking system. This court was established in 1980 to examine the concordance of laws and provisions of laws with the Shari'a. In their testimony to the FSC, the government's lawyers argued for a moderate view on interest, insisting that the Quranic riba is different from modern interest, especially interest on productive loans. They insisted that the Tradition of the Prophet is not conclusive over interest. They insisted that the commission for the Islamization of the system should resolve the issue.

Nevertheless, in November 1991, the court declared 22 legislative enactments and statutory provisions as "repugnant to Islam." Thus all kinds of interest, several legal tricks in banking, noncooperative insurance, and negotiable instruments were identified as contracts based on riba, even in transaction with non-Muslims. The verdict approvingly referred to a conclusion reached by the Islamic Academy of Jurisprudence in Saudi Arabia that was constituted under the Organization of Islamic States in 1985 (S. Ali 1991b: 27). The director of the School of Economics at Islamabad's International Institute for Islamic Economics and the court advisor, M. H. Choudhury, asserted that there could not be any other judgment and that the Quran "does not leave any room for interpretation" (World Press Review 1992: 43). He declared that Islamic banking in Pakistan has been realized only on paper and that all kinds of legal devices such as markup, housing loans made by the state based on a rent, and interest on government bonds are all un-Islamic. The only concession that Choudhury made, however, was that the ruling of the court against the payment of interest on foreign loans is not realistic in the short run (World Press Review 1992: 43).

On the other side of the debate, the finance minister, S. Aziz, insisted that "although riba is totally prohibited in Islam, unfortunately there is no universally acceptable definition of riba in the Muslim world according to which existing financial practices can be tested on the basis of Islamic law" (*The Economist* January 18, 1992: 34). The government did not appeal the judgment in order to avoid a direct clash with its Islamic supporters and only asked the court to reverse the verdict, calling it "an archaic interpretation of the Islamic injunction" (Khan 1993: 134–5). Finally, the government, insisting on its commitment to a riba-free banking, encouraged three banks to appeal to the Supreme Court in order to reverse the Shari'a Court's ruling on interest and postpone the crisis (S. Ali 1992: 18–19).

After the ruling of the FSC on interest payment the CIE came out with a report, reiterating the CII 1980 report's recommendation, including a profit-and-loss sharing scheme for government borrowing. The CIE also ruled that the existing insurance system was contrary to the Shari'a, and called for a system based on cooperative insurance. In reaction to the CIE report, one of the chief economists of the Planning Commission asserted that such recommendations were neither Islamic nor suitable for Pakistan in view of the fact that more than 85 percent of depositors had very little in their accounts, and they needed security and a positive return rather than the risk of a loss. It was argued that if riba is an exploitative income, it should apply more to a banking system based on profit-and-loss sharing scheme than to a system based on a fixed return (S. Ali 1992: 19).

In the meantime, after several proceedings that were extended over several years, and in the absence of solutions to replace interest in private and public transactions, the government successfully blocked the ruling of the FSC by lodging an appeal with the Shari'a Appellate Bench of the Supreme Court (SABSC) (Al-Omar and Abdel-Haq 1996: 98–9). Thus, in December 1999, after an extensive review of certain existing financial laws, and even laws dealing with government fiscal matters, such as deficit borrowing and indexation, that were excluded from 1991 ruling, the Appellate Court unanimously ruled that all forms of interest are contrary to Islamic injunctions. The ruling concluded that the financial system and contracts in Pakistan should be interest-free, and that some of the laws and provisions thereof dealing with the payment of interest will cease to be effective after March 31, 2000, and some other laws will cease to have effect from June 30, 2001. The ruling of the Court also directed the government to establish different commissions, boards, and committees, including a Shari'a board within the State Bank of Pakistan, for the evaluation and transformation of the financial system to an Islamic system (International Financial Law Review March 2000: 25–7). In reaction to the Court's ruling, the United Bank Ltd and two other civil and government applications were filed with the Supreme Court, seeking the review of the Shari'a Appellate Bench ruling and the extension of the time for its implementation (M. Ahmed 2002).

Based on the reports of different government committees and task forces that were set up for the study of a riba-free economy, in June 2002, in the Supreme Court, government lawyers claimed that the ruling of the Appellate Bench "was not practical or feasible and if implemented, will pose high degree of risk to the economic stability and security of the country" (M. Ahmed 2002). In reaction to government position, the lawyer of the Jama'at-i Islami severely criticized the stance of the government on riba and rejected the reports as misinterpretation of the Shari'a (Mukhtar 2002).

In their argument against the ruling of the Shari'a Bench, lawyers of the banks as well as the federal Government insisted on the fact that according to an established interpretation in Islam, the forbidden riba or the unjust riba is that which "doubled and multiplied." Government lawyers' argument concentrated on the misinterpretation of the Quran and the tradition of the Prophet by the Shari'a Court. This argument insisted that the Court's ruling had serious flaws. In their view the court's ruling amalgamated legal and moral aspects of riba in a legal ruling, and explicitly excluded riba al-fadl and its implications for the economy from its reasoning. They asserted that the ruling failed to define *qard* which is not the exact counterpart of the word loan in English, and that it violated the Islamic rules of interpretation by relying only on juristic inferences with respect to the pre-Islamic riba.

Government lawyers criticized the ruling of the Shari'a Bench for ignoring the views of Shi'i fiqh, interpreted by Baqir Sadr, and misreading the view of Sunni scholars such as Abduh, Rashid Rida, Sanhuri, Shaltut, Tantawi, and Khallaf. They insisted that the ruling wrongly applies the law of riba to non-Muslims, thus violating the Quran, the Tradition and ignores the non-Sunni views on the matter. They pointed out that the ruling forbids the use of legal Islamic tricks that are approved by classical and contemporary jurists, and except for the musharaka (equity sharing) contract, it wrongly declares the majority of the contracts used by the existing Islamic banks as un-Islamic. In short, government lawyers insisted that the ruling sided only with a specific interpretation of riba, and, therefore, was not objective, and that its implementation leads to chaos (M. Ahmed 2002).

After ten days of hearings, on June 24, 2002, the Supreme Court sent the 1999 rulings of the Federal Shari'a Court and the confirmatory order of the Shari'a Appellate Bench back to the former for a new ruling in light of the points raised during the arguments in review hearings. In a long order written by the Chief Justice and concurred by his colleagues, the Court held that the issues raised by different parties in the hearings require a thorough and elaborate research, as well as a comparative study of the financial systems in Sunni Muslim countries. In particular, the Court held that because the FSC did not present a definitive finding on all the issues involved, "it would be in the fitness of things if the matter is remanded to the Federal Shari'a Court" for the review of the case of riba and the Islamization of the whole economic system in a modern Muslim society (M. Ahmed 2002). Yet, while the Supreme Court's decision has warded off a financial-institutional crisis, it has prolonged an uncertain situation by not fixing any time frame for the disposal of the cases by the Federal Shari'a Court.

The Supreme Court's decision evoked mixed reactions. Jama'at-i Islami claimed that the government misrepresented the Shari'a in order to postpone the implementation of a riba-free system. The government and the central bank reasserted their demand that an Islamic financial system can be instituted gradually and with a proper groundwork. Commercial banks representatives were relieved and emphasized the practical aspect of the decision, and insisted on the superiority of a mixed or parallel banking system (M. Ahmed 2002).

Thus, the debate on a riba-free financial system in Pakistan, based on arguments that have been presented and represented in the past century mostly in Egypt, Turkey, Iran, India, and Pakistan, is still unresolved and awaits the verdict of the Federal Shari'a Court. In the meantime, foreign and national conventional banks that have already adopted many Islamic contracts as well as legal tricks, for their operation through Islamic windows, are not sure about the final outcome of the Islamization process. Even the existing Islamic banks, that is five commercial and investment banks, that use innovatory contracts as well as contracts that are legal in one interpretation (contracts based on legal tricks) but not Islamic according to radical readings of the Shari'a, have to live with the specter of a rigid interpretation of riba. Again, as in Egypt, the problem is not only legal or juristic. It is mixed with politics and ideology, complicating the problem of public policy even more than before. However, the government has reiterated its intention for establishing Islamic banking, and the central bank of Pakistan has announced the establishment of a Shari'a Board for the revision of the current modes of banking products in accordance with the Shari'a *(Business Recorder* June 11, 2002: 1).

The pragmatic view on riba in Iran

The problem of riba has never been an important political issue in Iran of the twentieth century, before as well as after the 1979 revolution. This does not imply that Iranian Shi'i ulama approve of riba or Islamic movements in Iran have not demanded the abolition of riba; it only means that unlike Egypt and Pakistan political and economic debates over Islamization were never focused on the issue of riba. For this reason one finds very little discussion, not to speak of a controversy, on riba from a legal, juridical, or constitutional view, and, after the implementation of Islamic banking, from a technical or economic point of view. It seems that Iranian Islamists and the Islamic government itself, have been content with mere formalistic changes and have left it at that. This situation might be envied by the Egyptian and Pakistani modernist Muslims, but, curiously enough, has also been referred to as an ideal case by many Islamic intellectuals who are not well informed about what has happened in Iran, partly due to the uncritical idealization and the historical and sometimes ideologically motivated research on the subject.

The first important modernist interpretation of banking and riba in Iran, distinct from the traditional understanding of it, was introduced in the early twentieth century. It was by Ayatollah Haeri, a prominent mujtahid, who defended the establishment of an Iranian bank in the constitutional and national movement in Iran, against the dominance of the British and Russian banks in Iran (Valibeigi 1992: 53). Later, in the 1927–32 period, the Iranian civil code that was a synthesis of western and Shi'i laws and was written by modernist Shi'is, prohibited usury, but in a timid manner recognized the legitimacy of interest (Amin 1986: 36–45).

However, in spite of differences in interpretation, various political tendencies of Shi'i Islam have always rejected riba. Navvab Safavi's interpretation of Islam and banking was political and radical. His political movement had a very rigid, simplistic, and militant orientation. This movement was in reaction to the onslaught of modernization after the Second World War that was uprooting traditional Islamic values, and had a categorical position on the abolition of riba from the modern banking sector. According to Navvab-Safavi, in a truly Islamic state Muslims would automatically and without any coercion accept obligatory financial prohibitions. Nevertheless, his group was for the forceful imposition of Islamic values and injunctions before the advent of an ideal Islamic state. For this reason, there was not much persuasive analysis about the prohibition of riba even within an Islamic intellectual framework (Rahnema and Nomani 1990: 73–96). Yet, in contrast to the simplistic views of Navvab Safavi, one of the first analyses of the possibility of an Islamic economic system and Islamic banking was presented in the 1960s and early 1970s by a Shi'i jurist in Najaf, Iraq, the late Muhammad Baqir Sadr.

Ayatollah Sadr's analysis of an Islamic economic system has been influential among Iranian Islamic movements before and after the Iranian revolution. His major work, *Our Economy* was translated in Persian and was published in two volumes (Sadr 1971, 1978). In this book Sadr was not interested in the study of an Islamic banking because in the late 1960s and early 1970s the intellectual priority of many Islamist scholars was to defend Islam as a viable economic system against what they conceived as communist influence and threat. However, in a very indirect way, he mentions that the use of mudaraba for manufacturing contracts is preferable to stock ownership (Sadr 1971: 591–2). In fact, in *Our Economy* Sadr does not even study the meaning and implications of riba in Islamic contracts, except for a very short reference to riba. Thus, in *Our Economy* riba in loans was condemned on distributive grounds and interest-free loan was recommended as the only acceptable loan contract (Sadr 1971: 544; Haneef 1995: 116).

However, in the 1970s, with the rise of oil income in Muslim countries, the problem of Islamic banking and the management of oil money without "openly flouting the shari'a" created a concern for Islamic banking (Mallat 1993: 164). Thus, in response to questions addressed to him from the Kuwaiti Ministry for Endowments, Sadr wrote his treatise on *Riba-free Banking*. In this treatise and in a later book on banking in Islamic countries, Sadr differentiates the establishment of Islamic banking in secular and semi-secular countries from the Islamic banking under a full-fledged Islamic state. In the latter case, interest-free banking is supposed to function only within a state banking system, while under the former context Islamic banking could be private Islamic banking, coexisting with conventional banking (Mallat 1993: 166–84).

Some Sunni as well as some Shi'i scholars have criticized the way Sadr has conceptualized the functioning of an Islamic bank in a parallel banking system. It is claimed that according to the pragmatic approach of Sadr an Islamic bank is only a financial intermediary that does not necessarily participate in productive activities; that Sadr permits the guarantee of mudaraba deposits by the bank, while Islamic law does not absolve depositors' liability to loss; that Sadr, like many Shi'i jurists, allows a banking prize for depositors as a percentage of Islamic time deposits; that Sadr's predetermined rate of profit for mudaraba deposits is compromising Islamic banking (Ahmad 1981: 223–4; Kahf 1993: 91–2). In short, according to the critics, Sadr's

> approach may fit in with some traditional interpretations in Islamic jurisprudence but it does not fit the Islamic economic theory or practice, since trying to make a workable set-up out of one whose long-term structure is based on legal tricks is obviously undesirable.
>
> (Kahf 1993: 93)

Like Sadr, all the other important personalities of Shi'i tendencies before the Iranian revolution, namely Murteza Mutahhari, Ali Shariati, and Mehdi Bazargan concentrated their effort in one way or another on an Islamic response to the spread of Marxism among Iranian intellectuals. Shariati's objective was to attempt to accommodate, co-opt, and eventually dissolve Marxism-Leninism in Islam. It is only within this perspective that Shariati is interested in the concept of riba. For him, and other leftist Islamists riba in Islam represents the exploitation of one class by another (Rahnema and Nomani 1995: 69–70). This conceptualization could not be left unanswered by religious scholars like Mutahhari, who had to argue for an Islam that was not only against secularists, but also against leftist tendencies within the Islamic movement. Thus, Mutahhari explicitly professes that the exploitation explanation of riba is not an Islamic but a socialist view. According to him, riba and exploitation are two different concepts, and the absolute prohibition of riba does not imply that Islam is against capitalism: "riba is unjust, but all injustices are not riba" (Mutahhari 1991: 89).

In general, Mutahhari's arguments on riba are very similar to the opinions of the majority of the Shi'i ulama. These arguments can be summarized in the following manner. Money is only a means of exchange and its transaction must not lead to an increase in the form of interest. However, if money capital in commercial or productive activities leads to an increase called profit, this profit is lawful because in such cases profit is a return to labor and the "excess" in commercial and productive activities is not a mere exchange of money. If bills of exchange and discounting are lawful in Shi'i Islam, it is because in such acts the lender "does not receive something extra, but less" (Mutahhari 1991: 40). According to Mutahhari, that which is forbidden in Islam is to demand something more than what has been given. Besides, sale on credit is not riba and is valid in Shi'i Islam because the substance of the act is the freedom of the seller to increase the price in case of a delay in payment.

Muttahari asserts that all kinds of riba, riba al-fadl, and riba al-nasia, are prohibited in Islam. Modern loans based on interest are equally forbidden as riba because the lender asks for a predetermined and fixed positive return. Thus, loans for consumption and for productive purposes, based on interest, are illicit. For this reason, according to Mutahhari, the view of those Egyptian Muslim scholars (Mutahhari does not identify these scholars but most probably he is referring to

Sanhuri) who differentiate between consumption and productive loans, "bad" or "good" riba is not admissible. In his view Shi'i jurists do not consider one type of riba to be less unjust than the other type, and, consequently, acceptable.

Mutahhari regards all legal tricks as invalid, even though the majority of Shi'i ulama find them legal. Therefore, for him the only legal way to increase a sum of money is by means of a mudaraba contract in which a "lender" shares in profit or loss of the enterprise of a "borrower." He asserts that the payment of interest on savings accounts and government bonds is riba, while the payment of bonuses on savings deposits are lawful if such bonuses are not predetermined. A guaranteed rate of return on a stock of an investment bank is legal since the bank is committing itself to a payment without asking the owner of the stock to agree to any condition in return; such a commitment is like what takes place in insurance contracts, which are in general legal. Finally, like the majority of Shi'i ulama, he permits the payment of interest to and receiving interest from non-Muslims (Mutahhari 1991: 87).

Mutahhari was a follower of Khomeini, and, therefore, the latter's legal opinion on the subject of riba was more or less the same. For example, according to Khomeini, paying an extra sum which is not to be determined at the time a savings account is opened or a promissory note is made, or giving a prize to depositors are all lawful (Rahnema and Nomani 1990: 149–50). However, the views of some other jurists in Iran, such as Milani, were even more pragmatic in relation to the needs of the modern financial system. Such jurists had come up with many legal tricks that would facilitate the effective payment of interest on loans, much to the dissatisfaction of clerics like Mutahhari. Such acceptable devices were management or service fees, discounting, markups, and hire-purchases, which were approved of even by Khomeini. However, the pragmatic Shi'i ulama came up with legal tricks that turned loans into a sale in a very formalistic manner. For example, according to Milani, instead of stating that I lend you $A and receive in a year $A + $B, one could say I sell this $A for $A + $B (Mutahhari 1991: 141). Since in Shi'i law the exchange of unequal quantities of things that are countable, for example money, are permitted, the act would be lawful.

Bazargan represented the Shi'i modernist view on riba. He, as a noncleric Islamic scholar advocated a tolerant religion compatible with liberalism and political democracy in a market system. He was familiar with the arguments of liberal modernists of Egypt and Pakistan and his position on riba follows their arguments. According to Bazargan, borrowing for consumption purposes by the needy should be free of interest. However, productive loans can receive simple interest because the interest on a loan is normally less than the profit received from the enterprise. He reiterates that only usurious interests have been forbidden by the Quran, and sales on credit with a rate of return that are like loans based on interest, are permitted by jurists. Nevertheless, Bazargan finds devices such as mudaraba and cooperative banks useful for modern banking (Mutahhari 1991: 89–94).

In 1979, the Shi'i clergy, under the leadership of Khomeini, came to power in Iran, and the official name of the country was changed to Islamic Republic of

Iran. During the uprising against the Shah in 1978, the religious movement did not present any Islamic economic program except general simplistic slogans about the end of "plundering and usurpation of wealth," autarky, and self-sufficiency; there were no slogans against banking based on riba or any reference to interest. The movement was focused against the Shah, and the clergy avoided concrete and controversial economic programs that have divided them since 1979 (Rahnema and Nomani 1990: 234–69).

According to the Constitution of the Islamic Republic the official religion of Iran is the Twelver Shi'i and all civil, penal, financial, and economic laws and regulations are to be based on the Islamic criteria of the Ja'fari school of law. Thus, jurists of the Guardianship Council were to judge the conformity of the laws and regulations with the Shari'a according to the Ja'fari school of Islamic law. The followers of Sunni schools of law were only given the right to conduct the personal affairs (marriage, divorce, inheritance, and wills) according to the rulings of their own schools.

Riba is prohibited and mentioned in two articles (43 and 49), along gambling, "monopoly, hoarding," and other "evil practices." Before the vote on the relevant article 43 on riba in the Assembly of Experts, only two comments were made. One was suggesting that the prohibition of riba is legally so evident that one could drop it from the Constitution. The second comment equated riba with exploitation and charging high prices. The article prohibiting riba was passed without any debate (61 representatives voted for, one against and two abstained) (*Soorat-e Mashrooh-e...* 1985: 1483–5).

Unlike the criminal law, the civil code and the general theory of contract of Iran, which were adopted in 1927–32, were Islamic in substance. Thus, the Islamic Republic could not change much in the civil and commercial laws (Amin 1986: 36–101, *Majmo'eh Nazariyat-e...* 1992: 292–3). All private banks and insurance companies were nationalized in 1979 (mainly because their owners had left Iran and they were nearly all insolvent). The Law of Riba-Free Banking was approved by the Parliament in August 1983. This law was similar to what the CII had presented in Pakistan in 1981, except that it was more pragmatic, allowing many legal tricks and few definitional differences.

The Islamization of banking took place in a gradual manner, again without any meaningful debate over the process or the articles of the Law. First, in 1981 interest on all asset-side transactions was replaced by a maximum "service charge" and a minimum "profit" rate. On the side of liability of banks, the interest on deposits was replaced by a guaranteed minimum profit. The Guardian Council approved the law immediately, except for one point related to gradual elimination of interest within a three-year period, which was accordingly dropped by the Parliament (*Majmoueh Nazariyyat-e...* 1992: 379–80). In 1988, the Guardian Council finally approved banking based on riba with non-Muslims, even though Iranian banks and authorities had been paying and receiving riba in their dealings outside of Iran without much fuss. Thus, according to the Council "collecting interest ... from foreign governments, organizations, companies and persons ... is permitted by Shari'a" (Amin 1989: 136).

The pragmatic approach of the Shi'i Islamic state in Iran is also reflected in the acceptance of a charge or paying of a "penalty" or "damages" for delayed payment of debt. Thus, in a ruling in 1983, the Council approved the inclusion of a "penalty" clause for unpaid debt at the rate of 12 percent per year by the consent of the borrower. Nevertheless, the same Council on different occasions in 1985, declared all forms of interest forbidden. The decision of the Council on the penalty clause instead of interest, has theoretically enabled the Islamic courts to accept a contractually arranged 12 percent rate of interest as a legal trick (Amin 1989: 128–30).

Unlike the majority of Sunni scholars and ulama, many of the Iranian ulama find the trading of debt (*bay' al-dayn*) at anything other than its face value licit. Thus, discounting of promissory notes and *bay' al-dayn* are common in Iranian Islamic banking. This pragmatism has encouraged even the official journals of the Islamic Republic to ignore the nomenclature of the Islamic banking and to talk about "interest rate" as well as the "rate of profit." Besides, there is the "un-Islamic" guarantee of a "positive" rate of profit on the savings and term investment deposits by Islamic banks, or payment of interest by municipal and government bonds which have rarely offended the Islamic clergy and public.[14]

These common practices based on explicit and implicit legal tricks and interest rates led a reputed clergy, Va'ezzadeh Khorasani, in his capacity as the chair of a research group on Islamic economics, to propose an explicit payment of interest. His proposal that has not given rise to any debate, for or against, is based on the following reasoning. He argues that the Quranic verses on riba are all related to private loans and exchanges, and contemporary riba is not like the riba that was practiced before the twentieth century. He asserts that in Iran all banks are state owned and the state is "totally" Islamic. Therefore, an Islamic state could pay and charge interest; the Islamic state bank can receive interest from loans granted to private or government sectors. "After all," he insists, "Shi'is do not consider riba to be exploitative when the practice is within the family," and state loans can be perceived as the transfer of money from the public to the representative of Muslims, that is, the Islamic state (Va'ezzadeh Khorasani 1991: 118). He believes that such a change in the existing institution of the banking system eliminates the "unethical" legal tricks like mudaraba or all kinds of banking partnerships and devices that are "formalistic," "cosmetic," and "farcical" in comparison to "real" riba-free contracts (Va'ezzadeh Kharasani 1991: 118, 119, 120). However, he neither discussed nor specified "real" riba-free contracts.

The pragmatic approach of the Shi'i state came to its height when the central bank officially started to use the guaranteed "profit rates," which are effectively interest rates, on profit-and-loss-sharing accounts of the nationalized banking system, as an instrument of monetary policy. In July 1990, the central bank increased the rates by 25 percent in order to reduce the private liquidity and attract private savings into savings deposits (*Iran Times* July 13, 1990). Obviously, traditional and moderate interpretations of profit-and-loss-sharing contracts in Islamic law assert that such increases should reflect the higher market profitability of investments related to these contracts. Yet, this decision of the central bank did not give rise to criticism or indignation on the part of Shi'i ulama.

In addition, once in a while there have been open and pragmatic innovations in interpretations of certain aspects of riba. For example, in a series of articles in the daily journal of *Salam*, Abedeeni raises the important and unresolved question of inflation and rate of interest in Islamic banking and fiqh. He contents that the traditional rejection of paying a positive, but variable, rate equal to the inflation rate as riba is itself the practice of riba.

Abedeeni tries to prove that due to lack of economic knowledge, ulama have not understood the difference between the acquired value of currency and demand deposits as modern money in contrast to the value of gold and silver used in the medieval period. According to Abedeeni, who relies on the legal opinion of Ayatollah Mussavi-e Bujnurdi, Islamic law recognizes compensation in the principle of *daman* (risk of loss, liability for loss, guarantee) if the Islamic government has created inflation by inappropriate fiscal and monetary policies. In such a situation the government, as the guarantor, is *damin* (guarantor). In the case of modern loans the value of today's money or its purchasing power, and not a given quantity of currencies, is borrowed. Therefore, according to a realistic interpretation of riba, the lender must at least receive the same value that was lent; otherwise, the debtors accumulate wealth unjustifiably in the aforementioned case. However, if the lender receives more than the purchasing power lent, he or she is engaging in a transaction that is riba. In the opinion of Abedeeni, modern currency is neither this nor that because both of these concepts apply to things that have value by themselves, while modern currencies only have an acquired value. Therefore, one could not apply the rules of riba to the case of compensation for a loan's loss of purchasing power (Abedeeni May 9, 11, 13, 16, 20, 25, 27, 1999).

After more than two decades of state Islamic banking in Iran, the share of ideally preferred Islamic contracts, in total outstanding assets of the banking system is very low (7 percent in 1999). In contrast, the share of certain other contracts, for example, installment sale that in the opinion of some radical clergies and Islamist intellectuals are legal tricks, is 57 percent (Statistical Center of Iran 1999: T. 12.13). And this is in spite of the pragmatic interpretation of mudaraba and musharaka contracts in Iran. Rate of profit on such contracts differ according to the duration of deposits. In the past two decades these rates have been changed by the Central Bank only three times despite the fluctuation in economic activities (which again poses the question about the "Islamic" authenticity of such practices).

However, rates of profit on mudaraba and musharaka contracts have been less than inflation rate in the last two decades, facilitating the transfer of private saving to the Islamic government and the availability of cheap loans to rent-seeking and bloated nationalized firms, quasi-public Islamic foundations and political cronies. Such practices, as well as the bureaucratic approach to banking and other structural flaws have led to the expansion of unregulated and informal bazaar lending based on mudaraba and/or conventional loans with high risk, and, therefore, very high rates.[15]

In fact, structural problems in the Iranian banking sector have led to a real pressure for banking reform in line with the Malaysian experience based on parallel Islamic-conventional banking (*Iranian Economics*, no. 43; Shahrivar 1381: 67–73). This is not a farfetched proposal because a parallel banking system is permitted by law in the Iranian free zones in the Persian Gulf for foreign banks and Iranian state banks, even though because of economic and political problems the experience has not been very successful.

An unresolved issue

Islamic banking is a growing economic sector in many Muslim countries, although it is still underdeveloped and fragmented by international standards (e.g. see Nigel 2001: 92–4, 96–7; Henry and Wilson 2004: 2–10). When Islamic banks came into existence in the 1970s, it was a phenomenon based on the combination of religion, politics, and oil money. This is still the case. Such a characteristic inevitably leads to controversies, varying interpretations, and religious compromises. This is demonstrated in the case of nationalized banking in Iran and private banking in Pakistan, and Islamic commercial banks in some Muslim countries, as well as some international and national banks that offer certain Islamic financial services and even some Shari'a advice.

The future expansion of riba-free Islamic banking and finance partially depends on the establishment of financial capital markets where long-term bank assets are invested in tradable securities and where banks can secure daily liquidity in money markets and inter-bank markets. However, none of these markets are faultless according to a strict interpretation of the Shari'a. And since there is no common interpretation of the law, the innovation of such new Islamic financial services will be continuously debated and contested. Yet, lack of innovation will be a serious economic constraint for the development of Islamic capital markets.

Some Islamic banks are slowly expanding into long-term investment based on Islamic contracts, but still a very important part of Islamic business is in debatable short-term finances, such as markup and leasing. To some extent this is because markup, which presents the lowest risk of all methods of Islamic finance available, might be cheaper than other finances, and traders are more at ease with it. Since most of banks liabilities in these contracts are short-term, banks are hesitant to tie up funds in medium or long-term assets. Besides, secondary markets for Islamic instruments are not yet developed and Islamic banks do not have access to the central bank lending facilities in countries where the whole banking is not Islamized.

Presently, some Muslim countries such as Iran and Sudan claim that the entire national banking is Islamic, and certain others like Saudi Arabia, insist that their banking has "always" been Islamic. However, the majority of Muslim countries, such as Egypt, have only permitted Islamic banks to coexist with conventional banks since the 1980s. Nevertheless, all these countries have been wary of the expansion of unregulated small private Islamic mudaraba funds. The high risk exposure and returns of the latter compared to regularized or state banks, has led to widespread bankruptcies and embezzlement. At least, this is what many full-fledged Islamic governments claim, and for this reason countries like Iran have forbidden their formation.

The most important financial activity of Islamic banks and conventional banks that offer Islamic services has been concentrated on short-term and less risky operations. Thus, markup and leasing prevail and the costs for providing funds are fixed in advance and limited to a fixed period, reflecting interest and traditional financial practices. Mudaraba and musharaka contracts for productive investment are rare. And this is in spite of the effective guarantees of the nominal values of these deposits even though such guarantees are incompatible with the rulings of the majority of jurists. The level of transparency of these banks, especially in countries like Iran where most banks are state banks, is almost nonexistent. However, depositors are guaranteed of their funds and are assured of receiving some nominal positive returns that in the majority of these countries are less than the rate of inflation. Despite the unconditional initial enthusiasm of some Muslim economists for these Islamic experiences in Iran and Pakistan, it is known by now that whatever these experiences are, they are neither recognized as Islamic by some of their own ulama, Islamic intellectuals, and Islamic judges, nor are they competitive.

In Iran, in 1994, in view of "excesses" and "flexible" interpretation of the prohibition against riba by state banks in recent years, Ayatollah Khamene'i, the supreme leader of the Islamic Republic, asked for the "reviving of the interest-free loan system" (*MEED* January 7, 1994). He has occasionally reiterated the same politically motivated call. Yet, at the same time former president Khatami, himself a religious scholar, insists that the Iranian banking system is totally riba-free (ISNA July 21, 2005).

The same type of conflict of views, religiously and politically motivated, is observable in other Muslim countries. In 1993, in Pakistan, with the consent of the government, some commercial banks appealed against the verdict of the Shari'a Court that demanded the elimination of riba from all financial instruments, public and private. That demand is still unsettled. Yet, in the meantime hundreds of millions of medium and low income families who are victims of inflation and negative real returns on their small deposits, should wonder whether it has not been a wrong historical moment for renouncing interest. Effectively, wherever total Islamic banking has officially been established, a massive redistribution of wealth takes place in favor of Islamic governments and state and private firms who can have access to interest-free loans, at the expense of millions of savers who receive negative real returns to their deposits.

Nevertheless, one must not forget that the problem of riba in Muslim countries is not only an economic question capable of social scientific scrutiny; it is also a religious dictum that can be interpreted differently, with varying politics and economic interest, nationally and internationally. Therefore, the weight and importance of the juridical-economic aspect of riba in relevant public policies rise with the relative decline of the legitimacy of the existing Islamic and semi-Islamic political and economic powers and movements, despite the relative independence of the religious factor in Muslim countries. As we have seen, this is clearly observable in the case of Egypt, Iran before and after the revolution, and Pakistan since its independence.

Yet, one must guard against passing judgment on the level of Islamization of the banking system in this or that Muslim country because such a judgment wrongly presupposes a unique concept of the Shari'a. In addition, if in Muslim countries some kind of Islamic banking is able to cater to the modern financial needs of believers, then the more suitable and efficient institutionalization of such a banking system would be a parallel banking system that is based on an innovative interpretation of the Shari'a and is able to compete internationally.[16] Such a system could act as an instrument for financial modernization in the Middle East and at the same time enable governments and central banks to bypass conservatism and noninnovatory tendencies of the existing banks. However, such a development requires a much more flexible and enlightened consensus on Islamic law and more independent, transparent, and active central banks within a democratic environment.

Notes

1 See Nomani and Rahnema (1994: 153–7), Warde (2000: 123–8), *Euromoney* (September 2001: 226), Henry and Wilson (2004: 2–14, 286–95), Kahf (2004: 22–31).
2 See Wilson (1997) for the prohibition of usury in Judaism, Christianity, and Islam.
3 See XXX: 39, IV: 161, III: 130–2 and II: 275–80. All references to the Quran are from A. Y. Ali (1989).
4 See the argument of al-Shafi'i on contradictory Traditions and the contradictory transmission of the Tradition (Khadduri 1987: 202–24, 325–6).
5 See Nomani (2002) for the details of the debate on the ambiguity of riba among classical jurists.
6 That is why there is no contemporary Sunni or Shi'i faqih (unlike some Islamic intellectuals) who would legally identify riba as economic exploitation or as economic rent (Rahnema and Nomani 1990: 146–50).
7 See Qadri (1986: 335–7), Schacht (1964: 79, 138), Mutahhari (1991: 265–9), and Doi (1984: 334–45).
8 See Schacht (1964: 155–7), Siddiqi (1987: 11–18), and Khan (1987: 48–9).
9 See Financial Institutions (1990), El-Ahdab (1992: 55–6), Davies (1984: 199, 220–1), Hill (1989: 159–63), and Ballantyne (1990: 153–7).
10 See Haque (1995: 48–52), and Rahnema and Nomani (1995: 74–80).
11 See www.islamicbanking.com/ibanking/ifi_list.php
12 See Khan (1987: 136–52); M. N. Siddiqi's comment in Z. Ahmed *et al.* (1983: 223–31).
13 See Umar Chapra's comments in Z. Ahmed *et al.* (1983: 212–14).
14 See Abrandabadi (1994) for a rare critical response to this issue.
15 See Miller (1999: 102–7) for the development of underground banking for foreign exchange in many Muslim countries.
16 See Aggrawal and Tarik (2000: 93–120) for an empirical analysis of Islamic banking that implicitly defends a parallel banking system in Islamic countries. See also Warde (2000).

Bibliography

Abdeen, A. M. and Shook, D. N. (1984) *The Saudi Financial system*, New York: John Wiley & Sons.

Abedeeni, A. (1999) *"Riba, Tavarrum va Daman,"* Salaam (9, 11, 13, 16, 20, 25, 27 May).

Abrandabadi, H. (1994) *"Molahezati dar bareh-e Oragh-e Musharakat,"* *Ressalat* (23 September).

Abu Saud, M. (1981) "Money, Interest and *Qirad*," in K. Ahmad (ed.) *Studies in Islamic Economics*, London: The Islamic Foundation.

Adams, C. C. (1968) *Islam and Modernism in Egypt*, New York: Russel and Russel.

Afzal-ur Rahman (1982) *Economics Doctrines of Islam* 3, Lahore: Islamic Publications Limited.

Aggrawal, R. K. and Tarik, Y. (2000) "Islamic Banks and Investment Financing," *Journal of Money, Credit and Banking* 32 (1): 93–120.

Ahmad, K. (1981) *Studies in Islamic Economics*, Leicester, UK: International Center for Research in Islamic Economics.

Ahmed, M. (2002) "Supreme Court sets aside judgments on riba," *Business Recorder* (25 June): 18–19.

Ahmed, Z., Iqbal, M., and Khan, M. F. (eds) (1983) *Money and Banking in Islam*, Islamabad: Institute of Policy Studies.

Algabid, H. (1990) *Les banques islamiques*, Paris: Economica.

Ali, A. Y. (tran.) (1989) *The Holy Quran*, Brentwood, MD: Amana Corp.

Ali, S. (1991a) "Shari'ah strains," *Far Eastern Economic Review* (2 May).

Ali, S. (1991b) "Question of interest," *Far Eastern Economic Review* (December 12).

Ali, S. (1992) "State and religion," *Far Eastern Economic Review* (February 13).

Al-Omar, F. and Abdel-Haq, M. (1996) *Islamic Banking: Theory, Practice and Challenges*, London: Zed Books.

Amin, S. H. (1985) *Islamic Law in the Contemporary World*, Glasgow: Royston Ltd.

Amin, S. H. (1986) *Commercial Law of Iran*, Tehran: Vahid Publications.

Amin, S. H. (1989) *Islamic Law and Its Implications for Modern World*, Glasgow: Royston Ltd.

Attia, G. (1986) "Financial instruments used by Islamic banks," in Butterworths Editorial Staff (eds), *Islamic Banking and Finance*, London: Butterworths.

Azzam, H. T. (1997) *The Emerging Arab Capital Markets*, London: Kegan Paul International.

Ballantyne, W. (1990) "A reassertion of the Shari'ah: the Jurisprudence of the Gulf States," in N. Heer (ed.) *Islamic Law and Jurisprudence*, Seattle, WA: University of Washington Press.

Biazar-e Shirazi, A. K. (1983) *Resaleh-e Novin* 2, Teheran: Nashr-e Farhang-e Islami.

Choudhury, M. A. (1986) *Contributions to Islamic Economic Theory*, London: Macmillan Press Ltd.

Commins, D. (1995) "Modernism," in *Oxford Encyclopedia of the Modern Islamic World* 3, Oxford: Oxford University Press.

Connors, J. (1986) "Towards a System of Islamic Finance in Malaysia," in C. Mallat (ed.) *Islamic Law and Finance*, London: Graham & Trotman.

The Constitution of the Islamic Republic of Iran, n.d. Teheran: Islamic Propagation Organization.

Coulson, N. J. (1990) *A History of Islamic Law*, Edinburgh: Edinburgh University Press.

Coville, T. (1994) *"La Banque Centrale d'Iran et la politique de liberalization"*, in T. Coville (ed.) *The Economy of Islamic Iran: Between State and the Market*, Teheran: Institute Français de Recherche en Iran.

Cragg, K. (1995) "Abduh, Muhammad," in *The Oxford Encyclopedia of the Modern Islamic World* 1, Oxford: Oxford University Press.

Davies, M. H. (1984) *Business Law in Egypt*, Deventer, Netherlands: Kluwer Law and Taxation Publishers.

DeLorenzo, Y. T. (1997) *A Compendium of Legal Opinions on the Operation of Islamic Banks*, London: Institute of Islamic Banking and Insurance.

Doi, A. R. I. (1984) *Shari'a: The Islamic Law*, London: Taha Publishers.

Edge, I. (1986) "Shari'a and Commerce in Contemporary Egypt," in C. Mallat (ed.) *Islamic Law and Finance*, London: Graham & Trotman.

El-Ahdab, A. H. (1992) "Interest in Islamic Law," *The ICC International Court of Arbitration Bulletin* 3 (May): 47–56.

El-Gamal, M. A. (2001) "An Economic Explanation of the Prohibition of *Gharar* in Classical Jurisprudence," *4th International Conference on Islamic Economics*. Online. Available HTTP: http://www.ruf.rice.edu/~elgamal

"Financial Institutions in OIC Countries of the Middle East" (1990) *Journal of Economic Cooperation among Islamic Countries* 2 (January–April): 1–261.

Galloaux, M. (1993) "*Réforme bancaire et finance islamique*," *Monde arabe Maghreb Machrek* 141: 53–67.

Galloaux, M. (1994) "*Économie islamique/occidentale*," *Les cahiers de l'Orient* 34: 49–70.

Gieraths, C. (1990) "Pakistan: Main Participants and Final Financial Products of Islamization Practices," in R. Wilson (ed.) *Islamic Financial Markets*, London: Routledge.

Haddad, Y. (1994) "Muhammad Abduh: Pioneer of Islamic Reform," in A. Rahnema (ed.) *Pioneers of Islamic Revival*, London: Zed Book Ltd.

Haneef, M. A. (1995) *Contemporary Islamic Economic Thought*, Kuala Lumpur: S. Abdul Majeed & Co.

Haque, Z. (1995) *Riba: The Moral Economy of Usury, Interest and Profit*, Kuala Lumpur: S. Abdul Majeed & Co.

Henry, C. M. and Wilson, R. (eds) (2004) *The Politics of Islamic Finance*, Edinburgh: Edinburgh University Press Ltd.

Heshmati-e Moulai, H. (1991) "*Bahsi Piramoun-e So'allat-e Matrohe dar Mored-e Nezam-e Bankdary-e Islam*," in *Majmo'eh-e Magalat-e Farsi: Siyasatha-ye mali*, Mashhad: Astan-e Gods-e Razavi.

Hill, E. (1989) "Islamic Law as a Source for the Development of a Comparative Jurisprudence, the Modern Science of Codification: Theory and Practice in the Life and Work of Abd Al-razzaq Ahmad Al-Sanhuri," in A. Al-Azmeh (ed.) *Islamic Law: Social and Historic Contexts*, London: Routledge.

Homoud, S. H. (1985) *Islamic Banking*, London: Arabian Information Ltd.

Islahi, A. A. (1988) *Economic Concepts of Ibn Taimiyah*, London: The Islamic Foundation.

Kahf, M. (1993) *The Islamic Economy*, Plainfield, IN: American Trust publication.

Kahf, M. (2004) "Islamic Banks: The Rise of a New Power Alliance of Wealth and Shari'a Scholarship," in C. Henry and R. Wilson (eds) *The Politics of Islamic Finance*, Edinburgh: Edinburgh University Press Ltd.

Kamali, M. H. (1991) *Principles of Islamic Jurisprudence*, Cambridge: Islamic Texts Society.

Kay, E. (1979) *Legal Aspects of Business in Saudi Arabia*, London: Graham & Trotman.

Kazarian, E. G. (1993) *Islamic Versus Traditional Banking: Financial Innovation in Egypt*, Boulder, CO: Westview Press.

Kerr, M. H. (1966) *Islamic Reform: Political and Legal Theories of Muhammad Abduh and Rashid Rida*, Berkeley, CA: University of California Press.

Khadduri, M. (trans.) (1987) *Al-Shafi'i's Risala*, Cambridge: Islamic Text Society.

Khan, R. S. (1987) *Profit and Loss Sharing*, Karachi: Oxford University Press.

Kuran, T. (1993) "The Economic Impact of Islamic Fundamentalism," in M. M. Marty and R. S. Appleby (eds) *Fundamentalism and the State*, Chicago, IL: University of Chicago Press.

Mahmood, M. (1973) *The Constitution of the Islamic Republic of Pakistan*, Lahore: Pakistan Law Times Publication.

Majmo'eh-ye Nazariyat-e Shoray-e Negahban (1992) 1, Teheran: Keyhan.

Malik, S. J. (1989) "Legitimizing Islamization – The Case of the Council of Islamic Ideology in Pakistan," *Orient* 30 (2): 253–65.

Mallat, C. (1986) "The Debate on Riba and Interest in Twentieth Century Jurisprudence," in C. Mallat (ed.) *Islamic Law and finance*, London: Graham & Trotman.

Mallat, C. (1993) *The Renewal of Islamic Law: Mohammad Baqer As-Sadr, Najaf and the Shi'i International*, Cambridge: Cambridge University Press.

MEED (January 7, 1994).

Miller, M. (1999) "Underground Banking," *Institutional Investor* 33 (1): 102–7.

Mills, P. S., Presley, J. R., and Mills, P. S. (1999) *Islamic Finance: Theory and Practice*, London: Palgrave Macmillan.

Mukhtar, A. (2002) "Riba Decision Evokes Mixed Reaction," *Business Recorder* (June 25): 2–3.

Mutahhari, M. (1991) *Mas'aleh-e Riba*, Teheran: Sadra.

Najjar, F. M. (1992) "The Application of Shari'a Laws in Egypt," *Middle East Policy* 1 (3): 65–70.

Neinhaus, V. (1986) "Islamic Economics, Finance and Banking – Theory and Practice," in Butterworths Editorial Staff (eds) *Islamic Banking and Finance*, London: Butterworths.

Nigel, D. (2001) "Islamic Banks Tap a Rich New Business," *Euromoney* (December): 21.

Nomani, F. (2002) "The Interpretative Debate of the Classical Islamic Jurists on Riba (Usury)," *Proceedings of the Middle East Economic Association* 4 (September). Online. Available HTTP: http://www.luc.edu/org/meea/vol4/NomaniRevised.htm

Nomani, F. (2003) "The Problem of Interest and Islamic Banking in a Comparative Perspective: The Case of Egypt, Iran and Pakistan," *Review of Middle East Economics and Finance* 1 (1): 37–70.

Nomani, F. and Rahnema, A. (1994) *Islamic Economic Systems*, London: Zed Books Ltd.

Pal, I. (1994) "Pakistan and the Question of Riba," *Middle Eastern Studies* 30 (January): 63–72.

Qadri, A. A. (1986) *Islamic Jurisprudence in the Modern World*, New Delhi: Taj Company.

Qaradawi, Y. (1995) *Le licite et l'illicite en Islam*, translated by S. Kechrid, Paris: Al-qalam.

Qureshi, A. I. (1970) *Islam and the Theory of Interest*, Lahore: Sh. Muhammad Ashraf.

Rahman, F. (1964) "Riba and Interest," *Islamic Studies* 3 (4): 34–41.

Rahman, F. (1980) *Major Themes of the Quran*, Minneapolis, MN: Bibliotheca Islamica.

Rahnema, A., and Nomani, F. (1990) *The Secular Miracle: Religion, Politics and Economic Policy in Iran*, London: Zed Books Ltd.

Rahnema, A. and Nomani, F. (1995) "Competing Shi'i Subsystems in Contemporary Iran," in S. Rahnema and S. Behdad (eds) *Iran after the Revolution: Crisis of an Islamic State*, London: I. B. Tauris.

Roy, D. A. (1991) "Islamic Banking," *Middle East Studies* 27: 427–56.

Sadr, M. B. (1971) *Eqtesad-e Ma*, vol. 1, translated by M. K. Musavi, Teheran: Intesharat-e Islami.

Sadr, M. B. (1978) *Eqtesad-e Ma*, vol. 2, translated by A. Espahbudi, Tehran: Intesharat-e Islami.

Saeed, A. (1997) *Islamic Banking and Interest*, Leiden: Brill.

Saleh, N. A. (1986) "Financial Transactions and the Islamic Theory of Obligations and Contracts," in C. Mallat (ed.) *Islamic Law and Finance*, London: Graham & Trotman.

Saleh, N. A. (1992) *Unlawful Gain and Legitimate Profit in Islamic Law*, London: Graham & Trotman.

Schacht, J. (1964) *An Introduction to Islamic Law*, Oxford: Clarendon Press.

Schacht, J. (1987) "Riba," in *First Encyclopedia of Islam, 1913–1936*, Leiden: E. J. Brill.

Siddiqi, M. N. (1981) "Muslim Economic Thinking: A Survey of Contemporary Literature," in K. Ahmad (ed.) *Studies in Islamic Economics*, London: The Islamic Foundation.

Siddiqi, M. N. (1987) *Partnership and Profit-Sharing in Islamic Law*, London: The Islamic Foundation.

Skovgaard-Petersen, J. (1997) *Defending Islam for the Egyptian State*, Leiden: Brill.

Sonn, T. (1995) "Rahman, Fazlur," in *The Oxford Encyclopedia of the Modern Islamic World* 3, Oxford: Oxford University press.

Soorat-e Mashrooh-e Mozakerat-e Majles-ye Baresi-ye Nahai-e Ghanoon-e Assasi 4 (1985), Tehran: Majles-e Shora-ye Islami.

Statistical Center of Iran (1999) *Iran Statistical Year Book: 1998–9*, Tehran.

Udovitch, A. L. (1986) "Kirad," in *Encyclopédie de l'Islam* 5, Leiden: E. J. Brill.

Va'ez-zadeh Khorasani, M. (1991) "*Tarhha-ye Jadid Baray-e Hall-e Moshkel-e Bankha*," in *Majmo'eh-ye Magalat-e Farsi: Siyasatha-ye Mali*, Mashhad: Astan-e Gods-e Razavi.

Valibeigi, M. (1992) "Banking and Credit Rationing under the Islamic Republic of Iran", *Iranian Studies* 25 (3–4): 51–65.

Warde, I. B. (2000) *Islamic Finance in the Global Economy*, Edinburgh: Edinburgh University Press.

Wilson, R. (1993) "Islamic Banking and Finance," in *The Middle East and North Africa*, London: Europa Publications limited.

Wilson, R. (1997) *Economics, Ethics and Religion: Jewish, Christian and Muslim Economic Thought*, London, Macmillan Press Ltd.

Wohlers-Scharf, T. (1983) *Les banques arabes et islamiques*, Paris: OCDE.

Ziadeh, F. (1968) *Lawyers, the Rule of Law, and Liberalism in Modern Egypt*, Stanford, CA: Stanford University Press. www.islamicbanking.com/ibanking/ifi_list.php (accessed June 5, 2005). www.isna.ir/Main/NewsView.aspx?ID=News-557560 (accessed July 21, 2005).

Appendix
Elements of Islamic law (Shari'a)[1]

Sohrab Behdad

Specific acts of Muslims and their religious rituals must be in accordance with the Islamic rules of conduct. These rules of conduct are called *Shari'a*. The primary sources of the Shari'a are the Quran and the Tradition (*Sunna*). The Quran, however, as a book of religious teachings contains many ambiguities and conflicting statements. The believers sought Prophet Muhammad's interpretation of the Quran during his lifetime. Soon after the death of the Prophet (AD 632), however, controversies arose on interpretation of the Quran, which gave rise to development of various schools of Islamic jurisprudence. The history of development of these schools has been studied elsewhere (Schacht 1982, 1985; Macdonald 1985; Calder 1993; Hallaq 1994). Here we are concerned with the basic elements of law in the major Sunni and Shi'i schools of jurisprudence.[2]

The process of deducing rules of *fiqh* (jurisprudence) from the primary sources of the Shari'a, that is, the Quran and the Sunna, in accordance with a set of principles and methods is known as *usul al-fiqh* (principles of jurisprudence). The person who makes these deductions is a *faqih* (jurist, *fuqaha* – plural). A faqih must be a *mujtahid*, that is a Muslim whose intellectual capacity and integrity has been recognized by the established mujtahids. The act of deducing a specific rule of conduct from the Shari'a is *ijtihad* (Kamali 1991: 362–92).

The bases of jurisprudence in the Sunni schools of fiqh are the Quran, Tradition of the Prophet (Sunna), Consensus *(ijma')*, and Analogy (*qiyas*). The ambiguities and conflicts in the Quran are to be resolved by the wisdom of mujtahid in the light of the philosophy of Islam and through the rules of jurisprudence established for utilizing the other sources. The most important source of the Shari'a after the Quran is Tradition. That is the conduct of affairs by the Prophet and statements attributed to him (*hadith*). The problem of application of the authority of Tradition stems not only from conflicting acts or statements of Muhammad but also from the existence of many false hadiths that have been circulated and transmitted. Therefore, Science of the Hadith (*ilm-al-hadith*) has become an element of Islamic jurisprudence. Complex rules of logical and historical scrutiny, and rhetoric have been established to recognize the genuine from false hadiths and to interpret Tradition for deducing Islamic rules of conduct (Aghnides 1969: 35–59; Kamali 1991: 44–82). This interpretation falls clearly in the domain of authority of mujtahids.

Thus, neither the Quran nor Tradition may be used by lay persons for advocating a position. The reaction of the fuqaha to the layman's application of the authority of the Quran and Tradition has been, historically, nothing short of condemnation. This condemnation has been particularly strong if the Quran or Tradition were relied upon to advocate a social or political action or change.

The other two bases of Islamic fiqh, Consensus and Analogy, are methods of interpreting Shari'a from the Quran and Tradition. According to Muhammad, Consensus among Muslims is the guarantee that the laws of God have been understood correctly (Aghnides 1969: 61). In the later periods, Consensus has been considered to be the agreement among the mujtahids of the past (Schacht 1982: 30).

Analogy is "the extension of the *shari'ah* . . . from the original case . . . to a new case, because the latter has the same cause as the former" (Aghnides 1969: 77). Islamic jurists believe that "extending the law" by analogy does not constitute "establishing a new law" (Kamali 1991: 198). The complexity of making Analogy is in the determination of the cause when the divine prescription has different attributes. Hence Analogy is a study in epistemology and logic and is constrained by the peril of abrogation in the divine prescriptions.

Within this jurisprudential framework, the new questions that may arise in the society of Muslims must be resolved by ijtihad. By the fourth century of Islam (tenth century AD), the view gained dominance, however, that all the essential questions have been clearly dealt with by the great mujtahids of the past (Schacht 1982: 69–75). According to this view, there would not be any need for independent reasoning in the Shari'a, and the duty of the future faqih would be limited to the interpretation of "the doctrine as it had been laid down once and for all" (Schacht 1982: 71). This is referred to as "closing of the gate of ijtihad" and is accepted in practice, if not in theory, by all major schools of sunni fiqih.[3] The muftis who issue religious rulings (*fatwa*) must rely upon the ijtihad of the great mujtahids of the past in a way not unlike judges in a system of common law.

Shi'i jurisprudence provides a somewhat wider scope for interpretation of the divine prescription.[4] Similar to Sunnis, Shi'is accept the Quran, Tradition, and Consensus. Shi'is, however, rely not only on the Tradition of Muhammad but also of the infallible Imams (Tabataba'i 1984: 3). This provides a longer period (lasting to the third century of Islam) and also a more varied sociopolitical context for Tradition, and is especially important because, with the exception of the first Imam, Ali, all other Imams considered the Islamic state illegitimate. (For a brief history of the life of Shi'i Imams see Momen 1985: 23–60.)

The most significant difference between Shi'i and Sunni jurisprudence is acceptance of Reason (*aql*), instead of Analogy, as a basis of fiqih in Shi'ism. Shi'i scholars maintain that Analogy "is possible only where there is a basic common denominator between . . . two cases inasmuch as one can be certain that the same reason which is behind the precept in the original case, covers the other case as well" (Tabataba'i 1984: 3). "Reason," however, is "categorical judgments drawn from pure and practical reason [and] whatever is ordered by reason is ordered by religion" (Tabataba'i 1984: 3–4).

Unlike many Sunnis, Shi'is consider "the gate of ijtihad" open. Every Shi'i mujtahid must make his view by personal investigation of the sources of Shari'a and may not imitate the opinion of another mujtahid (Tabataba'i 1984: 16). Thus, Shi'is may have, in theory, a wider latitude of interpretation of the Shari'a than sunnis. In practice, however, this latitude is significantly limited by the jurisprudential tradition of the great mujtahids of the past. Deviation from this tradition is heresy and is condemned by Shari'a (Aghnides 1969: 30).

Notes

1 I am indebted to Farhad Nomani for his constructive comments and suggestions. I am responsible for errors of omission and commission.
2 The Sunnis and Shi'is differ partly on the issue of the succession to Muhammad (Momen 1985: 11–22). The major Sunni schools of jurisprudence are Hanafi, Shafi'i, Maliki, Hanbali, and Zahiri. For a review of some differences among these schools see Doi (1984) and Qadri (1986). The main schools of Shi'i jurisprudence are Jafari, Zaidi, and Ismaili. See Momen (1985) for detailed elaborations.
3 Aghnides who considers the closing of the gate of ijtihad a fiction quotes a modern Turkish faqih saying "that the gate of ijtihad was not closed...by an external cause...but through the mere absence of mujtahids" (1969: 124). Hallaq (1984) is among the few modern scholars who believe the gate of ijtihad has never been closed in theory or practice. See also Kamali (1991: 366–92).
4 Here I am referring mainly to Usuli school of the Jafari Shi'ism, the dominant school of jurisprudence in Iran since the eighteenth century. For a discussion of the Usuli vs. Akhbari conflict, and of other schools within Shi'ism see Momen (1985: 220–32).

Bibliography

Aghnides, N. P. (1969/1916) *Mohammedan Theories of Finance with an Introduction to Mohammedan Law and a Bibliography*, New York: AMS Press.

Calder, N. (1993) *Studies in Early Muslim Jurisprudence*, Oxford: Clarendon Press.

Doi, A. R. I. (1984) *Shari'a: The Islamic Law*, London: Ta Ha Publisher.

Hallaq, W. B. (1984) "Was the Gate of Ijtihad Closed?" *International Journal of Middle East Studies*, 16 (1): 3–41.

Hallaq, W. B. (1994) *Law and Legal Theory in Classical and Medieval Islam*, London: Varriorum.

Kamali, M. H. (1991) *Principles of Islamic Jurisprudence*, Cambridge: Islamic Text Society.

Macdonald, D. B. (1985/1902) *Development of Muslim Theology, Jurisprudence and Constitutional Theory*, London: Darf Publishers.

Momen, M. (1985) *An Introduction to Shi'i Islam*, New Haven, CT: Yale University Press.

Mutahhari, M. (1983) *Jurisprudence and its Principles (Fiqh and usul al-fiqh)*, translated by Muhammad Salman Tawheedi, Albany, CA: Moslem Student Association, n.d.

Qadri, A. A. (1986) *Islamic Jurisprudence in the Modern World*, New Delhi: Taj Company.

Schacht, J. (1982/1964) *An Introduction to Islamic Law*, Oxford: Clarendon Press.

Schacht, J. (1985/1950) *The Origins of Muhammadan Jurisprudence*, Oxford: Clarendon Press.

Tabatab'i, H. M.(1984) *An Introduction to Shi'i Law: A Bibliographical Study*, London: Ithaca Press.

Index

Abbasids dynasty 5, 7–8, 14;
  main preoccupation of the state 7
Abdel Nasser, President Gamal 130, 133
Abduh, Muhammad 14, 33 n.16, 200,
  202–3, 205, 209
Abdul Hakim, Khalifa 1, 17
Abel 17–18
Abu Bakr, the Caliph 4–5, 171
Abu Dhabi 144–5, 162 n.1; commercial
  law in 145
Abu Dharr 5–7, 18–19, 24–6, 29–30
Abu Sufyan 5, 29, 32 n.6
Abu Ubaid al-Qasim 23
Abu Yusuf, Y. 7, 23, 31
Abu Zayd, Nasr Hamid 73
accumulation of wealth 1, 21, 25–9, 48
adultery 21–4, 70, 123
Afghanistan 1, 21, 51, 74, 85
agents of social renewal 39
age of marriage *see* marriage age
ahkam avvaliyya (primary rulings) 13
Ahmadinejad, Mahmoud 29, 82
Ahmed, Leila 91–2
al-Anfal, Sura 4, 30
al-Ashmawi, Said 73
Alavi 69
al Azhar University 74, 107, 151,
  203, 150
al-'Azm, Sadiq 73
al-Badawi, Ibrahim Zaki 201–2
al-Banna, Hasan 17
al-Bukhari 9
alcoholic beverages 23
al-Fajr, Sura 3
Algeria 31, 44, 55, 57, 89, 96, 98, 103,
  110, 135–7; Algerian women 89;
  labor law and Islam in 134; revivalist
  movement in 31; riba-free banking
  in 199

Ali, the Caliph 6–7, 15
al Ma'ida sura 4
al-Shafi'i, U. 33 n.14, 133, 160, 193,
  195–6, 219 n.4, 226 n.2
al-Turtushi (Ibn Randaqa) 8
amal 114
Amnesty International 83, 86 n.4, 90
amputation 21, 24, 70, 81, 207
Analogy 166, 169, 172, 224–5
Anderson, Sir Norman 143
An-Na'im, Abdullahi 72–3
an-Nisa, Sura 4
anticolonialist movement 14–15
anti-imperialist movement 15
anti-Islamic resistance 45, 55, 78
apostasy 70–3
Arab countries 102–6, 135, 146,
  176, 198; *see also separate
  country names*
Arab women 21, 24, 31–2, 44–9, 70–86,
  88–109, 113, 116, 119–136, 177;
  see also under Women
Aramco Arbitration 144
Arkoun, Mohammed 73
arrogant (*taghoti*) 26, 30
Atatürk 39, 58, 108
atheism 16, 18, 70
Atwood, Margaret 90
Aubi, Nazih 41
Ayub Khan, President 121
Ayyubids dynasty 8

Baathist 69
Baha'is 78
Bahrain 102–3, 122, 142–3, 148–9, 156,
  198; Bahrain Center for Human
  Rights 122; commercial law in 148;
  zakat in 173
Bangladesh 124; zakat in 173

Banking law 151, 155, 193, 199–200;
Abu Dhabi 193–219; Bahrain 198;
Bangladesh 173; Egypt 193–4, 198,
200–6, 210–13, 217, 219; Iran 194,
199, 210–19; Islamization 214;
Jordan 173; Kuwait 198, 211;
Pakistan 193–4, 199, 204–10, 213–14,
217–19; Qatar 148; Saudi Arabia 193,
199, 207, 217; Tunisia 108;
United Arab Emirates 102;
an unresolved issue 217–19
Barkat-Allah, Maulana 15–16
barley, riba on 194
bay' (exchange, sale) 194, 215
Bazargan, Mehdi 212–13
behavioral norms 58
Bharatiya Janata party (India) 98
Bhutto, Benazir 45, 55, 124
Bhutto, Zulfiqar Ali 24, 45, 118,
123, 125–6
Bin Laden, Osama 31–2
blasphemy 99
Bonyad-e Mustaz'afan (the Foundation
for the Oppressed) 25–6
bride price (*mahr*) 106
Buddhism 2
budget deficits, financing of 186–8
Bullock, Kathy 91
bureaucratic corruption 14
Byzantium 12

Cain 17–18
Cairo: Cairo University 99; employment
in 47; *see also* Cairo Declaration on
Human Rights
Cairo Declaration on Human Rights in
Islam 67–8; on ban on slavery 84; on
crime and punishment 70, 84;
on equality 70, 84; freedom to express
opinions 71; issuance of 68; prohibits
riba 71; on rights and freedom 70; on
rights of ownership 70; on right to
education 70, 84; on right to marry 70;
on right to privacy 70; on right to
education 70, 84; on right to marry 70;
on right to privacy 70; on Shari'a as the
only source of reference 70; *shari'a* as
the ultimate reference 71; on taking
away life 70; on torture 70, 84; on
wages 70; woman is equal to man in
human dignity 70
Canada 90–1
Canadian Council of Muslim
Women 90
Canadian Islamic Congress 90
capital accumulation 27

capitalism 15–17, 118–19, 133; capital,
globalization and the
internationalization, of Middle east 89;
capital-labor relations 114, 119, 127–8;
classical capitalism 11; Islam as
laissez-faire capitalism 1; Islamic
capitalism 19–25; Islamic movement
with 17; and labor relations 114–15;
modern capitalism 11; versus socialism
22; and work 161
censorship 45, 74
Center for Women's Counseling and
Legal Aid 94
centralization of the judicial system 7
Charter of the Organization of the Islamic
Conference (OIC) 67–71, 84, 86 n.1
chastity 30, 32, 96
Chhachhi, Amrita 98, 107
Chief Justice (*qadi al-qudat*), 7
child labor 11, 122, 125, 129, 138
child laborers 129, 136
Christians 78; Christian economics 52
Citizenship 96, 100–1, 109–11, 121
Civil Codes: of the Arab countries 146,
198; Egypt 154; Jordan 160; Kuwait
159; Oman 155
classless Islamic society 1
classless society 17–19, 25, 119
class privileges 21, 24
class society 2, 17–18, 30, 119
closing the gate of ijtihad 12, 33 n.13,
225–6, 226 n.3
collective action by employees 116, 184
collective bargaining 117, 123
collective life 22
collective welfare 8, 11, 22
collectivism 7, 19, 30
Commercial Code 151–3, 155–9, 162 n.3,
163 n.6, 199
commercial contracts 142, 144–5, 147,
155, 157, 160
commercial instruments 145
commercial law: Abu Dhabi 144–5,
162 n.1; academic and cultural
approaches 142; Bahrain 148, 155;
Bangladesh 173; Egypt 142, 151; Iran
146; Iraq 148; Jordan 149, 160;
Kuwait 148; Libya 148; Oman 149;
Pakistan 173; Qatar 142, 145, 149,
154, 158, 162 nn.2, 3, 4; Saudi Arabia
142–5, 150, 155, 162 n.3; Sudan 173–4;
Syria 148; Tunisia 130, 134–6;
uncertainty in commercial contracts 147;
United Arab Emirates 148, 156

Commission for the Islamization of the Economy (CIE) 207
communism 15–18, 35, 53, 57, 138
Communist Party of India 15–16
compound interest 198, 200, 202
concession agreement 144, 150
confiscation 23, 70
consensus (*ijma'*) 20, 57–8, 72, 84, 155, 171, 175, 187, 193, 219, 224–5
constitutionalism 66, 76, 82
constitutionalist movements 66
constitutions of Muslim states 67, 69, 71, 75, 85, 89, 107, 118
contractual negotiation 116, 132, 134
corruption 5, 14, 29–30, 40, 45, 56–7, 82, 85, 131–2
corrupt on earth 25
Council of Islamic Ideology (CII) 204–6
crucifixion 70
cultural imperialism 88
Cultural Revolution 28
culture and economic performance 50

daruriyyat 12
dates, riba on 194
death penalty 70
dependency 25, 50, 97, 108
dependent capitalism 25
depravation 25
Devotees of Islam (Fadalian Eslam) 81
dhimmi status 78
dislocation, economic and social 14, 30, 109
disputes between employers and employees 120
Dissolution of Marriages Act 107
Divine Legislator 144
divorce 58, 90, 92, 98–9, 101, 105–7, 128, 214; Dissolution of Marriages Act 107; Divorce Act in India 107; Shari'a on 105; woman's status after 106–7
domino effect 44–5
dower (*mahr*) 96, 106
Dworkin, Andrea 95

Ebadi, Shirin 72–3, 82
economics *see* Islamic economics
education, of women 104
egalitarianism 2, 7, 19, 29, 40, 56, 131
Egypt banking systems in 193; Civil Code in 154; commercial law in 142; debate on riba in 200–4; divorce in 106; Egyptian Trade Union Federation

(ETUF) 130; Egyptian women 91; employment in 47; health services at 42; Muslim women in 98; revivalist movement in 31; zakat in 173
El Fadl, Khaled Abou 73
employment: in Cairo 47; in Egypt 47; employers' and employees' rights and responsibilities 114–16; of females/women 113–20, 122, 125–36; in Turkey 47
enemies of the interior 28
equality of men and women 71–3, 77, 84, 89, 95, 98–9, 105, 136
equity 1, 154, 161, 180, 190, 209
Erbakan, Necmettin 49
Erdoğan, Tayyip, Recep 49
Esposito, J. 96, 123, 126
Essid, Y. 8–10, 33 n.9
exogamous marriages 97, 100
expatriate workers 121
Expediency Council (*Majma'-e Tashkis-e Maslahat*) 13
exploitation 1, 18, 25, 49, 113, 115, 121–2, 126, 139, 198, 206, 212, 214, 219; exploitive profiteering 25; of man by man 1, 25; of workers 27, 113, 115
expropriation 25–6, 51, 121
extortion 8

Fada'ian-e Islam (Warriors of Islam) 17, 81
fair price 10
fair wage 115–16
Family Code 98–9, 103, 105, 107
family law *see* Muslim family law
faqih (jurist) 26, 28, 80, 224–5
Fatemids dynasty 8
fatwa (ruling) 35, 83, 149, 203, 205, 225
Federal Shari'a Court (FSC) 207, 209
female labor force participation 120, 129, 134, 136
female religious endogamy 100
female's worth 96
feminist legalistic opportunism 89–95, 107
feudalism 1, 18, 22
fidelity 32, 96
financial contracts: classical views on 194–8
fiqh (jurisprudence) 224
floggings 21, 70, 79
Foda, Faraj 53
forbidden transactions 144, 159, 161–2
foreign workers 121, 136
forms of marriages 97, 100

France 80, 90
Fraud 8, 11, 23, 28, 30
free competition 23, 49
freedom of association 71, 122
freedom of press 71
freedom of religion 71, 78, 82, 83
Free Officers rule 131
free society, policy prescriptions for
    38–66; *see also* Islamic subeconomy
Front islamique de salut (FIS-Algeria) 98
fuqaha (jurists) 74, 146

gambling 23, 123, 196, 214
Gardezi, F. 93
gates of ijtihad 12
Gaza 102
gender and Islam 90
genuinely Islamic banks 54
gharar 147, 160–1, 193–6, 221; classical
    views on 194–8
Ghazali, Imam Muhammad 8, 12–13, 31
global economic order 51
globalization 98
God's ultimate ownership 26–7
Godwin, William 18
gold, riba on 194
Golden Age of Islam 3, 14, 166
grand mufti 20, 121, 200, 203
Guardian Council 13, 28, 82, 214

hadd 153
hadith 9, 11, 33, 37, 93, 114, 179,
    194–5, 205, 224
Hanafi school 100, 105, 196
Hanbali school 119, 144
haqq al-'abd 66
haqq allah 66, 162 n.5
Harun al-Rashid 7
Hayek, Friedrich 53
hegemonic imperialist discourse 95
Hessini, Leila 91–2
hijab 91
Hijaz 96
hijra 3
Hinduism 98
hisba 8
historical materialism 17, 19
hoarders/hoarding 5, 9, 11, 23, 122, 199,
    202, 214
Hoodfar, H. 91–2, 102
hoquq-e enlami 76
Hoseiniyeh Ershard 17
housewifely duties 77
human development index (HDI) 124

human rights policy and Islam 66–86;
    background 66–7; dubious Islamic
    authority of 69; human rights law
    67–8, 72, 77, 80, 82, 85; human rights
    theory 66; international principles 68;
    international standards 68, 72, 75, 132,
    217; Islamic alternatives 69; Islamic
    approach to 66; Islamic jurisprudence,
    see separate entry; in the Islamic
    Republic of Iran 74–82, *see also*
    separate entry; Islamic requirements
    68, 73, 76–7; Islamic rules 17, 69,
    77–8, 209, 224; to marry 70, 100, 103,
    105; Muslims attempt to elaborate 67;
    NGOs 68, 72, 129;
    non-Muslims 40, 53, 55, 70–2, 76–8,
    100, 166, 177–80, 207, 213–4;
    race 62, 70, 77, 109, 116; on religion
    convertion 70, 194; religious laws 71,
    78; rights of individual and rights of
    God 66; in Saudi Arabia 82–5, *see also*
    separate entry; secular norms 68; sex
    24, 47–8, 62, 70, 76–7, 81, 91, 98, 100,
    102, 111; social origin 77; theoretical
    problems 67–74; tribal origin 77;
    women rights denied 73; *see also* Cairo
    Declaration
Human rights policy in Saudi Arabia
    82–5; Article 5 (on monarchy) 83;
    Article 6 (in citizens duties) 83;
    Article 7 (on Quran and Sunna
    superiority over Basic Law) 83; Article
    26 (on human rights protection) 83;
    Saudi Basic Law 83–4; World Human
    Rights Conference 1993 83
Human rights policy in the Islamic
    Republic of Iran 74–82; on equality of
    men and women 77; on family
    safeguarding 77; on human rights 77;
    on Islamic criteria of all laws 76; on
    Islamic criteria of human laws 76;
    on minority religious associations 78;
    non-recognition of Baha'ism as a
    religion 78; post-revolutionary human
    rights 76; punishing women 80; on
    religious minorities 78; on rights of
    non-Muslims 78; UN critics
    of 82; women's dress code 79;
    women's rights in 79; on women's
    rights 76
Human Rights Watch 121, 139
huquq al-insan 66
Husayn (Ali's son) 6–7, 19, 24–5
hypocrites (*monafeqin*) 25

Ibn al-Qayyim 23, 160, 201–3
Ibn Qudamah al-Maqdisi 10
Ibn Qutayba 10
Ibn Taymiya, A. 9–11, 33 nn.11–12, 144,
   146, 160, 194, 196, 201, 203
Ibn Umar, Abu, Z. 8
ifta ([source of fatwa]) 149, 201
ijara (lease) 188, 196
ijtihad 12–13, 33 n.13, 143, 157, 162,
   167–9, 173, 224–6, 226 n.3
Ikhwan al-Muslimin (Islamic
   Brotherhood) 17, 98, 132
Imam Malik 9, 157
imitation (*taqlid*) 13, 26, 50
India 14–16, 20, 34, 95–6, 98, 107, 110,
   124, 139, 162 n.1, 210; Indian
   women 98; Islamic revivalist
   movements in 16–17; Muslim women
   in 98
individual freedom 11, 22, 90, 100
individual liberty 42
industrial conflict 117, 122–3
industrialization 14, 49, 62, 124
inheritance law 94
Inter-Collegiate Muslim Brotherhood 19
interfaith marriages 100–2
International Commission of Jurists
   (ICJ) 72
International Covenant on Civil and
   Political Rights (ICCPR) 74, 86
international human rights laws 67–8, 74,
   77, 80, 82, 85
international human rights principles 68
internationalization of capital 89
internationalization of the revivalist
   movement 31
International Labour Organization (ILO)
   128, 130
interventionist state 26–7, 132
Intifada 89
intoxicants 14, 24, 28
Iqbal, Muhammad 16, 19, 40, 54
Iran: child labor 129; economy 50;
   human rights in *see under* human rights;
   Human rights policy in 74–82; Iranian
   Constitution 76–7; Iranian Family
   Protection Act 77; Iranian revolution
   19, 25–7, 211–12, 139; Iranian women
   77, 79, 109; Islamic movements and
   labor law changes in 129–36; Islamic
   regimes and labor law in 118;
   Islamization of 30; labor law in 126–9;
   new labor code 128; pragmatic view on
   riba in 210–17; riba-free banking in 199;

weakening of labor's bargaining
   power 128; women's educational status
   in 128; workers and organizations
   in political transformation 126;
   zakat in 173
Iraq 5, 27, 29, 44, 69, 72, 82, 85, 104–5,
   127, 146, 148, 173, 176, 211;
   commercial law in 148; human rights
   in 69; polygamy encouraged in 105;
   zakat in 173
islah (rejuvenate) 13
Islam: classical patriarchy 96; and
   communism 15; conservative
   interpretation 18; egalitarianism 2, 7,
   19, 29, 40, 56, 131; emergence of 88;
   and human rights, clashes between 80;
   and human rights policy 66–86,
   see also under human rights policy;
   interpretations 2; Islam the rebellious
   2, 30; and labor law, some precepts and
   examples 113–37, *see also under*
   labor law; as laissez-faire capitalism 1;
   as a limitation on rights 71; as a
   monolith 95; of *mustaz'afin* 2;
   patriarchy, and the state, an alternative
   approach 95–9; populism 2, 7, 30–1;
   for profit sharing concept in work 115;
   public policy in 142, *see also*
   commercial law; rebellious Islam to Pax
   Islamicus 2; as religion 1; the religion
   versus the political movement 97;
   representations 2; restrictions on
   private property ownership 23;
   revivalism, and public policy 1–33;
   revolutionary Islam 25; as social
   movement 3; as 'third path' between
   capitalism and socialism 113; unitary
   conception of 8; women's productive
   and reproductive lives 88; work and
   capital relation in 161; workers wages
   and rights determination 11; zakat,
   taxes, and public finance in 165–89,
   see also separate entry; see also
   separate entries
Islamic banking: Abu Dhabi 145, 162 n.1;
   Bahrain 122, 173, 189 n.11, 198;
   criticisms 40; depositors encouraged
   by 39; and economics and religion
   40–4; Egypt 193–4, 198, 200–6,
   210–13, 217, 219; 'genuinely
   Islamic' banks 54; interest prohibition
   by 40; international oil market
   restructuring, impact on 61 n.9; and
   Islamism 39; Iran 194, 199, 210–19;

Islamic banking (*Continued*)
  Jordan 101, 104, 121, 130, 134–6, 173;
  Kuwait 173, 198, 211; as modern
  creation 55; 'nominally Islamic' banks
  54; Pakistan 193–4, 199, 204–10,
  213–14, 217–19; practice of 39; Saudi
  Arabia 193, 199, 207, 217; social
  significance 38–40; success of 39;
  Sudan 217; versus conventional
  banking 38, 41, 54
Islamic businessmen 23, 40, 45–6
Islamic capitalism 19–25
Islamic civilization 40, 72
Islamic clinics 42, 57
Islamic commerce 7, 25, 41
Islamic conglomerates 41
Islamic Consultative Assembly
  (Majlis) 26
Islamic culture, and Westernization 56
Islamic discourse 91
Islamic dress rules 79–80
Islamic economics: Ayatollah Sadr's
  analysis 211; careful listening to
  improve 56–9; on contemporary
  economies 42; economic behavior 40,
  53; economic choices 42, 51; economic
  disparities 21, 24; economic
  domination 25; economic
  illiberalism 49; economic Islamization
  51; economic justice 15, 32, 40;
  economic liberties/liberalism 29, 48–9,
  59, 128; economics, third path 113;
  Egypt 42; flaws and limitations
  exposure, to mitigate economic damage
  52–3; illiberal economic policies 49;
  Indonesia 42; Iranian economy 50;
  Islamism as economic instrument 45–8;
  limits of Islamist appeal, establishment
  54; networks of 46; organizational
  principles 23; political instability
  impact on 51; practical demonstrations
  of 41; rampant government corruption
  and widespread dishonesty in 45–6, 56;
  scholarly and intellectual debate on 28;
  threats to the global economy 48–51;
  vagueness 43–4
Islamic fashion industry 47
Islamic feminism/feminists 73–4, 86, 92
Islamic firms 41
Islamic fundamentalism 32, 38, 45, 51–2,
  56–7, 91, 97, 107
Islamic human rights 68, 71–3, 76,
  81–2, 85
Islamic identity 41, 46

Islamic ideology 1, 2, 74, 78, 127, 204–6
Islamic investment companies 41, 203
Islamic jurisprudence (*fiqh*) 2, 9–10, 20,
  53, 67, 69, 146–7, 155, 159, 212; basic
  texts of 117; and price fixing 10;
  schools of 53, 99–100, 103, 105;
  traditional jurisprudence 13–14, 31;
  women's right to 92
Islamic labor councils 128
Islamic labor policy 122
Islamic law: and Islam secular law public
  policy 141–63; banking law *see
  separate entry*; commercial law *see
  separate entry*; formulation 7; labor
  law *see under* labor law; on minimum
  wages 116–17; Muslim family law
  see separate entry; Shari'a; Women and
  family laws in Islam; *see also
  separate entries*
Islamic law of inheritance 23
Islamic legal culture 66
Islamic legal principles 118
Islamic-Marxists 18
Islamic militancy 51
Islamic movements and labor law changes
  129–36; alliance between the Islamists
  and the socialists 131–3; in Egypt
  130–3; and labor law 129; proposed
  changes to labor law 131
Islamic order 2, 22, 30
Islamic organization: organizational
  principles of an Islamic economy 23;
  Organization of Mojahedin Khalq Iran
  18; Organization of production 1;
  social-gender organizations, ideological
  forms of 97; *see also* Islamist
  organizations
Islamic orthodoxy 20, 27–9
Islamic penal code, enforcement 24
Islamic personal status law 68
Islamic pledge to social fairness and
  economic justice 15
Islamic populism 2, 7, 30
Islamic Protestantism 18
Islamic regimes and labor law 118–27
Islamic Republican Party (IRP) 127
Islamic revivalism 1, 2, 15, 17,
  29–32, 38, 64; Islamic revivalist
  movement 15–16; and
  socialism 15–25
Islamic rights and morality 77
Islamic Salvation Front 44, 55
Islamic services 43, 218
Islamic socialism 1

Islamic Society of North America
(ISNA) 90–1, 218
Islamic Solution 22
Islamic spirit 42
Islamic state: constitution 67, 69, 71, 75,
85, 89, 107, 118; control over
economy 56; financial crisis of 39,
121, 178, 203, 209–11; and gender and
class 88–109; in labor law 116–17; and
patriarchal relations 95–9; as the period
of reference 166; and public
expenditures 183–6; role 23
Islamic subeconomy 40–4, 46, 54, 59
Islamic symbolism 54, 90
Islamism: contemporary Islamism, and
pro- and antimarket ideologies 48; and
economic global order 51; as economic
instrument 45–8; and economics
38–66, *see also* Islamic banking;
modern Islamist movements 48–9; as
un- or anti-Islamic 45
Islamist ideologists, utopian claims of 38
Islamist obsession with veiling 47
Islamist organizations: income of 43; in
Iran 43; in Libya 43; in Saudi
Arabia 43
Islamists and the socialists 131–3
Islamization 1, 21, 24, 28, 30, 44, 51, 66,
73–4, 97–9, 199, 205–7, 209–10; of
banking systems 214; cultural and
symbolic dimensions 31; of Iran 30;
male hegemonies reinforced by 95
Israel 89, 97, 101, 134
istihsan (juristic preference) 12
istislah (consideration of public
interest) 12

Jafari 226 nn.2, 4
Jama'at-i Islami 1, 17, 19, 24, 40, 45, 55,
205, 207–9
Jenin, West Bank 134
Jews 78
Jinnah, Muhammad Ali 16, 40
jizya (poll tax on non-Muslims) 166,
177–180
Jordan 101, 104, 121, 130, 134–6, 160,
173; Jordan Civil Code 160; labor law
and Islam in 134; zakat in 173
Joseph, Souad 96, 100
Judaeo-Christian tradition 75
judges (*qadis*) 7
Jurists: classical jurists on Gharar 196;
classical jurists, on riba 194–5, 202;
and human rights policy 66, 68,

72, 74; interpretations of the Shari'a
by 12–13, 20, 33 n.14, 146, 165–70;
on Jizya 178; on mudaraba 197; on
polygamy 104; on private property 23;
on riba 151; on secular taxes 179–80;
Shi'i jurist 211–14; on zakat
levy 170–1, 175
Justice and Development Party
(AK Party-Turkey) 49
just price 11
just wage 115

Kamali, M. H. 12–13, 33 nn.10, 14, 177,
201, 203, 224–5, 226 n.3
Kandiyoti, D. 96–7
Kar, Mehrangiz 72
karo kari crimes 107
Kasravi, Ahmad 14, 17, 33 n.16, 81
Kerala (India) 96
Khalifa Abdul Hakim 1, 17
Khamene'i, Ayatollah Seyyed Ali 81, 218
kharaj (land tax) 166, 176–7, 179–80
Khatami, Muhammad 29, 82, 218
Khomeini, Ayatollah Rohollah 13, 25, 31,
48, 76, 78
Kidwai, Mushir Hosain 15, 17
Kuwait 143, 148, 152, 154–5, 158–9, 173,
198, 211; commercial law in 148, 159;
Islamic regimes and labor law in 118;
Kuwait Civil Code 159; Kuwaiti
Constitution of 1962 152

labor code 118–22, 125–6, 128–9, 135
Labor "flexibilization," 131–6
labor law and Islam 113–7; 1969 labor
code 120; Algeria 135–6; Arab world
133–6; Bahrain 122; Bangladesh 124,
173; capital/labor relationship 114;
changes and Islamic movements
129–136; contract employment 117;
Egypt 116–17, 125, 130–6; employers'
and employees' rights and
responsibilities 114–16; expatriate
workers, situation of 121; hiring
employees 116; in Iran 126–9, *see also
under* Iran; and Islam 113–37; Islamic
movements and labor law changes
129–36, *see also separate entry*; Islamic
precepts about 113–17; and Islamic
regimes 118–127, *see also separate
entry*; Islamic Republic of Iran 118;
Islamic views of work 114;
Jordan 121, 130, 134–6, 149;
Kuwait 118; Morocco 130, 134–6;

labor law and Islam (*Continued*)
in Pakistan 118–26, 129, 130, 135, *see also under* Pakistan; profit sharing 115; proposed changes to 131; role of state in 116–17; Saudi Arabia 117–27, *see also under* Saudi Arabia; strikes or lockouts 117; Tunisia 130, 134–6; United Arab Emirates 102, 142, 156, 163; wages 116; women as employees 116; workers and employers, clashes between 117; Yemen 118, 121
labor market 11, 116–18, 131, 134, 136, 138
labor militancy 117, 133
labor movements 129, 135–6
labor policy 118, 122–5, 127
labor process 26
labor rights 122, 125, 134, 136
labor unions 53, 117, 132, 134
Lahore 19, 94, 104, 108
Lahore-based Women Living Under Muslim Law (WLUML) 104
laissez-faire economics 1, 9, 19, 119, 128
lands 5, 7, 13, 17, 83, 94, 97–8, 115, 119, 123, 134, 169–173, 196; *kharaj* (land tax) 166, 176–7, 179–80; landlordism 1, 15, 22, 41, 175; land ownership, unlimited 22–4; *see also* property rights
Law of Adat (customary laws) 98
Law of Commercial Transactions 158
law of concession 144–5
law of contract 141, 162, 194
laws of the market (*ahkam al-suq*) 8
Lebanon 101, 106, 148, 198; divorce in 106
legal devices 195, 198, 207
Lenin, V. I. 16, 212
Lewis, Bernard 3–5, 9, 32 nn.6, 11, 50, 54
Liaquat Ali Khan 122
Libya: commercial law in 148; human rights in 69; polygamy in 104; riba-free banking in 199; zakat in 173
limits on ownership 22–3
Lumpenelite 131

McGuinty, Dalton 90
mafsada 12
Majlis 13, 26, 28
Malaysia 38, 98, 172–4, 177, 193, 199, 217; Malay women 98; riba-free banking in 199; zakat in 173
Maliki 33 n.14, 105, 193, 226 n.2

mandatory instruction in Islam 70
marginalized urban youths 47
market (*suq*): antimarket agenda 50; and contemporary Islamism 48; intervention 11; irregularities 11; Islamists' market-constraining enactments 49; and prices 9–12; rules of conduct of 8; stability 8
marriage age 102; *wali* (the male guardian) role in 102–3, *see also separate entry*
marriage contract 96, 102, 104–6
martial law 24, 123–4
maruf 8
Marx, Karl 16–19, 114, 212; Marxian analysis 18; Marxism 19, 114, 212
Mashhad University 17
maslaha, public interest 201; welfare 119
maslaha citizens' welfare 119
maslaha mursala (unrestricted public interest) 12–13, 33 n.15, 119, 201
maternal duties 77
matrilineal relations 96
Maududi, Sayyid Abul Ala (also transliterated as Mawdudi or Maudoodi) 1, 17, 28, 30–1, 31 nn.2, 11, 17, 40–1, 45, 48, 58, 60 nn.8, 9, 204–6; capitalism and socialism, distinguished by 22; on individualism 22; on Islamic law elements 20; Islamic society economic features 21–2; on private property rights/ownership 22–3; on Shari'a redefinition 19; on zakat 21–2; political theory of 19
mavazin-e eslami 76
Mecca/Meccans 3–6, 30, 32 n.6
Medina 3–7, 10, 14, 26; trade in 9
mercantillist policy 11
merchants 1, 3–4, 9–11, 14, 26, 28, 155, 158
Mernissi, Fatima 66, 73, 86 n.2, 91–3, 103
migrant workers 121
militant Islamism 51, 56, 60 n.2, 74, 123, 211
minimum age of marriage 77, 102
minimum standard of living 116, 180, 183
minimum wage 11, 115–17, 120, 125, 131–2, 134, 135; laws 116
Mirror for Princes', administrative literature 8; *Adab al-Kabir* (circa 750) 8; *Kitab al-Sultan* (889) 8;

Nasihat al-Muluk (1105) 8; *Siyasat Nama* (1091) 8

mixed marriage 100; between Muslim men and non-Muslim women 101; class backing 101; in Israel 101; marrying outside the faith 70, 100–1; Muslim women and non-Muslim men 101; in Palestine 101; in Turkey 101

modern Islamist movements 48–9

modernization 38, 50, 73, 98, 168, 171, 177, 179, 211, 219

Mojahedin (Organization of Mojahedin Khalq Iran) 18

monarchies 1

monarchization of caliphdom 18

monopolies 1, 11, 199

monotheism (divine unity, *towhid*) 18

monotheistic classless society 17–19

moral economy 118, 124, 133, 135, 139, 221

moral laxity 42

moral transgressions 115

Morocco 56, 101, 103–4, 130, 134–6, 148; labor law and Islam in 134; polygamy in 104; women labor force in 136

Mu'awiya 5–7, 15, 25, 30, 31 n.6

mudara'a (share-cropping) 196

mudaraba (*qirad*) 115–16, 196; advantages 197; in banking practices 200; confinement of 197; medieval mudaraba 197; profit sharing 115; rates of profit on 216; two-tier mudaraba 197

muhajjabat (veiled women) 92

Muhammad, Prophet 3–6, 10; from Mecca to Medina migration 3

muhtasib 8–9, 11, 24, 30–1

mujmal (ambiguous) 194

mujtahid 12, 27, 31, 210, 224–6, 226 n.3

Mumcu, U. 38–9, 45, 53, 57, 60 n.2

munker 8

musharaka (equity sharing) 196–8, 209; rates of profit on 216

Muslim Canadian Congress 90

Muslim family law 88–109; Algeria 96, 98; Arab countries 96, 101–6; Bahrain 102–3; Canada 109; Egypt 91–2, 97–8, 102; Gaza 102; and gender, class and state 88–109, *see also* Shari'a; Iran 92, 95, 99, 102, 104, 109; Iraq 104; Israel 89, 97, 101, 109; Lebanon 101, 106; Morocco 101, 103–4; Pakistan 93, 95,

101, 106–7; Sudan 93, 102–3; Syria 103–4, 106; Tunisia 95; Turkey 99, 101, 103, 108; West Bank 94, 104; Yemen 102

Muslim feminist scholarship 91; religious-cultural approach 91; secularist approach 31, 38, 41, 56, 58, 60, 91, 212

Muslim identity 40

Muslim society, Western culture impact on 14

Muslim values 92

Muslim women's resistance 91

mustaz'afin (oppressed) 2, 29–30

Mutahhari, Murtaza 27

Najmabadi, A. 99

Naskh (negation) 21

Natural resources 26–7, 115, 180

Navvab-Safavi, Mojtaba 17, 48, 81, 210–11

new Islamists 91, 104

nezam-e ruhaniyat 81

Nizam-i Mustafa 24

nominally Islamic banks 54, 188

non-Islamic labor organizations 128

non-tax revenues 180

Nuri, Abdollah 73

obligations of employers 116, 119

Occupational segregation 121

Oman 148, 149, 155; Civil Code in 155; commercial law in 149; Omani Banking Law 155

Ontario, Province of 90

Ordre public 142

organizational principles of an Islamic economy 23

Organization of Mojahedin Khalq Iran 18

Organization of production 1

Organization of the Islamic Conference (OIC) 67–71, 84, 86 n.1

Orientalism 88

Orientalists 2, 90, 93, 107

Özel, İ. 54, 58

Pahlavi Foundation 25

Pakistan: Bhutto government's labor policies 123–4; child labor in 125–6; debate on riba in 204–10; on human development and human rights 124; Islamic banking in 40, 193; Islamic movements and labor law changes in 129–136; Islamic regimes and labor law

Pakistan (*Continued*)
  in 118; Islamic revivalist movements in
  16–17; labor policy in 122–6; Pakistani
  women 101; riba-free banking in 199;
  under General Zia-ul-Haq 123;
  women's educational status in 125;
  zakat in 173
Pakistani People's Party (PPP) 123
Palestine 97, 101; Palestinian Intifada 89;
  Palestinian Territories 134
Pan-Islamic Society of London 15
parallel banking 209, 211, 217, 219 n.16
participatory management 123
Parwez, Ghulam Ahmed 17, 22, 30
patriarchal relations 92–3, 95–9, 106–7;
  classical patriarchy 96; neo-patriarchy
  96; and the state 95–9
patrilineal relations 96
Pax Islamicus 2, 4–7, 29–30
penal code of Islam (*hudud*) 24
People's Party of Pakistan 24
Persia 12
Personal Status Code 1956, abolishing
  polygamy 104
petty-producers 14
Peyman, H. 26–8, 30
pleasure-loving wealthy people 22
polarization: economic 51; social 51
police-state 1
political instability 51, 108
polygamy 90–1, 103–5; abolition in
  Tunisia 95; abolition in Turkey 95;
  to control women's bodies and
  reproductivity 104; as a form of
  security to women 90; as an
  indisputable Muslim rule 104; in Iraq
  104–5; in Libya 104; in Morocco 104;
  in Syria 104; in Tunisia 103;
  in Turkey 103
polytheism (*shirk*) 18, 30
populism 2, 7, 30–1
post-Orientalist Islamicists 2, 90,
  93, 107
predatory pricing 11
pre-Islamic Arab (tribal) society 96
price fixing 10; government's control over
  11; predatory pricing 11
price mechanism 10
price regulation 9–11
primacy of Islam 39, 42
primary ruling (*ahkam avvaliyya*) 13
private ownership 17–18, 48–9, 115;
  control over 96; ownership 23–4, 26–7;
  rights, unlimited 22; transition to 97

profits 39, 41, 115–16, 171, 187
profit sharing 115, 123, 126
prohibition of interest 52, 150, 187
Prohibition Ordinance 24
property rights 1, 13, 17–18, 22, 27–8,
  30, 51, 114
Prophet: role in taxation 166–170; in
  zakat fixing 172
proprietary rights 22
Protectionism 49, 59
Protestant Reformation 114
Protestant work ethic 114
public expenditures 181–6; allocation and
  level of support 182–3; assigned
  functions and expenditures 184–5;
  definitions and demarcations 181–3;
  and goals of an Islamic state 183–6;
  limitations for 186; mandatory
  functions and expenditures 183–4;
  necessary functions and circumstantial
  expenditures 184; practical significance
  of a categorization 185–6; relevance of
  classifications 185–6
public interest 12–13, 201–3
Public policy: in Islam 1–33, 142,
  see also commercial law; riba free
  banking in 193–211; secular law public
  policy 141–63; and urgency 12–13
public treasury 5
puritanical life style 47

Qabyle Berbers (Algeria) 96
qadi al-qudat 7
qadis 7
Qatar 142, 148–9, 154, 162 n.2, 164;
  commercial law in 145; Qatar Civil
  and Commercial Code 158
qazf 24
Quran: chapters (*suras*) of 3; precepts of
  Islam in 2; Quran schools 42;
  revelations of 4; on riba 40; women's
  position expressed in 94

Radicalism 1, 15, 25–30, 43, 50, 95, 176,
  199, 210–11, 216
Rahman, F. 50, 204–5
rahn (pledge) 195
Raja'i Khorasani, Sa'id 74–5
Ramadan, A. A. 17, 33 n.16, 42,
  119, 123
Reason (*aql*) 225
reformism and revivalism, Islamic 13–15
rejuvenate (*islah*) 13
religious fanaticism 17–18

religious liberation 17–18
renewal (*tajdid*) 14, 33 n.17
reordering of economic relations 43
return on industrial loans 39
revivalism: and anticolonialist and
    anti-imperialist movements 15;
    demands 1; internationalization of
    31–2; Islamic capitalism (Vision II)
    19–25; monotheistic classless society
    (Vision I) 17–19; power of 31;
    and reformism 13–15; and
    socialism 15–25; social order
    establishment by 2
revolutionary Islam (the rule of the
    oppressed) 25–9, 79
Revolutionary Islamic Courts 25
riba: in Algeria 199; categories 195;
    classical views on 194–8; debate on
    riba in Egypt 200–4; debate on riba in
    Pakistan 204–10; interpretation, in
    early twentieth century 198; in Iran
    199; legalization 195, 198; in Libya
    199; limited and broader definition of
    198–200; in Malaysia 199; meaning
    201; modern interpretation 198–217; in
    Pakistan 199; pragmatic view on riba in
    Iran 210–17; Quran's disapproval of
    194; *riba al-fadl* 195, 197, 201–2,
    205–6, 209, 212; *riba al-nasia* 195,
    197, 201–2, 204–6, 213; riba-free
    banking in Islamic public policy
    193–219, *see also* banking systems;
    Saudi Arabia 199; several devices
    for the evasion of the prohibition
    of 195; Shi'i modernist view on 213;
    on six articles 194; traditionalist and
    modern advocates of a broader
    definition of 199
ribawi (based on riba) transactions 150
Rightly Guided Caliphs: Abu Bakr 4–5,
    171; Ali 5–7, 15; Umar 5–7; Uthman
    4–7, 29
right of individual ownership 22
rights and responsibilities of employers
    and employees 113–16, 120, 123
rights of minorities 71, 76–8
rights of ownership 70
rights of women 32, 76, 136
rights of workers 11, 25, 118, 123
right to strike 122
Riyadh 83
Roozbeh (Abd Allah) Ibn al-Muqaffa 8
ruling oligarchy of Mecca 3–7, 25
Rushdie, Salman 78, 81

Sadr, Ayatullah Muhammad Baqir 27–8,
    33 n.23, 209, 211–12
Safavi Shi'ism 18
salam (salaf) future delivery 196
salt, riba on 194
sanctioning private property 1
sanctity of contract 143
sanctity of labor 114
Sanhuri, Abd al-Razzaq 141, 143–4,
    146–8, 150, 162 n.5, 163 n.11, 199,
    201–3, 209, 213
Saud al-Faisal, Prince 84, 86 n.12
Saudi Arabia: banking systems in 193;
    capital/labor issues 119; on classless
    society 119; commercial law in 145;
    educational status of women in 120;
    human rights in 69–70; Human rights
    policy in 82–5, *see also under* human
    rights policy; Islam and labor law in
    119–22; Islamic movements and labor
    law changes in 129–36; Islamic
    regimes and labor law in 118, 119–22;
    migrant workers treatment of 121;
    riba-free banking in 199;
    women's employment in 120;
    zakat in 173
Saudi Basic Law 83, 84
Sayyid Jamal al-Din Afghani 14
scarcity 10, 21
secularization/secularization policy 14,
    38, 40, 59, 101, 109
secular law public policy 141–63
secular left and Islamists 133
secular taxes 179–80
self-indulgence 22
Seljuks dynasty 8
seminary teachers (*modarresin*) 28
sexual immorality 14
Shafi'I school 10
Shahrour, Muhammad 73
Shari'a: approval and acceptance of the
    sukuk model by 188; in commercial law
    141–63; conflict in, and secular law
    public policy 141–64; on contract
    employment 117; in modern commercial
    law 148; Shari'a and commercial law
    141–64; Shari'a and constitution
    142–3, 148–59, 163 nn.7, 8, 9;
    Shari'a based family laws 143;
    Shari'a court 40, 88, 104, 109 n.1,
    207–10, 218; Shari'a law 66, 88, 90,
    93, 107, 162
Shariati, Ali 21–2, 25–8, 30, 33 nn.21,
    24, 25, 48, 212; on Islam 17;

Shariati, Ali (*Continued*)
  on Islamic liberation 18; on social
  structures 17–19; on war between
  Cain and Abel 17
Shariat-Sangalaji 14, 17
Sheikh, N. A. 17, 22, 30
Sheikh of al-Azhar 74
silver, riba on 194
Sismondian utopia 27
Siyasa: concept development 8; public
  policy 8–9
Smith, A. 19, 57
social and moral norms 57
social balance 27, 30–1
social contract 118
social-gender organizations, ideological
  forms of 97
socialism 1, 2, 19, 21–2, 24, 33, 35–6,
  113; European influence 15–16; by
  Indian Muslims 16; orthodoxy on 28;
  radical interpretation 27
social justice 1, 15, 17, 25, 29
social structure 1, 18, 56, 88
Socialist Labor Party (SLP) 132
Sorush, Abdolkarim 73, 81
Sources of Imitation (*Maraje' Taqlid*) 26
Soviet Union 16, 53
speculation 23, 28, 71, 168, 196,
  199, 202
Stalinism 16
standards of honesty 42, 46
state *see* Islamic state
stoning 21, 24, 70
stratified Muslim societies 2
structure of Abel 18
structure of Cain 18
subverting patriarchy 92
Sudan 21, 69, 73, 93, 102–3, 173–4, 193,
  217; human rights in 69; zakat in 173
sukuk 187–8, 189 nn.10–11
Sunna 3–4, 14, 83, 100, 106, 144, 148–9,
  152, 165, 177–84, 194–5, 224; on life
  and property 4; on marriage 100; on
  public expenditures 183; on riba 193;
  on transactions 144
Sunni 199
Sunni schools of jurisprudence 12, 203,
  209, 214–15, 224, 226 n.2
suras 3
Surplus 23, 27
Syria 5–6, 32 n.6, 69, 103–6, 148, 162
  n.4; commercial law in 148; divorce
  in 106; human rights in 69;
  polygamy in 104

Tablighi Jama'at 58
Taha, Mahmud Muhammad 73
Tajdid (renewal) 14
Taliban 1, 21, 51, 74
Tantawi, Mufti of Egypt 203, 209
taqlid (imitation) 13
tatfif (shirking) 114–15
taxation and public finance 166, 169–80;
  see also jizya; zakat
tax evasion 42, 77
temporary marriage 13, 77, 93, 131,
  184, 188
Third Way, the 127–8
tools of production 26–7
torture 70, 74, 76, 84, 86, 194
Toubia, N. 101–4, 106
Tradition (*Sunna*) *see* Sunna
Tunisia 95, 101–4, 107–8, 110–11, 130,
  134–5, 137; labor law and Islam in
  134; polygamy abolished in 103, 108;
  Tunisian women 108, 130; *wilaya*
  (male guardianship) abandoned in 103
Turkey: employment in 47; Islamist and
  Islamist-rooted political parties in,
  economic agendas 49; Muslim women
  in 99; polygamy abolished in 95,
  103–4, 108

ulama (or ulema) 20, 31, 74, 82,
  198–200, 202–6, 210, 212–13,
  215–16, 218
Umar, the Caliph 4–8, 32 n.6, 166, 176,
  178–9, 182, 194
Umayyads dynasty 5–8, 14, 30; main
  preoccupation of the state 7
uncontrolled economy of capitalism 21–2
underclass 14–15, 131
unemployment and official corruption, as
  Islamists problem 57
UN Human Rights Commission 72, 81
unionization of workers 24
unitary conception of Islam 8
United Arab Emirates 102, 142,
  156, 163
Universal Declaration of Human Rights
  75, 86 n.5
unlimited property rights 22, 186
urbanization 14, 45, 47, 100
urf Custom 154
urgency, and public policy 12–13
ushr (foreign trade tax) 24, 170, 178
ushur (import tax) 166, 178–9
ushur (on agricultural products) 178–9
Usmani, Shaukat 16

usul al-fiqh (principles of
   jurisprudence) 224
usury (riba) *see* riba
Uthman, the Caliph 4–7, 29
utopianism 14

veil (*hijab*) 21, 48, 80, 87, 91–2, 111;
   political and a practical meaning 91;
   see also veiling
veiling 15, 44, 47, 48, 49, 79, 80, 90, 92;
   veiling rules 79
Velayati, Ali Akbar 81
Vienna Conference 1993 84
Virtue Party (*Fazilet Partisi Turkey*) 49
von Mises, Ludwig 53

wa'd (burying female children at
   birth) 96
wages 11, 15, 70, 84, 116, 122–3, 126–8,
   131–2, 134, 196; minimum wage laws
   117; wage negotiation 116
Wahhabi 69
wali (the male guardian), role of: in
   Algeria 103; in Bahrain 103; in Egypt
   103; in marriage 102–3; in Morocco
   103; in Sudan 103; in Syria 103; in
   Tunisia 103
war on terrorism 32
welfare state 1, 116, 118, 120, 124,
   130–1, 133, 138
West Bank 94, 104, 134
Western civilization 40
Westernization 56, 62–3, 98
wheat, riba on 194
wilaya (male guardianship) 103
women: in agriculture 121;
   contextualization 89–90; in domestic
   service 121; educational status in Egypt
   130–3; educational status in Iran 128;
   in Egypt 98; as employees 116;
   employment in Iran 120; employment
   116, 120, 122, 125–6, 128–36;
   employment in Pakistan 120; and
   family laws 99–107, *see also separate
   entry*; in India 98; inheritance rights
   denied for 96; Islamic Republic's policy
   towards 128; in Malaysia 98; one
   dimensional analysis 95; participation
   in national liberation movements 89;
   polygamy as a form of security to
   women 90; Quran expressing the
   position of 94; in Saudi Arabia,
   educational status 120; in Saudi Arabia,
   employment 120; in Turkey 99;

The Veiled Revolution video 91;
   Women in Islam video 90; women of
   the Intifada 89; women's dress 44, 48,
   79–81, 99, 116, 123, 179; Women's
   education 104; women's status 73–9,
   84, 88, 91, 94–9, 103–8, 120, 125, 128,
   130; writings on 91
Women and family laws in Islam 99–107;
   age of marriage 102, *see also*
   marriage age; citizenship 100;
   divorce 105–7, *see also separate entry*;
   education 99; as a marginalized party
   104; marriage 100–3; marriage
   restrictions imposed on 101; mixed
   marriage 100; Muslim female mixed
   marriages 101
Women Living Under Muslim Law
   (WLUM) 86 n.2, 87, 90, 104, 111
worker participation program 123
workers' council (*showra*) 127
worker's strikes 24, 118–28, 131, 134
work ethics and Islam 114
working class 126, 132–5
World Conference on Human Rights 68

Yahya Khan, President 122
Yazdi, Ayatollah Mohammad 80–2,
   86 n.7
Yazid 6–7, 25, 30
Yemen 102, 110, 118, 121, 139, 149, 154,
   174; Islamic regimes and labor law in
   118; zakat in 173
young professional underclass 131
Yücel, Hasan Âli 58

zakat: on agricultural produce 174;
   Bahrain 173; Bangladesh 173;
   beneficiaries of 181; case law
   instead of general principles 168;
   contemporary practice, confusion
   and deficiencies 173; data of
   performance 50; "divine" character of
   167–8; duration of coverage 173;
   Egypt 173; expenditures 180, 181–7;
   on gold, silver, cash, and invisible
   wealth 174; immutable rates? 172–3;
   income subject to 182; income tax 170,
   177, 182; independent work subject to
   174; Iran 173; Iraq 173; Islamic state
   as the period of reference 166; Jordan
   173; Libya 173; on Livestock 174;
   Malaysia 173; methodology for an
   "Islamic system" 165–8; modernization
   of traditional zakat system 171;

zakat (*Continued*)
one full year of ownership, problem
with 171–2; Pakistan 173;
professionals subject to 174; on
productive or unproductive wealth?
171; on rice 174; rates 58, 102, 167,
169, 172–3, 175–80, 182, 188, 198,
202–3, 207, 215, 216; redistribution 48,
63, 174–6, 218; revenues 5, 29, 120,
174–7, 180–2; Saudi Arabia 173;
Sudan 173; tax base 166, 169–70, 177;
taxes, and public finance in Islam
165–89; wealth tax 170, 182;
Yemen 173; zakat, a wealth or income
tax? 170–1; *see also* public
expenditures

Zamindari system (landlordism) 22

Zia-ul Haq, General 24, 123,
126, 205

zina (extramarital sex) offence 24

Zoroastrians 78

Zulm 10

CPSIA information can be obtained at www.ICGtesting.com
Printed in the USA
BVOW04s0858070913

330530BV00002B/39/P